Louise Erdrich's
Justice Trilogy

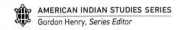

Louise Erdrich's Justice Trilogy

CULTURAL AND CRITICAL CONTEXTS

Edited by Connie A. Jacobs *and* Nancy J. Peterson

MICHIGAN STATE UNIVERSITY PRESS | *East Lansing*

♾ The paper used in this publication meets the minimum requirements of
ANSI/NISO Z39.48-1992 (R 1997) (Permanence of Paper).

Michigan State University Press
East Lansing, Michigan 48823-5245

LIBRARY OF CONGRESS CATALOGING-IN-PUBLICATION DATA
Names: Jacobs, Connie A., 1944– editor. | Peterson, Nancy J., editor.
Title: Louise Erdrich's justice trilogy : cultural and critical contexts /
edited by Connie A. Jacobs, Nancy J. Peterson.
Other titles: American Indian studies series (East Lansing, Mich.)
Description: East Lansing : Michigan State University Press, 2021. |
Series: American Indian studies series | Includes bibliographical references and index.
Identifiers: LCCN 2021001800 | ISBN 978-1-61186-403-8 (paperback)
| ISBN 978-1-60917-678-5 | ISBN 978-1-62895-445-6 | ISBN 978-1-62896-439-4
Subjects: LCSH: Erdrich, Louise—Criticism and interpretation.
Classification: LCC PS3555.R42 Z78 2021 | DDC 813/.54—dc23
LC record available at https://lccn.loc.gov/2021001800

Book design by Charlie Sharp, Sharp Designs, East Lansing, MI
Cover design by David Drummond, Salamander Design, www.salamanderhill.com
Cover image: Callahan/Shutterstock

Michigan State University Press is a member of the Green Press Initiative and is
committed to developing and encouraging ecologically responsible publishing
practices. For more information about the Green Press Initiative and the use of
recycled paper in book publishing, please visit www.greenpressinitiative.org.

Visit Michigan State University Press at *www.msupress.org*

CONTENTS

vii ACKNOWLEDGMENTS

ix INTRODUCTION. Visions of Justice in Louise Erdrich's Trilogy
Nancy J. Peterson and Connie A. Jacobs

1 The Aesthetics of Justice and Redress in *The Plague of Doves*
Debra K. S. Barker

17 Murder She Wrote, and Rewrote, and Rewrote: A Trilogy of Justices
Kenneth M. Roemer

43 Trauma and Restitution in Louise Erdrich's *LaRose*
Aitor Ibarrola-Armendariz

67 Family Trees: Land and Kinship in Louise Erdrich's Justice Trilogy
Ellen L. Arnold

87 You Aren't a Regular Dog, Are You? Dog as Intermediary
in Louise Erdrich's *LaRose*
Connie A. Jacobs

107   We Can Wade Grief: Ethics, Politics, and Relationality
in Louise Erdrich's *LaRose*
Silvia Martínez-Falquina

135   Narrative Design in the Justice Trilogy
Nancy J. Peterson

159   *Debwe, Onaakonige gaye Nanaandawi'iwe*: Finding Justice
in the Language of Louise Erdrich's Novels
Margaret Noodin

183   Honoring Our Relatives
Gwen Nell Westerman

187   A Reader's Guide to the Novels of the Justice Trilogy
Peter G. Beidler and Gay Barton

259   The Art of Fiction No. 208: Louise Erdrich, from the *Paris Review*,
No. 195 (Winter 2010)

283   SELECTED BIBLIOGRAPHY

289   CONTRIBUTORS

293   INDEX

ACKNOWLEDGMENTS

The editors would like to acknowledge the anonymous readers for the press; their comments on the original manuscript were especially valuable to us and all of the contributors in guiding our revisions for the final volume. Most important, we would like to offer a special thanks to Gordon Henry for his interest in our work at the earliest stages and for his support during the process of bringing this volume into print.

We also wish to thank Peter London of HarperCollins, Tucker Smith of the Wylie Agency, and Heidi Heller of the Minnesota Historical Society for assisting with the permissions process for the following:

- Family tree of characters, hand-lettered by Martie Holmer and designed and composed by Elliott Beard, from *The Last Report on the Miracles at Little No Horse*, by Louise Erdrich. Copyright © 2001 by Louise Erdrich. Used by permission of HarperCollins Publishers.
- Ojibwe bandolier bag decorated with spot-stitch floral beadwork with a deer in the mid-panel, ca. 1890. Source: Minnesota Historical Society Collections, Accession No. 8701.1.

Visions of Justice
in Louise Erdrich's Trilogy

Nancy J. Peterson and Connie A. Jacobs

n 1984, a few months before *Love Medicine*, her first novel, was published by Holt, Rinehart, and Winston, Louise Erdrich published a fascinating short story titled "The True Story of Mustache Maude" in *Frontiers: A Journal of Women Studies*. Even though the publication of the short story and the novel fell close together, the story's titular character, Mustache Maude, would not be part of Erdrich's first novel—or her second, third, fourth, or fifth (and so on), for that matter. Mustache Maude does not reappear in one of Erdrich's novels for thirty-some years, when readers encounter her in *The Plague of Doves*, published in 2008, the first novel in a trio that we now refer to as Erdrich's "justice trilogy."

Like "Mustache" Maude Black in Erdrich's 2008 novel, who is described as "a giant woman dressed in the clothing of a man" (*Plague* 16), Mustache Maude in the 1984 short story is a strong woman, able to thrive on the frontier because she is a skilled sharpshooter and a wily rustler. In fact, the 1984 short story dwells on Maude's androgynous gendering and brings same-sex desire into her depiction. In the short story, Mustache Maude steals "a rare blue sow" from another woman—the Countess Svagmadda, who has come to the Badlands from a small, ruined country in eastern Europe after having a vision of a "withered tower of stone" (63). When the Countess comes to reclaim her prized sow, the two women agree to settle the score with an honor duel designed for women from the Countess's country of origin. This duel involves sewing weapons (steel bits, saws, rapiers, wristlet blades, etc.) into their clothing and running at each other until someone is bleeding profusely or dying. When Mustache Maude and the Countess Svagmadda engage in their duel, they are equally matched: they end up cutting off each other's clothing, disarming each other, and then, in their nakedness, they embrace. They live together, and love each other, until they grow into old age and the Countess dies.

While this fabulous story of the Countess and Maude is not directly part of Erdrich's 2008 novel, it is a story worth pondering for a moment, for it reveals how Erdrich's interest in certain kinds of material can take years to ripen and become part of her full-length novels. In interviews she has given over the years, Erdrich talks about how important it is for her to write out the first drafts of her novels by hand on notebook paper, eventually transferring a cluster of pages onto the computer so that she can edit them and continually revise. She tells interviewer Lisa Halliday of an incident when she was out for a walk near her home in Minneapolis when an idea for the end of *Shadow Tag* came to her. She was desperate to write it down but didn't have any paper with her; by chance, her sister Heid appeared driving her car nearby, and so Louise raced over to flag her down and beg for pencil and paper ("Art of Fiction" 156). (In the same interview, Erdrich confesses to writing while driving when inspiration strikes, or to stopping the car on the side of the road when she feels the inexorable pull of words.) Erdrich is also a keeper of notebooks in which she records ideas and phrases that can serve as fodder for later writing projects. She describes them as "my compost pile of ideas. Any scrap goes in, and after a number of years I'll get a handful of earth" ("Art of Fiction" 157). In other words, well before she had any idea that she would become absorbed in the questions of justice that connect her trilogy—*The Plague of Doves* (2008), *The Round House* (2012), and *LaRose* (2016)—Erdrich was already gathering materials that would form her overarching narrative, as well as various stories that intersect with them. As it turns out, Mustache Maude was a character out of North Dakota history who piqued Erdrich's interest years before she actually began working on *The Plague of Doves*. Even the plague of doves that opens the first chapter of that novel was inspired by a news clipping that Erdrich stumbled upon years earlier, along with the story of the lynch mob that haunts her novel, as she revealed to host Liane Hansen when she appeared on NPR's *Weekend Edition Sunday* in May 2008 ("*Plague of Doves*").

Looking back at the short stories that were published earlier and then later incorporated into Erdrich's 2008 novel, we see a visionary writer at work, returning to previously published material, revising it in new ways, and weaving together individual stories that previously stood by themselves as artful works of fiction. "The True Story of Mustache Maude" from 1984 offers the first glimpse of a colorful minor character who would become part of the fictional universe of *The Plague of Doves*, but other early stories—"Satan: Hijacker of a Planet" from 1997, for instance, "Sister Godzilla" from 2001, or "Shamengwa" from 2002—also provide evidence of Erdrich's capacity to reimagine and reinvigorate earlier work. Following the voices of characters who speak to her, plumbing her notebooks for news clippings and phrases and images she wanted to keep track of, constantly writing and rewriting, Louise Erdrich has become one of the most widely read and highly regarded authors of our time. The justice trilogy pulls readers into Erdrich's fictional universe in an unprecedented way and demonstrates the historical, ethical, and tribal vision that lays the foundation for all of Erdrich's fiction. It brings together key themes and issues that run throughout her work, but this time in three novels directly connected by the force and the friction of Indigenous people wanting to hold onto their homelands and preserve their traditions and communities in the face of settler colonialism.

Louise Erdrich is an enrolled member of the Turtle Mountain Band of Chippewa, and she is also of German and French ancestry. Erdrich is a prolific author: she has published seventeen novels to date (the most recent is *The Night Watchman*, which appeared in March 2020), along with three collections of poetry, two memoirs, numerous short stories, and seven children's/young adult books. Her work—especially her novels—has been read and discussed widely, by reviewers and scholars, students, and general readers. Much of the growing body of scholarship on Erdrich focuses on earlier novels. In particular, *Love Medicine* (her debut novel, which won the National Book Critics Circle Award for Fiction in 1984 and the American Book Award in 1985), *Tracks* (1988), and *The Last Report on the Miracles at Little No Horse* (2001) have garnered considerable critical attention. This collection of essays focuses specifically on the three novels that constitute the justice trilogy—*The Plague of Doves* (2008), *The Round House* (2012), and *LaRose* (2016)—not only to comprehend their strengths as individual novels, but to tease out the complex interrelations among them and to highlight the visionary fictional world Erdrich has created in northern North Dakota, where small towns and reservation life bring together a vibrant cast of characters who are shaped by history, by community, by the forces of desire, by their fragile and resilient humanness.

Given the sustained and deeply engaging portrait that emerges in the justice trilogy, it is no wonder that all three novels have been recognized by notable awards: *The Plague of Doves* was a finalist for the Pulitzer Prize and won the 2009 Anisfield-Wolf Book Award; *The Round House* won the National Book Award for Fiction in 2012 and an American Book Award for 2013; *LaRose* won the 2017 National Book Critics Circle Award for Fiction. During this same period of time, Erdrich has been honored as the recipient of several highly prestigious awards, including the 2016 National Museum of the Indian Arts Award, the Library of Congress Prize for American Fiction (2015), the PEN/Saul Bellow Award for Achievement in American Fiction (2014), and the Dayton Literary Peace Prize Richard C. Holbrooke Distinguished Achievement Award (2014). Clearly, Erdrich's justice trilogy is being recognized as a major achievement, one worth exploring in depth via the essays in this collection.

It is worth noting that, while scholars and readers now commonly use the term "justice trilogy" to signal the thematic connections among *The Plague of Doves*, *The Round House*, and *LaRose* in terms of justice (and injustice), Erdrich did not originally intend to write three closely related books. Just after *LaRose* was released in March 2016, Erdrich was interviewed numerous times, and she began to discuss the evolution of the trilogy, revealing that she was surprised when she realized that the novels were related. For instance, Erdrich comments to Emily Gray Tedrowe in a May 2016 interview, "I knew I was working on the subject of justice when I wrote the first book, and then I realized I had to write about jurisdictional issues for the second book . . . and then I understood that I had to continue this theme. So the books are thematically linked—there's no order to them, and very few of the characters are connected. But they are thematically about justice" ("Sunday *Rumpus* Interview"). Also in May 2016, she explains to Laurie Hertzel, a reporter for the *Minneapolis Star Tribune*, that "I didn't find them related internally until I was about halfway through *The Round House*. . . . But one question led to another, and then I realized, ah, you know, I'm really writing something thematically linked." Accordingly, Hertzel uses the term "accidental trilogy" in her article to describe the three novels.

While the term "accidental" captures Erdrich's honest reflection about not originally intending to write a deliberately planned group of novels, nonetheless, as questions of justice, injustice, and jurisdiction became paramount for Erdrich, the three novels serendipitously began to interconnect, to make up a trilogy, and thus inspired the use of the term "justice trilogy" to refer to them. Erdrich points out that justice "is the foundation of a trusting society. It's the foundation of going forward and making a life. Justice is an enormous issue for this country" (Hertzel)—especially given the treatment Native peoples have received in the United States, past and present. Erdrich's trilogy is committed to raising thorny issues revolving around justice—and oftentimes the lack of justice—especially as they involve Native American history and the losses, inequities, violence, and tragedy that have resulted through US interventions. In fact, in an interview with Erica Rivera, Erdrich directly links tragedy to her interest in justice—"usually what precedes a dramatic justice . . . is a pretty dramatic tragedy" ("Louise Erdrich")—and all three novels in the trilogy open with a horrific scene of violence and/or death.

As Maria Russo observes in her review of *The Round House*, "Law is meant to put out society's brush fires, but in Native American history it has often acted more like the wind." The novels of Erdrich's trilogy often reference legal precedents involving Native America and thus dramatically expose the injustices of history and the ways that principles of Indigenous sovereignty have unfortunately been questioned and eroded over many years. For an Indigenous fiction writer such as Erdrich, tackling the concept of "justice" is in itself noteworthy. Writing for a general audience, Erdrich makes the most of her opportunity to educate her readers about historical policies and inequities that are often omitted from American history textbooks. Erdrich's published body of work mentions or dramatizes the effect of such things as treaties made by US governmental officials with the intent to never fulfill them; brutal removals from homelands and tribal lands confiscated by policies such as Manifest Destiny and the Dawes Act; the creation of reservations as another way to take land from tribes; Native children sent to "Christian" boarding schools as a way to save their souls and to erase their Native heritage; US laws forbidding Natives to practice their religion or to perform sacred ceremonies; US policies that determined for Native people what "blood quantum" was required to be listed on a tribal roll; denial of the right of US citizenship until 1924; the relocation policy of separating Native Americans from their home communities and resettling them in urban areas to assimilate; the policy of termination, which terminated federal recognition of an Indian nation as a sovereign entity; the practice of seizing Indian children from their own families and homes and adopting them out to non-Native parents. And so much more.

Many of Erdrich's earlier novels (in particular, *Tracks* and *The Last Report on the Miracles at Little No Horse*) portray these kinds of devastations and losses, and questions of justice and injustice run throughout Erdrich's published work. But the justice trilogy, along with Erdrich's newest novel, *The Night Watchman*, dwells upon the legacy of injustices Native Americans have faced. *The Plague of Doves* has been described as exploring vengeance or revenge as a kind of justice, and indeed the novel includes memorable and haunting phrases surrounding this theme, such as "rough justice" to describe the hanging mob's actions (297) or Mooshum's pained exclamation that "there is no justice here on eart" as he laments loss of tribal land and Métis historical losses (55). *The Round House* looks at unachieved justice because of issues related to jurisdiction and sovereignty, and late in the novel, readers are told that the round house was given to the people as a way to keep the community together "since justice was so sketchily applied on earth" (315). The Judge himself argues that "there are many kinds of justice" and draws a distinction between "ideal justice" and "best-we-can-do justice" (306). The novel also offers alternative possibilities of conceptualizing justice. Joe wonders if perhaps "Murder, for justice" (280) can be carried out. And the possibility that "traditional Anishinaabe justice" (196) or "wiindigoo justice" (187) might be more effective than Euro-American law and US justice fuels the tension at the heart of the novel. Justice is referred to less prominently in *LaRose* than in the other two novels of the trilogy, though, significantly, the novel refers to "an old form of justice" (36) to explain the act of gifting a son from one family to another to make up for an accidental death. In the Acknowledgments section at the end of *LaRose*, Erdrich recalls hearing a story from her mother about "an Ojibwe family who allowed parents enduring the loss of a child to adopt their child—a contemporary act that echoes an old form of justice" (373). She describes *LaRose* as involving "a traditional act of reparation" ("Sunday *Rumpus* Interview"). Her use of the word "reparation" echoes other comments she has made about *LaRose*'s narrative arc as portraying "the working out of justice" and enacting "restorative justice" ("After Tragedy").

As she grappled with issues of justice and injustice, Erdrich also had to reckon with the presence of real evil in the world. *The Plague of Doves* dramatizes what Debra K. S. Barker identifies in this volume as a kind of "frontier justice" as it recounts the practice of killing Natives when they got in the way of settlers—tactics similar to the ones the KKK used against African Americans. In a 2008 profile, Erdrich reveals, "It's against my nature to believe how evil people can be. I didn't see cruelty a lot growing up. When it became apparent that the world was different from what I had known as a child, it took me a long time to understand it" (Freeman). Erdrich's unflinching look at evil in the world unfolds on many levels—the land grab of the surveying party that lays claim to tribal lands and founds the town of

Pluto, the brutal murder of members of the Lochren family, the unfair accusation that four Ojibwe men are the murderers, the hanging of innocent Ojibwe men for the murders—and these long-past events continue to leave scars and inflict trauma on families of not only the victims but also of the murderers, up to the present moment of narration. Reckoning with evil, as well as understanding the terrible damage one group of people can inflict on another, reverberates throughout *The Plague of Doves*.

The Round House, the second book of the trilogy, reveals disparities in the law that allow a nontribal member to rape and murder Indigenous women on their own lands and to escape prosecution because of jurisdiction issues. Geraldine's and Mayla's abuse and assault at the hands of Linden Lark dramatically exposes the lack of justice available to Native women who are victims of heinous crimes, and so a terrifying awareness of injustice for Native women suffuses the novel, culminating in a profound moral dilemma for readers to ponder. The white perpetrator is shot and killed in an act of vigilante justice, but is this justice or revenge? Through this agonizing situation, Erdrich's novel calls attention to an ongoing contemporary issue of the violence and abuse experienced by many—too many—Indigenous women in the United States and Canada, as memorialized in the Missing and Murdered Indigenous Women and Girls movement (#MMIWG). *The Round House* was released in October 2012, and on February 27, 2013, Erdrich published an op-ed for the *New York Times* titled "Rape on the Reservation." In that piece, she cites a glaring statistic that propels her novel: "More than 80 percent of sex crimes on reservations are committed by non-Indian men, who are immune from prosecution by tribal courts." This legal conundrum means most of these predators go unpunished since tribal courts have no jurisdiction, while state or federal authorities, who do have jurisdiction, rarely follow through with any investigation that could lead to an arrest. In her op-ed, Erdrich contributes her eloquent voice and a compelling argument in favor of reauthorizing the Violence Against Women Act (VAWA), which would restore limited jurisdiction to tribal police and tribal courts to handle sex crimes perpetrated against Native women by non-Natives. VAWA was originally passed in 1994 and, after much debate, did gain enough votes in Congress for reauthorization in 2013 (though attempts to reauthorize VAWA's grant programs and extend its reach in 2018 and 2019 failed).

LaRose, the final book of the trilogy, depicts the lifelong trauma caused by broken families, by boarding school experiences, and by the human propensity for envy, cruelty, and selfishness. But the novel also shows us an alternative school designed to address the needs of struggling Native students, includes a resident priest who cares deeply for his parishioners, and depicts strong and healthy reservation families that function with love and support. The novel begins with a death, an accidental shooting that shatters families and the community, and that allows revenge plots to multiply because of various grievances. In *LaRose*, as is the case for much of the justice trilogy, revenge feels like the only way to have agency against injustice, but by the end of *LaRose* traditional ways of healing prove efficacious, stories are passed on from elders to educate a new generation, and a young boy takes his place as the one sent to heal historical and intergenerational trauma.

While Erdrich's trilogy develops a heart-wrenching look at loss and tragedy, it is also important to recognize that marvelous comic scenes intervene to offer some relief from the sense of foreboding and the dire revelations that unfold in each novel. Often humor emerges from incidents featuring food or bawdy talk, and in scenes involving Catholicism or other spiritual traditions. In *The Plague of Doves* when Marn Wolde escapes from Billy and the kindred with her children, they take refuge at the 4-B's café, indulging in breakfast specials with dessert. But Bliss tracks them down and confronts Marn, inciting not only a fight but a huge comic mess that breaks out when all the ketchup bottles Evelina has carefully balanced on top of each other, to consolidate the ketchup into fuller containers, are jostled, then upset onto the floor, rolling and scattering, spraying ketchup everywhere. And who can forget the appalling stew the Judge concocts in *The Round House* to convince Geraldine that she should leave her bedroom and rejoin the family, or the scene when Mooshum's birthday cake, decorated with a hundred or so lit candles and whiskey-laced icing, bursts into flames? Along with food, the sex talk of Grandma Ignatia Thunder, in *The Round House* and in *LaRose*, interjects laughter and humanity into several scenes.

Not only food and sex talk, but spirituality and religion become ripe for humor in Erdrich's trilogy. Mooshum and Shamengwa's pestering the Catholic priest, Father Cassidy, in *The Plague of Doves* results in a debate that Mooshum wins by following a line of logic that reaches the conclusion that "the Eucharist is a cannibal meal" (40), to which the Father responds, "All right, be a pagan, burn in hell!" (a not very priestlike retort, made in the heat of the moment, perhaps because they've all been drinking together). In *The Round House*, Father Travis becomes enraged when he learns Cappy and Zelia have made love in the church basement, and he provokes laughter from onlookers as he chases Cappy around the reservation to confront him. Even Ojibwe spiritual traditions are occasionally subject to comic treatment, as when Randall in *The Round House* adds a special powder to the sweat-lodge ceremony he is performing for his friends, and the special "medicine" turns out to be Pueblo hot pepper, which makes everyone run naked from the lodge with their eyes (and other body parts) stinging.

As several essays in this collection point out, along with all the forces that cause pain and inflict trauma on the families, individuals, and tribal nations in Erdrich's justice novels, there are also forces that bring people together. Near the end of *The Plague of Doves*, the Judge and Geraldine marry; surrounded by family, this joining together signifies a hopefulness that relationships can be restored, that families will endure, that the tribal nation will have strong members to shape its future. Near the ending of *The Round House*, justice for Geraldine and Mayla is carried out not by following the law, but by following Ojibwe tradition. Moreover, the community absolves Joe of the crime of murder in various ways, and readers know Joe will grow up to marry an Ojibwe woman, Margaret, from the Nanapush family, and that he will become a lawyer who can carry on the work of preserving legal sovereignty for his people. The culmination of Erdrich's justice trilogy in *LaRose* represents the most hopeful, sustaining vision of community and resilience among the novels, as the people gather together to celebrate Hollis's graduation from high school. Old antagonisms are set aside for this happy day. Romeo attends, even though the celebration is at the Iron house, and he shows himself to be a caring father. Likewise, Nola and Peter are there with Maggie, so the two families that were plunged into tragedy at the beginning of the novel begin to find a way forward. The ancestors come too, though only LaRose (and perhaps the dog) can see them. So the community is made whole.

The overview of the justice trilogy outlined above does not, of course, do justice to the rich detail, the interlaced storylines, and the profound imagination of Erdrich's novels, but it does set the stage for the essays that follow. The essays gathered together in this volume illuminate and emphasize Erdrich's storytelling abilities; the complex relations among crime, punishment, and forgiveness in her novels; and Anishinaabe perspectives that underlie her presentation of character, conflict, and community. As editors, we have drawn together a variety of approaches to the novels of the justice trilogy: some essays focus primarily on a single novel, while others discuss the full trilogy. Some essays analyze the texture of Erdrich's craft, while others examine the critical, philosophical, historical, and tribal contexts of the trilogy. All of the essays maintain a focus on what Erdrich's trilogy reveals about the possibility of achieving justice.

The essays fall into three groups, connected by the related issues they explore. The first group of essays highlights injustices in the trilogy—lynchings, murders, and other acts of violence, land loss, boarding schools, and other traumatic experiences. Debra K. S. Barker's "The Aesthetics of Justice and Redress in *The Plague of Doves*" explores the ways in which Erdrich's aesthetics can be read as counter-colonial strategies that lay bare the ideology of white supremacy that dispossessed Native peoples of their land and that all too often led to acts of "frontier justice." At the same time, Barker's analysis reveals how Erdrich's deliberate aesthetic choices resist stereotypical images of Indians and humanize her Ojibwe characters. In addition, Barker pays close attention to the ending of *The Plague of Doves*, which, she argues, reaches a sense of closure by foregrounding survival as a key aesthetic for Indigenous art. Kenneth M. Roemer's essay, "Murder She Wrote, and Rewrote, and Rewrote: A Trilogy of Justices," takes up the issue of crime, in particular murder, as a critical lens to approach the three novels of the justice trilogy. Roemer's analysis pinpoints the ways in which Erdrich does, and does not, follow the genre expectations of crime fiction or the murder mystery novel, and he argues that Erdrich innovatively adapts the genre to bring issues of social justice for Indigenous peoples to the foreground and to reimagine justice. In "Trauma and Restitution in Louise Erdrich's *LaRose*," Aitor Ibarrola-Armendariz emphasizes the historical injustices, intergenerational and collective trauma, and various tragedies imposed on the characters of *LaRose*. His analysis makes clear that, for much of the novel, revenge or punishment seems to be the only means to address or express the grievances that follow in the wake of traumatic experiences. We expect a tragic outcome. And yet, as Ibarrola-Armendariz details, *LaRose* turns to "alternative solutions to grievances" to achieve a meaningful sense of restoration and restitution by the end.

The second group of essays highlights the move from trauma to healing in the novels of the trilogy by emphasizing relationality and kinship as significant cultural resources to restore community and to repair various rifts caused by injustices. Ellen L. Arnold's "Family Trees: Land and Kinship in Louise Erdrich's Justice Trilogy" examines Erdrich's justice trilogy from the perspective of finding relations across species, across a range of living things, including humans, animals, plants, and trees, to characterize Erdrich's fictional world as composed of reciprocal and caregiving relations. In particular, Arnold calls attention to the significant presence of trees in all three novels, especially the hanging tree that appears in *The Plague of Doves* and in *The Round House*, and the climbing tree in *LaRose*. As Arnold argues, trees serve as the embodiment of justice in Erdrich's trilogy; they help bind the

Anishinaabeg to their land and to their history. By analyzing trees as relatives, as family, in Erdrich's trilogy, Arnold delineates an ethical understanding of kinship and justice from an Indigenous perspective that unfolds from novel to novel. The essay by Connie A. Jacobs, "You Aren't a Regular Dog, Are You? Dog as Intermediary in Louise Erdrich's *LaRose*," expands kinship relations to animals, specifically dogs. As Jacobs shows, dogs in Erdrich's fiction are special presences. To develop this argument, she turns to the long and interesting history of Indigenous peoples and dogs, and then discusses the dog who adopts the Ravich family in *LaRose* as central to the narrative's working out of justice and forgiveness. Silvia Martínez-Falquina's essay, "We Can Wade Grief: Ethics, Politics, and Relationality in Louise Erdrich's *LaRose*," focuses on the profound sense of grief that haunts the main characters of *LaRose* for much of the novel. The weight of this grief flows from the dramatic opening scene of the novel, when Landreaux Iron accidentally shoots Dusty Ravich. But, as Martínez-Falquina demonstrates, the novel finds ways to work through that grief by calling upon Anishinaabe traditions, teachings, and ceremonies, especially those emphasizing relationality, and the boy LaRose has a central role to play in reforging community relations and in reestablishing order.

One vital goal for this collection of essays is to provide insight into the ways that Anishinaabe culture informs the novels of Erdrich's justice trilogy, and the third group of essays emphasizes Ojibwe culture and language as healing ways to restore balance and effect justice. In "Narrative Design in the Justice Trilogy," Nancy J. Peterson argues that Erdrich's narrative intricacies are illuminated by comparing them to the balanced asymmetrical designs found in Ojibwe beadwork, especially the kinds of floral designs that began to appear on bandolier bags (*gashkibidaaganag*, plural, in Ojibwemowin) in the late nineteenth century. By drawing comparisons to beadwork, Peterson insists on the importance of absorbing all the colorful details and characters, as well as the flowing narrative lines of each novel, but the most satisfying perspective comes from seeing the complete design as it comes together in the trilogy as "one big book" that moves toward forgiveness and healing. Margaret Noodin's essay for this volume, "*Debwe, Onaakonige gaye Nanaandawi'iwe*: Finding Justice in the Language of Louise Erdrich's Novels," explores Erdrich's use of Ojibwemowin, as well as other languages, in the justice trilogy. Noodin argues that Erdrich's trilogy "create[s] justice through a multilingual landscape," and the glossary Noodin includes of words in languages other than English is invaluable. Moreover, Noodin pays particular attention to Erdrich's use of Ojibwemowin to highlight an Anishinaabe ethos that shapes the presentation of history, land

and the environment, spirituality, and community in the novels—all of which come together to create a sense of justice. Gwen Nell Westerman's "Honoring Our Relatives" is a personal essay that takes up the issue of language justice that Noodin addresses. In her essay, Westerman eloquently pays tribute to Louise Erdrich as a mentor and shares one of her own poems that moves between Dakota language and English to emphasize the importance of Indigenous language revitalization.

The essays in the volume will have much to say to scholars of literature, to Native studies specialists, to teachers, to students, and to avid readers of Erdrich's work. The volume concludes with materials designed to provide accurate details and appropriate contexts for understanding the justice trilogy. Peter G. Beidler and Gay Barton have extended the reach of their previously published *A Reader's Guide to the Novels of Louise Erdrich* (1999; rev. ed. 2006) to focus on the novels of the justice trilogy. Each novel—*The Plague of Doves*, *The Round House*, and *LaRose*—is treated in a separate section that presents an overview of key themes, a list of chapters, a chronology of major events, relevant family trees, and a dictionary of prominent characters. The final contribution of the volume is the interview Louise Erdrich gave to Lisa Halliday for the *Paris Review* in 2010. This interview was conducted when Erdrich had just published *The Plague of Doves* and was at work on *The Round House*, and so it gives us a valuable sense of issues that were on Erdrich's mind at the moment and provides fascinating details about her habits as a writer.

The essays of this volume trace some of the most prominent themes that shape the novels of Erdrich's justice trilogy. More importantly, considered together, the essays suggest the visionary ways in which Erdrich repairs and revises ideas of justice to serve the claims of Indigenous peoples. *The Plague of Doves*, *The Round House*, and *LaRose* draw readers into Erdrich's fictional universe in such a way that we come to share the belief that justice must serve as "the foundation of a trusting society" (Hertzel), which necessarily involves what Erdrich describes as "reparation" or "restorative justice" ("After Tragedy"). As Erdrich's trilogy affirms, this kind of justice advances Native sovereignty and calls for acts of human compassion and forgiveness.

WORKS CITED

"After Tragedy, 2 Families Find Their Own Justice in Louise Erdrich's *LaRose*." *All Things Considered*, National Public Radio, 11 May 2016, www.npr.org/2016/05/11/477518606/after-tragedy-two-families-find-their-own-justice-in-louise-erdrichs-larose.

Erdrich, Louise. "The Art of Fiction No. 208: Louise Erdrich." Interview with Lisa Halliday. *Paris Review*, no. 195, Winter 2010, pp. 133–66.

———. *LaRose*. HarperCollins, 2016.

———. "Louise Erdrich on Mercy and Vengeance, Addictions, and the Twin Cities' Bookshop Renaissance." Interview with Erica Rivera. *CityPages*, 9 May 2016, www.citypages.com/arts/louise-erdrich-on-mercy-and-vengeance-addictions-and-the-twin-cities-bookshop-renaissance-8257955.

———. *The Plague of Doves*. HarperCollins, 2008.

———. "Rape on the Reservation." *New York Times*, 27 Feb. 2013, p. A25.

———. *The Round House*. HarperCollins, 2012.

———. "The Sunday *Rumpus* Interview: Louise Erdrich." Interview with Emily Gray Tedrowe, 29 May 2016, therumpus.net/2016/05/the-sunday-rumpus-interview-louise-erdrich/.

———. "The True Story of Mustache Maude." *Frontiers: A Journal of Women Studies*, vol. 7, no. 3, 1984, pp. 62–67.

Freeman, John. "Louise Erdrich: Secrets in the Indian File." *Independent*, 6 June 2008, www.independent.co.uk/arts-entertainment/books/features/louise-erdrich-secrets-in-the-indian-file-841027.html.

Hertzel, Laurie. "Minneapolis Author Louise Erdrich Finds Writing Humor Is the 'Hardest Thing.'" *Minneapolis Star Tribune*, 5 May 2016, www.startribune.com/minneapolis-author-louise-erdrich-on-family-justice-resilience-and-humor/378195271/.

"*Plague of Doves*, Multigenerational Murder Mystery." *Weekend Edition Sunday*, National Public Radio, 4 May 2008, www.npr.org/templates/story/story.php?storyId=90167624.

Russo, Maria. "Disturbing the Spirits." Review of *The Round House*, by Louise Erdrich. *New York Times Book Review*, 14 Oct. 2012, p. 9.

The Aesthetics of Justice and Redress in *The Plague of Doves*

Debra K. S. Barker

> Only one thing here is worth much, to pass your life in truth and
> justice, and show benevolence even to liars and unjust men.
> —Marcus Aurelius, "Meditations," Book 6.47

In her early critical scaffolding of Louise Erdrich's unsettling narrative aesthetics, Catherine Rainwater argues that all of Erdrich's novels challenge certain readers who come to her work with an eagerness to capture and contain a definitive comprehension of the subjects of her novels: "For some contemporary American Indian writers such as Erdrich, to change a reader's habits of interpretation amounts to a subtle, counter-colonial, and reappropriative act" (30–31). In the first of what we now deem Erdrich's justice trilogy, *The Plague of Doves* dramatizes a field of issues around racial violence, murder, and the legacy of settler colonialism, mediated through Erdrich's deft management of authorial subversion.[1]

The opening scene of the eleventh and arguably one of the most complex of

---

Parts of this article appeared in a previously published version, titled "There Are No Burning Wagons, Beads, or Feathers in Louise Erdrich's *The Plague of Doves*." *Critical Insights: Louise Erdrich*. Edited by P. Jane Hafen. Salem Press, 2013.

Louise Erdrich's North Dakota novels, *The Plague of Doves*, takes us back to the early twentieth century with the 1911 mass murder of a white family living outside fictional Pluto, North Dakota. Accused of the crime, four scapegoated American Indians, including a thirteen-year-old boy, are summarily lynched by the founding fathers of Pluto in an act of frontier justice. Only one of the accused victims survives, (Mooshum) Seraph Milk, whose granddaughter, Evelina Harp, will later tease out family and community secrets as she explores the interrelationships between the descendants of both the lynching victims and the immigrant lynch mob: the Buckendorfs, the Wildstrands, and the Peace characters. Later, in the throes of a nervous breakdown, haunted by the memory of the lynching story, Evelina realizes one ineluctable theme both of her life and of this novel: "history works itself out in the living" (243). As history does so, within what I argue is ultimately a moral universe, readers may discern the management of a macro-level process of justice that entails the redress of settler colonial encroachment, as well as the redress of crimes narrated in the early part of the novel. Meanwhile, Erdrich reappropriates aesthetic expectations that certain readers may harbor as they engage with this complex novel offering levels of counternarratives that challenge colonial aesthetics around manifest destiny and the daily lives of surviving Indigenous families.

As I develop my discussion of *The Plague of Doves*, I argue that this is one of Erdrich's novels that performs a rich tour de force of subversion on many levels—subversion that unsettles the authority of non-Native readers tempted to ahistoricize American Indians in time within an imaginary "reservation" space unresponsive to time or the forces of history. Likewise, this novel challenges certain readers' tendency to romanticize the settlement of the American frontier and then ignore the consequences for the Indigenous inhabitants of that frontier. Clearly the forces of history have shaped not only the material circumstances of the American Anishinaabeg as a nation but also the consciousness of the community members who have survived to see the twentieth century. This essay will later devote attention to political issues around the colonial invasion and conquest of Pluto, North Dakota, tracing that legacy into the present time, ultimately mediating the conflicts presented in the acts of injustice and dispossession narrated in the earlier portions of the novel.

The Plague of Doves, a 2009 Pulitzer Prize finalist, has slowly aggregated a critical reception that has remained overwhelmingly positive since its release. One of the few Native critics writing about this novel, Anishinaabe scholar Margaret Noori, situates the work within the tradition of Erdrich's other polyvocal novels, layering plots and subplots, shifting seamlessly between generations and interwoven narrative contexts. Noting Erdrich's prodigious stylistic influences, Noori points out, "Although many read her work as Native American, with each successive novel she challenges that boundary by writing more like Ernest Hemingway, William Faulkner, Albert Camus, or Arturo Pérez-Reverte than like N. Scott Momaday, Leslie Silko, James Welch, or Simon Ortiz" (12). Arguing for the sovereignty of Native artistic production, Noori asserts, "She has earned the right to write according to her own expectations" (12). Erdrich's artistic self-expectations have continually ranged across the widening terrain of her reading and lived experiences, which Steven Leuthold argues in *Indigenous Aesthetics* precisely describes "aesthetic behavior": "Not simply a logical construct or link in a philosophical system, the term 'aesthetic' refers to real aspects of lived experience that have a social dimension" (6). Leuthold goes on to broaden the application of the terms "art" and "aesthetics," connecting "art, ethics, and spirituality" while also "counter[ing] the materialism, ethno-centrism, and specialized uses of the term often found in recent Western theory" (9).

Erdrich is a postmodern author writing to audiences who can appreciate that although American Indians may appear to some non-Indians as surviving vestiges or living relics of a vanishing, mythic race, they are in fact complex American citizens who have hauled into this millennium a great amount of unique cultural, political, and historical baggage. Erdrich is entitled to the assertion of aesthetic sovereignty regarding not only her narrative style but also her choice of subject matter, including the representation of Native American family life in the mid-twentieth century. One of the many accomplishments of this novel lies in its challenge to readers to interrogate their assumptions about American Indians and class. Indeed, rarely have critics explored the subject of middle-class Indians in fact, perhaps because, as Dr. Jack Forbes points out in his essay "Colonialism and Native American Literature: Analysis," "critics or scholars sometimes seem to want modern-day chants and lots of symbolic beads and feathers. They want to read about the mystical, about rituals and ceremony. . . . They seem to be less interested in reading about genocide and politics or love and sex" (21).

In *The Plague of Doves* Erdrich normalizes American Indians by situating her characters within domestic contexts already familiar to many readers of Erdrich's generation. For instance, she develops a series of Native characters, none of whom is looking stoic, wearing feathers, or bemoaning liminal identities. In fact, she repositions American Indians within a broader historical, racial, and socioeconomic context so non-Native readers new to Erdrich's fiction might elide knee-jerk, stereotypical responses to a novel featuring American Indian characters: first, that Indians—and middle-class Indians at that—really did and do exist, and they make enormous contributions in the world broadly, alongside their settler neighbors. Erdrich, in fact, subtly decolonizes her readers' aesthetics or aesthetic expectations. Second, Indians do not inhabit a space called "plight." For example, while Evelina notes that her mother's and aunt's clothing was purchased secondhand, her parents nevertheless occupy a socioeconomic stratum not unknown to the majority of middle-class Americans during the 1960s. She tells us early in the novel, "We are a tribe of office workers, bank tellers, book readers, and bureaucrats. The wildest of us (Whitey) is a short-order cook, and the most heroic of us (my father) teaches" (9).

Evelina's new uncle, mixed-blood Judge Antone Bazil Coutts, reads the Stoics—as in the classical Stoic philosophers Marcus Aurelius and Epictetus—but he himself is not stoic in the least. Even as he refers to himself as "the clichéd mixed-blood" (114), the irony in his tone is clear: Judge Coutts holds both a law degree and enrollment in his tribe, quite mindful of the benefits his status has afforded him. And while Evelina grows up aware of the historical processes of colonization and dispossession, this dimension of her family background does in no way dominate her consciousness or contain her within a marginalized category. Indeed, as she grows up and goes to college, Evelina expresses multiple identities as a college student during the early 1970s, when drug and sexual experimentation, as well as membership in countercultural collective households were not at all uncommon.

In the twenty-first century, Erdrich's novel performs the work of resolving the conflicts of internalized ideologies by cultural normalization of racial representations. This normalization serves as a key aesthetic element of Erdrich's representation of contemporary Indigenous life. Erdrich's representation of American Indians challenges readers by the very nature of their complexity, their humanity, normalizing American Indians as a racial category. The novel explores a twentieth-century childhood and coming of age through the eyes of Evelina, a curious, passionate girl who enjoys *The Three Stooges*, is learning French, dreams of going to Paris, and is discovering her sexual identity. If readers come to *The Plague of Doves* curious about the ethnographic dimensions of Indigenous family life in the 1960s, they will be disappointed to discover that background elements of this novel resonate with those of *To Kill a Mockingbird*, for instance, or 1960s television programs featuring benign and preoccupied "Ward and June" parental figures moving along the vague periphery of the stage that foregrounds the dramatic inner lives of their children. Evelina suffers dramatic, romantic crushes not only on Corwin Peace but also on her teacher, Sister Mary Anita Buckendorf. Her brother, Joseph, collects stamps and loves science. In every respect the siblings' experiences reflect the influence of mainstream American pop culture. Finally, what Erdrich accomplishes is a type of aesthetic redress, a corrective to representations of Native people found in 1960s Hollywood Westerns and Euro-American pop culture in general.

Frontier Justice

With the exception of John Rollin Ridge, Erdrich is the only Native writer to draw attention to the lynching of Indians, a subject that has remained largely ignored, except by Western American historians. In crafting *The Plague of Doves*, Erdrich anchors the novel's central plot in historical events, after having read a newspaper account of the lynching of three American Indian males in her native North Dakota in the aftermath of the mass murder of a farm family. The headline of the 1897 *New York Times* article reads as follows: "Mob Law in North Dakota: Three Indians Lynched for the Murder of Six Members of the Spicer Family." The caption goes on to announce, "The Courts Were Too Slow. The Alleged Ringleader of the Murders Had Obtained a New Trial after Having Been Sentenced to Death." The *New York Times* reports that the vigilante group was composed of forty masked men, all members of the fraternal Lodge of the Woodmen, who adjourned their meeting to carry out their self-appointed civic duty. The 1897 article narrates the events in some detail: "The lynching apparently had been planned carefully, and was carried out without a break in the programme [*sic*]"; the accused men were lynched from a slaughterhouse "windlash" (a device used to suspend slaughtered cattle) in Williamsport, North Dakota, and left to hang. Readers are also told that a period of time elapsed before the arrival of the coroner, and no one came to claim and bury the bodies ("Mob Law in North Dakota"). In his 2008 review of the novel, Jeff Baenen reports, "No one in the lynch mob ever was prosecuted, and two other suspects, who were jailed miles away in Bismarck, N.D., were released after the lynching." However, there was no direct evidence or, for that matter, circumstantial evidence, establishing beyond a reasonable doubt that Paul Holy Track committed or participated in the murders of which he was accused.

In *Murdering Indians: A Documentary History of the 1897 Killings That Inspired Louise Erdrich's The Plague of Doves*, Peter G. Beidler presents his deeply researched history of the Spicer murders, contemporaneous newspaper articles, and court records from the trial. Beidler provides as well valuable historical context that gives readers an insight into the genocidal impulses of the settlers living near the Standing Rock Sioux Indian reservation at the end of the nineteenth century.

One witness photographed the lynching, capturing for posterity this sensational local event. On its website, in anticipation of a 2005 auction, Cowan's Auctions featured a grainy black-and-white photograph, titled "Photograph of North Dakota Triple Lynching," capturing the image of the three victims, hanging from a windlass. After identifying the victims' names and summarizing the events leading up to the hanging, the annotation for the photograph concludes with a memorialized narrative:

> Eventually all were caught, and jailed. Technicalities, a hung jury and the belief that all three would be set free prompted a November 13, 1897 "visit" to the Williamstown jail by 40 masked men. The jailer was quickly overpowered and the doomed trio was pulled from their cells. The mob attempted to hang the three first from a well curbing, then a log cabin, and finally succeeded using the beam of a beef windlass at the rear of the Williamsport Hotel. Although the identities of most of the vigilantes were known, none were ever prosecuted.

Suggesting a kind of poetic justice in effect, a rather satisfying aesthetic conclusion in that, the catalog copy concludes, "Significantly, neither Winona—the town where the Spicer's [*sic*] lived, or Williamstown—the place where the murderers were lynched—exists today." The photograph sold at auction for $3,105.00 under the category "Historic Americana" (Cowan's Auctions). A second photograph of the five accused, titled "Degraff Photograph of Indians Implicated in the Spicer Murder," sold for $352.50 at auction in 2009, a sale no doubt prompted by the opportune publication of Erdrich's novel. The names of the accused are identified as follows: Black Hawk, Phillip Ireland (Standing Bear), Paul Holy Track, George Defender, and Alex Coudot (Cowan's Auctions).

According to Ken Gonzales-Day's *Lynching in the West*, the number of American Indians lynched in the late nineteenth century rose exponentially in relation to the relentless encroachment of settler populations, anxious to claim and establish land rights, citing California as a region where Indigenous people were not only "driven from their lands but shot on sight" (83). Gonzales-Day points out, "The fact that due process was rarely extended to 'Indians' was complicated by their legal status. Because they were rarely brought to trial, one will never know the truth of the charges" (83).

Readers new to American Indian literature may be surprised to learn that at this time, the Indigenous inhabitants of what is now known as the United States were not legally recognized under United States law as American citizens and therefore could be denied the legal protection enjoyed by undocumented Euro-American immigrants. Legal recognition and enfranchisement would not be conferred until 1924, and then only under the pressure of European governments noting the battlefield valor of the American Indian soldiers who fought during the First World War. Peter Nabokov writes, "At long last, on June 2, 1924, the Indian Citizenship Act was passed—in large measure because Congress had become embarrassed over the obvious discrepancy between Indian status at home and Indian courage overseas" (382).

The status of American Indians has been determined, since contact with European settlers, by the ideologies of race and racism that sank their roots into the rocky soil of the early Puritan colonies. Indeed, the Puritans racialized early American society and its social systems around its need for slave labor and land. George Lipsitz explains, "The colonial and early national legal systems authorized attacks on Native Americans and encouraged the appropriation of their lands" (72). Categorized as nonpersons by virtue of their race, American Indians weathered a genocidal assault that reduced their total numbers to 265,683 by 1910, according to the 1910 US Census. Invoking Herman Melville's expression from *The Confidence-Man*—"the metaphysics of Indian hating" (149)—to characterize a particular strand of racial animus in early America, Richard Drinnon historicizes the "deadly subtleties of white hostility that reduced native peoples to the level of the rest of the fauna and flora to be 'rooted out.' It reduced all the diverse Native American peoples to a single despised nonwhite group and, where they did survive, into a hereditary caste" (xvi). The racial animus dramatized in Erdrich's novel is reflected in Dr. Cordelia Lochren's refusal to provide medical treatment to Indians, suggesting a long-held ideology that finds expression in ambivalence. She is drawn to, repelled by, and yet guilty about the presence of Native people in her community in a space that her ancestors seized and settled. While she has desired and retained Antone Bazil Coutts as her lover in a long, surreptitious love affair, she will not marry him, nor will she be seen with him in public.

The Plague of Doves prompts readers to reflect on the origins and historical consequences of American racial ideologies and the purposes that racial animus served as the frontier was settled. Drinnon maintains that the dehumanization of Indians in relation to white Christian social systems was a step in the process of colonial conquest, which was "in a real sense the enabling experience of the rising American empire: Indian-hating identified the dark *others* that white settlers were not and must not under any circumstances become, and it helped them wrest a continent and more from the hands of these native caretakers of the lands" (xvii–xviii).

In *The Plague of Doves*, the dispossession of ancestral, tribal land assumes the power of a psychic wound within Evelina's family. A tactless question posed by her Aunt Neve Harp, a non-Indian and self-appointed Pluto historian, prompts Evelina's dawning recognition that she too will inherit the historical trauma of dispossession. Mooshum, incredulous at Neve's question, responds: "What you are asking . . . is how was it stolen? How has this great thievery become acceptable? How do we live right here beside you, knowing what we lost and how you took it?" (84). Neve's desire to hear an Ojibwe elder explain to her how the pioneer town of Pluto came to be situated within the boundaries of the reservation strikes the reader as a display of callous ignorance born of her own white privilege, given that she has not considered the moral implications of how the land she enjoys has come at the expense of her homeless, landless Ojibwe neighbors. Like many Indian reservations that have fallen prey to land loss based on spurious treaty agreements and settler greed, the pioneer town in proximity to Evelina's reservation home had been pried from her ancestral land base.

Ironically, there are few Indians living in Pluto, North Dakota, a town situated within the reservation boundaries. In an emotionally nuanced scene capturing her recognition of her elders' quiet distress in response to Neve Harp's question, Evelina begins to internalize the effect of the historical processes and patent injustice of American imperialism:

> [B]oth men's [demeanors] became like Mama's—quiet, with an elaborate reserve, and something else that has stuck in my heart ever since. I saw that the loss of their land was lodged inside of them forever. This loss would enter me, too. Over time, I came to know that the sorrow was a thing that each of them covered up according to their character—my old uncle through his passionate discipline, my mother through strict kindness and cleanly order. As for my grandfather, he used the patient art of ridicule. (84)

Here Erdrich captures an intimate, domestic moment that the early New England colonists certainly could not have imagined or projected into a twentieth-century tableau—a Native American front-porch scene. As she comes of age, Evelina's dawning comprehension of the effects of these historical processes rendered on the generations of her family emerges, introduced with no drama and certainly no polemics.

The ideology of white supremacy wrested more than ancestral land from Evelina's forefathers; it dispossessed them of their own sense of personhood. At the opening of the novel, it is clear that by the early twentieth century, Native people have internalized colonial oppression. Evelina's young grandfather, along with the other individuals who come upon the murdered Lochren family, already feel helpless to evade what appear to be certain inevitabilities attending their very presence in their own land. When Mooshum and the others stop to care for the one human survivor of the massacre, drawn by compassion to the wailing, dehydrated Lochren baby and the "bawling" of unmilked cows, one heard "scream[ing] like a woman in pain" (61), they know they will regret their act of human kindness. Asiginak, the great-uncle of the young Holy Track, rejects Cuthbert Peace's suggestion that they notify the sheriff of the existence of the surviving baby. Incredulous, he asks, "You're not drunk, so why do you say this? We are no-goods, we are Indians, even me. If you tell the white sheriff, we will die" (63). Young Mooshum adds, "They will hang us for sure" (63). Later, as they are taken to be hanged, Cuthbert pleads, "We found those people already dead. . . . We found them, but did not kill them. We milked their cows for them and we fed the baby. I, Cuthbert, fed the baby! We are not your bad kind of Indians! Those are south of here!" (74–75). Clearly, they have internalized the ideology of white supremacy, along with the social and political inequities that attend being an American Indian in a world in which the settlers have normalized Euromerican racial practices and justified murder as a civic practice complementing legal justice. At this point in early twentieth-century America, Cuthbert Peace is powerless to protest the degraded status not only of American Indians in the region but also of himself and his companions.

Justice and the Ethic of Rapacity

Another key act of counter-colonial, aesthetic subversion on Erdrich's part is her repositioning of American Indians within a broader historical and racial context that initially defamiliarizes conventional historical paradigms that have shaped the way Anglo settlers have viewed Indians vis-à-vis the frontier and the conquest of the American West. With her recounted history of the founding of Pluto, Erdrich presents, through the narrative of Judge Antone Bazil Coutts, a critique that deromanticizes colonial exploration and conquest. Critic Seamus Deane, in refining his definition of colonialism, explains: "To disguise its essentially rapacious nature, colonialism has been represented in literary, historical, and political discourses as a species of adventure tale, dominated by an ethic of personal heroism that is embedded in a specific national-religious formation" (354). Erdrich's "adventure tale," embellished by details of blizzards, starvation, the temptations of cannibalism, and persistent lower gastrointestinal miseries, provides readers with a dark comedy rather than a saga of frontier heroics. Moreover, it presents a story dominated by an ethic of rapacity with Judge Coutts's reference to the Pluto "town-site expedition" as "a bunch of greedy fools" engaged in a "hideous trial" that nearly kills them. Speculating on the eventual construction of a railroad line extending westward of the eastern border of Dakota territory, the expedition party, dreaming of the "millions" they would make, sought to "survey and establish claim by occupancy on several huge pieces of land that would most certainly become towns, perhaps cities, when the railroad reached that part of the world" (*Plague* 97).

In Erdrich's hands, Joseph Coutts's narrative foregrounds the true heroes of the tale, the Native guides, Henri and Lafayette Peace, who preserve the lives of the hapless white land speculators and venture capitalists who have hired them and who have chosen to time their departure in midwinter, thus securing a clever advantage over any competing expeditions seeking to claim the wealth of the plains for themselves. Before long, having eaten their oxen, the food for the oxen, and then their own shoes, the men come to rely on a drug remedy one of the men brought along, "Batner's Powders" (105), which Erdrich later reveals to be opium.

In a 2010 interview with Lisa Halliday for the *Paris Review*, Erdrich discloses that this fictional expedition was based on a documented one that found its conclusion in Wahpeton, North Dakota, her hometown. Erdrich explains, "I knew the exact route they took, and my description was based in reality. Daniel Johnston, who wrote the account, recorded that the party had bowel troubles and so took 'a remedy.' Then it only remained for me to look up what remedy there was at the time, and it was laudanum" ("Art" 155). The Peace brothers, familiar with winter-weather camping, set up camp, enticed and stalked bison, and deployed inherited survival skills to enable the party's survival. Meanwhile, their employers hallucinated, considered eating one of their deceased comrades, and coped with incessant diarrhea. One expedition survivor, Joseph Coutts, would pass on to his grandson, Antone Coutts, this decidedly unromantic conquest narrative. Joseph Coutts would pronounce himself cured of "town fever" and decide to "take up the law" (*Plague* 113).

Erdrich's Unsettling Aesthetics

Native cultural studies scholars have already noted the degree to which American Indian imagery and cultural references have been appropriated by the dominant culture to promote everything from Leinenkugel's beer to Land O Lakes butter. In an exercise of subversion and aesthetic sovereignty, Erdrich draws freely on potent American pop culture indexical signs to underpin allusions signaling their parallel engagement with pop culture. Asserting her aesthetic sovereignty and thereby agency in shaping or frustrating colonial expectations of Native American coming-of-age stories, Erdrich appropriates signifiers of baby boomer literary and pop culture, drawing on hybrid cultural materials to provide unexpected cultural textures, thereby shaping the zeitgeist that informs the consciousness of Evelina Harp, the central narrator of *The Plague of Doves* and a descendant of one of the lynch party's victims.

The chapter Evelina narrates of the lynching tragedy presents a field of allusions that organizes the novel's layers of pathos and irony. The legacy of racial violence sorted out by its inheritors suggests the Southern Gothic of William Faulkner's and Harper Lee's imaginary communities. Faulkner's middle name was Cuthbert; by appropriating that name for Cuthbert Peace, Erdrich implies broad cultural connections between race relations in the American South and those on the Western frontier. By naming one of the lynching victims Cuthbert, Erdrich likewise lends an aesthetic and political poignancy to the lynching tragedy of 1911. Erdrich's novel, initiated by the author's shock at reading the newspaper story, in fact, prompts one to wonder if Harper Lee might have constructed her own novel around an actual story of a thwarted lynch mob that sought an innocent scapegoat such as Tom Robinson.

A common motif relates *To Kill a Mockingbird* and *The Plague of Doves*: an eccentric stranger provides odd little gifts to children. Thinking about the folded dollar bills Warren Wolde left for the orphaned child of the family he murdered, then later tried to give to Evelina (as if to provide reparations for the scapegoated victims of the lynchings) in Erdrich's novel, readers may recall the small gifts Boo Radley secreted in the tree for Scout and Jem in Lee's novel. Furthermore, like Scout and Jem, young Evelina and her brother, Joseph, are introduced to the reality of racialized violence, shocked out of their innocence by Mooshum and initiated into their town's secret history of murder and racial hatred. As Evelina contemplates the implications of the lynching—that her own great-grandfather, John Wildstrand, was a leader and her beloved grandfather, Mooshum, an implied abettor in the discovery of the accused men—she realizes that the story had "its repercussions—the first being that I could not look at anyone in quite the same way anymore" (86). Later, as a patient in the state mental hospital, Evelina recalls one of Mooshum's old stories of her ancestors' will to survive not just hunger but the rapacity of colonial domination that sought to control the indocile, the land. Evelina recalls, "Mooshum told me how the old buffalo hunters looked beneath the robe of destruction that blanketed the earth. In the extremity of their hunger they saw the frail crust of white commerce lifting, saw the green grass underneath the burnt wheat, saw the buffalo thick as lice again, saw the great herds moving, flattening that rich grass beneath their hooves" (244). The imagery of recovery and renewal of the natural world echoes descriptions of Ghost Dance visions. As leaders of the Indigenous religious movement of the late nineteenth century, the Ghost Dance prophets taught believers to dance in prayer for a cataclysmic transformation of the world, praying for the disappearance of the white settlers, the renewal of the land, and the return of the bison. They prayed for the supernatural hand of justice to render apocalyptic justice.

History Works Itself Out in the Living

Living out the history of Pluto, the sole surviving member of the Lochren family massacre eulogizes the dying town, once a proud and hopeful outpost of colonial civilization. The "white commerce" that Mooshum refers to in his apocalyptic story to Evelina has indeed been drawn back to reveal the Indigenous frontier's reclaiming the space once platted and mapped by the venture capitalists, who could never have imagined one-stop shopping centers, interstate highways, or big-city entertainment. An infant in the opening chapter in the novel and now an elder in the closing one, Dr. Lochren concludes the novel with this prediction: "The wind will blow. The devils rise. All who celebrate shall be ghosts. And there will be nothing but eternal dancing, dust on dust, everywhere you look" (313). Narrator Cordelia Lochren envisions Pluto as "empty at last" and her house "reclaimed by earth" (310). With no tax base, the town yields to disrepair. Pluto will return to the rhythms of time, which beat for the ghost dance of posterity. Both she and Judge Coutts eulogize the quiet apocalypse they are witnessing, understanding, nevertheless, that the everlasting spirit of the land will prevail.

Both narrators' meditations lend an eschatological cast to the conclusion of the novel, suggesting that Pluto has collapsed under the weight of its own history. The displaced Indigenous inhabitants of this region, the Ojibwe and the Dakota, understood the power of the earth, seeing themselves as its stewards, rather than its masters. They understood the futility of attempting to partition and control the earth, respecting the spirits and the moral universe that oversee ephemeral human endeavors. Critic Anne Ursu points out, "Place has a sentience in Erdrich's prose; it murmurs memories and whispers fortunes." Western historian Patricia Limerick, assuming the perspective of a self-reflective descendant of frontier settlers, comments, "We live on haunted land, on land that is layers deep in human passion and memory" (73). Within a moral universe the symmetry of the birth and death of Pluto affords readers an aesthetic pleasure of closure, resolution, justice.

Judge Antone Bazil Coutts, recalling his grandfather's perspective on the siren call for easy wealth, which nearly cost him his life during the original Pluto site expedition, reflects on the futility of conquest:

> As I look at the town now, dwindling without grace, I think how strange that lives were lost in its formation. It is the same with all desperate enterprises that involve boundaries we place upon the earth. By drawing a line and defending it, we seem to think we have mastered something. What? The earth swallows and absorbs even those who manage to form a country, a reservation. (115)

His discerning observation lays the groundwork for the resolution of the novel. The conclusion of *The Plague of Doves* challenges readers' expectations in unexpected ways, given the identity of the narrator who knots together the conclusions of the multiple story lines of the novel. Moreover, we are left with a sense that this is a rare Erdrich novel that meets an expectation of closure. Sister Mary Buckendorf gives Evelina Paul Holy Track's shoes to return to the hanging tree, and the Buckendorf family line ends with her eventual death. The deadly beauty of Corwin Peace's violin music overtakes Warren Wolde, whose 1911 crime precipitated the lynching of Corwin's ancestor, Cuthbert Peace. And John Wildstrand goes to prison, thanks to the work of his accomplice, Corwin's father, Billy Peace. The injustices of history are ultimately rendered through the destinies of the living as agents of a moral universe.

One of my uncles, Albert White Hat, Sr., taught us that Lakota spirituality is "reality-based," that our religious and philosophical practices are very much rooted in the land and in lived experiences. In that sense we imagine that Indigenous art springs from the collective memory of Indigenous survivors who bequeath the stories that chronicle the survival of Native people. Survival must be appreciated as an aesthetic dimension of Indigenous art. It certainly marks a significant aesthetic of the three novels that constitute Erdrich's justice trilogy. Readers are asked to ponder at length the persistent legacy of economic, spiritual, and judicial oppression bequeathed through the generational politics supporting the colonial presence of immigrant settlers both in real America and in Erdrich's North Dakota world.

The Plague of Doves stands as a work that successfully humanizes American Indians within a racial category previously deemed mythic, without denying the racism that remains to this day as the shared legacy of both the Native and non-Native descendants of the early denizens of colonial settlements like Pluto, North Dakota.

WORKS CITED

Aurelius, Marcus. "Marcus Aurelius: Meditations." Book 6.47. *Marcus Aurelius and His Times: The Transition from Paganism to Christianity*, published for the Classics Club by Walter J. Black, 1945, pp. 65–66.

Baenen, Jeff. "A Dark Event Inspires Erdrich's New Novel." *Indian Country News*, 30 May 2008, http://indiancountrynews.net/index.php/culture/books-music-reviews/3557-a-dark-event-inspires-erdrichs-new-novel.

Beidler, Peter G. *Murdering Indians: A Documentary History of the 1897 Killings That Inspired Louise Erdrich's* The Plague of Doves. McFarland, 2014.

Cowan's Auctions. "Photograph of North Dakota Triple Lynching." 2005. www.cowanauctions.com/lot/photograph-of-north-dakota-triple-lynching-29677.

Deane, Seamus. "Imperialism/Nationalism." *Critical Terms for Literary Study*, edited by Frank Lentricchia and Thomas McLaughlin, 2nd ed., U of Chicago P, 1995, pp. 354–68.

Drinnon, Richard. *Facing West: The Metaphysics of Indian-Hating and Empire-Building.* U of Minnesota P, 1980.

Erdrich, Louise. "The Art of Fiction No. 208: Louise Erdrich." Interview by Lisa Halliday. *Paris Review*, no. 195, Winter 2010, pp. 133–66.

———. *The Plague of Doves*. HarperCollins, 2008.

Forbes, Jack. "Colonialism and Native American Literature: Analysis." *Wicazo Sa Review*, vol. 3, no. 2, 1987, pp. 17–23.

Gonzales-Day, Ken. *Lynching in the West: 1850–1935*. Duke UP, 2006.

Leuthold, Steven. *Indigenous Aesthetics: Native Art, Media, and Identity*. U of Texas P, 1998.

Limerick, Patricia Nelson. *Something in the Soil: Legacies and Reckonings in the New West*. Norton, 2000.

Lipsitz, George. "The Possessive Investment in Whiteness." *White Privilege: Essential Readings on the Other Side of Racism*, edited by Paula S. Rothenberg, 4th ed., Worth, 2012, pp. 71–94.

Melville, Herman. *The Confidence-Man: His Masquerade*. Edited by Hershel Parker and Mark Niemeyer, 2nd ed., Norton, 2006.

"Mob Law in North Dakota." *New York Times*, 15 Nov. 1897, www.nytimes.com/1897/11/15/archives/mob-law-in-north-dakota-three-indians-lynched-for-the-murder-of-six.html.

Nabokov, Peter. "Glimmerings of Sovereignty, 1915–1924." *The Native Americans: An Illustrated History*, edited by Betty Ballantine and Ian Ballantine, Turner, 1993, pp. 377–83.

Noori, Margaret. "The Shiver of Possibility." Review of *The Plague of Doves*, by Louise Erdrich. *Women's Review of Books*, vol. 25, no. 5, 2008, pp. 12–13.

Rainwater, Catherine. *Dreams of Fiery Stars: The Transformations of Native American Fiction*. U of Pennsylvania P, 1999.

Ursu, Anne. "The Lay of the Land: Louise Erdrich." *City Pages* [Minneapolis, MN], 9 Sept. 1998.

Murder She Wrote, and Rewrote, and Rewrote

A Trilogy of Justices

Kenneth M. Roemer

n 2008, the Arts & Letters Live series in Dallas hosted a public interview with Louise Erdrich conducted by Randy D. Gordon and Catherine Cuellar. During the Q & A session, Erdrich revealed two characteristics of her writing processes that fascinated me. She keeps voluminous lists of possible character names. That comment inspired me to spend months researching her English, Métis, and Anishinaabe character names.[1] Later, she confessed that she was well into writing *The Plague of Doves* (2008) when she realized that she was writing a murder mystery and that she needed to add clues. The last clue she added—indeed, the last part she composed for the novel—was the sensational "Solo" that raises many questions about a horrendous murder that had just been committed and might continue with infanticide (Interview, Gordon and Cuellar).

As Connie Jacobs's paper "'Move Over Tony Hillerman'" emphasizes, there are quite a few Native American authors writing mysteries.[2] In Erdrich's case, her interest in mysteries raises an intriguing question: what might be the implications of combining a focus on social justice with the conventions of a murder mystery—in a "suspense novel masking a crusade," as she described the combination for *Time* magazine (Luscombe)? *The Plague of Doves*, *The Round House* (2012), and *LaRose* (2016) are not primarily mystery novels. But they include killings, attempted murders, murders, and mysteries about these events. Murder-mystery conventions certainly have the potential to enhance social justice narratives. The crimes committed and the mysteries posed—Who done it? To whom? When? Where? Why? And will there be justice?—raise significant concerns about conditions on reservations, interactions between on- and off-reservation populations, and multiple questions about jurisdiction and sovereignty. As Julie Tharp (28) and early reviewers suggest, mystery elements may also entice readers not familiar with Indian Country or Native authors to learn some of the territory. On the other hand, mystery conventions could become distractions from social justice problems or result in narratives marred by the types of contrived clues and unrealistic motives and solutions that Raymond Chandler criticized in his classic essay "The Simple Art of Murder" (1950).

Erdrich's social justice novels avoid these pitfalls, especially because her mysteries demonstrate her ability to adapt mystery conventions to explore an impressive variety of social justice challenges ranging from the very personal psychological responses of perpetrators and victims, to the need for alternative forms of restorative justice that question the validity of established legal systems, and to expansive considerations of the historical legacies of centuries-old racism and settler-colonial paradigms. This spectrum—beginning with the personal and ending with the expansive historical—helps to explain why I discuss the novels in reverse order of publication dates. *LaRose* focuses on the complex effects of a killing on an individual, a family, and their neighbors. It also makes less use of conventional mystery questions, since most of the who-done-it questions seem to be answered in the first few pages. *The Round House* makes the most obvious uses of who-done-it mystery questions, explores the psychological impact of a rape and attempted murder on an individual and her family, and expands the range of questions relating to heinous crimes to include explicit examinations of the legal parameters of jurisdiction and sovereignty in the late twentieth century. The murder mysteries in *The Plague of Doves* raise the most expansive questions of historical legacies by dramatizing how "history works itself out in the living" (243), that is, in the lives of contemporary Ojibwe people impacted by centuries of settler colonialism, Manifest Destiny, and prejudice.

My genre studies approach is influenced by murder-mystery guidelines established decades ago by masters of the form, especially Raymond Chandler ("Simple Art") and S. S. Van Dine ("Twenty Rules"), as well as by more recent criticism by well-known critics, including Fredric Jameson. These general studies are valuable interpretive road maps for me, but what especially fascinates me is Erdrich's ability to ground her representations of comprehensive social justice issues firmly and believably in the complex psychological responses of specific perpetrators, victims, and Ojibwe communities immersed in local circumstances. These representations are particularly intriguing because of Erdrich's ability to vary the amount and kind of detail used to describe perpetrators and victims, her careful attention to revealing and withholding significant information and to pacing her clues and false clues, and the narrative voice offering the details and the revealing, withholding, and pacing. These variations often invite readers to adopt strong emotional and/or intellectual feelings and thoughts about victimization, oppression, and, to use Gerald Vizenor's term, survivance. Hence my foray into Erdrich's use of murder-mystery conventions is as much character, narrative structure, focalization, and reader-response analysis as it is a genre study.

Exonerated, Guilty, and (Almost) Framed

Should *LaRose* even be included in a discussion of murder mysteries and social justice fiction? Where's the mystery? Where's the murder? In the opening pages, we learn who shot whom and when and where. One key element of standard definitions of murder is premeditation. That element is absent in the killing of Dusty Ravich. Romeo, Landreaux Iron's nemesis, knows that the community believes that Dusty's death is "an open-and-shut sort of thing, a tragic accident" during a deer hunt (273). The deer-like colors of Dusty's hair and T-shirt further point toward an accident (5). In this case, the fact that the coroner's report indicates that the 1999 event occurred "a few dozen yards" on the reservation side (275) doesn't pose jurisdiction problems (a key concern in *The Round House*). No mysteries there, either.

But there are at least three significant questions related to the consequences of killing a human being that are examined in greater depth in *LaRose* than in the other two social justice novels and thus justify its inclusion: How does shooting someone affect the killer's psyche and family dynamics? If the legal system exonerates a killer whose psyche tells the perpetrator that s(he) is guilty of a crime as horrendous as murder, are there alternative Indigenous justice customs that can heal the "criminal's" conscience? Finally, how do we determine guilt? To be more specific, in attempts to establish guilt when someone is killed, to what degree can an investigator utilize and/or abuse the rational methods of induction and deduction typically lauded by real-life detectives and mystery writers (Moretti 144; Van Dine, Rule #5)?

Erdrich's portrayal of Landreaux's psychological battles after Dusty's death represent her most thorough examination of how killing affects the killer. Her narrators in *The Round House, The Plague of Doves,* and *LaRose* offer scant insights about the post-event psyches of the vigilante lynchers in *Plague,* Marn in *The Round House,* and Wolfred, who poisons Mackinnon, in *LaRose.* We do get glimpses of traumatic effects of murder on Warren Wolde in *Plague* (e.g., 245–46), in Linden's outbursts after the rape of Geraldine (160–62), and in the nightmares that haunt Joe and Cappy in *The Round House* (307). But in *LaRose,* the central mysteries are: How will Landreaux handle his guilt? Will he relapse into substance abuse? Will he commit a murder-suicide?

During a three-year period, readers witness Landreaux's attempts to respond to these questions with combinations of self-help and seeking help. He's briefly tempted by liquor (9–10), talks to and prays with Father Travis (8), and enters the sweat lodge (10, 51–54). None of these attempts at healing work completely. Only a willingness to accept help from unexpected sources and the act of defining his guilt alleviate some of his demons. Both these approaches fall outside the bounds of traditional Catholic (confession, formal prayer) or Ojibwe (sweat baths, ceremonies) practices. One of the sources is unexpected: two squabbling daughters. Their bickering over one sister's crush on their adoptive brother distracts Landreaux, and then their fake fight with him shakes him out of his self-absorption and temptation to escape his guilt with pills (286–88).

The other source comes from a revelation. Kate Shanley has argued that many Native rejuvenation processes begin with the individual's ability to define his or her guilt ("Healing Efficacy").[3] Landreaux must define his wrongdoing. He knows he did not intend to kill Dusty and that he was not under the influence of alcohol or drugs. But he concludes that he is guilty of "a crucial lack of attention" (149). This might seem to be a minor crime, but to Landreaux, it is a sacrilege that represents a premeditated attempted murder. The buck that he had carefully stalked for years appeared that morning. He should have realized that it "was trying to tell me something" (149). Like the deer Sam Fathers reveals to the boy Ike McCaslin in Faulkner's "The Old People" (184–85), this deer should not have been hunted. It was "a bridge to another world" (*LaRose* 149). Landreaux's definition of the event does not vanquish his guilt; it may even deepen it. But it helps Landreaux to conceptualize his sickness. His transgression is no longer a nebulous "blur"—the word he initially used to define his perception of his act of killing (4).

These two private movements toward healing are overshadowed by the major manifestation of alternative social justice in *LaRose*. Most of the narrative after Landreaux's release from custody directly or indirectly relates to Landreaux's decision to atone for his guilt in a way Erdrich's mother told her was not "totally unusual" (McGrath). It was an "old [Anishinaabe] way" (*LaRose* 16). Landreaux and Emmaline explain, "Our son will be your son now" (16), as they give their five-year-old son, LaRose, to the Ravich family as a replacement for Dusty, which Erdrich has described as an "act of restoration" in hopes of restoring "decency" and "balance" (Interview, Makkai). This answers one mystery question: Are there ways of atonement for someone cleared by the law but plagued by feelings of guilt?—but raises another question: Will this form of alternative justice work?

At first it doesn't. Landreaux's wife and daughters violently oppose losing LaRose: "My family hates me," Landreaux tells Randall (51). LaRose's new sister, Maggie Ravich, maliciously tells the boy, "your dad murdered my little brother" (108). But gradually over a three-year period, Landreaux's traditional form of restoration eases tensions, as the families work out a flexible schedule of sharing LaRose and as LaRose's childlike innocence and beneficent maturity bring peace between the families. Even Maggie softens: "There could be a whole revenge plot going on between our families. But now I don't think there ever will be" (131). LaRose is sweet but also practical. When he senses that Maggie's mother is suicidal, he removes the ammunition from the guns in the Ravich home, an act that saves his father's life when, near the end of the narrative, Maggie's father tries to shoot Landreaux.

Landreaux's movement toward healing is almost derailed by a revenge-maddened vigilante detective, Romeo Puyat. According to S. S. Van Dine (William Huntington Wright), the creator of the famous detective Philo Vance, and to Franco Moretti, one of the hallmarks of a conventional murder mystery is an investigator who exposes the culprit by discovering "the causal links between events" (Moretti 144) using careful inductive reasoning and "logical deductions" (Van Dine, Rule #5). Romeo grounds his conclusions in meticulous research, imaginative deductions, and a fierce desire for revenge. His investigation is a form of what Fredric Jameson defines as "dishonest" detective work. In his discussion of Raymond Chandler's murder mysteries, Jameson proposes several types of investigators, including the "dishonest detective," an investigator with a severely limited vision: "His job boils down to the technical problem of how to succeed on [a] given assignment" (72). Romeo Puyat (his last name should alert Erdrich readers to be wary of him)[4] is an extreme incarnation of Jameson's "dishonest detective." He is a frightening warning about how warped methods of investigative induction and deduction can threaten justice.

When readers first meet Romeo, he is in training for his detective work. He knows the criminal mind. Erdrich has called him a "super scam artist" (Interview, Makkai). He is a petty thief who lacks educational and job-training credentials; he is severely disabled; and he is a substance abuser. He has decided that his only route to power is information acquisition: "He was a spy, but a freelancer. Nobody ran him, he ran his one-man operation for his own benefit" (90). In her review of the novel, Mary Gordon perceives how Romeo's possession of secrets enables him to create "quilt[s] of deception" (26). He methodically collects information around communal coffee pots, night shifts at hospitals, ambulance crews, and from medical records, trash dumpsters, and obituaries. He knows how to get something "on" many people (alcoholics, opioid junkies, wife abusers). To him, this information gives him a power "superior to any other form of power" (91).

After Dusty's death, Romeo becomes possessed by a desire to destroy Landreaux. He blames Landreaux for his mangled arm and leg and for the loss of the love of his life and of his son's affections. Readers know that Romeo's accusations are distortions of the truth. But for this maimed, drug-addicted revenge seeker, Landreaux is the White Whale that crippled him. To borrow and hype Jameson's language, his "one job boils down" to one "assignment" (72): "to get something solid on Landreaux to bring him down" (*LaRose* 219). For Romeo, the killing is a welcome opportunity to frame Landreaux by transforming an accident into a murder.

Romeo knows that circumstantial evidence abounds. Landreaux's parents were alcoholics (89), and Landreaux has a history of some "wild years" of drinking and pills (8). Indeed, that reputation follows Landreaux into the sweat lodge, where the traditional healer Randall asks him about the shooting and his potential guilt: "Were you high?" . . . "You off the booze?" . . . "Pills?" (53). Similarly, Romeo knows Landreaux's psyche is tortured and fragile. Romeo's meticulous evidence-collecting skills gain him access to information in the coroner's report, which he combines with other evidence: "I put it all together" (334). In Romeo's reconstruction of the killing, Landreaux's shot didn't kill the boy; rather, shrapnel from the breaking branch of the "climbing tree" caused severe bleeding. Romeo thus concludes, if Landreaux had stayed with Dusty or sought medical aid immediately instead of deserting Dusty to go to Dusty's mother, he could have saved him (333–34). Instead, he left the boy to die a slow and painful death. (This accusation in fact echoes Romeo's grudging claim that Landreaux deserted him after Romeo's tragic fall in

Minneapolis.) Romeo shares this narrative, spiced with hints of Landreaux's drug use, with Dusty's father, Peter, knowing that this reconstruction of the killing will enrage Peter enough to want to kill Landreaux and that Landreaux is guilt-ridden enough to let Peter perform his execution. Romeo won't even have to throw a harpoon. "My work is done" (330).

Erdrich could have turned Romeo into a one-dimensional dishonest detective or worse. After all, when he was young, Romeo attempted to kill Landreaux while he slept to get his money (31–32). Instead, she complicates his portrait and creates a character who resembles Shakespeare's Iago or Malvolio (Gordon 26). He has a history that, in Erdrich's words, created a "very wounded human being" (Interview, Makkai). He was a good student at the boarding school, and before the tragic fall that maims him, he once saved Landreaux from a fall. Furthermore, Erdrich elevates his voice with occasional profound breakthroughs. His language and thoughts are commonplace compared to the thoughts and language of Melville's Ahab, another monomaniac seeking revenge for a crippling injury, but in Romeo's soliloquy on the Iraq war, Erdrich endows him with an Ahab-like perception of truth seeking: "Behind all the flimsy bits of pretend truth there must be a real truth so terrible it would cause a stock market crash. But what if the truth is some kind of bubble truth? What if behind the truth there is nothing but a heap of pride or money or just stuff?" (276). The devastating complication for Romeo is that during his drug-infused confession to Father Travis, the priest reads the coroner's report that Romeo provides as evidence and discovers that Romeo's version of the truth is a horrid misreading of evidence, an investigation warped by drugs and the desire for revenge (334–35). Father Travis breaks this news to Romeo and rushes off to tell Peter before Peter can shoot Landreaux. Disillusioned and in a suicidal drug delirium, Romeo hurls himself headfirst down the church cement steps—and astonishingly becomes healed.

Erdrich's novel ends by making things right: Romeo is redeemed as a character, and the ambiguity of Landreaux's shooting of Dusty is resolved. In the final festive gathering scene (347–72), Romeo reappears sans injury. He even thinks the suicidal church-steps fall cured his disability. Furthermore, he is resurrected as a father figure and solves one of the few remaining mysteries in *LaRose*, the identity of his son's mother (a woman who is never introduced to readers; she quickly disappears from the text). Gordon compares the actions in this scene to the concluding scenes in "great Shakespearean comedies of forgiveness" (26), but Erdrich has declared she doesn't comprehend the nature of forgiveness and prefers "act of restoration" to describe this scene (Interview, Makkai). I find Romeo's (imagined?) healing and sudden fatherliness a disappointing literary denouement to the tale of this tragically flawed investigator.

But this less-than-convincing denouement shouldn't overshadow Erdrich's fascinating combination of murder-mystery elements and a social justice narrative. The injection of a complex dishonest detective into the narrative allows Erdrich to expose the potential misuse of evidence-based accusations of murder. And despite the lack of major who-done-it conventions, Erdrich presents readers with her most sustained examination of the psychological impact of killing a human and the most radical form of alternative justice in her trilogy, one that reaches beyond the bounds of conventional law and beyond Catholic and Ojibwe ceremonial means of restoring decency and balance: the offer of an exceptional five-year-old child and Landreaux's willingness to modify his offer by negotiating a sharing of LaRose.

A Murderous Rape, a Criminal beyond Redemption, and a Young Murderer Exonerated

More than *LaRose* or *The Plague of Doves*, *The Round House* focuses on one who-done-it mystery narrative, and in this case the initial identification of the crime is Geraldine's rape, not murder. It is only near the conclusion of the narrative that readers discover that the rape and murder of Mayla Wolfskin occurred probably on the same day (305, 310). The placement of Mayla's murder revelation and the limited space devoted to it suggests that in this novel, Erdrich wanted to put emphasis on rape, not murder. This is one of several unique elements of Erdrich's use of murder-mystery conventions in *The Round House*. Another is that Erdrich enhances the detective story with an accelerated coming-of-age story (Miller). One of the primary investigators is Joe, a thirteen-year-old boy who, as Erdrich has commented, is placed in a "terrible situation." He must decide "if [in this case] revenge is the only form of justice" (Interview, Cornish). Another difference is the emphasis on the complex legal systems that help to shape the mystery and determine the degree of justice possible.[5] For instance, as early as page 2, the narrator mentions Felix S. Cohen's *Handbook of Federal Indian Law*, and this tome is referenced throughout the novel. The legal context of events of *The Round House* represents a striking departure from the legal frames of conventional detective narratives. Franco Moretti argues that in a traditional murder mystery, the criminal represents individual actions as contrasted to the more just "social organism['s]" laws represented by the detective (134). In Indian Country, that formula often doesn't apply: "Law [may be] meant to put out society's brush fires, but in Native American history it has often acted more like a wind" (Russo 9). Judge Coutts reveals the injustice of Indian law to his son in mini-lectures (142–43, 196–97) and with his descriptive transformation of the rotting layers of a casserole into a metaphor for the history of Indian law (227–30).

The dual narrative voice Erdrich uses is important to the interrogation of law and justice in *The Round House*. Instead of the adult Dr. Watson narrator of Sherlock Holmes's stories and instead of the multiple narrators of *The Plague of Doves* or the omniscient/limited omniscient narrator of *LaRose*, there is/are the voic(es) of Joe Coutts. He speaks as a thirteen-year-old during the year 1988, when the rape and murder occurred, and he also speaks as a mature adult who, sometime in the early twenty-first century, followed his father's career path and became a lawyer. (Judge Coutts once predicted, "You'll be a lawyer if you don't go to jail first" [228].) This complex narrative perspective is reminiscent of Sherwood Anderson's narrative viewpoint in "Death in the Woods" or even Neihardt's representation of Black Elk in *Black Elk Speaks*. In all three, the narrator has firsthand experience with a tragedy (a rape and an old woman's solitary death in Anderson's story) or a wonderful but frightening experience (the Great Vision in Neihardt), but he is too immature and too close to the event to process it and shape it into a narrative. The narrators in "Death in the Woods" and *Black Elk Speaks* are explicit about this reason for delaying the telling. Joe is not explicit, but it is reasonable to assume that, as a thirteen-year-old, he would have great difficulty telling the story of his mother's rape and its consequences.

The telling of the mystery through a dual perspective, which is enhanced by a third perspective used whenever Joe reconstructs his father's legalistic explanations, enables Erdrich to represent the rape (and later the murder) within the authoritative contexts of legal knowledge, while the thirteen-year-old voice gives the mystery the immediacy of the witness. Russo argues that the boy's voice gives the novel "the momentum and tight focus of a crime novel" (9). It obviously also creates the illusion of the freshness of the childhood "innocent eye," and the exuberant sense of justice characteristic of Twain's young fighters for justice, Huck Finn and Tom Sawyer. Another advantage to the dual perspective is that it allows Erdrich to conclude the narrative with sadly realistic events—the car accident, Cappy's death, Joe's speculation that he didn't have to kill Linden ("he'd have gone to jail for life anyway" for murdering Mayla [310]), and the premature aging of Joe and his parents

(317)—while the readers can close the book with a more optimistic realization. They know that Joe survived 1988 and has gone on to continue the good fight his father fought, most likely with the determination he exhibited when he attacked those roots that threatened the foundation of his childhood home (1).

As in *The Plague of Doves* and *LaRose*, the opening of *The Round House* sets all the major mysteries in motion, in this case with a middle-of-the-road strategy: much more is revealed than in the "Solo" opening of *The Plague of Doves*, but less than readers witness in the first pages of *LaRose*. A mother is missing. The son and father are worried, though the son longs for a bit of excitement, "something out of the ordinary" (5). A reader doesn't have to be a mystery connoisseur to know that Joe's longing is a red-flag warning: Be careful what you wish for. You may get it. What Joe discovers is that his mother has been brutally raped. Joe's close relation to the victim and his age (onset of puberty?) make the impact of the rape especially traumatic.

By the end of the first section, readers assume they have learned a tantalizing clue (Joe smelled gasoline on his mother [7, 15], and they have answers to key elements of the mystery: Who is the victim? (Geraldine Coutts), When did it happen? (1988), What was the motive? (forced sex). Much later readers discover several other motives (see pages 299–300). But the adult narrator withholds several key elements: Who was the rapist? Where did he commit the rape? (He put a pillowcase over Geraldine's head so she wouldn't know [159].) Later, we discover he took her to a place where "tribal trust, state, and fee" land converge (160), thus complicating the legal jurisdiction for prosecutors. And the crucially withheld question is: Will there be justice? Joe is especially concerned about justice, but his father's response to this question is not reassuring: "I can't think that far ahead now" (11).

In the sections that follow the opening, one response readers receive to Joe's question about what will happen involves knowledge of the suffering of the victim. In *The Plague of Doves* readers get only vague pronouncements about the sights and smell of blood after the slaughter at the Lochren farm, but no details, and readers get a restrained description of the physical effects of the hanging of the three innocent Ojibwes. In *LaRose* there are no detailed descriptions of the impact of Landreaux's bullet on Dusty's little body. But in the opening and multiple sections in *The Round House*, readers find vivid descriptions of the physical and psychological results of Geraldine's rape. Joe and his father first spot Geraldine "riveted" and "fixed, rigid, wrong" as she drives home (5–6). When she arrives, they see vomit down the front of her dress and dark blood stains on the car seat (7). Her lips are cracked and bleeding (7). After she returns from the emergency room, her black eyes make her look "like a raccoon," her temples are "dark green," her jaw "indigo," and "the white of the left eye was scarlet" (23, 35). (Also see pages 159–62 where she describes the brutal scene.) Geraldine was not murdered, but several times, Joe describes his mother as if she is a murder victim: her "spirit" "severed" "from her body" (45); she could be a "frozen" or a "raging corpse" (43, 90). When Linden Lark is incarcerated, she shows signs of recovery, but when he is released (two-thirds of the way through Joe's narrative), she relapses (226). Her sanity and life are still in doubt. Except for the gruesome description of the physical effects of the poison Wolfred administers to Mackinnon in *LaRose* (119), there are no descriptions in the justice trilogy to equal the horrid embodiment of suffering we see in Geraldine. (The Mackinnon description in *LaRose* and its postscript of dogs devouring his body are much shorter [147].) Geraldine's suffering lasts for more than two hundred pages. Tharp speculates that she may never fully recover (29). In the context of a social justice/mystery narrative, the emphasis on the suffering of the victim invites readers to sympathize with her, to perceive rape as a crime as heinous as murder, to long for retribution and justice, to feel anger about the impediments to justice, and, of course, to despise the perpetrator.

After Judge Coutts considers one false lead on the perpetrator (the Francis Whiteboy case [53–54]) and after some really bad detective work by Joe and his friends on another false lead (Father Travis [104–08]), the Judge, Joe, and readers follow a trail of clues leading to Linden Lark. There are minor clues, like Linden's golf-club matchbook discovered near the scene of the crime (27). The major clues relate to Linden's hatred for Indians and Judge Coutts in particular. In two cases the Judge ruled against the family: in the first case he strikes down the 20 percent surcharge the Larks assessed Indian customers on items sold in their gas-station store, and in the second, he refuses to grant guardianship to Mrs. Lark over Linda Wishkob, a baby she abandoned at birth even though she was a twin to Linden. The Judge sees through the guardianship ploy and realizes that it is an unjust attempt to claim Wishkob land. The subsequent consequences are also significant: the Indian community boycotts the Lark family store, Sheryl Wishkob helps Whitey secure funding to establish an Ojibwe-owned gas station and store, and Linden's mother dies shortly thereafter. Linden, unassisted, has done a fine job of messing up his life. But like Romeo in *LaRose*, he scapegoats: Indians, the Indian-run gas station, and Joe and his parents, they caused all his sorrows. As Linden's sister tells Joe, "he hated your family" (299).

Linden Lark is the most despicable villain in the social-justice and murder/rape mysteries, possibly in all of Erdrich's novels. She obviously fashioned him to be an object of hatred: a murderer beyond redemption, juxtaposed against his severely suffering victim. The details of his life are damning. Before readers meet Linden for more than a chance glimpse, they learn that he has been fired as a postal worker, inherited his mother's "venomous" poison of "emotional violence" (52), and wrecked his substance-abused kidneys (127). Readers finally meet him up close when his twin sister, Linda, speaks to him as she prepares to give him one of her kidneys. Instead of expressing gratitude to a twin he has totally avoided, he brags about the "perfect murder[s]" he could have committed on his mail route and berates her, calling her "disgusting" and expressing revulsion at having an organ in his body from an "ugly person" (124–25). Linden's own pride in the premeditation makes the rape particularly insidious: he has "bon[ed] up on Indian law," places a pillowcase over Geraldine's head so that she won't know where she is, picks a place where "three classes of land meet" (160), and plans to douse her, his girlfriend Mayla, and possibly her baby, with gasoline and burn them to destroy the evidence. Geraldine escapes in a way that is probably unique to murder mysteries. Linden's matches are in a pocket in his discarded pants, and she urinates on the pocket so that he can't light the gasoline. She manages to free herself as he goes for more of his golf-club matches.

Readers discover near the end of the novel that Linden does succeed in murdering Mayla, (305, 310) but spares the baby (212). No doubt Erdrich withheld this information and the details of complex mystery subplots—the paternity of Mayla's baby (the South Dakota governor[6]), the hush money paid, Linden's desire to get the money and Mayla's enrollment document naming the baby's father, and Geraldine's frantic effort to return to her office to get the document—because she wanted to make the murderous rape, the suffering victim, and the monstrous villain the primary interests in the novel.

Considering Linden's despicable villainy, it is not surprising that one reviewer defined him "as one-dimensionally monstrous as the baddie in a paperback thriller" (Miller). Because of the limited tribal jurisdiction laws in 1988, this monster is set free after a brief incarceration.[7] What may further horrify readers is that the freed Linden may be more than a crime-novel, one-dimensional "baddie." As Jacob Bender and Lydia Maunz-Breese argue, Linden may represent a sub/superhuman Ojibwe *wiindigoo* or even the oil slick Armus that takes on human form in season 1 of *Star Trek: The Next Generation*.[8] Some of the parallels with the *wiindigoo* that Bender and Maunz-Breese don't emphasize are especially convincing. Erdrich leaves a trail of clues to build this connection, beginning with Linden's "deceitful eyes" (124) and further describing him as a "big brown-haired, sunken-eyed white man" (170). Most telling, early in the novel, during a sweat lodge ceremony, Randall, one of the traditional leaders in the community, has a troubling vision of "a man bending over you [Joe], like a police maybe, looking down on you, and his face was white and his eyes deep down in his face" (40). Then, one night after the rape, Joe's dog wakes him and stares out the bedroom window, and Joe sees a figure that is "neither human nor entirely inhuman." Before it vanishes, Joe sees that it has "deep-set eyes under a flat brow" (79–80, 307). Those eyes are *wiindigoo* eyes.

Then Mooshum tells a "white *wiindigoo*" Liver-Eating Johnson story (236–39) that is different from the one he tells in *The Plague of Doves*. In both narratives, the story is comic, but in *The Round House* the tale takes on much more sinister overtones because of Linden's presence. Linden's twin sister knows there is a "monster" in him, an endlessly "hungry" monster (300). And this monster is a threat to the entire community because of the proximity of Linden's crimes to the round house. Mary Paniccia Carden (95, 97, 99) as well as Bender and Maunz-Breese (145) stress the connections between the round house and Ojibwe narratives that feature the round house as a manifestation of the body of Old Buffalo Woman who offered her body to encircle and protect Nanapush. The round house is a sacred protector of the Ojibwe, and it has been violated by a "white *wiindigoo*." An unjust legal system has set this monster free. As in *LaRose*, a form of traditional Anishinaabeg justice provides a response to injustice. *Wiindigoos* must be killed (306).

Joe decides to be the agent of that traditional justice. He plans and, with the help of his friend Cappy, kills Linden on the golf course (another landscape that shares reservation and non-reservation space). His decision and this murder set off the final mystery questions of the narrative: Is this a just killing? What type of justice is appropriate to deal with Joe's and Cappy's act? One clear answer that the novel offers is that Joe evidently never serves time, not even the juvenile sentence he expected. Cappy is killed in a car accident, but Joe the child narrator and Joe the adult narrator give no indication that Cappy is being punished for delivering the shot that finished Linden off. They are not formally punished, but both Joe and Cappy are haunted by terrifying nightmares. Has the *wiindigoo* shape-shifted into their dreams, or are the dreams frightening psychological manifestations of guilt for committing murder?

The clearest answer to these questions concerning appropriate justice comes from the Native community's protective reaction. First of all, "Whitey vouched for us"—Whitey provides an alibi, claiming Joe and Cappy stole his booze and got drunk (293). Vince Madwesin, a tribal policeman, discovers and returns a pickle jar Joe had left at the crime scene. He tells Geraldine to "wash it out." Vince has thus engineered the erasure of Joe's fingerprints (294). Linden's twin sister makes sure that the murder weapon is completely disassembled and the parts scattered over a wide area from Missouri to North Dakota (301).[9] Joe's father does ask Joe directly if he knows "anything" about the murder. Joe has prepared for this question and responds with a calculatedly childish flurry of words, words that tell the truth and yet do not answer the question: "Dead? I wanted him dead, okay. In my thoughts. If you're telling me he's dead, then I'm happy. He deserved it. Mom is free now. You're free. The guy who killed him should get a medal" (292). Judge Coutts, who has decades of experience interrogating criminals with probing questions, drops this interrogation immediately: "Alright, my father said. Enough" (292).

Joe's family, important representatives of the community and law enforcement, and the sister who prolonged Linden's life all protect Joe. As in *LaRose*, the mystery narratives in *The Round House* validate alternative systems of justice that issue a verdict more just than the tangled injustices articulated in Cohen's *Handbook of Federal Indian Law*. Because the family and community exercised an alternative justice towards him, Joe avoids arrest and becomes a lawyer, determined to root out the endless injustices of Indian law with the legal skills his father demonstrated over decades. Readers do witness one impressive act of justice performed by Joe as an adult: his telling of the round house tale of 1988.

The Long Shadow of Grotesque Murders and the Survival of the Stories

As previously mentioned, the opening "Solo" was the last section of *The Plague of Doves* Erdrich wrote (Interview, Gordon and Cuellar). She obviously knew all the answers to the mysteries "Solo" presents and how one crime would lead to others, but she chose to withhold this information from readers. We do learn a few facts as the novel opens. The shooter is a man; he has fired multiple shots; there are multiple victims and at least one shot left; the gun jams; he pauses to fix the gun, fixes it, and raises his rifle; there is a baby still alive in the "closed room" (1). In between the jamming and the fixing, the man is attracted to a gramophone and plays a violin solo once, and then three more times, listening to its "strange sweetness" (1). We don't know the man or his motives, where or when the event occurs, and how many victims there are. Despite the "odor of raw blood . . . all around him," we don't even know if the victims are dead; we don't know who is giving us this account or if we witness the event's closure, or if this is only part of an event that leads to the baby's death and other events (1).

It's not until fifty-four pages later that we realize that we did and didn't witness closure. The gunman slaughtered a family, but, as in *The Round House*, a baby survived. Still, the slaughter of innocents continues with the hanging of three Ojibwe men falsely accused of the murders. Mooshum, who is old, but younger than in *The Round House*, tells the story of the hanging of the men who saved the baby after the murderer fled. Not until page 297 do we learn from another narrator (the baby, now the elderly woman, Cordelia Lochren) that the non-Native Lochren victims were "parents, a teenage girl, and an eight- and a four-year-old boy."

As a storyteller, Mooshum provides many details about the innocent Ojibwe before their tragic deaths. Mooshum partakes of a storytelling tradition at least as old as Shakespeare's portrayal of Macduff's wife and children in *Macbeth*: if you want your audience to be particularly sympathetic to particular murder victims, humanize them before they are slaughtered. Mooshum's story does not represent closure, not only because he does not initially disclose why he was spared from hanging (another mystery), but also because the deaths of the innocent family and of the innocent Indians haunt the town right up until the closing page of the narrative. Cordelia Lochren, who became a doctor and is now an aging town historian, reveals what readers have probably already figured out (Uncle Warren Wolde murdered the Lochrens) and proclaims with heavy irony and a mix of gallows humor that there should be a "town holiday to commemorate the year I saved the life of my family's murderer" (311). Years earlier, she had indeed cured Warren Wolde after he suffered a serious wound (309).

For a mystery novel, it makes sense for Erdrich to present "Solo" as an un-completed event that raises many questions for readers to solve. But for most of the novel the emphasis is not specifically on discovering the murderer, though Erdrich does tease readers with false leads. Early in the narrative readers meet Mooshum's brother, Shamengwa, who is devoted to his violin. Could he be capable of murder and, in the midst of a heinous act, take time out to listen to a violin solo? That possibility withers quickly as readers get to know him as a kind musician who participates in the long-standing Métis tradition of violin playing (Sing 114, 120–21). Then there is a young man, Tobek Hoag, who fled the area the day after the murder. Many years after the slaughter of the Lochrens and near the end of the narration, Cordelia discovers new evidence revealing that Tobek was a false lead. But long before that, Erdrich has introduced readers to the Woldes, with an oddly behaved Uncle Warren and his great-niece, Marn, who is dangerously attracted to a charismatic, controlling cult founder. Readers cannot help but wonder how these peculiar characters might connect to the murder and perhaps other crimes.

In the section narrated by Marn (137–79), Uncle Warren seems to be just a grotesque sideshow to the terrifying rise and sudden fall of Billy Peace, a descendant of one of the lynched Ojibwe. Billy combines the worst of a demoniacal evangelist, Melville's Ahab (Ahab uses the corposants; Billy uses a lightning strike to gain a supernatural aura), and Melville's White Whale (Billy's enormous size and uncanny color). Billy's sensational fall comes at the snake-venom-empowered hands of Uncle Warren's great-niece, Marn. The killing is premeditated—a murder that most critics have presented as a case of rough justice administered by a woman who has endured severe physical and psychological abuse by Billy and has witnessed his abuse of the children, including their own children, and adults among Billy's community of followers (Madsen 23; Roemer 122–23, 129). Deborah Madsen offers an alternative reading of the murder in her nuanced narratological reading of Erdrich's discontinuous narrative (23–24, 27–45). Emphasizing covert evidence, Madsen represents the murder as an unjust reenactment of settler-colonialism land greed. She stresses a turning point in the Billy-Marn relationship when Marn concludes that Billy longs to reclaim the Wolde farmland that was once reservation land. In Madsen's reading Marn becomes possessed by a *wiindigoo*-like hunger to keep the land for herself, a goal she achieves by murdering Billy and disguising his death as a suicide (*Plague* 178–79). After she leaves Billy's compound, she is attacked by Billy's faithful secretary (186–87), but Marn is never arrested. She eventually comes away from the crime with the land, Billy's money, and her children.

Madsen's emphasis on settler-colonialism greed is a welcome expansion of the meanings of Billy's murder beyond the scope of personal revenge. But her approach reduces the murder motive to a land-grabbing fixation and thus obscures the powerful feminist implications of the act and the importance of the Ojibwe community's response to Billy's death. Instead of comparing Marn to the possessed murderer Pauline in *Tracks* (37–38), she could have compared Marn to the strong young (Evelina) and old (Cordelia and Neve) women in *Plague* or to Fleur in *Tracks* (1988) and *Four Souls* (2004). (She does mention Fleur but only in a brief footnote [48].) While there is much more evidence of the community protecting a murderer (Joe) in *The Round House*, in *The Plague of Doves* we see the community protecting

Marn. Evelina's and Mooshum's family takes in Marn and her children, and, when Marn contacts Judge Coutts to get the land deed, there is no indication that she is in legal trouble. The evidence for a Native community-approved, necessary killing of a *wiindigoo* is much stronger in *The Round House*, but the implications for such a killing are also evident in *Plague*.

Marn's narrative focuses on her relationship with Billy, but her section also provides significant clues about the deeply troubling dimensions of Uncle Warren, a character reminiscent of the grotesques in the fictions of Sherwood Anderson, William Faulkner, and Carson McCullers: "[M]y uncle Warren . . . would stare and stare at you like he was watching your blood move or your food digest. Warren's face was a chopping block, his long arms hung heavy. He flew into disorderly rages and went missing, for days sometimes. We'd find him wandering the farm roads bewildered and spent of fury" (139). In retrospect, Uncle Warren's behavior and Erdrich's language ("watching your blood," "chopping block," "rages," "spent of fury") raise many (bloody) red flags.

The clues build, then climax dramatically, convincing the reader that, to quote the creator of Philo Vance, "the solution had, in a sense, been staring [the reader] in the face" (Van Dine, Rule #15). At a prayer meeting led by Billy, the airing of the "plenitude and triviality" of Marn's mother's sins and the proclamations of the sins of congregation members trigger a strong reaction in Uncle Warren: "his eyes grow pleading and he seems to cringe beneath the weight of all he hears" (153). "Cringe" and "weight" suggest that his sins, which he keeps secret, may not be so trivial. A few pages further, a version of his "killing" mantra begins. Taking on a Melvillian Elijah-like role, he tells Marn that she is "gonna kill" (158, 177), thus predicting her murder of Billy. Then Uncle Warren almost vanishes from the narrative.

The clues and building tension about Uncle Warren resume in Evelina's last narrated section when she has an internship in a psychiatric ward where Uncle Warren is a patient. His mantra has taken its final compulsive form. As in the past, he is still a wanderer. From early morning, he can be found "strolling up and down the corridors, crisscrossing the commons room, in and out of every bedroom. To everyone he met, he nodded and said, 'I'll slaughter them all.' The patients answered, 'Shut up.' The staff didn't seem to hear" (228). He sometimes complements his mantra with an offering to Evelina and others of "dollar bills folded fine in a peculiar way" (229). These bills become a key clue when Cordelia recalls that, as a child living with her adoptive parents, the Hoags,[10] she and they would find peculiarly folded bills around their house. The dollar-bill clincher-clue is that, after Warren's death, the lawyer representing his sparse estate presents Cordelia with a box containing "hundreds upon hundreds of wadded bills . . . and of course I recognized the folded pattern as identical to the bills that had turned up for me all through my childhood" (310). Obviously, when Cordelia had treated Uncle Warren for an infected wound years earlier, he must have realized that he was being treated/saved by the baby he had orphaned. She could see the horror in his eyes then: at the first visit "he reacted to the sight of me with horror unprecedented in my medical experience" (309). After his death, she recalls that look and connects it with the bills from her childhood and the final atonement gift box of bills.

The one obvious unsolved part of the mystery is Uncle Warren's motive. When Evelina is working in the psychiatric ward, Uncle Warren almost gives her and the readers a motive. As he tries to offer her a folded bill, in desperation he pleads, "'Please' [take the bill]. His old eyes begged, moist and red. 'I did it because they told me . . . ,' but he choked on what he might say" (233). Like the falsely accused young man, Tobek Hoag, did Warren love the Lochren teenage daughter, and did she and the family reject him? If so, was he rejected because the Lochrens thought he was a raging, wandering misfit? Or was he "normal" before the rejection and that rejection drove him to murder and that act changed him into a raving, wandering, fury-filled grotesque? We will never know, but Uncle Warren's response to Evelina's rejection to his plea to take the bill is revealing. He "recoil[s]" (an obvious gun term) and plunges into a "waking dream": "he began taking apart some invisible thing on his lap" (234). Alert mystery readers would immediately know that Evelina's rejection has triggered Uncle Warren's memory of a possible past rejection ("'they told me . . .'"), and this new rejection has triggered a reenactment of his frantic motions to unjam his gun. Readers can see this because the sensational opening is only a couple of hundred pages ago, but Evelina and the psychiatric staff in the late twentieth century can't see this clue or hear his confession of slaughter because that event happened decades ago (on page 92, readers finally get a date, 1911). To them he is just an old senile man to ignore and once again reject.

Does a murder mystery originating in a sensationalistic opening, involving a fascinatingly grotesque murderer, a tantalizingly unexplained motive, and a concluding box of bills detract from or enhance a social justice message? The answer to that question will obviously depend on the lens through which the readers approach the book. If readers are looking for examples to enhance the social justice/injustice theme, then the clues do complement this theme. First, and most obviously, the mystery of the slaughter of the Lochren family triggered the vigilantes to act out rough and unjust lynching justice—an injustice legitimatized by centuries of white settlers dehumanizing Indigenous peoples and, in *Plague*, more recently, in the unjust appropriation of vast tracts of Indian land, which readers witness in Judge Coutts's flashback narrative of the nineteenth-century land-grab expedition (96–112).[11] In her afterword (313), Erdrich draws readers' attention to the factual grounding for both the land grab and the lynchings. Thus, the mystery narrative becomes an invitation to examine justice unfulfilled on a macro-land-grab scale and on the micro-personalized scale of the deaths of three Ojibwe.

The web that Erdrich spins out from the sensationalistic slaughter-mystery narrative also dramatizes at least three other angles on justice unfulfilled and fulfilled. The mystery raises a blind-justice irony, not unlike the one Poe creates in "The Purloined Letter." The evidence is right in front of readers and the fictional community. How can a community be so blind as not to see that the murderer is right in their midst? Uncle Warren does live on "the farthest edges of our land," according to Cordelia (309), and he doesn't fulfill one of Van Dine's recommended characteristics for a murder-mystery perpetrator, which is that he or she must play "a more or less prominent role" in the narrative (Rule #10). But Uncle Warren does wander all over the place, even when he is confined in a psychiatric ward. The community doesn't see him as a suspect—because the vigilante activist group is blinded with fury by the savage horror of the crime (73, 78); because they leap to conclusions based on the flimsy evidence (especially Holy Track's tracks and an offhand remark by Mooshum about their presence at the Lochren farm); and, most significantly, because they have been conditioned by generations of stereotypes of Indians as bloody savages. While the community gradually realizes the injustice of murdering those who did not slaughter the Lochrens (92), the vigilantes are still allowed to thrive ("the Buckendorfs got rich, fat, and never died out" [82]) because of these same prejudices, amplified by the fear of reopening old wounds involving respected families. The community also had the convenient out of blaming (again on flawed evidence) an individual, Tobek Hoag, who can't be punished because he is dead. Then, as I suggested previously, there is the impact of time. By the time Uncle Warren is in the psychiatric ward, the patients, staff, and most of the community have forgotten, or more likely thoroughly repressed, knowledge of a 1911 slaughter, so even when the murderer, in effect, walks the halls confessing his crime, he is ignored or told to shut up. This time-lapse phenomenon for Erdrich's characters in the "present" corroborates Jameson's praise for Chandler's ability to invite readers to consider the legacy/obscurity of murders: "the underlying crime is always old, lying half-forgotten in the pasts of the characters before the book begins" (86).

Where is the social justice in this murder mystery? The Ojibwe community evidently approved of Marn's act as a form of necessary justice, especially if Billy is a *wiindigoo*. But the grotesque murderer of the Lochrens and the hate-filled vigilantes never go to jail. The Judge mentions to Geraldine that the vigilantes later admitted they hanged the wrong people (92), but readers don't witness any "shared guilt" among these murderers, a phenomenon that Slavoj Žižek relates to suspects in murder mysteries (59). And there is no retribution for the theft of millions of acres of Indian land foreshadowed by the nineteenth-century land speculation expedition narrated by Judge Coutts. There may be some form of justice in the fact that the "fat" and "rich" lives of the descendants of those who took the land and lynched innocents is ending as the town of Pluto withers. But that dying is certainly a pale version, a ghost, of justice.

Erdrich does, however, weave together a web of complex graphic and symbolic justices that grow out of the Lochren murders. The nurse who found Uncle Warren dead informs Cordelia that it wasn't a stroke or heart failure that killed him; it was Corwin's solo violin performance (310). The death of Uncle Warren is poetic justice on at least three levels. The music obviously triggers Uncle Warren's memory of the "solo" "strange [violin] sweetness" he heard and reheard that murderous day (1), and his aging body and mind couldn't withstand the traumatic memory. Second, Corwin Peace is a descendant of Cuthbert Peace, one of the innocents lynched, and Corwin's skill in playing owes a great debt to one of the clear manifestations of justice in *Plague*. In his wayward days, Corwin stole Shamengwa's legendary violin. He was an immediate suspect, soon caught, and faced Judge Coutts's innovative sentence: to study the violin with the victim of the crime. This just punishment enables the aging Shamengwa to pass on his art, helps to rehabilitate Corwin, and enables him to indirectly and unintentionally avenge the death of his ancestor, Cuthbert Peace, in a way that will never be prosecuted.[12]

There are also the linked mystery/justice tales of the two sole survivors. From the viewpoint of almost all the vigilantes, Mooshum should have been hanged along with his three innocent companions, and Uncle Warren's mantra indicates that he intended to slaughter "all" of the Lochrens, including the baby. Chance intervened in both cases. Kinship chance in Mooshum's case: Mooshum married Junesse, the daughter of a vigilante, Eugene Wildstrand, who abandoned her, and Wildstrand's aversion to hanging a son-in-law evidently outweighed his hatred for Indians.

Mooshum's salvation is believable but certainly not fair. Holy Track, Asiginak, and Cuthbert just weren't lucky enough to have wed the daughter of an Indian hater. Cordelia too is saved by chance—by a jammed gun and the interruption of a violin solo. In at least one sense, she is also not a worthy survivor: for her entire medical practice, she refused to treat Indians because she thought they had slaughtered her family.

Besides chance salvation, there is another powerful connection between these two unworthy survivors of murders: like the adult Joe in *The Round House*, they are both storytellers. Mooshum passes on the stories of the lynchings, especially to Evelina, who also takes in the historical and contemporary accounts offered by Judge Coutts. Of all the members of her late-twentieth-century generation presented in *Plague*, she seems the most passionate about learning the stories that haunt her community, and she is the most likely to continue the story of unfulfilled justice into the future. Mooshum is a powerful storyteller who knows how to pick the right audience—an audience who, as Erdrich no doubt knew, is the most likely surrogate for readers of her novel.

As a storyteller, Cordelia recounts stories of Pluto's haunted past in the town's historical newsletter and in conversations with elderly close friends like Neve Harp. The newsletter and conversations confirm Jameson's belief that the best murder mysteries should involve a return to the beginning (85). In her final newsletter, Cordelia returns to the Lochren slaughter and the murderer. Cordelia and Neve share their reminiscences of this and other events of town history as they "wear our orbit into the earth" walking the perimeter of their little planet, Pluto, nightly: "the air is so black I think already we are invisible" (311). This vanishing American act performed by Native and non-Native citizens, combined with the fact that the newsletter's subscriptions have declined so sharply that Cordelia is discontinuing publication, would seem to suggest that, unlike Mooshum, Cordelia has no audience with agency. Her narratees (to borrow Gerald Prince's term [57]) are disappearing.

But there are real readers beyond the fictional readers of Pluto, and more than the other three narrators in *Plague*—Evelina, Judge Coutts, and Marn Wolde—Cordelia seems to be speaking/writing directly to them as she ruminates on the legacies of the Lochren murders, the lynchings, the land grabs, and Pluto's decline. These ruminations offer convincing answers to "who done it" and "who didn't." But in her telling, solving specific mysteries is much less important than grappling with the way the past plays out in "living histories" (243). Cordelia's somber stories taken in combination with the success, potential impact, and rehabilitation stories of

Judge Coutts, Evelina, and Corwin, invite real readers to grapple with the roots and realities of suffering and survivance in Indian Country. If they accept the invitation, Cordelia has indeed found an appropriate audience for her stories.

Murder She Wrote, and Rewrote, and Rewrote for Social Justice

Louise Erdrich's social justice novels are, of course, much less than—and much more than—classic murder mysteries. Erdrich certainly doesn't fulfill all of Van Dine's credo of "Twenty Rules" of murder mysteries. Moretti would be annoyed at Erdrich's undermining of the criminal individual vs. just social organism binary. Chandler would no doubt criticize Erdrich's use of convenient coincidences (Uncle Warren coming to Cordelia for treatments), clues that hint of contrivance (all those folded bills), the mixing of rape and murder crimes in one mystery, and Landreaux's guilt grounded in ignoring a sacred deer's message. Furthermore, conventional mysteries, especially the classics of the 1920s and 1930s, are expected to be end-game narratives. Moretti claims that in a detective murder mystery, the "ending is the end indeed: its solution is its true sense" (149). Chandler concurs and is even more prescriptive: at the end of the narrative, "there is nothing left to discuss" (2). Moretti and Chandler might be pleased with the concluding feast in *LaRose*. That gathering does tie up loose ends about a missing mother, a snatched body, and young love. Dusty and some of LaRose's ancestors even gather. But long after that feast is over, two good friends will still carry guilt—about killing a child, ignoring a holy messenger, and pulling the trigger of a (fortunately unloaded) gun aimed at a friend. In the other social justice novels, the narratives avoid the trap of a closed (dead) ending by opening up expansive questions about the impact on individuals, families, and Native and non-Native communities of murders, rape, complex and unjust legal systems, alternative forms of justice, and the legacies of tragic events.

It is tempting to present Erdrich's appropriations and transformations of classic murder formulas as acts of subversion that challenge the closed narrative championed by Moretti and Chandler. In my opinion, that would be a constricting approach to Erdrich's ingenious uses of conventional expectations about murder mysteries. More appropriate are the resonances of the title that Gloria Bird and Joy Harjo picked for their anthology *Reinventing the Enemy's Language*, and Simon Ortiz's belief in "the creative ability of Indian people" to take the "many forms of socio-political colonizing force which beset them and to make these forms meaningful in their own terms" (8). True, Erdrich's transformations involve subversion, but subversion alone may imply a goal that is too limited: the decolonization of a specific non-Native genre. Reinvention and transformation imply goals that go far beyond questioning of a genre and, in Erdrich's case, question long-standing injustices against Native Americans and celebrate examples of individual, family, and community acts of survival.

Could all these questions be raised and demonstrations of survivance be achieved without the readers wondering, will Landreaux survive a murderer's guilt, will Romeo frame him, will Geraldine's rapist be punished, will the Lochrens' murderer be caught, will/should Pluto come out from under the shadow of the lynchings? Of course they could. But the adaptations of mystery elements serve important purposes. They charge the narratives with suspense and with invitations to become intellectually involved in figuring out who done it, why, and what then, and they allow readers to become emotionally and intellectually engaged with perpetrators and victims. In other words, there is a greater possibility that readers will experience the "living histories" of Indian Country and the continuing quest for justice through Erdrich's transformations of murder-mystery elements.

NOTES

1. See Roemer, "Naming Native (Living) Histories."
2. In "Move Over Tony Hillerman," Jacobs discusses mysteries by A. A. Carr, Louis Owens, Devon Abbot Mihesuah, Drew Taylor, and Anna Lee Walters.
3. Shanley mentioned this in an aside while she was delivering "The Healing Efficacy."
4. In Erdrich's early reservation novels, Puyats routinely mean trouble.
5. For background on the complexities of Indian law, especially jurisdiction laws, see Erdrich's 2013 op-ed, "Rape on the Reservation"; Jasmine Owens's "'Historic' in a Bad Way"; Sierra Crane-Murdoch's "On Indian Land"; and Julie Tharp's "Erdrich's Crusade" (25–27).
6. William Janklow was the governor involved in the scandal. See Tharp (34–36).
7. Soon after the publication of *The Round House*, the reauthorization of the Violence Against Women Act extended tribal jurisdiction involving nonreservation perpetrators. But as Tharp indicates, tribal jurisdiction is still limited (36–37).
8. As Bender and Maunz-Breese note, the chapter titles of *The Round House* come from *Star Trek*, and there are specific references to Armus (143, 149–51). Carden draws parallels between Linden and Warren Wolde as villains, but these are not fully convincing

(109–10).

9. Bender and Maunz-Breese note Whitey's and Vince's protective acts but omit Linden's sister's meticulous disposal of the murder weapon (148); Carden does make brief mention of her actions (112).

10. The Hoag name may be a veiled reference to the bestselling author of suspense thrillers Tami Hoag. I thank Trudi Beckman for this suggestion.

11. For a discussion of the loss of land, see Jacobs ("History" 29–30) and Roemer (127–28). For a listing of selected reviews and articles on *Plague*, see Roemer, endnotes 18 and 21 (133).

12. Another just sentence is John Wildstrand's incarceration for planning the kidnapping of his wife, Neve Harp (134).

WORKS CITED

Anderson, Sherwood. "Death in the Woods." *The Portable Sherwood Anderson*, revised ed., edited by Horace Gregory, Viking, 1972, pp. 410–24.

Bender, Jacob, and Lydia Maunz-Breese. "Louise Erdrich's *The Round House*, the Wiindigoo, and *Star Trek: The Next Generation*." *American Indian Quarterly*, vol. 42, no. 2, 2018, pp. 141–61.

Bird, Gloria, and Joy Harjo, eds. *Reinventing the Enemy's Language: Contemporary Native Women's Writing of North America*. Norton, 1998.

Carden, Mary Paniccia. "'The Unkillable Mother': Sovereignty and Survivance in Louise Erdrich's *The Round House*." *Studies in American Indian Literatures*, vol. 30, no. 1, 2018, pp. 94–116.

Chandler, Raymond. "The Simple Art of Murder: An Essay." 1950. *The Simple Art of Murder*, Ballantine Books, 1972, pp. 1–21.

Crane-Murdoch, Sierra. "On Indian Land, Criminals Can Get Away with Almost Anything." *Atlantic*, 22 Feb. 2013, https://www.theatlantic.com/national/archive/2013/02/on-indian-land-criminals-can-get-away-with-almost-anything/273391/.

Erdrich, Louise. *Four Souls*. HarperCollins, 2004.

———. Interview. Conducted by Audi Cornish. *All Things Considered*. National Public Radio, 2 Oct. 2012.

———. Interview. Conducted by Randy D. Gordon and Catherine Cuellar. Arts & Letters Live, Charles W. Eisemann Center, 12 May 2008, Richardson, TX.

———. *LaRose*. HarperCollins, 2016.

———. "*LaRose*: An Evening with Louise Erdrich." Interview conducted by Rebecca

Makkai. Chicago Humanities Festival, 24 June 2016, https://www.youtube.com/watch?v=gywvfuPsZtY.

———. *The Plague of Doves*. HarperCollins, 2008.

———. "Rape on the Reservation." *New York Times*, 27 Feb. 2013, p. A25.

———. *The Round House*. HarperCollins, 2012.

———. *Tracks*. Holt, 1988.

Faulkner, William. "The Old People." *Go Down, Moses*, Modern Library, 1942, pp. 163–97.

Gordon, Mary. "A Boy's Fate." Review of *LaRose*, by Louise Erdrich. *New York Times Book Review*, 22 May 2016, pp. 1, 26.

Jacobs, Connie. "A History of the Turtle Mountain Band of Chippewa Indians." *Approaches to Teaching the Works of Louise Erdrich*, edited by Greg Sarris, Connie A. Jacobs, and James R. Giles, MLA, 2004, pp. 23–31.

———. "'Move Over Tony Hillerman': Decolonizing American Indian Mystery Writing." Native American Literature Symposium, 22 March 2013, Mystic Lake Casino, Prior Lake, MN.

Jameson, Fredric. "On Raymond Chandler." *The Critical Responses to Raymond Chandler*, edited by J. Kenneth Van Dover, Greenwood, 1995, pp. 67–87.

Luscombe, Belinda. "Ten Questions for Louise Erdrich." *Time* magazine, 14 Jan. 2013, p. 60.

Madsen, Deborah. "Discontinuous Narrative, Ojibwe Sovereignty, and the *Wiindigoo* Logic of Settler Colonialism: Louise Erdrich's Marn Wolde." *Studies in American Indian Literatures*, vol. 28, no. 3, 2016, pp. 23–51.

McGrath, Charles. "Obsessively Mining a Familial Landscape: Louise Erdrich on Her New Novel, *LaRose*, and the Psychic Territory of Native Americans." *New York Times*, 7 May 2016, p. C1.

Miller, Laura. Review of *The Round House*, by Louise Erdrich. *The Guardian*, 18 May 2013, https://www.theguardian.com/books/2013/may/18/round-house-louise-erdrich-review.

Moretti, Franco. "Clues." *Signs Taken for Wonders: On the Sociology of Literary Forms*, translated by Susan Fischer, Verso, 1983, pp. 130–56.

Neihardt, John G. *Black Elk Speaks, Being the Life Story of a Holy Man of the Oglala Sioux*. Introduction by Vine Deloria Jr., U of Nebraska P, 1979.

Ortiz, Simon J. "Towards a National Indian Literature: Cultural Authenticity in Nationalism." *MELUS*, vol. 8, no. 2, 1981, pp. 7–12.

Owens, Jasmine. "'Historic' in a Bad Way: How the Tribal Law and Order Act Continues the American Tradition of Providing Inadequate Protection to American Indian and Alaska Native Rape Victims." *Journal of Criminal Law and Criminology*, vol. 102, no. 2, 2012, pp. 497–524.

Prince, Gerald. *A Dictionary of Narratology*. U of Nebraska P, 1987.

Roemer, Kenneth. "Naming Native (Living) Histories: Erdrich's Plague of Names." *Studies in American Fiction*, vol. 43, no. 1, 2016, pp. 115–35.

Russo, Maria. "Disturbing the Spirits." Review of *The Round House*, by Louise Erdrich. *New York Times Book Review*, 14 Oct. 2012, p. 9.

Shanley, Kathryn. "The Healing Efficacy of Reclaiming Indigenous Space." Native American Literature Symposium, 23 March 2018, Mystic Lake Casino, Prior Lake, MN.

Sing, Pamela. "Ancestral Songs and Sorrowful or Joyous Shreds of Imagination in Contemporary Métis/Mixedblood Stories." *A Usable Past: Tradition in Native American Arts and Literature*, edited by Simone Pellerin, UP of Bordeaux, 2010, pp. 111–23.

Tharp, Julie. "Erdrich's Crusade: Sexual Violence in *The Round House*." *Studies in American Indian Literatures*, vol. 26, no. 3, 2014, pp. 25–40.

Van Dine, S. S. (William Huntington Wright). "Twenty Rules for Writing Detective Stories." *American Magazine*, Sept. 1928, www.thrillingdetective.com/trivia/triv288.html.

Vizenor, Gerald, ed. *Survivance: Narratives of Native Presence*. U of Nebraska P, 2008.

Žižek, Slavoj. *Looking Awry: An Introduction to Jacques Lacan through Popular Culture*. MIT P, 1992.

Trauma and Restitution in Louise Erdrich's *LaRose*

Aitor Ibarrola-Armendariz

> Connecting the past with the present is inherent in many cultural traditions. Historical trauma theory contextualizes "time and place." It validates and aligns itself with the experiences and explanatory models of affected populations and recognizes issues of accountability and agency.
>
> —Michelle Sotero, "A Conceptual Model of Historical Trauma"

Michelle Sotero has developed a helpful conceptual model of historical trauma that shows, among other things, how it originates; the kind of impact it has on the direct victims, or primary generation; and how its effects are invariably prolonged to generations to come. One of the most disturbing aspects of this psychosocial hazard is that in its latest phase, and to make its appearance in subsequent generations, it needs to be sustained by present-day stressors and grievances. According to Sotero, successive generations may come to experience "vicarious traumatization" through the collective memories and storytelling tradition of the group. What is crucial, though, is that "They may also experience original trauma through loss of culture and language, as well as through proximate, first-hand experiences of discrimination, injustice, poverty, and social inequality" (Sotero 100). To put it briefly, for the unresolved grief and chronic trauma to continue reemerging among the younger generations, the gross historical violations need to be accompanied by new afflictions reinforcing their feelings of powerlessness, shame, and guilt. It is no coincidence, of course, that this scholar should choose to focus on American Indians and Alaskan Natives as a case study to test her theory, for they seem, as a group, to display most conspicuously—and tragically—many of the effects deriving from this psychosocial condition. As the epigraph to this chapter suggests, the fact that Native American cultures are keen on finding continuities between past and present, and that they are also closely attached to the land, may in fact have made them more vulnerable to intergenerational trauma. Nevertheless, as the epigraph also makes clear, historical trauma theory has learned to see how families, communities, and tribes have managed to reframe and work through those traumatic memories by means of coping strategies often related to the oral transmission of their ethnic identity. In Aaron Denham's words, "The way narratives are constructed and told, in addition to their content and meaning, communicate specific resilience strategies. . . . This ethic of sharing narratives generates and connects a cycle of listening and learning that culminates in sharing their wisdom with others" (393).

Although Denham and others have primarily focused on the oral tradition as a source of resilience, Native American fiction writers have also sought to represent the effects of settler domination and the resulting intergenerational trauma in their works, as well as the strong resistance practiced by their communities in the form of ceremonies, trickster narratives, family histories, and the like. Authors such as James Welch, Leslie M. Silko, Gerald Vizenor, and Linda Hogan have shown great interest in delving into the psycho-wounds—uprootedness, helplessness, self-denial, alcoholism, abuse of others, etc.—that a long history of oppression and genocide have left on their peoples, and in devising tactics, both traditional and new, that could be used to reverse, at least partly, the devastating effects of those historical processes. In *Native American Renaissance*, Kenneth Lincoln rightly observed more than thirty years ago that, relying on tribal heritage, those tactics should combine elements of history, song, Native spirituality, performance, ethics, politics, and the arts, but always with the objective of cultural survival (14). It is perhaps Gerald Vizenor's concept of *survivance* (= survival + continuance) that best captures the effort of Native American writers to achieve continuity and survival in the contemporary world by dint of contesting and revising the legacy of victimization and tragedy advanced by the dominant culture and its literature. Referring to Native writers, Vizenor (White Earth Anishinaabe) states:

"The postindian warriors bear their own simulations and revisions to contend with manifest manners, the 'authentic' summaries of ethnology, and the curse of racialism and modernism in the ruins of representation." And he emphasizes, "The wild incursions of the warriors of survivance undermine the simulations of the unreal in the literature of dominance" (Vizenor 82). All of the aforementioned Native authors have managed, in their own way, to challenge those "simulations of the unreal" and to contribute to the survivance of their cultural identity, but few have done so with the critical accolades and international recognition that Ojibwe writer Louise Erdrich has accrued. As Jessa Crispin remarked a few years ago in the *Guardian*, "Her books, which remain consistently excellent in the third decade of her career, are reviewed lovingly, and her audience is enormous and loyal." Among the key reasons for Erdrich's popularity are her ability to translate the cultural specificities into universal concerns and her acute ability to tap into issues—such as racism, injustice, revenge, atonement, or love, to mention but a few—that will resonate with most readers.

Louise Erdrich's fifteenth novel, *LaRose* (2016), has been acclaimed for its "rich but plain" (Gordon 1) prose style and the "blunt, clear-eyed realism" (Athiakis) with which she represents the phenomenal struggles and grief of a Native community in the confusing aftermath of an awful accident. As is the case with the two novels leading up to *LaRose*—*The Plague of Doves* (2008) and *The Round House* (2012)— the story is set near the border town of Pluto in North Dakota, where an Ojibwe reservation, state, and federal land converge. Numerous critics and reviewers (see McGrath; Charles) have highlighted the exhaustive knowledge that the author— often compared to Cather and Faulkner in this regard—proves to have of both the landscape and its people. What is especially interesting about this knowledge is that place and characters are not confined to one particular historical period, but the past and the characters' forebears keep coming back to intersect with—and frequently haunt—the present time. Quite often the reader realizes that places and characters become some sort of palimpsest on which several historical episodes have been inscribed and which, therefore, carry all kinds of nuances regarding affections and aversions. Note, for example, the kind of feelings that two of the main characters of *LaRose* have developed toward their dwelling place:

> Landreaux and Emmaline's house contained the original cabin from 1846, built in desperation as snow fell on their ancestors. It satisfied them both to know that if the layers of drywall and plaster were torn away from the walls, they would find

the interior pole and mud walls. The entire first family—babies, mothers, uncles, children, aunts, grandparents—had passed around tuberculosis, diphtheria, sorrow, endless tea, hilarious and sacred, dirty, magical stories. They had lived and died in what was now the living room, and there had always been a LaRose. (86–87)

Eminent fiction writers of the stature of Toni Morrison and Philip Roth have praised Erdrich's power to reveal concisely and in astoundingly precise ways "the dark knowledge of her place" (Roth, qtd. in McGrath).

In her most recent novels, Erdrich has been trying to tackle the thorny issue of how anybody should respond fairly or justly to such terrifying events as racist mob executions (*The Plague of Doves*), rape and murder (*The Round House*), or a child's death by gunfire (*LaRose*), which seem to unleash the ghosts of intergenerational trauma in the community and for which neither conventional justice nor Christian religion seem to offer ready solutions. Indeed, the young boy LaRose is sent to intervene in this kind of traumatic wounding: "That name would protect him from the unknown, from what had been let loose with the accident. Sometimes energy of this nature, chaos, ill luck, goes out in the world and begets and begets. Bad luck rarely stops with one occurrence. All Indians know that. To stop it quickly takes great effort, which is why LaRose was sent" (105). In *LaRose*, the author succeeds in bringing some kind of unstable balance back to the collectivity by resorting to some of the old ways (of reparatory justice) that Anishinaabe tradition affords and by the healing presence of the title character. As Konnie LeMay has concluded, Erdrich "excels at conveying the painful histories of generations past and present, while weaving in the realities of the spiritual realm and the possibilities of healing and love."

To explore these issues fully, this chapter focuses on trauma, revenge, and restitution in *LaRose*. It is divided into three sections. The first section focuses on the calamitous hunting accident that opens the book—in which a five-year-old boy is killed—and the stringent effects it has not only on the two affected families, but also on the rest of the community. As will soon become clear, some of the ideas put forth by historical and cultural trauma theory will be invaluable to fully understand why the accident reverberates so intensely on the reservation. The second section investigates the resentment, troubling memories, shameful feelings, and vengeful attitudes that, despite the characters' best efforts, gush forth in their relationships and that recurrently threaten to spur the story toward "blood everlasting," as the novel describes it (5). In fact, most of the main characters—with the exception of

LaRose—are assailed by desires of revenge and retaliation as a shortcut to recover their personal emotional stability. The third section discusses the central role played by restitution—or reparation—as part of Ojibwe cultural heritage and as resilience strategy, in the healing process and survival of the whole community. Mei Wan has recently identified the tradition of "spiritual reparation" among the Anishinaabe—which in the novel takes the form of child adoption, power acquisition through naming and kinship, and sacred rituals—as essential to "the survivance of a Native culture" (1182). Finally, the chapter concludes by considering the applicability of certain strategies and ethical principles shown in the novel to combat grief, collective trauma, and retaliatory impulses. Although Debra Holt (and others) has argued that Native American literature "does not depend on the resolution of conflict" (150), nor does it aspire to come up with viable solutions to the ordeals faced by most human beings, *LaRose* may have a great deal to offer concerning reparatory justice and conflict management as recently considered and discussed by several legal scholars (see du Plessis and Peté).

Unexpected Tragedy and Collective Trauma

Like the two preceding books in the "justice trilogy," *LaRose* begins with an unexpected and shocking event that shakes the foundations not only of the families directly involved, but also of the rest of the Native community in North Dakota. In the fall of 1999, while hunting a deer near the edge of his land, Landreaux Iron accidentally kills his neighbors' five-year-old son, Dusty Ravich, who had been playing on the low branches of a tree. Needless to say, Landreaux is utterly horrified when he realizes what he has done, for not only have the Raviches and the Irons been close friends for a long time—sharing food, clothes, and rides into town—but Dusty was his youngest and favorite son, LaRose's, best friend. As Crispin remarks, despite the reservation's persistent struggles with poverty, ill health, addictions, and despair, "the repercussions of the young boy's death are felt throughout the community." Naturally, it is the two families who see their lives most deeply affected by Dusty's demise, and the parents' relationships quickly begin to deteriorate as none of them seems to know how they are "going to go on living" (*LaRose* 6). Although the four parents show evident signs of mental volatility during the mourning process, it is probably Nola, Dusty's mother, who has the most difficult time coping with the situation:

The parents didn't want it, but Christmas came for both families. Nola woke a week before the twenty-fifth, picturing her heart as a lump of lead. It lay so heavily in her chest that she could feel it, feebly thumping, reasonlessly going when she wasn't interested in its efforts. But Christmas. She turned over in bed and nudged Peter—she resented that he could sleep at all. (45)

Although Nola Ravich and Emmaline Iron, Landreaux's wife, are half-sisters, intense resentment appears between the two of them as their families are rocked by Dusty's death, which brings another area of conflict to light—their degree of attachment to a Native way of life is radically different. Moreover, Nola has an extremely strained relationship with her only remaining child, Maggie, whose aloof and sometimes rebellious personality does not help much in terms of filling the unbearable void in her mother's life. Not even her kind husband, Peter, seems able to assuage the uncontrollable agony and outrage in her: "He stroked her shoulder. She pulled violently away. The black crack between them seemed to reach down forever now. He had not found the bottom yet" (14).

After seeking guidance from both an Ojibwe tribal tradition (via a visit to the sweat lodge) and the Catholic Church (by means of a meeting with the local priest), Landreaux and Emmaline Iron decide to give up their own five-year-old son, LaRose, in an attempt to somehow compensate for the pain inflicted on their neighbors. Father Travis Wozniak tries to comfort the couple by offering them the conventional religious explanations for the catastrophe: "*Incomprehensible, His judgments. Unsearchable, His ways*" (7). However, it is the ceremony they perform at the sweat lodge that becomes revelatory of the way to proceed: "Emmaline had songs for bringing in the medicines, for inviting in the manidoog, aadizookaanag, the spirits. Landreaux had songs for the animals and the winds who sat in each direction" (11). In spite of Emmaline's initial reluctance to admit the meaning of their visions, she finally yields:

> He calmed her, talked to her, praying with her. Reassuring her. They had sundanced together. They talked about what they had heard when they fell into a trance. What they had seen while they fasted on a rock cliff. Their son had come out of the clouds asking why he had to wear another boy's clothing. They had seen LaRose floating above the earth. He had put his hand upon their hearts and whispered, *You will live*. They knew what to make of these images now. (11)

Connie Jacobs has cogently explained the centrality of Ojibwe traditions in Erdrich's fiction, and she has also insisted on their relevance to better understand the "importance of families in Indian culture and stories" (105 ff.). The Irons' generous gesture of relinquishing their youngest son at the end of the first chapter ("The Door") is a perfect example of how the two topics are indissolubly connected in most of Erdrich's novels: "Our son will be your son now," Landreaux explains to Peter. "It's the old way" (16).

Not being aligned with Native American customs and traditions, the Raviches are quite perplexed by the Irons' intimation of atonement and solidarity. It is Nola, deeply disturbed by suicidal thoughts, who benefits the most from the presence of LaRose, on whom she dotes obsessively. Curiously, after a not-too-welcoming first night together, fierce Maggie decides to adopt her new brother as a co-conspirator, as she realizes that he is the only one able to keep her mother's dark moods at bay: "After the first weeks, LaRose tried to stop crying, around Nola at least. Maggie told him the facts again, why he was there. His parents had told him, but he still didn't get it. He had to hear it again and again" (33). Although Nola and Peter Ravich come to love LaRose very much, they are never completely comfortable with the arrangement. Peter, in particular, suspects that his wife does not see LaRose so much as an "unspeakable gift" (15) of beauty and sacrifice, but rather as a payback that would inflict the kind of grief they themselves are suffering on the Irons. And then, there are Emmaline and LaRose himself, who, as Peter explains to Landreaux, must be going through true hell on account of the unnatural severance:

> I think it does [help]. I know it does. Help. As long as we're with LaRose we're thinking about him, and we love him. He's a decent boy, Landreaux, you've raised him right. Him being with us helps Nola. Helps Maggie. It does help . . . but what's it doing to him? I mean, he's holding Nola together. Big job. Meanwhile this is probably tearing Emmaline apart. (75; ellipsis in original)

Although Landreaux has been told by his friend Randall—who runs sweat lodges, is some sort of medicine man, and teaches Ojibwe culture in the tribal high school—that he did right in following the old ways and should be concerned neither about Emmaline nor LaRose ("He has it in him. He's stronger than you think" [53]), he eventually follows Peter's advice, and LaRose is allowed shared visits with his birth family. Nevertheless, even though LaRose's name and charming character prevail as the elders had predicted, the bad vibes among the main characters continue. Mark Athiakis wonders in his review of the novel if all those voices (a stray dog's, woods spirits', Dusty's, the demons', etc.) that the characters hear mostly in their interior monologues are "just grief talking, or something deeper." As a matter of fact, these voices and several other ominous symbols skillfully distributed throughout the novel suggest that the whole community has been a victim of some harrowing events in the past that makes them particularly susceptible to dark moods:

> The green chair had rested in the barn for two months and nobody noticed that it was gone from the kitchen. Nola was ready to say that she was going to restore it, if Peter asked. But it was just a green wooden chair, and who cared? Yet this painted chair was key. It would be the last solid thing her feet touched. She'd push off and kick the backrest down. (112)

Most readers of *LaRose* would agree that one of the fundamental achievements of the novel is its immensely rich cast of mostly tormented characters whose fate is undoubtedly linked to their capacity to overcome current trials, but who also live under the burden of a turbulent history. As Erdrich puts it in the novel, "Loss, dislocation, disease, addiction, and just feeling like the tattered remnants of a people with a complex history. What was in that history? What sort of knowledge? Who had they been? What were they now? Why so much fucked-upness wherever you turned?" (51). Theorists of historical trauma, such as Maria Yellow Horse Brave Heart, would appreciate this description of the kind of disorientation that invades the collective consciousness of a human group after they have been the object of massive and gross historical abuses. As will become evident in the section below, one of the immediate consequences of the accident at the beginning of the novel is precisely that families are fractured and the sense of communal safety and a shared heritage is crippled, as personal grudges and bitterness take up most characters' time and energies. In Holt's view, the effects of this displacement can be fatal: "In the Native American universe, the self is not so distinct from its environment; conversely, it consists of other people, places, and experiences. To forget or to deny that which makes up the self, then, is to lose the self" (153).

Revenge Plots in Human Relations

Jane Hafen, among other scholars, has established a direct connection between Erdrich's landscapes, peoples, and their historical memories: "Erdrich has created a vision of the Great Plains that spans the horizon of time and space and ontologically defines the people of her heritage" (321). Indeed, in *LaRose*, the distressing events of the present, such as Dusty's death, the fears of catastrophes at the turn of the millennium, or the run-up to the Iraq war in the news, are played out against extensive recollections of the protagonist's grandparents and even earlier generations. As Gordon notes, "With a touch so light as to be almost casual, Erdrich includes details of Indian history that force the reader to acknowledge the damage that has extended through generations" (26). In the chapter "The Passage," for instance, young LaRose is told by his grandmother about the disastrous effects that attending boarding schools had on her mother and her people: "Look at this picture, said Mrs. Peace. Rows and rows of children in stiff clothing [with their braids already cut off] glowered before a large brick building" (70). She explains to her grandson that the government was aiming for nothing short of extermination in those days and tells him to read from a newsprint clipping by Frank Baum—author of *The Wizard of Oz*—published in 1888 in the *Aberdeen Saturday Pioneer*:

> . . . the nobility of the Redskin is extinguished, and what few are left are a pack of whining curs who lick the hand that smites them. The Whites, by law of conquest, by justice of civilization, are Masters of the American continent, and the best safety of the frontier settlements will be secured by the total annihilation of the few remaining Indians. Why not annihilation? Their glory has fled, their spirit is broken, their manhood effaced, better that they die than live as the miserable wretches they are. (*LaRose* 70–71; ellipsis in original)

Statements such as this, and the repressive actions that accompanied them, contributed decisively to what Jeffrey Alexander calls "the acute discomfort" that enters the "core of a collectivity's sense of its own identity" (10).

No doubt, the boarding schools that Native children were subjected to in the nineteenth century were a significantly oppressive force. Miriam Schacht has analyzed at some length the presence and significance that Indian boarding schools have in Erdrich's fiction, and considered the light in which they are presented. Her conclusions coincide broadly with what the reader sees in *LaRose*, where, although we occasionally hear about the first LaRoses receiving food and useful lessons for survival in these institutions, the focus is on brutal physical abuse, deep emotional trauma, and harsh cultural erasure. Again, it is Mrs. Peace who, when half-unconscious because of the drugs she is receiving to relieve her pain, remembers how she and her ancestors inscribed their name in hidden places of the schools in an attempt to conjure away the damage that they were doing:

> Chamberlain. Flandreau. Fort Totten and Fort Totten. We left our name in those schools and others, all the way back to the first school, Carlisle. For the history of LaRose is tied up in those schools. Yes, we wrote our name in places it would never be found until the building itself was torn down or burned so that all the sorrows and strivings those walls held went up in flames, and the smoke drifted home. (134)

Despite the elders' efforts to find antidotes to the poison that the schools regularly doled out among the young Native population, it is quite evident that the members of the older generation in *LaRose* are still suffering from the psycho-wounds inflicted by the system (see Broida). This becomes most conspicuous in the kind of resentment and vengeful sentiments that they develop toward each other, and which disrupt unequivocally their sense of community and shared future.

Most critics and reviewers have agreed that the theme of revenge is very central, not just in *LaRose*, but in the other two novels of the trilogy (cf. Kurup 100). It gains its import because, after episodes of unexpected violence, the community seems unable to find redress and to recover its balance in the absence of any assistance from official justice. In an article on *The Round House*, I have claimed that the young protagonist of that novel, Joe Coutts, sees himself prematurely—and unfairly—driven to the adoption of vigilante methods when neither the legal system nor the Church provides any instruments to protect his family against a *wiindigoo* who, after having raped his mother, is trying to eat them all (Ibarrola-Armendariz 270–71). In *LaRose*, we learn about several revenge plots, some of which are fully carried through, while others, fortunately, are never accomplished. Intertwined with the story of the effects of the hunting accident and the subsequent exchange, we are told the story of the first LaRose, an Ojibwe girl who was sold by her mother in 1839 to Mackinnon, the owner of an isolated trading post. Although the girl is cared for and protected by the clerk at the post, Wolfred, the latter can do little to stop the trader from physically and sexually abusing her. After some time, though, a revenge plan begins to take shape in the girl's mind:

The daughter of Mink brooded on the endless shifting snow. *I will make a fire myself,*
as the stinking chimookoman [Mackinnon] won't let me near his fire at night. Then I
can pick the lice from my dress and blanket. His lice will crawl on me again if he does
the old stinking chimookoman thing he does. She saw herself lifting the knife from
his belt and slipping it between his ribs.

    The other one, the young one [Wolfred], was kind but had no power. (63)

Eventually, after much hardship in the clutches of the trader, the first LaRose
manages to kill the brute—with the help of the clerk—by using her Native knowledge of natural poisons. Although we watch the first LaRose go voluntarily to
residential school, fight off tuberculosis, and happily marry Wolfred, it is never clear
whether the couple are able to overcome the trauma that the murder of the trader
left in their minds. Very much like Joe Coutts after the wiindigoo is shot down in
The Round House, brave LaRose and her partner are regularly haunted by disturbing
images of the vicious abuser:

Wolfred followed her gaze and saw it, too. Mackinnon's head, rolling laboriously
over the snow, its hair on fire, brightly twitching, flames cheerfully flickering.
Sometimes it banged into a tree and whimpered. Sometimes it propelled itself along
with its tongue, its slight stump of neck, or its comically paddling ears. Sometimes
it whizzed along for a few feet, then quit, sobbing in frustration at its awkward,
interminable progress. (132)

A similar point could be made about the parents in the Ravich and Iron families
who, although never mistreated in such despicable ways and never carrying out
their darkest thoughts, are still caught in a cycle of vengeful feelings that prevent
them from seeing each other and the world in objective ways. Social psychologist
Ian McKee has shown how it is the desperate struggle to retain a sense of dignity,
self-esteem, and status that pushes people into the maelstrom of revenge when
they feel that they have been wronged and, therefore, some sort of power has been
taken from them. This is further complicated if those individuals have the feeling
that the honor and the cultural heritage of their community has been historically
desecrated (Alexander 11). It is Nola and her half-sister, Emmaline, who see their
psychosocial stability most clearly jeopardized by the animosity that Dusty's demise,
and its aftereffects, causes in both of them. Even their husbands, who have kept a
long friendship and have created ties of mutual respect and solidarity, seem deeply

affected by the disturbance, although for different reasons. The reader is particularly dismayed by the thoughts and impulses that often encroach upon Peter Ravich—an otherwise patient and good-hearted man—who is also sporadically troubled by temptations of revengeful action that he knows he would later regret:

> Peter looked down on his parted hair, the long tail of it, the loose power of Landreaux's folded arms. A sinuous contempt gripped him and he thought of the rapture he would feel for an hour, maybe two hours, after he brought down his ax on Landreaux's head. Indeed, he'd named his woodpile for his friend, and the mental image was the cause of its growing size. If not for LaRose, he thought, if not for LaRose. Then the picture of the boy's grief covered his thinking. (76)

The clearest example of a character driven by vengeance in the whole novel is, no doubt, Romeo Puyat, who is described by the Catholic priest as a satanic presence on the reservation. Romeo nurses a quasi-Shakespearean grudge against Landreaux due to an accident that occurred after they had run away from a boarding school during their childhood—an accident that left Romeo crippled. Not only that, but the handicapped man, who has grown addicted to prescription drugs, is fully convinced that Landreaux stole Emmaline's heart from him. Although most reviewers have claimed that one of Romeo's primary functions in the novel is to provide comic relief in a narrative that is mostly cloaked in grief (Gordon 26; Charles), his subplot grows in importance in the second half of the book, as the story nears its climax, and his perverse intentions are seen to increasingly threaten the gradual recovery process of the two families:

> Landreaux believed he was outside of Romeo's reach and interest. But no, he wasn't. Landreaux was so full of himself, so high on himself that even now he did not remember those old days of theirs. Far back when they were young boys hardly older than LaRose. That's how far back and deep it went, invisible most times like a splinter to the bone. Then surfacing or piercing Romeo from the inside like those terrible fake pills the old vultures had tricked down him. (141)

The allusion to the "terrible fake pills" in this passage refers to one of those comic episodes in which a group of elderly tribal women decide to punish Romeo for pilfering their drugs by preparing a mixture that gives him uncontrollable diarrhea and an unstoppable erection.

But besides these occasional humorous touches, Romeo keeps stealthily putting together his plan to achieve revenge on Landreaux. In order to do so, he reforms and changes his old habits, so that people in his workplace and the community begin to trust him: "He began to like following the rules! He loved wearing rubber gloves! People began to think he had sobered up, and he let them think that" (214). By exploiting this new trust and making others believe that he was one of "the success stories," Romeo uses his jobs at the assisted-living home and the local hospital to gather (misleading) information that he thinks will convince Peter Ravich that Dusty's death was not a mere accident. Although he feels more positive about his role in the community and his relationship with his son, Hollis—who was adopted at an early age by the Irons—Romeo's long-standing resentment does not seem to recede. He compares himself to President George W. Bush, who is, in his estimation,

> No one to trifle with, Slot Mouth. Nor am I. Nor am I, ol' buddy ol' pal Landreaux Iron. According to my exceedingly detailed memories of our so-called runaway escape, said Romeo to a sky blue dream catcher with iridescent threads, the reason which I am rubbing Icy Hot into my sad ol' leg, you Landreaux Iron have much to answer for, things you never have addressed! (218)

Romeo's Iago-like blanket of deception brings us to the climax of the story: reinforced by Romeo's ill-intentioned revelations, Peter Ravich is faced with the tough decision of unleashing his own revengeful feelings on Landreaux, seeing "all he has kept himself from seeing. . . . the sickness rising out of things. The phosphorous of grief consuming those he loves" (342). It is only LaRose's lucky intervention that, almost miraculously, prevents both of his fathers from completing Romeo's malevolent plot. In an interview with magazine writer Claire Hoffman, Erdrich declared Romeo Puyat to be one of the most interesting characters in the novel because he embodies the struggle "between decency and brutality." And, indeed, it is the most deeply traumatized characters in the book—Nola Ravich, Landreaux Iron, Maggie, or Romeo—who appear to benefit from the counterplot of redemption and reparation primarily orchestrated by the protagonist of the novel.

Alternative Solutions to Grievances: The Role of Restitution

While Erdrich's novel abounds with references to drug abuse, marital disappoint-
ments, menial employments, adolescent yearnings, and old-age discontent, it is also
true that these negative forces are often leavened with the occasional amusements
and ordinary joys of family and tribal life (cf. Campbell). In her interview with
Hoffman, Erdrich clarifies that, despite the unmistakable evidence of tragedy and
grief in the novel, she always intended to write about common lives and normal
people: "I think that's the way life is. I think we experience the most ordinary
circumstances and the heightened realm of experience when huge things happen
to us. We also have to tend to what people are going to eat, where they are going to
sleep, all of the small things." Indeed, much attention is paid in the novel to the food
people eat, the hobbies they have, the jokes they make, or the traditional rituals
some of them perform. Even an outsider such as Father Travis comes to appreciate
and enjoy some of the distinctive habits that the Ojibwe keep, and which, regardless
of the poverty and other adversities on the reservation, he feels somehow connected
with: "He loved it here. He loved his people. They were his people, weren't they?
They drove him nuts, but he was inspired by their generosity. And they laughed so
much. He hadn't known funny before. So with or without his savior, or his sanity,
he wanted to stay" (110). As Father Travis observes, it is remarkable that, in the face
of horrific disruptions, the people seem to find the traditional ways and resilience
tactics to bring back peace and harmony.

One interesting point to be made about *LaRose* is that, unlike in the other two
novels of the trilogy, the key disruption does not come from outside the boundaries
of the community, but is generated from within the ethnic group—and even
within the family. Jacobs has underlined that the (circular) narrative structure of
Erdrich's novels is generally motivated by a family's story "and the reverberations
of its history upon the life of the community" (108). This ripple effect is very
clearly observed in the case of the Iron and Ravich families, who happen to share
a common lineage, but seem to relate to it in very different ways, thus causing the
massive schism that lies at the heart of the novel. This schism finds its deepest
roots, as will be seen below, in the degree of assimilation to the Western culture
each of the families has experienced, and the type of ties they have been able to
maintain with their Native heritage (see Broida; Shelton 310). This kind of schism
is apparent when Nola sarcastically remarks to Peter: "How generous you are,
Emmaline, what a big-time traditional person to give your son away to a white man

and almost white sister who is just so pitiful, so stark raving. So like her mother that Marn who had the snakes. People never forget around here. And they will never forget this either. It will be Emmaline Iron the good strong whaddyacallit, Ogema-ikwe" (234).

A majority of critics and reviewers have noted that *LaRose* is, above anything else, a book about the possibility of atonement and reparation, even in cases in which the pain inflicted appears to be completely unmanageable. Interestingly, however, it is the family more deeply rooted in Native culture that has caused the grievance and that is, therefore, responsible for taking the first step in terms of restitution. Fortunately, the Irons seem to have more resources than the "victims," as the plight of the Raviches confronting their affliction is one of utter powerlessness. The former count on their strong cultural heritage, a lively and loving family that has already taken in and nurtured an adopted child, Hollis Puyat, and, of course, the most important asset of all, the protagonist of the book. Landreaux and Emmaline "had resisted using the name of LaRose until their last child was born. It was a name both innocent and powerful, and had belonged to the family's healers. They had decided not to use it, but it was as though LaRose had come into the world with that name" (11). Although his parents suspect from the beginning that there is something special about their youngest son, they cannot be sure that the invisible cloak of "power and wisdom" that is associated with the name will suffice to get him through the trial of moving into a family deeply aggrieved and fatally crumbling to pieces. Nonetheless, despite some uncertain steps at the beginning, it soon becomes clear that the young hero is completely up to the task of healing the severe wounds in his surrogate family and the community at large.

LaRose's special role in the novel brings up the need not just for vengeance or punishment in the form of justice, but for something more significant and restorative, which some commentators have described as reparative justice. In an article on the increasing importance that reparative or restorative justice is gaining for peoples who have been historically abused and decimated, Felipe Gómez-Isa clarifies that while reparation should not be viewed as "a panacea" that will solve all the problems of afflicted communities, it is by its very nature progressive: "The important aspect is not only the objects that form part of the victims' reparation but 'the process' that takes place around the object" (272). In Erdrich's novel, the act of restitution or compensation generously enacted by the Irons when they surrender their son to the Raviches is not enough by itself to reconstruct the families and community. Although LaRose seems to have an almost immediate curative impact on some of the characters—Nola, most obviously—the majority of them take a while to see themselves transformed by this adorable charmer.

One remarkable advantage that LaRose has over all the other characters in the novel is that besides the care and counsel he receives from his parents, he is also in close communion with elders, especially his maternal grandmother, and with some forebears. In his vision, he sees "a group of people. Half were Indians and half were maybe Indians, some so pale he could see light shining through them. They came and made themselves comfortable, sitting around him—people of all ages" (210). If LaRose is able to become a bridge or a kind of ambassador between the two families (cf. McGrath), it is because he is attentive to the particular needs each of his closest kin has and tries to afford them what they most require. In this sense, he does not just offer restitution for the victims, who are at least partly restored to their original condition before the calamity happened, but also comfort and rehabilitation for those who were not so directly injured by the grievance.

Dinah Shelton has argued that it is people who insist on dwelling excessively on past injuries that have the hardest time in facing the future without resentment, as they habitually develop "a culture of victimization" (308). This may be the case for characters in *LaRose* such as Romeo or Mrs. Peace, who are so deeply engrossed in their personal and tribal past that it is difficult for them to conceive that any type of reparation is possible. Nevertheless, thanks primarily to LaRose's healing and bridging skills, the younger generation seems to build up alternative perspectives and strategies to deal with the future. Notice, for example, the radically different stances Hollis and his father, Romeo, take when the former informs the latter that he is thinking of joining the National Guard:

> Ever since they hit the Towers, said Hollis, I've been thinking. My country has been good to me.
>
> What? Romeo was scandalized. You're an Indian!
>
> I know, sure, they wiped us out almost. But still, the freedoms, right? And we got schools and hospitals and the casino. When we fuck up now, we mostly fuck up on our own.
>
> Are you crazy! That's called intergenerational trauma, my boy. It isn't our fault they keep us down; they savaged our culture, family structure, and most of all we need our *land* back. (214)

Of course, it is difficult not to see the irony in the fact that one of the few references to intergenerational trauma in the novel should come from a character who is perceived by the rest of the community as a good-for-nothing who has done little to make life on the reservation more tolerable. The closing section of the novel, appropriately entitled "The Gathering," reveals the partial recovery of those most deeply hurt, such as Nola and Romeo, and makes clear LaRose's uncanny powers to bring reconciliation and balance to his people: "Soon the dog ambled up and settled down, leaning incrementally closer to Nola's ankle until he touched and she let him stay. She had decided to come to the party. Strictly speaking, it did not make sense. Yet there was someone here with Nola's body, voice, name. Soon she was eating a plate of barbecue with a dog warm along her ankle" (365).

Although LaRose could pass for a regular boy at school and on the reservation, neither too bright nor too physically deft, he proves to have astonishing discernment to see beyond what everybody else can manage to see. Peter Ravich does not fully understand LaRose's power until after he has pulled the trigger of his rifle several times against Landreaux and "Nothing happened." Then he sees: "The picture of those small capable boy hands now fills Peter. Those hands curving to accept the bullets. Loading and unloading his gun. And the ropes, the poisons. Those hands taking them from their places and getting rid of them. The missing rat poison, strychnine, the missing bleach. LaRose saving him now, saving both his fathers" (342). In this way, the boy LaRose represents simply an embodiment of one of the essential forces in the spiritual life of the Anishinaabe: restitution as a form of atonement to restore tribal cohesion. As Erdrich explained to McGrath, the book originated in a casual comment by her mother about the common practice among Native Americans of adopting children from other families and how this fact made their view of family much more "elastic." No doubt, LaRose, being an "old soul" (*LaRose* 52), represents this perfect materialization of a tradition that allowed many tribes to survive under the pressure of a government and a culture that did not understand and punished such practices. As the novel shows, the protagonist slowly learns to make the best out of his bewildering situation suspended between two severely wounded families:

He had learned from his birth family how to snare rabbits, make stew, paint fingernails. . . . He had learned from the old people how to move between worlds seen and unseen. Peter taught him how to use an ax, a chain saw, safely handle a

.22. . . . Nola taught him how to paint walls, keep animals, how to plant and grow
things. . . . Maggie taught him how to hide fear, fake pain, how to punch with a
knuckle jutting. (208)

Through his careful attention and care for the people who surround him, LaRose
becomes a healing force, ready to use all his competencies as a sensitive child and
a conciliator: "In all of these things, LaRose was precise and deliberate. He was
becoming an effective human being" (208).

Balancing Trauma and Restitution

As LeMay points out, Erdrich's novel tells a story of "life understood and experienced
by many in Indian country, where the pain and the triumphs of the past are not
forgotten but become part of the foundation on which the present and the future
are built." Indeed, we have already seen how buildings, objects, and even people
contain layer upon layer of history that turn them into much more than what they
seem to be at first sight. Even the name "LaRose" contains many layers of history:

> There are five LaRoses. First the LaRose who poisoned Mackinnon, went to mission
> school, married Wolfred, taught her children the shape of the world, and traveled
> the world as a set of stolen bones. Second, her daughter LaRose, who went to
> Carlisle. This LaRose got tuberculosis like her own mother, and like the first LaRose
> fought it off again and again. Lived long enough to become the mother of the
> third LaRose, who went to Fort Totten and bore the fourth LaRose, who eventually
> became the mother of Emmaline, the teacher of Romeo and Landreaux. The
> fourth LaRose also became the grandmother of the last LaRose, who was given to
> the Ravich family by his parents in exchange for a son accidentally killed. (290)

This passage indicates the importance of names in Native traditions, in which
they denote identity, status, and heritage. As Wan explains, "giving a newly-born
child a spirit name is thus a sacred action for the child and the tribe as well" (1184). It
is for that reason that the Irons at first hesitated to name their fourth child "LaRose,"
knowing very well the kind of power—but also the responsibility—that it bears.
But after they have heard from Randall and the elders of the last LaRose's healing
powers, it is easy to understand why Landreaux and Emmaline decide to surrender

their last son for adoption to the Raviches as some form of compensation for the damage—or trauma—they have caused in their family: "LaRose is powerful both in name and in origins and can survive traumas and preserve Ojibwe traditions" (Wan 1184).

It is important to note that the protagonist's name, which travels through bloodlines and has a mysterious power to help the community recover from their grief, also evokes several references to boarding schools and their injurious influence on the family history. Joseph Gone has described in great detail the "horrific instances of violence and violation perpetrated against" Native children in those institutions and how they yield "a harrowing legacy of distress and disability for contemporary Native peoples" (752). In a way, the Irons' beautiful and altruistic act of giving up their youngest son is also an attempt at correcting the deracinating aftermath that those schools had on the older generation, as each of them is marked by that experience in a different way: "low self-esteem, victim identity, anger, self-destructive behavior, and substance abuse" (Brave Heart 7). It is perhaps Emmaline Iron who is most aware of the pernicious impact of boarding schools on her peoples, and so she decides to establish an alternative "on-reservation boarding school for crisis kids" (105):

> The radical part was that, unlike historical boarding schools, this one would be located on the reservation. Pre-K through grade 4. After that, kids could board but go to regular school. This new/old sort of boarding school, equipped to pick up the parenting roles for families that went through cycles of failure and recovery, became Emmaline's mission. (105–106)

As a crisis-intervention project, Emmaline understands that this school's primary aim and mission is "Heartbreak mitigation" (106)—that is, to provide calm and stability in the face of collective trauma, to achieve dependable household structures, to combine education with traditional cultural practices, and, above all, to afford coping strategies for those who see their lives disarrayed by unexpected accidents awakening old fears. Of course, she is quick to realize that her own mitigating program at the school could be productively transferred to her own home when the Ojibwe tradition of restitution spurs them to hand over their son for the benefit of the whole community. Although it is painful at first, she understands the need to go through the "trauma process" (Alexander 22), which involves confronting and understanding the trauma, releasing the pain by resorting to cultural rituals, and transcending the trauma to move beyond (Brave Heart 5). As the ending of the novel demonstrates, even those most deeply hurt may begin to show signs of recovery if these basic principles are pursued. Even if the process may be tortuous at stages and the invaluable presence of a powerful "healer" may be imperative at times, there is hope that the community will regain its balance. As "those other people"—their forebears—tell LaRose and Dusty near the end of the book: "*We love you, don't cry. Sorrow eats time. Be patient. Time eats sorrow*" (371).

Frances Washburn notes that one of Erdrich's main strengths as a writer is her ability to represent the violent culture clash between Native American tribes and Euro-American colonizers, and to still endorse a cross-cultural view of history: "Erdrich addresses historical injustice, yes, but she complicates and explicates presenting nuanced stories that are closer to truth, if there is such a thing as one single truth" (124). *LaRose* presents just such a story in which the boundaries between saints and sinners, traditionalists and assimilationists, savages and civilized are constantly problematized. At one point in the novel, the young LaRose hears "old stories" from Ignatia Thunder, one of the female elders in the novel, and he feels quite frustrated because he cannot find a "moral" in those tales. So he is given a teaching: "'Moral? Our stories don't have those!' Ignatia puffed her cheeks in annoyance" (293). Ignatia's response holds true for the novel as a whole, since it provides only tentative solutions to the complicated issues that most of the characters need to deal with. *LaRose* explores the different responses that a diverse set of human beings give to grievances—grievances that can be very immediate or that may throw us back in time into historical traumas that have hardly been properly assimilated. These diverse responses range from vehement revenge plots to those that rely on atonement and restitution to try to bring human relationships back to harmony. In the end, reparative strategies seem to get the upper hand, but one cannot be completely sure that such healing tactics would have worked under any other circumstances—especially without the crucial presence of the last LaRose.

Besides the superb achievement of allowing readers to identify with her characters in an intimate manner, Erdrich's novel also advances ways to address such huge problems as historical injustice and intergenerational trauma. Legal scholars such as Daniel Butt (2008) and Francesco Francioni (2008) have dwelt upon the complications of applying reparatory or rectificatory justice today. Complex issues related to legitimacy, non-retroactivity, or redistribution often get in the way when "the most serious breaches of human rights and humanitarian law," such as slavery or Native genocide, are involved and are shown to clamorously require reparatory action (Francioni 43). Although Native legal experts have demonstrated that most of the current demands for reparation and restitution from Indigenous peoples are based on the violation of treaties signed by the United States during the nineteenth century (see Deloria 4–5), only minor steps have been taken to rectify the situation. In her justice trilogy, Erdrich illustrates in thought-provoking ways how those historical abuses reemerge on Indian reservations in current forms of dysfunction and inequality. Scholar David Stirrup notes that as Erdrich's career has developed, her novels engage "the political-milieu" in significant ways: "her late work revisits . . . terrain with a much more pronounced political edge to it, and a keener eye for the devastating and often paradoxical legacy of communities, values, lifeways, and economies clashing, 'cracking apart', merging, and reforming" (204). If the frequent references to Y2K, 9/11, the Iraq War, and the National Guard were not enough to make us conscious of that political edge in *LaRose*, we always have the wise words of Ignatia Thunder right before she dies, telling the protagonist of the novel what Native American history has always been all about:

> It is *about* getting chased, said Ignatia, with a long suck on her oxygen. We are chased into this life. The Catholics think we are chased by devils, original sin. We are chased by things done to us in this life.
>
> That's called trauma, said Malvern.
>
> Thank *you*, said Ignatia. We are chased by what we do to others and then in turn what they do to us. We're always looking behind us, or worried about what comes next. We only have this teeny moment. Oops, it's gone! (294)

WORKS CITED

Alexander, Jeffrey C. "Introduction: Toward a Theory of Cultural Trauma." *Cultural Trauma and Collective Identity*, edited by J. C. Alexander et al., Grove Press, 2000, pp. 1–30.

Athiakis, Mark. "Hunting Accident Propels Tragic Erdrich Novel." Review of *LaRose*, by Louise Erdrich. *USA Today*, 2 June 2016, www.usatoday.com/story/life/books/2016/05/14/larose-louise-erdrich-book-review/84039990/.

Brave Heart, Maria Yellow Horse. "From Intergenerational Trauma to Intergenerational Healing." *Wellbriety!*, vol. 6, no. 6, May 2005, pp. 2–8.

Broida, Michael. "*LaRose* by Louise Erdrich: Brilliant, Subtle Exploration of Tragic Stories." *Philadelphia Inquirer*, 20 May 2016, www.inquirer.com/philly/entertainment/20160522__LaRose__by_Louise_Erdrich__Brilliant__subtle_exploration_of_tragic_histories.html.

Butt, Daniel. *Rectifying International Injustice: Principles of Compensation and Restitution between Nations*. Oxford UP, 2008.

Campbell, Ellen Prentiss. Review of *LaRose* by Louise Erdrich. *Fiction Writers Review*, 30 May 2016, fictionwritersreview.com/review/larose-by-louise-erdrich.

Charles, Ron. "Louise Erdrich's *LaRose*: A Gun Accident Sets Off a Masterly Tale of Grief and Love." *Washington Post*, 9 May 2016.

Crispin, Jessa. "*LaRose* by Louise Erdrich Review—Tragedy and Atonement from One of America's Great Writers." *Guardian*, 25 May 2016, www.theguardian.com/books/2016/may/25/larose-by-louise-erdrich-review.

Deloria, Vine, Jr. *Behind the Trail of Broken Treaties: An Indian Declaration of Independence*. 1974. Revised ed., U of Texas P, 1985.

Denham, Aaron R. "Rethinking Historical Trauma: Narratives of Resilience." *Transcultural Psychiatry*, vol. 45, no. 3, Sept. 2008, pp. 391–414.

Du Plessis, Max, and Stephen Peté, eds. *Repairing the Past? International Perspectives on Reparations for Gross Human Rights Abuses*. Intersentia, 2007.

Erdrich, Louise. "Interview with Louise Erdrich." Interview conducted by Claire Hoffman. *Goodreads*, 2 May 2016, www.goodreads.com/interviews/show/1124.Louise_Erdrich.

———. *LaRose*. HarperCollins, 2016.

Francioni, Francesco. "Reparation for Indigenous Peoples: Is International Law Ready to Ensure Redress for Historical Injustices?" *Reparations for Indigenous Peoples, International and Comparative Perspectives*, edited by F. Lenzerini, Oxford UP, 2008, pp. 27–46.

Gómez-Isa, Felipe. "Repairing Historical Injustices: Indigenous Peoples in Post-Conflict Scenarios." *Rethinking Transitions: Equality and Social Justice in Societies Emerging from Conflict*, edited by G. Oré-Aguilar and F. Gómez-Isa, Intersentia, 2011, pp. 265–300.

Gone, Joseph P. "A Community-Based Treatment for Native American Historical Trauma: Prospects for Evidence-Based Practice." *Journal of Consulting and Clinical Psychology*, vol. 77, no. 4, 2009, pp. 751–62.

Gordon, Mary. "A Boy's Fate." Review of *LaRose*, by Louise Erdrich. *New York Times Book Review*, 22 May 2016, pp. 1, 26.

Hafen, P. Jane. "'We Anishinaabeg are the keepers of the name of the earth': Louise Erdrich's Great Plains." *Great Plains Quarterly*, vol. 21, no. 4, 2001, pp. 321–32.

Holt, Debra C. "Transformation and Continuance: Native American Tradition in the Novels of Louise Erdrich." *Entering the 90s: The North American Experience*, edited by Thomas E. Schirer, Lake Superior UP, 1991, pp. 149–61.

Ibarrola-Armendariz, Aitor. "Negotiating Traumatic Memories in Louise Erdrich's *The Round House*." *Memory Frictions in Contemporary Literature*, edited by M. J. Martínez-Alfaro and

S. Pellicer-Ortín, Palgrave Macmillan, 2017, pp. 255–76.

Jacobs, Connie A. *The Novels of Louise Erdrich: Stories of Her People*. Peter Lang, 2001.

Kurup, Seema. "From Revenge to Restorative Justice in Louise Erdrich's *The Plague of Doves*, *The Round House*, and *LaRose*." *American Revenge Narratives: A Collection of Critical Essays*, edited by Kyle Wiggins, Palgrave Macmillan, 2018, pp. 99–117.

LeMay, Konnie. "Louise Erdrich's *LaRose*: Two Families Bound by Death, Love and Healing." *Indian Country Today*, 11 May 2016, https://indiancountrytoday.com/archive/louise-erdrich-s-larose-two-families-bound-by-death-love-and-healing-rcjc1WNEgUillW3kkDfefQ.

Lincoln, Kenneth. *Native American Renaissance*. U of California P, 1983.

McGrath, Charles. "Obsessively Mining a Familial Landscape: Louise Erdrich on Her New Novel, *LaRose*, and the Psychic Territory of Native Americans." *New York Times*, 7 May 2016, p. C1.

McKee, Ian. "Revenge, Retribution, and Values: Social Attitudes and Punitive Sentencing." *Social Justice Research*, vol. 21, no. 2, June 2008, pp. 138–63.

Schacht, Miriam. "Games of Silence: Indian Boarding Schools in Louise Erdrich's Novels." *Studies in American Indian Literatures*, vol. 27, no. 2, Summer 2015, pp. 62–79.

Shelton, Dinah. "The World of Atonement: Reparations for Historical Injustices." *Netherlands International Law Review*, vol. 50, no. 3, Dec. 2003, pp. 289–327.

Sotero, Michelle M. "A Conceptual Model of Historical Trauma: Implications for Public Health Practice and Research." *Journal of Health Disparities Research and Practice*, vol. 1, no. 1, Fall 2006, pp. 93–108.

Stirrup, David. *Louise Erdrich*. Contemporary American and Canadian Writers Series. Manchester UP, 2010.

Vizenor, Gerald. *Manifest Manners: Postindian Warriors of Survivance*. Wesleyan UP, 1994.

Wan, Mei. "Culture Survivance and Religion Healing: On Ojibwe Spirituality in Healing Trauma in *LaRose*." *Journal of Literature and Art Studies*, vol. 8, no. 8, August 2018, pp. 1181–87.

Washburn, Frances. *Tracks on the Page: Louise Erdrich, Her Life and Works*. Women Writers of Color Series. Praeger, 2013.

Family Trees

Land and Kinship in Louise Erdrich's Justice Trilogy

Ellen L. Arnold

> In Anishinaabe culture trees have long been considered markers
> of meeting places and messengers to other dimensions.
>
> —Margaret Noodin, *Bawaajimo*

The three novels in what has come to be known as Louise Erdrich's justice trilogy, *The Plague of Doves* (2008), *The Round House* (2012), and *LaRose* (2016), are linked not only by their entangled human genealogies and shared examinations of the intergenerational effects of settler colonial violence, but also by their illumination of the way violent histories are manifested through place beyond human intention and memory. While the characters and events that dominate the human stories in *The Plague of Doves* are only vaguely remembered by the human characters in *LaRose*, there is a specific location central to all three novels where the effects of the crimes narrated in *The Plague of Doves*—the murders of the Lochren family, the lynching of innocent Native men (one just thirteen years old), and the land theft that underlies these crimes—are vividly remembered and unraveled: a site at the boundary between the large tract of farmland claimed by the German immigrant Wolde family and the fictional North Dakota reservation of which it was originally part. As Christopher Schliephake notes in his exploration of the intersections of literary place and cultural memory, which includes a discussion of *The Round House*, "the natural world . . . is not merely . . . the background to cultural processes . . . but a central actor in them" (596). In Erdrich's trilogy, the land is no passive object of greed and theft, but plays a potent role in events, particularly through important tree characters. Considering these trees as protagonists in the three novels traces a trajectory from violence to healing that is broader than the human lives it encompasses and expands our understanding of both kinship and justice.

The most commanding tree presence in *The Plague of Doves* is the hanging tree, a native oak already ancient in 1911 when white settler vigilantes used it to hang Natives Mooshum (Seraph Milk), Asiginak, Cuthbert Peace, and the boy Holy Track, for the murders of the white Lochren family. The oak had "grown there quietly for a hundred years" on "the edge of Wolde's land," just beyond the Ojibwe reservation boundary; it has "a generous spread," including a branch "that ran straight on both sides of the tree and then bent upward, as if in a gesture of praise" (77), a structure that ironically makes the oak ideal for hanging.[1] The location of the hanging tree on Wolde land—previously part of the reservation allotted to the Ojibwe Peace family (152)—highlights the fact that the lynching had its roots in the already tangled history of racism and greed that fueled the original theft of the land. Some of the connections are direct; Emil Buckendorf, a leader of the lynching party, was part of the "town-site expedition" that first laid claim to the land (97), and victim Cuthbert Peace was brother to Henri and Lafayette Peace, the Métis guides who led the expedition party to the area and kept them alive through a bitter winter.

The hanging oak stands alone, separated from its woodland relations by the theft and clearing of the land for farming; as Emil Buckendorf remarks while the vigilantes are searching for a hanging site, "All the good trees is back of us, over the reservation line" (74). Isolated but unmolested, the oak inhabits the stolen land peacefully until it is appropriated in this act of settler violence. In her essay "Discontinuous Narrative, Ojibwe Sovereignty, and the *Wiindigoo* Logic of Settler Colonialism," Deborah Madsen explores Erdrich's "discursive reappropriation of indigenous history . . . played out through the symbolic value of the hanging tree" (40) in *The Plague of Doves* and *The Round House*; bedecked with prayer flags in remembrance of the victims, the tree becomes an "assertion of indigenous sovereignty" (40–41). But the tree is more than symbol; its presence just beyond the reservation boundary stakes an active claim on the stolen land. And the oak stands not only at the boundary of Indian and white worlds, but between earth and sky, at the intersection of material and spiritual worlds; it is harbor to and conduit of spirit, through which it acts to shape the course of events.

The tree's connection with a powerful holy spirit in the form of a bird first becomes apparent in the minutes before the hanging. On the way to the tree, Mooshum observes in a sky "the sweetest color of blue . . . the clouds were delicate, no more than tiny white breast feathers way up high" (75); at the moment of his death, Holy Track opens his eyes to the sky and sees the same "wisps of clouds, way up high," which "resolved into wings" that "swept across the sky now, faster and faster" (79). A sign of peace and comfort to the victims, these wings in the sky echo the titular "plague of doves" that swarmed the area and stripped the fields of their crops fifteen years earlier in 1896, doves that remain associated with the hanging tree throughout *The Plague of Doves*. Several critics have read the doves as symbolic of the white settlers: John Gamber, for example, describes them as "an excessively large, migrating, white mass of life clamping down on the American landscape" (144); Margaret Noori observes that "all that whiteness descending on Chippewa reservation farmland, hungry and destructive, is also a metaphor for the myth of manifest destiny" (12). However, while the Catholic priest Father Cassidy may describe the Holy Spirit as "a pure white dove" (Erdrich, *Plague* 212), those that plague the land are actually "brown doves" (8)—more likely, as Mooshum's granddaughter Evelina later points out, "the passenger pigeons of legend and truth, whose numbers were such that nobody thought they could possibly ever be wiped from the earth" (19). The doves are often linked in the novel with the buffalo and with the Indigenous people whose lives are intertwined with them, all threatened with extinction. When Mooshum begins narrating the story of the hangings to his grandchildren, he marks the beginning of the story as a time when the doves and the buffalo, "which he'd been told were once limitless," had been "killed off" (57).[2]

The birds that plague the white settlers and the Natives who farm among them bring a "vision of the Holy Spirit" to Mooshum in the form of his future wife Junesse when he is struck in the head by a "bird hurtled from the sky with such force that it seemed to have been flung directly by God's hand" (8). It is largely because of his marriage to Junesse, daughter of one of the lynchers, that Mooshum is cut down before he is hanged "*to death*" (82). More than half a century later, as Mooshum tells the story to Evelina and her brother Joseph, he comments urgently to his brother Shamengwa, "*I saw the same thing as Holy Track, the doves are still up there*" (83). Obsessed with tracing the lineages of lynchers and victims, Evelina, on a visit home from college in 1974, learns the truth about her grandfather's role in the lynching; drunk, he revealed to his father-in-law, Eugene Wildstrand, that he and his companions had visited the Lochren farm and found the bodies. Forced finally to acknowledge his betrayal of the other victims, Mooshum enlists Evelina to take him to the hanging tree for a ritual act of contrition, the rehanging of Holy Track's boots; on their arrival, "a thousand birds startled up at the same instant . . . sucked into the air" (253). Even now, "Everybody knew where the tree was. The tree still grew on Marn's [Marn Wolde's] land, where Billy Peace's kindred used to stay. . . . The tree took up the very northwest corner of the land, and it was always full of birds" (253). Evelina describes the oak in awed terms: "Alone in the field, catching light from each direction, the tree had grown its branches out like the graceful arms of a candelabra. New prayer flags hung down—red, green, blue, white. The sun was flaring low, gold on the branches, and the finest of new leaves was showing" (253). More than sixty years after the hangings and the extinction of the passenger pigeons, the tree stands a living memorial to both, a beacon of pilgrimage. Evelina throws the boots into the tree for Mooshum, but she doubts the significance of the act; "This is sentiment instead of justice," she tells her grandfather (253). "Awee, my girl," Mooshum responds. "The doves are still up there" (254). The continuing presence of the spirit doves in the tree suggests to Mooshum the possibility of a different kind of justice, a "blanket of doves [that] had merely lifted into the stratosphere and not been snuffed out" and are awaiting their return to earth (255).

Evelina does not come to trust her grandfather's vision until she experiences her own crisis of identity; recovering in a mental hospital from a bout of depression, Evelina mulls over "how history works itself out in the living," as the descendants of lynchers and victims have intermixed until "there is no unraveling the rope" (243), making human justice impossible. At the same time, Evelina recalls Mooshum's account of how the last of the buffalo hunters "looked beneath the robe of destruction that blanketed the earth" and "saw the frail crust of white commerce lifting, saw the green grass underneath the burnt wheat, saw the buffalo thick as lice again, . . . flattening that rich grass beneath their hooves. Looking up, they saw the sky darkening with birds that covered it so that you could not see from one end to another" (243–44). The doves are a promise that the land will be restored, a promise already beginning to take shape in the dying town of Pluto, once located inside the reservation boundaries, and on Mooshum's fallow allotment land, where "sage and alfalfa and buffalo grass stood heavy" (267), awaiting the return of the buffalo. The perpetrators of land theft and murder may go unpunished and thrive on their stolen land, but eventually the land will reclaim itself. Judge Coutts understands this as well; as he reflects on the dying town, he comments on the "desperate enterprises that involve boundaries we place upon the earth. By drawing a line and defending it, we seem to think we have mastered something. What? The earth swallows and absorbs even those who manage to form a country, a reservation." Yet, the Judge continues, "there is something to the love and knowledge of the land and its relationship to dreams—that's what the old people had. That's why as a tribe we exist to the present" (115). It is this kinship *with* the land more than the possession of it that Evelina begins to understand when she describes Mooshum's and Shamengwa's withdrawal from town historian Neve Harp's insensitive questions about how the town of Pluto was stolen: "I saw that the loss of their land was lodged inside of them forever. This loss would enter me, too" (84). In her room at the mental hospital, she feels both the loss and the promise: "Sometimes doves seem to hover in this room. At night, when I can't sleep, I hear the flutter of their wings" (244).

The intermixing that Evelina ponders means human attempts at justice for the loss of Indian lives and lands play out in convoluted and unexpected ways in *The Plague of Doves*; the attractions that draw descendants of perpetrators and victims together in hopeless tangles of passion, revenge, and penance are explored insightfully by Susan Strehle in her essay "'Prey to Unknown Dreams': Louise Erdrich, *The Plague of Doves*, and the Exceptionalist Disavowal of History." Taking her title from Judge Coutts's musing, "[W]hat is the difference between the influence of instinct upon a wolf and history upon a man? In both cases, justice is prey to unknown dreams" (*Plague* 117), Strehle suggests that the "unknown dreams" that "deform relationships" among the Native, European, and mixed-blood inheritors of land theft and murders are the emergence of repressed histories and "disavowed events" of Manifest Destiny and American exceptionalism (Strehle 110). But the land has its own ways of addressing loss and achieving justice, and on a less symbolic level, these "unknown dreams" could be understood to arise from the land itself, working through humans to accomplish its own ends. In Erdrich's earlier novel, *The Last Report on the Miracles at Little No Horse*, the character Mashkiigikwe observes angrily that the white men "take all that makes us Anishinaabeg. . . . First our land, then our trees" (100). *Last Report* closes with this meditation by Nanapush on Anishinaabe identity:

> If we call ourselves and all we see around us by the original names, will we not continue to be Anishinaabeg? Instead of reconstituted white men, instead of Indian ghosts? Do the rocks here know us, do the trees, do the waters of the lakes?

Not unless they are addressed by the names they themselves told us to call them in our dreams. Every feature of the land around us spoke its name to an ancestor. Perhaps, in the end, that is all that we are. We Anishinaabeg are the keepers of the names of the earth. (360–61)

For traditional Anishinaabeg, dreams and visions are the location of their most intimate exchanges with the natural world, where they learn the true names of the world's other inhabitants and, in relationship with them, their own identities. It is this intimacy that is disrupted by the removal of Indigenous people from their land, cut off by the drawing of artificial boundaries that declare human possession. In *The Plague of Doves*, it is through the visions and dreams of both Natives and settlers, some of which seem to be directed through the hanging oak, that the land begins to reclaim itself and the humans who have been lost to it.

When Ojibwe evangelist Billy Peace, a descendant of lynching victim Cuthbert Peace, marries Marn Wolde, he is at first interested more in her visions than her land. But, as Madsen notes, Marn's visions are tied to the family land, and she has "trouble with the pictures" when she is away from it (31; quoting *Plague* 147). After their marriage and their three years "in the desert" (147) assembling a following, the land calls Marn home; she longs for "all that flat land, green crops, those clouds . . . the blue fields. The yellow mustard fields. Sunflowers turning all day to catch the light" (148–49). She persuades Billy to return using the land as bait, and he becomes fixated on the idea of repossessing the land and returning it to the reservation. However, the land does not respond well to Billy's desires; there is drought when he first visits the farm, and drought when he returns. The day sixteen-year-old Marn meets Billy, she stands on the stricken land staring out at "the great oak across the field," which "reared out, its roots sucking water from the bottom of the world." The hanging oak, previously described as peaceful, even gracious, takes on a threatening presence. When rain seems imminent, Marn, sitting on the deck of her house, "could almost feel the timbers shake under [her] feet, as its great searching taproots trembled" (*Plague* 137). Thus begins an ominous association among Marn, Billy, and the hanging tree that ends with Billy's death. Almost immediately upon their return, Marn feels the great bird spirit hosted by the tree settle within her: "Half-awake and drifting, I feel the stark bird that nests in the tree of the Holy Ghost descend and hover. . . . The wings flutter lower, scored white, and the down of its breast crackles faintly as the sparks jump between us" (151). As the spirit enters her, Marn is filled with unintelligible words in the voice of her uncle Warren, who, as we learn at the end of the novel, is the real killer of the Lochren family. The description of fluttering wings and downy breast feathers recalls Mooshum's and Holy Track's visions of wings in the sky above the hanging tree, but there is no sense of peace or blessing here. Like Warren Wolde, who more than once has told Marn, "It's on you . . . you're gonna kill" (158, 177), the hanging tree sees the killer in Marn as well and orchestrates Billy's death by sending its holy bird spirit and snake messengers to work through her.[3]

The electrically charged scene of Marn's possession is echoed when Billy attempts to end the drought by commanding the rain. A "rain prayer meeting" draws thunderclouds (155), and Billy sits on an iron bench, allowing himself to become "the locus of blue bolts that spark" among the iron fixtures in the yard (156). Finally "a rope of golden fire snakes down and wraps Billy twice," evoking the sparks that fly between Marn and the presence that enters her as well as the snakes she handles, and reduces him to a "mound, black and tattered, . . . [a] snuffling creature of darkness burnt blind." Though Billy is resurrected larger than life, "swollen with unearthly power" (156), the lightning strike is the beginning of his end. It is at this point Marn realizes Billy must be stopped. His rapacious, controlling behaviors become more extreme, and the land continues to turn away from him and the hungry kindred. "We tried to grow hothouse and hydroponic produce and failed," Marn recounts. "Our chickens were picked off by hawks. Our turkeys looked up in the rain and drowned. The geese flew off. The goats ate the garden. Weasels got the baby pigs and coyotes got the calves" (174). Soon, bitten by one of her snakes, Marn feels the poison "bloom" in her, "fruit of the tree of power" (162). Finally, in a vision, Marn feels "that bird moving in the cage of my ribs" (177), and her serpents instruct her how to kill Billy with their venom. Guided by her vision, she strings him up from the rafters of their bedroom to make his death look like suicide, a bizarre reenactment of the lynching that took Billy's uncle Cuthbert's life in the hanging tree just across the field. Marn's first thought after escaping with her children is to repossess the land that is now in Billy's name.

Both Billy and Marn have been identified by critics as wiindigoo. Gina Valentino details the stages of Billy's transformation from a sympathetic Native man attempting to regain his family land to a "figure of excessive consumption, predatory sexual appetites, and greed" (131), possessed by desire for power over his family, his followers, and the land. Madsen argues that Marn also succumbs to "the *wiindigoo* pathology of insatiable land hunger" (48) associated with settler colonialism, and "acts to aggrandize herself by taking the children, the money, and the land" (38). However, Marn is much closer to the land than Billy and ultimately acts in its interests, defying Madsen's portrayal of her as another wiindigoo. Like her father, who "loves his land" (138) and knows how to plant a seedling tree with "knowledge, tender and offhand, of the ways roots took hold in the earth" (139), Marn has an intimate relationship with the land that goes back to her childhood and deepens during her runs about the farm after her return. When she begins to question her relationship with Billy, it is "[g]rass, water, summer fireweed and thistle" she calls on to save her; "I didn't call on god, though. He was on my husband's side" (164). Clearly Marn knows which is more powerful. On her final run before the "schedule," the punishment she takes in her son's place that produces her vision of Billy's end, she stops and turns a ceremonial invocation "in six circles. Sky over me, sky under me, sky to my north and south. Sky to my west." She runs "for the pure joy of moving in the air, in this life, in this goodness soaking up through the dirt" (176). Her father's knowledge is more about making the land produce, but Marn feels herself part of the land: "I was everything the mountain knew. I was the unturned stone. And the snake under it, that too" (166). The hanging tree has chosen her as the instrument of the wiindigoo Billy's death and the land's deliverance. Through Marn, we learn in *LaRose*, the land is passed on to her mixed-blood daughter—half Peace, half Wolde—enabling the eventual reconciliation of land and Ojibwe community that comes about at the end of that novel. The land will be restored to the people on its own terms, rather than by any human redrawing of boundaries or transfer of ownership. Human crimes in *The Plague of Doves* may go unpunished, but the original crime at the foundation of all the others, the breaking of kinship between the Ojibwe people and the land, is redressable; it is this particular form of justice, the restoration of an intimate, reciprocal relationship with its Indigenous kin, that the land and its tree agents work to accomplish throughout the rest of the trilogy.

While *The Plague of Doves* focuses on the devastating effects of boundaries drawn between settlers and Native peoples and on the land, *The Round House* concerns itself more with the confusion and violation of boundaries—the boundaries of land, identities, and bodies. The living legacy of the 1911 lynchings in the central crimes that occupy *The Round House*—the kidnapping and murder of Mayla Wolfskin and the rape of Geraldine Coutts in 1988—is emphasized by the appearance of the hanging oak at the heart of the novel, still draped with "prayer flags, strips of cloth. Red, blue, green, white, the old-time Anishinaabe colors of the directions. . . . [s]ome . . . faded, some new" (140). More than a decade after Mooshum and Evelina rehang Holy Track's boots, and three-quarters of a century after the lynchings, the oak still bears witness to the ongoing historical traumas of land theft and murder.

"This was the tree where those ancestors were hanged," young Joe Coutts recalls. "None of the killers ever went on trial. I could see the land of their descendants, already full of row crops" (140). Confusions of land class and jurisdiction regarding the location of Joe's mother's rape make it similarly unlikely that Geraldine's rapist will be tried for his crime. But the connection is even more specific. As Judge Bazil Coutts explains to Joe, Linden Lark is a descendant of a member of the lynching party and inheritor to his Indian-hating sense of entitlement: Lark "[k]nows we can't hold him. Thinks he can get away. Like his uncle." Judge Coutts recognizes that the lynching is an "old brutality that hadn't yet bled itself out" (211). In addition to keeping the memory of the lynchings alive, the hanging tree becomes the scene of new betrayals, heirs to that crime, when Joe and his aunt Sonja choose it to mark the hiding place of Joe's stolen blackmail money, which is in turn stolen by Sonja to enable her escape from a violent relationship.

The native oak stands in contrast to the "invader" seedlings that frame the novel—"ash shoots, elm, maple, box elder, even a good-sized catalpa" (1)—whose roots Joe fruitlessly tries to dig from the foundations of his reservation home on the day of his mother's rape and to memories of which he returns at the end of the novel. Signaling an important theme of the novel, Joe comes to understand that these invader seedlings are not evil in themselves but become so when they settle in the "wrong place" and fail to become part of the local ecosystem. Looking back as the novel closes on the events of his mother's rape and its consequences, Joe recalls, "I kept going back to the day I dug the trees out of the foundation of our house. How tough those roots had clung. . . . And how funny, strange, that a thing can grow so powerful even when planted in the wrong place" (293). The pairing of twins Linden and Linda Lark, children of a white couple who exploited the Ojibwe with their reservation gas station, similarly illustrates the importance of human integration with community and place. Rejected by her birth mother, taken in by a loving Ojibwe family, given a home on the reservation and a role in the community, having been cleansed in Doe Lafournais's sweat lodge and feasted by his son Randall, Linda Lark Wishkob is nurtured to become a kindhearted, forgiving person. Her brother Linden, left to inherit his mother's "warped hatreds" (123) and desire for revenge on the Indians she believes stole the family business, becomes an empty, rootless man, driven, like Billy Peace, by insatiable hungers to possess, control, and punish. Erdrich's naming of Linden Lark is ironic in a novel filled with examples of the generosity of trees. The linden, or American basswood, is a native tree with edible leaves and flowers and abundant nectar, but the human Linden attempts to put roots down in the "wrong places" through the domination of Indian land and bodies. In an echo of the hanging oak and the winged spirits it is home to, his name also connects this native tree with the lark, a North American songbird with both imported European and native American species.

Comparison of the twins' lives underlines the futility of Geraldine Coutts's task as tribal enrollment specialist to "parse the ever more complicated branching and interbranching tangle of each bloodline" (149) to determine questions of tribal membership. Even as Geraldine's work brings back children who grew up off-reservation and "facilitates the reknitting of clans" (Carden 103), the forced focus on linear blood descent defies traditional Ojibwe practices of *making* kinship, which are evidenced by the acceptance into the tribe of Mooshum's Métis family when they flee Canada after Louis Riel's defeat in *The Plague of Doves*; the adoption of Linda Lark into the Wishkob family and the community in *The Round House*; or the raising of Hollis Puyat by the Iron family in *LaRose*. The trees and shrubs on the reservation model this kind of kinship-making; invaders and imports commingle with natives, sometimes establishing themselves within networks of interconnection and thriving (such as Geraldine's beloved lilacs, planted by the reservation farm agent at the edge of her yard [*Round House* 85]), while others are placed or settle in the "wrong place" and fail to interweave themselves into the community (such as Clemence's "struggling blue Colorado spruce" that finally succumbs to Mooshum's "snoose" in *The Plague of Doves* [55]). Once Geraldine names Linden Lark a wiindigoo (*Round House* 248), thirteen-year-old Joe decides he must undertake the responsibility of removing this invader to protect his mother's life and restore balance in the community.[4]

Joe's preparation for his task is guided by his great-uncle Mooshum's dream stories about the legendary Nanapush, stories that illuminate how traditional Anishinaabeg define themselves in relationship to land, animals, and community. From within his sleep, Mooshum tells Joe how twelve-year-old Nanapush was tasked with the killing of his own mother Akiikwe, labeled wiindigoo by a few men during the times of starvation when the Ojibwe had been confined to the reservation and game was scarce. Nanapush refuses to believe she is a wiindigoo and helps her escape; assisted by fish and rabbit, who with all the other animals "miss the buffalo" and "the real Anishinaabeg too" (182), they call the last buffalo, Old Buffalo Woman, "back from over that horizon" (183) where the buffalo have retreated (as the spirit doves retreated to the hanging tree in *The Plague of Doves*). The old buffalo gives her body to Nanapush and shelters him inside her ribcage in a blizzard, returning not only to provide food for the people but also important instructions on how to live: "She said wiindigoo justice must be pursued with great care. A place should be built so that people could do things in a good way" (187). She instructs Nanapush in the building of a round house where the people will gather to make such important decisions as when and how to pursue wiindigoo justice. "Your people were brought together by us buffalo once. You knew how to hunt and use us. Your clans gave you laws. You had many rules by which you operated. Rules that respected us and forced you to work together," she tells him. "The round house will be my body, the poles my ribs, the fire my heart" (214).

Following Nanapush's directions, the community, among them the young Métis Mooshum, constructs the round house, a "log hexagon" (59) oriented to the sacred directions and used for ceremonies disguised as social gatherings or Bible study during the years that the practice of Native religions was outlawed. The round house, like the hanging oak, still stands in Joe's time as a site of Native remembrance and resistance, though its location is no longer central, and its abandonment and the trashing of its adjacent woodlands suggest how far the people have grown from their roots. Because the round house is no longer used, Joe has no formal community to guide him in his pursuit of wiindigoo justice and must rely on an ad hoc community composed of his best friend, Cappy, who supports his decision unquestioningly; Mooshum and Father Travis, who offer indirect counsel; and the trees that surround and sustain them all. Like the buffalo, the trees have given their lives to the people and their bodies to the round house, and they shelter and protect the reservation. Trees are integral to the fabric of Erdrich's entire fictional world,[5] but *The Round House* is especially replete with their presence and their gifts; they guard the road to the round house, surround the cemetery in Pluto where the lynching victims and other ancestors are buried, provide arbors for powwow gatherings, frames and fuel for sweat lodge ceremonies, the medicine tea with the "sharp taste of bark" (133) that Clemence credits with keeping Mooshum alive to the ripe old age of 112. With the help of the trees, Joe's quest to protect his mother and bring justice to her rapist also becomes the remaking of his identity *with* the land.

Considering Father Travis Wozniak as a candidate for the rapist, Joe stands "rooted": "I put my back against a tree and leaned there—not slumping. I was filled with that odd energy. I was allowing the tree to help me think" (98). Thinking with the tree, Joe realizes he needs proof before wishing the priest dead. Once he knows the rapist's identity and goes to the round house to search for evidence, Joe hears "a low moan of air . . . through the cracks in the silvery logs" (59), a cry of grief that confirms his suspicions that the rape occurred in this location. Despite its appropriation for acts of racist oppression and violence and its abandonment by the people, the round house actively participates in Joe's quest to bring the rapist to justice. Having made up his mind to kill Linden Lark, Joe sits long hours under a particular native oak, watching across the reservation boundary for Lark to appear on the golf course below. Every morning he awakes at sunrise, makes a ceremonial run through the woods to his place of vigil, and removes his stolen rifle from its hiding place beneath the tree. Sometimes as he "sat against the oak tree," Joe recalls, "there were moments I forgot why I was there." Gradually, his awareness is altered; heading home one evening after his ritual of watching, he recalls, "I looked at every tree I passed and it amazed me with its detail and life" (281). Even as Joe is executing a traditional form of justice by killing the wiindigoo, he is being reclaimed by the land; like his grandfather Joseph, a member of the land-claim expedition recounted in *The Plague of Doves*, Joe returns from his quest with a new sense of interrelationship with the land and its nonhuman beings and devotes his life to the legal struggle for Ojibwe land and sovereignty.

As does *The Round House*, *LaRose* opens with trees: "Where the reservation boundary invisibly bisected a stand of deep brush—chokecherry, popple, stunted oak—Landreaux waited." Landreaux Iron is standing in the general area of the hanging oak, at the boundary between the reservation Peace land now belonging to his wife Emmaline Peace and the "big farm cobbled together out of what used to be Indian allotments" (3), the Wolde farm. Passed down to Nola, daughter of Marn Wolde and Billy Peace and half-sister to Emmaline (Billy's daughter by the fourth LaRose[6]), the Wolde land is now farmed by Nola's husband of Russian-German descent (76), Peter Ravich. Landreaux and Peter, hunting buddies, are comfortable in this boundary area, but their half-sister wives never cross it, estranged by the blasted history left behind by Billy Peace and his many wives. The hanging oak is not named in *LaRose*, but it is tempting to assume it is the lightning-struck oak located between the Iron and Ravich houses that "killed the smaller trees in a circle" as fire moved through their interconnected roots (14). Equally difficult to resist is a comparison of the tree's demise to that of Billy Peace, who served in the U.S. Army and returned to South Dakota possessed by an evangelical vision that gathered a following of non-Native kindred; dis-placed from kin and communities, altered by their use for purposes of settler colonial violence, both oak and man become host to a somewhat ambiguous holy spirit they seek to use as a tool of vengeance, and both meet fiery ends that simultaneously destroy the new communities that formed around them. Whether or not the lightning-struck oak is the hanging tree, it is clear that the hanging tree's time, the time for retribution, has passed. Between Geraldine Coutts's rape in 1988 and the death of Dusty Ravich in 1999, the lynching itself seems to be mostly forgotten, at least by the characters of *LaRose*, recalled for readers in the names of its inheritors—Peaces, Wildstrands—and in the ongoing effects of intergenerational trauma it engenders.

Other trees located within the reservation boundary in the old-growth woodlands "still considered uncanny" (*LaRose* 14) by the Ojibwe take the hanging tree's place as central characters in *LaRose*. The "climbing tree" that "with its low crotch and curved limbs was irresistible" (22, 23) to seven-year-old Dusty Ravich, shot accidentally by Landreaux Iron as he hunted a buck, echoes the hanging tree most closely. Dusty, accompanied by the special dog who adopts his family, was guided to this tree, to be met by the buck; something important was in the making for Dusty that Landreaux's ill-fated shot interrupted. Perhaps Dusty was being led to the tree to "seek a dream or vision" to discover within himself a talent to "bring into fulfillment and reality," a quest traditionally undertaken by young Anishinaabeg in a sacred place (Noodin 130, quoting Basil Johnston). The tree continues to draw the grieving after Dusty's death, but unlike the hanging tree, it inspires its visitors to remain, to become part of its web of being and begin to heal. Peter Ravich lies down on the spot "where Dusty's life had flowed into the earth" and has a vision of how the accident happened. He "listened to the sound of the woods around him," the voices of "chickadee . . . nuthatch . . . crow"; from the "scent of sweetgrass, tobacco, kinnikinnick, offerings" (23), Peter knows Landreaux has been there too, bringing him understanding and easing his anger. The climbing tree becomes a memorial "where dead flowers, tobacco ties, loose sage, and two small rain-beaten stuffed animals" (103) remember Dusty. There LaRose Iron and his sisters gather for a reading of Dusty's favorite book, *Where the Wild Things Are*, another story about a young boy accompanied by a dog who makes a dream journey to an inspirited forest and befriends the wildness there and within himself. As the story ends, the siblings stand "in the resounding sweetness of birdcall" (103). The birds that haunt the hanging tree, which signify to Mooshum both the devastation of extinction and the promise of rebirth, are echoed in these woodlands, but these birds do not lift and disappear when humans approach; they accept them into their lives.

Three years after Dusty's death, the climbing tree again calls LaRose. "[C]ompelled to sleep on the spot of ground where the boy he replaced had died" (207), LaRose not only takes Dusty's place in Dusty's family in an "old form of justice" (36), he also undertakes Dusty's interrupted quest. Amidst the singing of birds, he lies down under the climbing tree among the disintegrating objects of remembrance, offers a song and water to the four directions. Hungry, thirsty, in the deep darkness, he is visited by ancestor spirits who promise to teach him the gift of the LaRoses, to fly. Dusty's spirit visits LaRose here as well and tells him he is "*not really*" okay (211), but LaRose makes a play date with him, promising Dusty he can be Seker (seeker?) in their action-figure games. Later, Nola overhears them playing across the boundaries of time and death: "An epic battle between light and darkness. Forms passing through the material of time.... Shapes of beings unknown merging deeply with the known. Worlds fusing. Dimensions collapsing" (271–72). LaRose and Dusty are "complet[ing] the universe" (271), living out the elder Ignatia's origin story about the two sons of the woman who loved a snake (echoed in Dusty's grandmother Marn), who are given the power to create "a river, fire, a mountain, a forest of thorns" (292) and together create "the first people, Anishinaabeg" (293). The boys' interaction across dimensions, enabled by the climbing tree, brings "the inner and the outer worlds" into alignment (272), allowing Dusty's spirit to find identity and meaning and bringing his mother a measure of peace.

Dusty's older sister, Maggie, is also called by trees, from which she observes animal and human activity on the reservation, and in one of which she is inhabited by an owl spirit whose "soundlessness" and "authority" (222) enable her to intervene in her mother's suicide attempt. Like Joe in *The Round House*, Maggie has been walking the woods, sitting with trees, watching, listening, and learning, until she feels "more at home outside than inside." Like her grandmother Marn, she allows a great bird spirit "into her body," an owl "with great golden eyes ... [that] fixed her with supernatural hunger" (221), but this bird spirit guides her to save a life rather than to kill. It is to "this place ... my place," an "old oak so huge that it had choked out all other brush but the long pale grass" (338–39), that Maggie brings her boyfriend, Waylon, for her first voluntary sexual experience, at the end of which she looks out of the owl's eyes and is "right at home with herself" (340). By choosing this act in a place sacred to her, Maggie reclaims control over her life after her assault by the "Fearsome Four"—a group of boys who take revenge on Maggie for punishing a brother of one of the boys for an act against LaRose. Maggie's assault carries echoes of both the lynching in *The Plague of Doves* (the attackers include a Wildstrand and a Peace) and Geraldine Coutts's rape in *The Round House*, but Maggie stops the cycles of revenge by using the owl's power to redefine herself and remake her connections with her human and nonhuman reservation kin.

As the feet of the Irons and Raviches walking back and forth between their homes erase the boundary between reservation and Wolde land, LaRose and Maggie, with the help of the trees, are remaking their community's broken relationship with the land and bringing the ancestor spirits back to the people. It is the trees who remember, who shelter the spirits, where the songs that allow the LaRoses to fly are "waiting in the leaves" (291); they draw those who will listen to themselves, teaching them how to be native to the land again. It is this broken intimacy with the land that is central to Landreaux's guilt in Dusty's death: "The buck knew, Landreaux thought.... If he had listened, or understood, or cared to know what he understood, he would never have hunted that buck. Never. He would have known the animal was trying to tell him something of the gravest importance. The deer was no ordinary creature, but a bridge to another world" (*LaRose* 149). Though he possesses the land through his marriage with Emmaline, knows its topography well through hunting, "had songs for the animals and winds who sat in each direction" (11) and uses them in ceremony, Landreaux realizes he has lost the heart of his traditions, the subtle interconnections that weave him into the life of the woodlands, attune him to the interactions and intentions of nonhuman lives and spirits.

By the end of *LaRose*, the settler colonial crimes of *The Plague of Doves* have indeed worked themselves out in the living, as Evelina Harp predicted. Complicated by intermixing and diffused through time, the once well-defined boundaries between invaders and Ojibwe have fractured and reassembled into the internal divisions among family and friends that are the intergenerational inheritance of historical trauma. As Romeo's and Peter's attempts at revenge against Landreaux play out anticlimactically, and Father Travis finds himself wishing for Landreaux's death to leave Emmaline free, each man faces the worst in himself and turns away from it, clearing the way for new life. Even LaRose fails at his superhero effort to avenge Maggie's assault and instead discovers his gift, his ability to fly. The "old brutality" has finally "bled itself out" (*Round House* 211); scrub oak and wild raspberry grow up where the hanging tree once dominated; things are "growing all over" beneath the climbing tree where Dusty's blood soaked the ground (*LaRose* 108). Even the buffalo have returned, albeit as tourist attractions; though Romeo Puyat sees "the dreadful message of their extinction" glowing in their hearts, he knows they, like "us"—the Ojibwe—are "a symbol of resistance" (335). Decolonization requires the erasure of boundaries not only on the land and within the hearts of individuals that divide human kin and community, but also those that separate humans from the other living communities that constitute their place.

As does *The Round House*, *LaRose* also closes with trees, but in contrast to Joe Coutts's meditation on things that take root where they do not belong, the final section of *LaRose*, "The Gathering," describes a restoration of belonging, a rerooting in place and remaking of kinships, as the community, including the Raviches, gathers at the Irons' home to celebrate Hollis Puyat's graduation. A redeemed Romeo Puyat, who has reconnected with his estranged son and the Irons who raised him, "stood looking off into the deep green woods. That is our home, he thought, where we came from" (366). Romeo is newly "aligned" and "[r]ooted, he was rooted right there" (368). LaRose makes a plate of food as offering to the spirits: "He . . . stepped off into the trees, put the plate down at the base of a birch tree. He stood beside the tree, staring through new leaves, toward the spot he'd fasted, where Dusty and all of the others had visited him" (367–68). When Sam Eagleboy presents Hollis with an eagle feather and prays in Ojibwe to close the ceremonies, LaRose feels the spirits come out of the woods: "He watched as they moved together and apart, frowned or laughed, in a dance of ordinary joy" (371). The networks of kinship that have been remade among the human characters across boundaries of blood descent, history, guilt, and resentment have expanded to include the actual trees—*family* trees—whose roots and branches are intertwined with the human characters across the generations as actors in the narratives, co-creators of place and memory, and sites of interaction across material and spiritual dimensions. By reclaiming their human kin, the trees have become instrumental in the process of restoring a traditional Anishinaabe identity *with* the land.

Catherine Rainwater, in her ecocritical analysis of *The Plague of Doves*, explores how the novel "de-centers the human," developing "a radically non-Western conception of personhood" (165) that "is inextricable from an intricate web of site-specific interrelationships" (157). Erdrich goes a step beyond, however, asking readers not only to recognize human embeddedness in a living web of inspirited beings, but also to attempt to perceive the point of view and agency of some of these other beings. It is not insignificant that Erdrich's tree characters speak to us from within her justice trilogy at a time when science is finally beginning to glimpse the intricate worlds in which trees exist as interconnected social beings that exchange many different kinds of information, support each other physically and biochemically (Wohlleben), "sing" (Haskell), and "think" (Kohn). Eduardo Kohn, in his effort to build an "anthropology beyond the human" (11) that does not separate humans from the nonhuman worlds in which they are embedded, asks us to reflect on how "[n]onhuman life-forms also represent the world" (8).

"That other kinds of beings see us changes things," Kohn states; "encounters with other kinds of beings force us to recognize the fact that seeing, representing, and perhaps knowing, even thinking, are not exclusively human affairs" (1) and that "meaning, broadly defined, is part and parcel of the living world beyond the human" (20). Human lives cannot be "disentangled" (19) from their human histories and relationships, nor from the web of other lives and spirits that constitute their location in place and time. Erdrich's writing has always been filled with trees, but in this trilogy, Erdrich goes beyond describing their presence, their roles in human lives, their centrality to Anishinaabe identity as a woodland people; she recognizes their individuality, their subjectivity, their abilities to remember and plan, their interests in making a world of mutual care and remembrance. Erdrich asks her readers to reconceptualize our place in the world, to recognize that any form of justice that really matters must also consider our inextricable interconnectedness within a world that is made up of sentient, also thinking and acting, nonhuman beings who participate in generating the knowledge and care humans need to live in the world in a balanced way. By making and remaking kin beyond blood ties, beyond species boundaries, humans can participate in building new communities of shelter and strength toward a livable future.

NOTES

1. Deborah Madsen notes that the hanging tree is likely a bur oak, the only oak indigenous to North Dakota (31).

2. Passenger pigeons, often confused with their dove relatives, became extinct in 1914, just three years after Erdrich's fictional lynching, which is based on a historical 1897 lynching.

3. As Kenneth Roemer points out in his examination of naming in *The Plague of Doves*, Evelina ("Evey") Harp's name associates her with the "Judeo-Christian Eve" (116) who is tempted by "forbidden knowledge" from a "tree of knowledge that is a lynching tree" (121). Evelina is further connected to the tree of knowledge through the serpents that appear to her in acid-induced visions of a "Reptile Garden" (*Plague* 221) and the spirit doves that visit her in the mental hospital (244). Marn is even more powerfully associated with the oak as the biblical tree of knowledge through references linking her both to Eve (the fruit with which she covers the tip of the syringe of venom she uses to kill Billy is "the apple of good and evil" [178]) and to Lilith, the first wife of Adam, who was expelled from the Garden of Eden for refusing to be subservient to him. Madsen explores at length subtexts linking Marn to Lilith, who, like Eve, is widely portrayed in

relationship to a powerful tree inhabited by serpents (Madsen 33). These intertextual references implicate Marn's serpents as emissaries of the hanging tree.

4. Given that he is the same age as Holy Track, and the wiindigoo who becomes his prey is descended from one of the lynchers, Joe's actions also enact a symbolic retribution for Holy Track and the other lynching victims.

5. See especially *Tracks* and *Four Souls*.

6. Mrs. Peace is fourth in a line of five LaRoses in the novel, all spirit walkers and healers. The original LaRose, daughter of Mink, married trading-post employee Wolfred Roberts in the mid-1800s and was sent to boarding school in Michigan (*LaRose* 145). Her daughter, the second LaRose, was recruited by Richard Pratt to attend Carlisle Indian School (198): "She was a teacher and the mother of a teacher. Her namesake daughter [the third LaRose] became the mother of Mrs. Peace" (202). It is unclear but likely that Mrs. Peace is Geraldine Coutts's boarding-school friend LaRose in *The Round House*, who "had so many husbands that nobody kept track of her last name anymore," but who "started out a Migwan" (*Round House* 172). The fifth LaRose is, of course, young LaRose Iron, grandson of Mrs. Peace and son of Emmaline and Landreaux Iron.

WORKS CITED

Carden, Mary Paniccia. "'The Unkillable Mother': Sovereignty and Survivance in Louise Erdrich's *The Round House*." *Studies in American Indian Literatures*, vol. 30, no. 1, 2018, pp. 94–116.

Erdrich, Louise. *Four Souls*. HarperCollins, 2004.

———. *LaRose*. HarperCollins, 2016.

———. *The Last Report on the Miracles at Little No Horse*. HarperCollins, 2001.

———. *The Plague of Doves*. HarperCollins, 2008.

———. *The Round House*. HarperCollins, 2012.

———. *Tracks*. Henry Holt, 1988.

Gamber, John. "So, a Priest Walks into a Reservation Tragicomedy: Humor in *The Plague of Doves*." *Louise Erdrich: Tracks, The Last Report on the Miracles at Little No Horse, The Plague of Doves*, edited by Deborah L. Madsen, Continuum, 2011, pp. 136–51.

Haskell, David George. *The Songs of Trees: Stories from Nature's Great Connectors*. Viking, 2017.

Kohn, Eduardo. *How Forests Think: Toward an Anthropology beyond the Human*. U of California P, 2013.

Madsen, Deborah L. "Discontinuous Narrative, Ojibwe Sovereignty, and the *Wiindigoo* Logic of Settler Colonialism: Louise Erdrich's Marn Wolde." *Studies in American Indian Literatures*, vol. 28, no. 3, 2016, pp. 23–51.

Noodin, Margaret. *Bawaajimo: A Dialect of Dreams in Anishinaabe Language and Literature.* Michigan State UP, 2014.

Noori, Margaret. "The Shiver of Possibility." Review of *The Plague of Doves,* by Louise Erdrich. *Women's Review of Books,* vol. 25, no. 5, 2008, pp. 12–13.

Rainwater, Catherine. "Haunted by Birds: An Eco-critical View of Personhood in *The Plague of Doves." Louise Erdrich: Tracks, The Last Report on the Miracles at Little No Horse, The Plague of Doves,* edited by Deborah L. Madsen, Continuum, 2011, pp. 152–67.

Roemer, Kenneth M. "Naming Native (Living) Histories: Louise Erdrich's Plague of Names." *Studies in American Fiction,* vol. 43, no. 1, 2016, pp. 115–35.

Schliephake, Christopher. "Literary Place and Cultural Memory." *Handbook of Ecocriticism and Cultural Ecology,* edited by Hubert Zapf, De Gruyter Mouton, 2016, pp. 569–89.

Strehle, Susan. "'Prey to Unknown Dreams': Louise Erdrich, *The Plague of Doves,* and the Exceptionalist Disavowal of History." *Literature Interpretation Theory,* vol. 25, 2014, pp. 108–27.

Valentino, Gina. "'It All Does Come to Nothing in the End': Nationalism and Gender in Louise Erdrich's *The Plague of Doves." Louise Erdrich: Tracks, The Last Report on the Miracles at Little No Horse, The Plague of Doves,* edited by Deborah L. Madsen, Continuum, 2011, pp. 121–35.

Wohlleben, Peter. *The Hidden Life of Trees: What They Feel, How They Communicate.* Greystone, 2013.

You Aren't a Regular Dog, Are You?

Dog as Intermediary in Louise Erdrich's *LaRose*

Connie A. Jacobs

Dogs are pervasive in the novels of Louise Erdrich. While they are minor characters, often unnoticed as they unobtrusively appear in the storyline, their role is always significant. There is the Black Dog, death/devil, found in *Tracks*, *The Bingo Palace*, *The Antelope Wife*, and *The Last Report on the Miracles at Little No Horse*, but the majority of dogs in the novels are loyal companions and helpers. In *The Antelope Wife*, dogs save lives—Windigo Dog saves Klaus Shawano from being run over by a large commercial grass mower, and in a canine genealogy as complicated as any of Erdrich's human families, a dog named Sorrow and her offspring are essential secondary characters to the survival of Blue Prairie Woman's descendants. During a brutal attack by the US Cavalry on her village, Blue Prairie Woman straps her infant daughter on the back of a bitch camp dog who carries the infant to safety. The grieving mother, who was nursing her baby, in desperation nurses one of the dog's pups, Sorrow. When Blue Prairie Woman later sets out to find her lost child, Sorrow follows and offers up her body to be eaten

---

The quotation in my title comes from a scene in *LaRose* when Peter Ravich says this to the mongrel dog (61). Though I focus on discussing the dog in *LaRose* in this essay, I also want to acknowledge the significant role that dogs play throughout Erdrich's fiction.

by the starving mother and child. One of Sorrow's offspring, Almost Soup, saves a very ill Callie, a great-granddaughter of Blue Prairie Woman, from the Black Dog by taking Callie's spirit into its body to keep it safe.

In three novels, *The Master Butchers Singing Club*, *The Round House*, and *LaRose*, the dog's role is to protect and aid the young, most especially the boys, and as such, serve not only as sentinels but also as spirit guides. The dog Schatzie, a white German shepherd, in *Master Butcher* stays with and guards Eva when she falls ill, and after her death, she becomes the guardian dog of Eva's sons, Markus, Erick, and Emil. In *The Round House*, Uncle Whitey brings Pearl to live with Joe and his parents while the rapist of Joe's mother is still at large. Pearl has one function: to protect the family. She is part wolf, not a companion dog, unwilling to play ordinary dog games with Joe like "fetch," and with her keenly honed awareness of imminent danger, she feels the malevolent presence of a ghost outside Joe's bedroom window. Additionally at the novel's close, Pearl senses when Joe goes on the impromptu road trip with his friends Cappy and Zack that tragedy will join them on that journey. Schatzie from *The Master Butchers Singing Club* is similar to the rusty mongrel in *LaRose*: they both serve as intermediaries to the spirit world; Schatzie escorts Eva to the other side when she dies, and the mongrel dog in *LaRose* becomes an intermediary between the boy Dusty in the spirit world and his cousin LaRose, who is from a long line of powerful healers.

There are other dog characters of seeming unimportance in Erdrich's novels yet critical to the plot development and eventual outcomes for their humans. In *Tracks*, Lily Veddar's "stumpy mean little bull" (18) loyally never leaves Lily's side and freezes to death with him when Pauline bolts them into the meat locker. Pepperboy, Candice Mauser's dog in *Tales of Burning Love*, becomes the catalyst for her failed marriage to Jack Mauser, who inadvertently kills her beloved canine. Another Pepperboy, found in *LaRose*, is the dog Romeo and Landreaux encounter at a remote farmhouse whose sole occupant is a blind woman who feeds the boys and takes them in. Her old dog Pepperboy, not sensing danger from the two runaways, does not bother them. In *The Birchbark House*, Old Tallow's wolflike dogs hunt with her and protect her, and in *The Plague of Doves*, English Bill's little terrier saves the expedition from starving to death by digging up thirty-six frozen snow buntings and finding two big catfish, a squirrel, and a snapping turtle. In *Shadow Tag*, the two shepherd mixes protect the family from Gil's ferocious temper and help maintain a balance in the household.[1] There are three dog helpers in *The Night Watchman*. One is Thomas's dog Smoker, who divides his duties as watchdog between Thomas's home and the home of Biboon, Thomas's elderly father. Two other dogs assist in finding and helping heal Vera, Pixie's sister who has been "lost" in Minneapolis. As in *LaRose*, one dog mind-talks to Pixie, relaying critical information.

Erdrich not only writes repeatedly of this special connection to dogs in her novels, but she also embraces it herself. If readers go to her Birchbark Books website, one link under "Staff" is "Our Dogs." Here you find the various "owners" of the staff working in the bookstore talking about themselves, their humans, and, of course, recommending books. At any time, it is possible to find ten or more such "chatty" canines on the dog blog. Of special interest to Erdrich readers is Maki (*Ma'ingan* is Ojibwe for wolf), "owner of Louise."

Erdrich's many dog characters play various roles in her novels: protector, companion, helper, and healer. The dogs' special bond with their human companions enriches her novels by giving focus to the long-standing human-dog connection. Although Erdrich does not anthropomorphize her dog characters, noted Anishinaabe writer and critic Gerald Vizenor takes issue with Erdrich's, as well as N. Scott Momaday's, Gordon Henry Jr.'s, Leslie Marmon Silko's, and Louis Owens's use of animals in their work. He reads what he terms "authored animals" as "wild tropes, fantastic creatures, and . . . mundane similes of domestication" ("Authored" 663). He continues his critique: "The presence of authored animals in these selected novels are *real* as tropes of the imagination. The creatures in native literature are seldom mere representation of animals in nature or culture, wild, domestic, generic, or otherwise" ("Authored" 678). In addition, he insists that the "animals of literature must depend upon the turns of tropes, the practices of similes, metaphor, and metonymy, as the necessities of authored nature" ("Authored" 669). He holds metaphor as the highest of the comparative literary arts as it requires the reader to undertake the job of parsing out connections. His critique of Erdrich's use of animals, especially dogs in *Tracks*, positions her animal characters "closer to the literal or prosaic simile than to the obscure metaphors of motivation: the other authors mentioned here seldom used the literal style of simile" ("Authored" 675).

What are readers to make of Vizenor's dismissive analysis? The quotes I use are from a 1995 article, but even in his 2009 book titled *Native Liberty: Natural Reason and Cultural Survivance* (and Erdrich by this time had written an additional seven novels), Vizenor continues to dismiss Erdrich, characterizing dogs in *Tracks* as nothing more than her use of a prosaic animal simile to describe human behavior. Vizenor is an Indigenous intellectual as well as an Anishinaabe tribal member. To read him against Erdrich, also an Anishinaabe tribal member as well as a best-selling and award-winning author, challenges both readers and critics. This article counters Vizenor's critique of the dogs in Erdrich's work, citing Anishinaabe historical and cultural memory. We as readers are presented with two competing narratives that require us to discern the truth in both positions. One helpful guide through these conflicting approaches is found in the current burgeoning field of animal studies, especially the relationship of animal studies to Indigenous literature, which "examines the moral and philosophical complexities of the many kinds of connections that occur among Indigenous human and nonhuman animals . . . [and] engage[s] the aesthetic possibilities of those same complex connections" (Allen).

A definition of animal studies is a helpful point of entry to this recent interdisciplinary field where researchers and academics from various disciplines examine the human relationship to nonhuman species and consider our responsibilities in this interdependent relationship. Editors Wendy Woodward and Susan McHugh in the abstract to their book *Indigenous Creatures, Native Knowledges, and the Arts: Animal Studies in Modern Worlds* provide this overview: "Traditionally imagined in relation to spiritual realms and the occult, animals have always been more than primitive symbols of human relations. Whether as animist gods, familiars, conduits to ancestors, totems, talismans, or co-creators of multispecies cosmologies, animals act as vital players in the lives of cultures." The journal *Studies in American Indian Literatures* devoted a 2013 special issue to the topic of animal studies, and the contributors added to our understanding of the human and nonhuman connections in Indigenous literatures.[2] Among the most salient points are comments from Brian K. Hudson (Cherokee), a co-guest editor, who observes in his Introduction that "many Native ideologies do not define humans as categorically different from or superior to nonhuman animals" (3). Hudson also draws on the work of Linda Hogan (Chickasaw), who writes in "First People" that the "relationship between human people and animals is still alive and resonant in the world" (qtd. in Hudson 8). In that same special issue, Maureen Riche discusses Erdrich's short story "Father's Milk," and describes how in this work, "Nonhuman animals participate in the narrative as often and as actively as the humans, both as characters and as storytellers" (49). She points out that Erdrich's writing "offers us many examples of interactions across species lines in her writing" (48), and she cites the work of Thomas King (Cherokee), describing how "members of most Indigenous North American cultures believe that humans and animals coexist, not in a hierarchical relationship of dominance and submission, but rather as partners in the more complex network of 'all my relations'" (Riche 48). In Erdrich's justice trilogy, the human-dog bond, partnership, is vital, and is especially important in *LaRose*, where a mongrel dog serves as more than a prosaic simile by helping drive the action and assisting in the ultimate resolution.

How does understanding the long human-dog connection benefit our reading of the justice trilogy and serve as a counter-approach to Vizenor's reading of Erdrich's dogs? This discussion will begin in the present with our love of our dogs and journey back to archeological evidence that confirms our long connection to our dogs from at least 11,000 BC. Erdrich writes out of this historical record as well as the Anishinaabe cultural context throughout her fictional work.

Our contemporary human connection with dogs is pervasive and deep. In the United States, the American Veterinary Medical Association (AVMA) estimates that 38.4 percent of American households have dogs, and other references list up to as much as 60 percent of households with dogs. Americans are, of course, not alone in their love of dogs, although percentage-wise there are more American households with dogs than in any other countries in the world. That said, the Petfood Industry website figures that 33 percent of households worldwide have dogs. Why so many dogs? Dogs love us, guard us, hunt with us, herd our flocks, pull sleds, search out drugs and bodies for the police (K-9s), serve as part of American Armed Forces (MWD, Military War Dogs), serve as guide and therapy dogs, and even act in movies and on television. Most of all, they are our companions. Jeffrey Moussaieff Masson and Art Wolfe affirm, "Our relationship with dogs is the single most important symbiotic relationship between humans and another species on the planet. . . . The special bond we share is one that seems to confer . . . survival benefits on both species" (1). We love our dogs, and more recently have wanted to understand them better. In a 2019 *New York Times Book Review* essay, Vanessa Woods and Brian Hare discuss the explosion of books on "dog cognition, spanning the fields of psychology, anthropology, and neuroscience." They point out, "Since 2000, books exploring dog minds have proliferated at an astonishing rate."[3] According to their count, "Currently more than 70,000 dog books are listed on Amazon," including novels[4] and books of poetry.[5]

Recently in the field of archaeology, significant attention has been given to the human-dog bond, and theories abound as to when this relationship began. Scientists do not argue the basic premise that the human-dog bond is a very old one, but just how old is hotly debated. The research of K. Kris Hirst suggests that "The earliest confirmed domestic dog anywhere so far is from a burial site in Germany called Bonn-Oberkassel, which has joint human and dog interments dated to 14,000 years ago. . . . Danger Cave in Utah is currently the earliest case of dog burial in the Americas, at about 11,000 years ago."

But, before there were dogs, *Canis lupus familiaris*, there was their ancestor, the wolf, *Canis lupus*, and that is where the real story of our contemporary domestic dog begins. While it is not hard to find ancestor wolf in German shepherds, Malamutes, Siberian Huskies, Czechoslovakian Wolfdogs, and Canadian Eskimo dogs, those wolf genes seem hard to imagine in a Chihuahua, Cavalier King Charles Spaniel, Pekingese, Bichon Frise, and Shih Tzu. Paleontologists, archaeologists, geneticists, and evolutionary biologists research when, where, how, and why dogs were domesticated from wolves, and not surprisingly, come up with different conclusions. Most relevant to this discussion is the research of ecologist and evolutionary biologist Raymond Pierotti and environmentalist Brandy Fogg who privilege an Indigenous perspective,[6] and I invite interested readers to delve into the many other theories on the topic.[7]

Pierotti and Fogg conclude that there were four domestications that occurred at different places and at different times: Europe 32,000 YBP (years before present) and Central Asia, 33,000 (YBP). These dates correspond to most archaeological evidence that points to domestication, which happened at least 15,000–40,000 YBP. Pierotti and Fogg offer, "Domestication of wolves appears to have taken place in various locations at various times, including Europe, the Middle East (Levant), central Asia, and eastern Asia, and probably India and North America" (14). Additionally, "The striking phenotypic and genetic diversity of dogs clearly indicates that their founders were recruited from a large and varied wolf population" (44), but how and why certain wolves, most especially the gray wolf,[8] associated with humans, hunted with them and eventually became domesticated is another complicated and fascinating story with many answers as well as many unsolved questions. Scientists generally can agree that as humans moved out of Africa into Europe, the Middle East, and the Far East, they encountered groups of wolves with whom they began to interact, suggesting that diverse groups of people confronted indigenous wolves in different areas and at different times in history.

A long-standing theory of the human-wolf bond promoted by Ray and Laura Coppinger suggests that wolves became domesticated by hanging around human camps and eating their refuse and thus became domesticated (cited in Bekoff). This "dumpster theory" has been replaced by more recent theories that suggest a gradual cooperative evolution in hunting between wolves and humans. Since both species are predators and are capable of hunting cooperatively, this theory appears more likely. According to wildlife biologist Amy Purdie, "Any predator can be a scavenger, but scavengers are not necessarily predators." Pierotti and Fogg conclude, "Examination of the archaeological records suggest that around the world, multiple groups of people had close relationships with wolves that over varying lengths of time led to domestication and eventually to animals being recognized as dogs" (87).

For Indigenous people, especially people of the Great Plains, the wolf-human bond through time has been mostly positive and reciprocal. Important to understanding the human-wolf story is that wolves resemble humans in several important aspects: they cooperate in a pack and with other species (often ravens; see Pierotti and Fogg 56–58), stay within a self-determined boundary, live in single family groups, and are dedicated to the survival of their pack (family). Pierotti and Fogg suggest that a lone wolf, similar to a lone human, does not survive as well as those within a group or pack (61). Stories, both apocryphal and proven, abound of humans being abandoned by their human family and raised by wolves. The story of Romulus and Remus, mythic founders of Rome, as well as contemporary accounts exist throughout the world, and most relevant for this essay, there are numerous Indigenous stories of humans being cared for by wolves, especially among the Plains tribes.[9]

Joseph Marshall III, Sicangu Lakota, who was raised traditionally, relates, "In the past, the wolf and the first people of Turtle Island lived and moved on the same earth. We coexisted. . . . we always respected one another's right to be" (25).[10] He adds, "the wolf and his virtues are still woven into the life and cultures of many contemporary native North American tribes" (15). This close connection of brother wolf to Indigenous people is borne out in creation stories where wolves are both teachers and spiritual guides, clan animals, and names of special societies. The Skidi Pawnee are known as the Wolf People, and the Gros Ventres, Ogalala Lakota, and Cheyenne have warrior societies that are called Wolf Societies.[11] Before the horse was brought to the Americas by Euro-American settlers, the Blackfeet "credited wolves with teaching them how to hunt using buffalo drives" (Fogg, Howe, and Pierotti 270), and the Shoshone, Comanche, Pawnee, Salish, and Lakota, among the Great Plains tribes, used wolf-like dogs to carry their belongings from their summer and winter camps on a sturdy travois. Pierotti and Fogg detail other Indigenous tribes having a close bond with the wolf: among the Haida and Tlingit in the Pacific Northwest, Wolf is considered as a creator figure (156–57), as well as among the Quileute and the Kwakiutl, whose stories describe how their people were transformed from wolves. Additionally, for the Shoshonean tradition, which includes "Comanches,

Paiutes, Utes, and Gosiutes, Wolf is considered the benign creator figure" (Pierotti and Fogg 143). The close tie between the wolf and Indigenous people is especially found in clan animals, where the wolf clan pan-tribally is regarded as one of the most important and the most powerful.[12]

For the Anishinaabeg, various versions of the origin story tell of their close connection with Brother Wolf. In *LaRose*, Ignatia Thunder,[13] a wise (and cranky) elder, wanting to instruct LaRose in traditional ways of knowing and understanding his history, as well as his importance to the ongoing tribal story, relates her version of the origin story. As Anishinaabe scholar Lawrence Gross emphasizes, "storytelling encourages the strong voice and empowers children . . . and "[t]he Anishnaabeg are using stories to help them control their destiny" (8). Ignatia tells LaRose of two brothers who become separated when escaping from their mother's vengeful rolling head. The older brother becomes Nanabozho, who creates the Anishinaabeg, and his younger brother turns into a wolf, who, according to Ignatia, "was always by his side" (293). There are various versions of the Nanabozho–Brother Wolf story, which include Basil H. Johnston's account of two lost fishermen who are rescued by a giant who protects them from an evil windigo. Giant sends his pet, a doglike creature who could change shapes and swim across a large body of water with the vulnerable men and who, once safely reaching their camp, stays with the men to continue to protect them (see Johnston 36–39). Other stories tell of a helpless human, in most cases Wenabozho, who is taught to hunt by the wolves who have taken pity on him, and realizing Wenabozho needs his help to survive, one wolf stays with him as his companion. In the Earth Diver story, as retold by Gross, Wenabozho and his wolf companion are so successful that they overhunt the area, which angers the animals, who seek revenge by asking Water Monster, Michibizhii (Misshepeshu in Erdrich's novels), to kill the wolf, which he does. In a retaliatory act of vengeance, Wenabozho kills Michibizhii. The animals, attempting to stem this cycle of vengeance, flood the earth, which Wenabozho then must rebuild, this time with the help of the muskrat who dives down far enough to bring up enough earth to begin the creation of Turtle Island.[14]

Gross's account and the stories Ignatia tells LaRose all underscore the close connection through human time of the human-dog (wolf) connection as well as the degree to which vengeance can disrupt, weaken, and ultimately destroy a community. Erdrich's justice trilogy reflects not only this cultural history but also the timeless story of revenges that can span decades, even a century. That is why in *LaRose*, the concluding book of the trilogy, a special young boy needs to know the old stories and to understand that he has been sent to arrest the ever-present threat of vengeance with the help of a dog who shows up at his parents' house when he is most needed. In fact, the dog's role becomes crucial in turning aside the revenge plots that readers find throughout the trilogy.

The theme of revenge begins with the first book of the trilogy, *The Plague of Doves*, the beginning of the story that details "frontier justice," where innocent Natives are helpless victims of an enraged group of Slavic settlers who wrongly believe that the Indians are responsible for the death of a neighboring farm family.[15] The lives of descendants of the lynching mob, the Wildstrands and Buckendorfs; of the victims, the Peaces and the almost-victim, Mooshum; and of the original town party, the Coutts and Peaces—all are interwoven through marriages, in the schools, and as neighbors. But the injustice of the hanging lives deep in the blood of the victims' families, unsettled, unresolved. While there is no justice for the victims, there is some ironic justice in the fact that the town of Pluto, which was originally the territory of the Anishinaabeg, by contemporary times is dying:

> The bank has become an all-day breakfast place, the 4-B's, and now serves as the municipal building where the affairs of the town are conducted. Shopping is done 68 miles south. Major businesses have pulled out: the fertilizer plant and the farm-implement dealer. Agricultural products are no longer transported by train because the Interstate has taken over as the railroad dwindled. Many of Pluto's houses and lots are abandoned, and the cemetery has more occupants than the town. (Jacobs)

What survives is the neighboring reservation and its families.

The Round House, the second book in the justice trilogy, is the story of a brutal rape of an Anishinaabe woman, Geraldine Coutts, on reservation land. It is her thirteen-year-old son Joe Coutts who seeks justice for her, and when he finds the name of the rapist, Linden Lark, takes justice into his own hands. Joe is compelled to avenge his mother's rape because of "legal black holes" (Russo)—Lark is not a tribal member; the tribal courts cannot prosecute him; and in state and federal courts, it is difficult if not impossible for Indigenous victims to find justice. When Joe and his friend Cappy track down Lark and eventually shoot him, a type of vigilante justice is again enacted, this time by a young Native boy. Is Joe's act justified? Absolutely. Is it morally supportable? That is the question Erdrich leaves with readers at the end of the novel. When is revenge an acceptable act?

In her May 2016 *New York Times Book Review* assessment of *LaRose*, Mary Gordon touches on this issue and points out, "Erdrich has always been fascinated by the relationship between revenge and justice, but while *The Round House* suggested the allure of revenge, *LaRose* comes down firmly on the side of forgiveness" (26), which would seem impossible given that six-year-old Dusty Ravich is accidently shot and killed by his uncle, Landreaux Iron, who was deer hunting on the reservation. Revenge becomes the story line as multiple characters seek to right their wrongs, perceived or actual. Nola, the mother of the dead boy, initially thinks of nothing but revenge. When she hears the horrific news she screams, "Execute him! Execute the son of a bitch. . . . She wanted her husband to bludgeon Landreaux to death. . . . she wanted blood everlasting" (*LaRose* 4–5). Nola is the daughter of Marn Wolde, who poisoned her husband (and Nola's father) Billy Peace in revenge for his infidelities, meanness, gluttonous appetite for food, sex, and power (as well as confiscation of her family's farm to use as the headquarters for a radical religious cult he founded whose followers rigidly adhered to his "Manual of Discipline" [*Plague* 159]). Therefore, it is little wonder that Nola is screaming for a blood revenge. However, her husband Peter's role is to try to keep Nola together, to moderate her poisonous hatred for Landreaux. As a solitary man with only Landreaux who he can call a friend, Peter is caught in a maelstrom of feelings: he wants to somehow make Landreaux pay for his son's life, he is deeply in debt over his stockpiling of goods he thought necessary to weather Y2K, yet his love for his wife is deep and true, even when she is out of control. Peter by necessity is a peacemaker in his household, whose calm and steadfast love for his wife and his daughter help balance out their dark moods. Also, given that Dusty was Nola's favorite child, Peter senses the degree to which his family is unraveling. He holds himself together for the sake of his family until Romeo Puyat, seeking his own revenge against Landreaux, poisons Peter's mind with his wild and flawed theory of how Landreaux could have prevented Dusty from dying.

Romeo is one of Erdrich's most flawed and unlikable characters, similar to his relative, Pauline Puyat; both Puyats wreak havoc on the lives of those around them, stemming from their misguided sense of what the world owes them as well as their delusional sense of the righteousness of their actions. Gordon compares Romeo to some of Shakespeare's great but malevolent characters. "Like Iago and Malvolio, Romeo gets his power from his possession of secrets" (26). However, as Romeo lives in his own drug-induced sense of reality, his judgment and reasoning are deeply flawed. Romeo's life since boarding school, when he and Landreaux were best friends, has been a quest for vengeance against Landreaux, who he feels is responsible for Romeo's lame arm and leg caused by an accident when the two boys ran away. Additionally, Landreaux is married to Emmaline, whom Romeo has loved since they were children. Based on a faulty report Romeo construes and relates to Peter, Romeo feels he can finally enact revenge by feeding Peter his concocted story of how Landreaux could have saved Dusty. Only then does Peter lose his self-control and set out to kill Landreaux.

And there are more revenge plots in play in this nuanced and powerful novel. Maggie gets even with Dusty Veddar, who has been bullying LaRose. She succeeds in nearly killing him by stuffing an Almond Joy bar down his throat at recess, and in revenge, his older brother and his friends lure Maggie to their clubhouse and molest her. When she eventually confides what has happened to her to LaRose, he vows to avenge her and punish the Fearsome Foursome (Tyler Veddar, Curtains Peace, Brad Morrissey, and Jason "Buggy" Wildstrand), who are now in high school.

The act of revenge that has unsettled the lives of this Anishinaabe community for over a century begins with the first LaRose and Wolfred poisoning the trader Mackinnon, whose vengeful rolling head follows the first LaRose throughout her life and eventually causes her death. Ignatia Thunder in the third "Old Story" cautions LaRose, "We are chased by what we do to others and then in turn what they do to us" (291). It is the accidental death of Dusty Ravich that unleashes the vengeance plots and stirs up old wrongs, alleged and real.

That is the role the little boy LaRose is given, to stop the revenge plots and to heal his two families. His name, Mirage (Ombanitemagad), "would protect him from the unknown, from what had been let loose with the accident. Sometimes energy of this nature, chaos, ill luck, goes out in the world and begets and begets. Bad luck rarely stops with one occurrence. All Indians know that. To stop it quickly takes great effort, which is why LaRose was sent" (105). He needs to bring peace to his two families and to the community at large and is aided in this work by spirit helpers and a stray dog, who initially shows up at the Iron house and then follows LaRose when he is given to the Ravich family.

Skeptical readers might question a child and dog who can heal and communicate with spirits, but this is fully consistent with Indigenous beliefs, as scholars and Indigenous people confirm. Anthropologist Robin Ridington writes,

> Power comes from a person's conversation with the supernatural. It comes from an encounter with sentient beings with whom humans share the breath of life. It

appears when a human makes contact with the non-human persons of the cosmos. It comes to a person when he or she is humble and pitiable. It comes to children. . . . Power comes to people who listen carefully to the storied world around them. . . . Power comes when a person realizes a story that already exists. (471)

And in A. Irving Hallowell's seminal article "Ojibwa Ontology, Behavior, and World View," he argues the idea of "other-than-human" beings who possess "such attributes as self-awareness and understanding. I can talk with them. Like myself, they have personal identity, autonomy, and volition . . . and some of them have more power than I have . . . and help me when I need them" (168).

The boy LaRose is from a family of powerful healers, and as with the first LaRose, a dog appears at the crucial time so both human and dog can fulfill the roles they were sent to play. Flashbacks throughout the novel reinforce the connection from the original LaRose to the contemporary story. The first LaRose and Wolfred, the clerk at the trading post, escape Mackinnon's malevolent rolling head with the help of a cur dog from Mackinnon's trading post. The dog shows up to aid the escape and guard their camps, always alerting LaRose and Wolfred to the presence of the vengeful head. When the fleeing couple reach a small settlement and find safety, the dog disappears, having played its part in the story.

The dog in *LaRose* comes with its own medicine, healing powers, and connection to the spirits. As Sicangu Lakota scholar Debra K. S. Barker explains, her Lakota elders taught her that animals have agency and can step in to play a particular role when needed. LaRose needs the dog to work with him to carry out the mission for which he has been sent. With both families grieving, the little boy cannot be everywhere to heal the sufferings and protect the families from danger. LaRose works between the two families while the dog is needed most at the Ravich house.

LaRose saves and heals both his families, especially his fathers. He reminds Landreaux that both of them have been gifted with a special connection to animals. As a traditional, "Landreaux had songs for the animals" (*LaRose* 11) and could connect with the dog if he tried. LaRose, attempting to take the weight of the killing from him, urges his father to do so, to communicate with the dog who was present at the accident. "Dusty fell from a tree branch, said LaRose. I saw the place. One night in my dream I saw the whole thing. Dusty followed the dog into the woods. The dog saw you. Ask the dog. . . . Dusty told me you shot him on accident" (151). LaRose's biological family with their traditional practices, abundant love of parents for their children, as well as the closeness of the siblings, are better able than the Raviches to hold together as a family as they support each other and heal together.

This is not the case at the Ravich house, where Nola's grief turns to rage and eventually an attempted suicide as she strikes out against all in her household: Maggie, her daughter, and Peter, her husband. LaRose's work is to heal all of them by taking the place of Dusty in the family and, along with the dog to keep watch over them, to comfort and to save them all from their worst instincts. He keeps Peter from harming Landreaux and himself by methodically removing bullets from his rifle and by disappearing any household item that could potentially harm: ropes, bullets, poisons. At the same time, the dog becomes Peter's emotional support, because no one else is able or willing to do so. Peter is the most approachable member of the Ravich family and immediately recognizes, "You aren't a regular dog, are you?" (61). Later when Peter returns to the place in the woods where Dusty died, the dog is there: "It [the dog] was still, as if waiting for him . . . the dog studied him" (22), waiting for the man to initiate contact. Peter, without knowing why, instinctively feels the need to keep the dog. "He's got a story. He's come from somewhere" (64), to which the dog mind-talked to him telling him why he had come: "I saw Dusty that day. . . . I carry a piece of Dusty's soul in me" (64). Vine Deloria, Jr., the noted Lakota scholar, discusses the possibility of such occurrences: "When we begin to gather stories of talking with other creatures, we find three kinds of communications are involved. The first instance is when another creature appears in an encounter with the sacred and plays a vital role in the unfolding scenario" (108).[16] The dog has come to heal, and Peter accepts his comfort since the dog is the only one to whom he can express his deepest feelings, including his heartbreaking recognition that "Dusty is gone" (319), to which the dog "leaned into his [waiting] arms" (319). The dog also acts to keep Peter from resorting to violence, as when Peter and Landreaux are fighting inside the house, the barking of the dog outside helps bring them to their senses.

Nola requires intense vigilance and forbearance from both LaRose and the dog to keep her safe and to bring her to a place where she is able to begin healing. Nola's family history has made her hard, inflexible, and predisposed to avenge those who wrong her. She is the daughter of Billy Peace, whose rapacious appetites and domineering personality prompt Marn Wolde, her mother, to use the venom from her beloved pet snakes to poison him. With Billy and Marn as her parents, Nola grew up bound by rules, strict discipline, and then a new identity when Marn flees Billy's cult. When both LaRose and the dog become part of the household, they first have to learn Nola's rules and always abide by her decisions, traits inherited from her father. But rule following isn't enough to keep Nola from resorting to the vengeance she learned from her mother—vengeance on others as well as turning on herself.

Sensing his new mother's fragility, LaRose goes through her kitchen and removes any and all sharp and potentially harmful items: knives, scissors, and bleach. He and Maggie team up to keep Nola under their surveillance by passing between them a "watching" rock, their mutual alert to potential danger. This is where the dog plays one of the most vital roles in the novel. Nola never wanted it, but "that ugly dog wouldn't leave her alone" (272); he couldn't. When Nola finally decides that suicide is her only option, it is the dog who alerts Maggie to the potential tragedy taking place in their barn, and Maggie is able to talk her mother down from the rope she has wrapped around her neck. Without the dog's frantic barking, Nola most likely would have killed herself.

LaRose and the dog help Nola in other ways. LaRose stays connected to Dusty in the spirit world, talks to him, and even still plays their favorite games. When Nola comes upon them in one such play session, she begins to realize, "Something good he [LaRose] was doing for her by playing with her son from the other kingdom" (272). And gradually the presence of LaRose begins to mitigate her loss, and with the dog who remains by her side to the point that she gradually accepts him, Nola begins to heal. Her "old self stirred . . . and she felt unalone" (272), so that by the time of Hollis's graduation picnic, a time of reconciliation for the community and especially for the Iron and Ravich families, Nola, with the dog settled next to her, is vaguely able to sense when Dusty and the other spirits come to bless the event.

LaRose's new sister, Maggie, is one of Erdrich's most complicated and complex characters. An interesting note on the development of this character came up at the March 2014 Native American Literature Symposium, when Erdrich was the keynote speaker discussing her new book (*LaRose*): Erdrich confessed that she was stuck and didn't know where to go. What she did know, however, was that the Maggie character was a surprise, and she didn't know where she came from. Erdrich introduced us to this character by reading the "Almond Joy" chapter, which emphasizes Maggie's meanness and penchant for revenge. Even then, Erdrich called her "a piece of work." In the published book, Maggie is just that, but she also describes herself as "a wounded wolf" (139) and a "broken animal" (140) who is in desperate need of LaRose's ability to heal. Maggie notices "how the animals are drawn to LaRose" (140) as he cares for and comforts them. It is this gift that enables LaRose to gradually penetrate the fiercely protective barrier Maggie has erected, to temper her worst instincts, and to soften her enough to be able to care about others, especially her mother.

However, Maggie has no use for the dog, and from the first when the dog comes to live at the Ravich home, the dog is wary of the "restless meanness" (33) he senses in her. And with good reason. Maggie gets the dog drunk and even wants to shoot it to show LaRose what death looks like. However, she remembers in her dream when Dusty came to her that he had "showed her a stuffed dog that looked . . . just like that orange dog out there" (33). Could even she wish to harm a creature that connects her to her deceased brother? While she never really likes the dog, she learns to tolerate it to where the dog gradually becomes a part of her daily life. It is her growing up, changing to the reservation school, feeling a close family bond with LaRose and his sisters/her cousins Snow and Josette, and especially taking up volleyball that enables Maggie to grow into a softer, more likable person. The dog even goes to the barn to watch her practice her jumping for volleyball, as it is there that Maggie and the dog had come together to save Nola from her attempted suicide. The most intriguing part of this incident is that Maggie had been up in a tree when "she allowed an owl into her body" (221), the owl for the Ojibwe being both an agent of bad medicine and also a protector and healer (see Pomeldi 97, 102). With LaRose's steadying presence and good influence, her maturity, and her new owl power, Maggie finally comes into her own best self, aided in her transformation especially by LaRose but also by the dog's watchful presence over the entire household.

While LaRose is clearly the central character in the novel, it is the dog who is present at all the pivotal events and some key minor ones: the dog is at the tree when Landreaux accidently shoots Dusty; at the time of the accident, he had been hanging around the Iron house and then follows LaRose to live at the Ravich home; when Peter visits the tree where his son died, the dog is there; when Nola attempts suicide in the barn, the dog is nearby to alert Maggie; as Peter leaves to find Landreaux to relate all Romeo's poisonous theories on how Landreaux could have saved Dusty after he was shot, the dog is "shuffling in the undergrowth" (326); and at "The Gathering," Hollis's graduation party, the dog is there with the Ravich family. When LaRose invites the spirit people to come, "Nobody noticed Dusty was there except the dog and perhaps Dusty's mother" (371).

It would be easy for readers to overlook the dog's importance in the novel while being drawn into the multilayered story, time shifts, traditional stories, beautiful poetic language, characters who infuriate and delight, families who hold together and those who come apart, humor, Erdrich's lists, and the overriding event of an accidental killing of a young boy and how that tragedy plays out in the community. But to underestimate the dog's importance in *LaRose* would be to miss the many ways in which the dog as agent is crucial to the novel's resolution.

The novel is about healing, about the various ways in which healing can take place and the various agents of healing who appear when they are needed. Two boys, one living and one dead, and a dog: LaRose, Dusty, and the mongrel dog are inseparably linked. Dusty lives through LaRose, who can communicate with him in the spirit world, and the dog carries a piece of Dusty's soul. "According to Anishinaabe scholar Lawrence Martin, animals bless human beings; they are power spirits who are connected to and are mutually dependent upon other power spirits" (qtd. in Pomeldi xxvi). The dog, companion to Indigenous people through time, in the novel is an intermediary between the power spirits and the humans badly in need of both healing and protection. He is carrying on his traditional role, supporting the two families with his presence and aiding the human beings he has been sent to help.

NOTES

With thanks to Drs. Debra K. S. Barker for her guidance with this paper; Ellen Arnold for her careful editing; and Jill Patton for her research assistance with the long human–dog connection.

1. With thanks to Peter G. Beidler and Gay Barton for the *Reader's Guide to the Novels of Louise Erdrich*, an invaluable resource for finding all of her dog characters.
2. The special issue of *Studies in American Literatures* was guest-edited by Brian H. Hudson and Dustin Gray: see *Studies in American Indian Literatures*, "Special Issue: Animal Studies," vol. 2, no. 4, 2013, pp. 3–99. Also see *PMLA*'s special issue on Animal Studies, edited by Marianne DeKoven: *PMLA*, vol. 124, no. 2, Mar. 2009, pp. 361–575.
3. See especially, Csányi, *If Dogs Could Talk*; Franklin, *The Wolf in the Parlor: How the Dog Came to Share Your Brain*; Kessler, *The Secret Language of Dogs: Stories from a Dog Psychic*; Masson and Wolfe, *Dogs Make Us Human: A Global Family Album*; and Simon, ed., *The Dharma of Dogs*.
4. Classics and best-selling fiction books on dogs include Burnford, *The Incredible Journey*; Cameron, *A Dog's Purpose*; Rawls, *Where the Red Fern Grows*; and Stein, *The Art of Racing in the Rain*.
5. For example, see *Dog Songs* by Mary Oliver.

6. "Our goal was to examine the relationship that nondomestic wolves had with Indigenous people by studying how the Indigenous peoples themselves described and characterized that relationship" (Pierotti and Fogg ix).

7. See especially the work of Darcy Morey and Stanley Olsen, two acknowledged experts on dog domestication.

8. Scientists generally believe that the dog evolved from the gray wolf since it "is the only large Canid that has lived in all of the places where dogs are presumed to have originated" (Pierotti and Fogg 16).

9. Twenty-six of these traditional stories have been collected by Paul Goble in *The Woman Who Lived with Wolves and Other Stories from the Tipi*. Other accounts are found in Marshall's *On Behalf of the Wolf and the First People*, as well as in Fogg, Howe, and Pierotti's "Relationships between Indigenous American Peoples and Wolves 1: Wolves as Teachers and Guides."

10. Pierotti and Fogg pointedly observe, "This privileging Western concepts and inability to imagine relations between wolves and humans in other than contemporary Western terms (Euro-bias) leads to a number of difficulties" (14). The "difficulty" that comes immediately to mind is when the early Western cattlemen and ranchers urged the government to exterminate the wolf in order to protect their livestock, and by the 1920s, the wolves in Yellowstone had all been killed. However, since 1995, there has been a concerted effort to restore wolves to Yellowstone in order to rebalance the ecosystem.

11. Scholars have noted how often early Euro-American settlers unfamiliar with the close connection between wolves and people recorded these various Wolf Societies as Dog Societies or Dog Soldiers (see Fogg, Howe, and Pierotti 266).

12. The Pillager family, especially Fleur, of the powerful Wolf Clan, are central figures in Erdrich's North Dakota novels.

13. Ignatia's name recalls *Night Flying Woman: An Ojibway Narrative*, Ignatia Broker's account of her great-great-grandmother, Night Flying Woman, who lived in the nineteenth century. Erdrich calls this "One of my favorite books."

14. For various versions of the Flood Story, see Brown and Brightman's *The Order of the Dreamed: George Nelson on Cree and Northern Ojibwa Religion and Myth*, 1823.

15. See Peter G. Beidler's *Murdering Indians: A Documentary History of the 1897 Killings That Inspired Louise Erdrich's The Plague of Doves* for a full account.

16. See page 68 in Deloria's *The World We Used to Live In: Remembering the Powers of the Medicine Man* for the two other kinds of animal communication.

WORKS CITED

Allen, Chadwick. "From the Editor." *Studies in American Indian Literatures*, vol. 25, no. 4, 2013, p. vii.

Barker, Debra K. S. Personal communication, 4 Nov. 2019.

Beidler, Peter G. *Murdering Indians: A Documentary History of the 1897 Killings That Inspired Louise Erdrich's* The Plague of Doves. McFarland, 2014.

———, and Gay Barton. *A Reader's Guide to the Novels of Louise Erdrich*. Expanded and rev. ed., University of Missouri Press, 2006.

Bekoff, Marc. Review of *The First Domestication: How Wolves and Humans Coevolved*, by Raymond Pierotti and Brandy R. Fogg. Animal Emotions blog post, 11 Dec. 2017, www.psychologytoday.com/us/blog/animal-emotions/201712/the-first-domestication-how-wolves-and-humans-coevolved.

Broker, Ignatia. *Night Flying Woman: An Ojibway Narrative*. Borealis Books, 1983.

Brown, Jennifer S. H., and Robert Brightman. *The Orders of the Dreamed: George Nelson on Cree and Northern Ojibwa Religion and Myth, 1823*. Minnesota Historical Society P, 2004.

Burnford, Sheila. *The Incredible Journey*. Vintage, 2013.

Cameron, W. Bruce. *A Dog's Purpose*. Forge, 2019.

Csányi, Vilmos. *If Dogs Could Talk: Exploring the Canine Mind*. North Point P, 2000.

Deloria, Vine, Jr. *The World We Used to Live In: Remembering the Powers of the Medicine Man*. Fulcrum, 2006.

Erdrich, Louise. *LaRose*. HarperCollins, 2016.

———. Reading from *LaRose*. Native American Literature Symposium, 29 March 2014. Mystic Lake Casino, Prior Lake, MN.

———. *Tracks*. Henry Holt and Company, 1988.

Fogg, Brandy R., Nimachia Howe, and Raymond Pierotti. "Relationships between Indigenous American Peoples and Wolves 1: Wolves as Teachers and Guides." *Journal of Ethnobiology*, vol. 35, no. 2, 2015, pp. 262–85.

Franklin, Jon. *The Wolf in the Parlor: How the Dog Came to Share Your Brain*. St. Martin's Griffin, 2009.

Goble, Paul. *The Woman Who Lived with Wolves and Other Stories from the Tipi*. World Wisdom, Inc., 2011.

Gordon, Mary. "A Boy's Fate." Review of *LaRose*, by Louise Erdrich. *New York Times Book Review*, 22 May 2016, pp. 1, 26.

Gross, Lawrence W. *Anishinaabe Ways of Knowing and Being*. Routledge, 2016.

Hallowell, A. I. "Ojibwa Ontology, Behavior, and World View." *Teachings from the American Earth: Indian Religion and Philosophy*, edited by Dennis Tedlock and Barbara Tedlock,

Liveright, 1975, pp. 141–78.

Hirst, K. Kris. "Dog History: How and Why Dogs Were Domesticated." www.thoughtco.com/how-and-why-dogs-were-domesticated-170656.

Hudson, Brian K. "Introduction: First Beings in American Indian Literatures," *Studies in American Indian Literatures*, vol. 25, no. 4, 2013, pp. 3–10.

Jacobs, Connie A. "Louise Erdrich's *Plague of Doves*: The Story of a Town." Native American Literature Symposium, 28 March 2008, Mystic Lake Casino, Prior Lake, MN.

Johnston, Basil H. *Tales the Elders Told: Ojibway Legends*. Royal Ontario Museum, 1981.

Kessler, Jocelyn. *The Secret Language of Dogs: Stories from a Dog Psychic*. Hampton Roads, 2013.

Marshall, Joseph, III. *On Behalf of the Wolf and the First Peoples*. Museum of New Mexico P, 1995.

Masson, Jeffrey Moussaieff, and Art Wolfe. *Dogs Make Us Human: A Global Family Album*. Bloomsbury, 2011.

Morey, Darcy F. *Dogs: Domestication and the Development of a Social Bond*. Cambridge UP, 2010.

Oliver, Mary. *Dog Songs*. Penguin, 2015.

Olsen, Stanley J. *Origins of the Domestic Dog: The Fossil Record*. U of Arizona P, 1985.

"Pet Ownership Internationally." Petfoodindustry.com.

Pierotti, Raymond, and Brandy R. Fogg. *The First Domestication: How Wolves and Humans Coevolved*. Yale UP, 2017.

Pomeldi, Michael. *Living with Animals: Ojibwe Spirit Powers*. U of Toronto P, 2014.

Purdie, Amy. Personal conversation, 15 May 2019.

Rawls, Wilson. *Where the Red Fern Grows*. Yearling, 1996.

Riche, Maureen. "'Waiting Halfway in Each Other's Bodies': Kinship and Corporeality in Louise Erdrich's 'Father's Milk.'" *Studies in American Indian Literatures*, vol. 25, no. 4, 2013, pp. 48–68.

Ridington, Robin. "Voice, Representation, and Dialogue: The Poetics of Native American Spiritual Traditions." *American Indian Quarterly*, vol. 20, no. 4, 1996, pp. 467–88.

Russo, Maria. "Disturbing the Spirits." Review of *The Round House*, by Louise Erdrich. *New York Times Book Review*, 14 Oct. 2012, p. 9.

Simon, Tami, ed. *The Dharma of Dogs: Our Best Friends as Spiritual Teachers*. Sounds True, 2017.

Stein, Garth. *The Art of Racing in the Rain*. HarperCollins, 2008.

Vizenor, Gerald. "Authored Animals: Creature Tropes in Native American Fiction." *Social Research*, vol. 62, no. 3, 1995, pp. 661–83.

———. *Native Liberty: Natural Reason and Cultural Survivance*. U of Nebraska P, 2009.

Woods, Vanessa, and Brian Hare. "Why So Many Books about Dogs?" *New York Times Book Review*, 5 May 2019, p. 19.

Woodward, Wendy, and Susan McHugh. Abstract for *Indigenous Creatures, Native Knowledges, and the Arts: Animal Studies in Modern Works*. Springer International Publishing, 2017, doi.org/10.1007/978-3-319-56874-4.

We Can Wade Grief

Ethics, Politics, and Relationality in Louise Erdrich's *LaRose*

Silvia Martínez-Falquina

With *LaRose*, Louise Erdrich culminates her justice trilogy and offers an illuminating proposal on how to wade grief—to borrow Emily Dickinson's well-known collocation—through an affirmation of Anishinaabe relationality. Connecting Puritan-stock, Amherst-based Emily Dickinson with Louise Erdrich may seem far-fetched, even, arguably, problematic. Erdrich does not make any explicit reference to Dickinson or her poetic vision of grief in this novel—although she does incorporate several direct references to Dickinson's poetry in *The Night Watchman*—and the contextual and epistemological differences of the two authors' works are self-evident. Needless to say, Dickinson's idea of pain as leading to empowerment in "I can wade Grief—" cannot be easily extrapolated to a member of a people who are vindicating reparation for their historical unresolved grief, derived from white settler colonialism. However, the reclusive poet may be taken to exemplify an understanding of grief that Erdrich converses with

The author gratefully acknowledges the support of the Spanish Ministry of Economy, Industry and Competitiveness (MINECO) and the European Regional Development Fund (DGI/ERDF) (code FFI2017-84258-P); the Government of Aragón and the European Social Fund (code H03_20R); and the University of Zaragoza and the Ibercaja Social Fund (code JIUZ-2019-HUM-02), for the writing of this essay.

and tellingly departs from. The novel shares with the nineteenth-century poem an emphasis on the centrality of grief in everyone's life and the human capacity to handle a great deal of suffering. Moreover, both texts suggest the complex relation of grief to happiness. But most significantly, they conceive of pain as a transformative force. Pain makes us human, and it also connects us to the cycles of nature. For all that, one basic difference separates the two texts: Dickinson focuses on the need to remain stranded, isolated. To her, this is the only way one can stay strong and wade grief, "Whole pools of it—" (Dickinson 2). Erdrich, on her part, and as evidenced throughout this essay, finds a possibility to alleviate pain in relationality. Deliberately recovered as an exercise of Indigenous resurgence, with some specifically Anishinaabe elements to characterize it, relationality here refers to the understanding of being as *being with*, as part of a system of interdependence and reciprocity that includes not only humans—living, dead, or still unborn—but also the land and all its creatures, animate or inanimate, visible or invisible. Thus, in *LaRose*, the answer to an overwhelming load of grief is offered by what Dickinson—which in this sense is representative of the individualistic, white-stream US tradition—most rigorously denied herself: kindness, generosity, and companionship.

Whole Pools of Grief: Tough Choices at the Crossroads

Erdrich strategically sets the accidental death of Dusty Ravich at the hands of his father's friend and neighbor, Landreaux Iron, at a narrative, geographical, and chronological intersection. Several of the chapter titles for the first part of the novel—"The Door," "The Gate," "The Passage," "The Crossbeams"—announce different junctions. The terrible event is presented at the very beginning of the text, just as we are crossing the door into the book. The place from which Landreaux is waiting for the deer he has been tracking down all summer is located at the border between his property and that of his neighbors, "[w]here the reservation boundary invisibly bisected a stand of deep brush" (3). Landreaux is a man who is used to crossing boundaries and following diverse beliefs: he is "a devout Catholic who also followed traditional ways, a man who would kill a deer, thank one god in English, and put down tobacco for another god in Ojibwe" (3). Finally, it is the transitional year 1999, and Dusty's father, Peter, is preparing himself for the millennium. Before the accident that would kill his son, he "thought that something would happen, but not what did happen" (3). The world may not literally conclude once the year 2000 starts, but the death of Dusty does mark the end of a kind of life and the beginning of a new one, where everyone in the two families will be defined by the way they deal with grief and by how they rebuild their lives accordingly.

The death of Dusty is so devastating that there is nothing to say "about what had happened—an unsayable thing" (6). Emmaline "did not know how she or Landreaux or anyone," especially Dusty's mother and Emmaline's half-sister, Nola, "was going to go on living" (6). Mortified by the burden of what he has done, Landreaux—who is an example of "how some people would try their best but the worst would still happen" (8)—makes "fierce attempts to send himself back in time and die before he went into the woods. But each time he closed his eyes the body was still ruined in the leaves" (9). The man looks for solace first in a visit to Father Travis, where he prays together with his wife Emmaline; he is then expectedly tempted by alcohol, an addiction he has recovered from, but which still haunts him; and he finally turns to Ojibwe tradition, preparing a sweat-lodge ceremony with Emmaline and with the help of his five-year old son, LaRose, a friend of Dusty. While in the sweat, Landreaux and Emmaline sing songs for inviting the spirits, the animals, the winds, and the ancestors to help them. The two communicate without speaking, and Emmaline understands Landreaux's thoughts, although she resists accepting what she feels is forming in her husband's mind:

> They had sundanced together. They talked about what they had heard when they fell into a trance. What they had seen while they fasted on a rock cliff. Their son had come out of the clouds asking why he had to wear another boy's clothing. They had seen LaRose floating above the earth. He had put his hand upon their hearts and whispered, *You will live*. They knew what to make of these images now. (11)

The account of Landreaux and Emmaline's decision is briefly interrupted by a narrative section describing "an isolated Ojibwe country trading post in the year 1839" (12), where we are introduced to the first LaRose. This interlude, the first of several that cover the history of four generations of LaRoses, announces the interwoven nature of the present and the past. Back in the narrative present, we follow Landreaux and Emmaline walking towards the Ravich house, bringing LaRose with them. They are received by Peter, who still keeps the "instinct" of his friendship with Landreaux (14) but is "charged with exhaustion" (15), and by Nola, transformed by an anger that will make her bitter and suicidal. Between the bereaved parents, a "black crack . . . seemed to reach down forever now" (14), the first of many examples of dissociative processes derived from grief. At the door, which they are not invited to cross, Landreaux and Emmaline stand with LaRose and his small suitcase. "Our son will be your son now," says Landreaux. "It's the old way. . . . He said it very quickly, got the words out yet again. There was a lot more to their decision, but he could no longer speak" (16). Peter tries to protest, but then he looks at Nola and sees "that her face had broken open. All the softness was flowing out. And the greed, too, a desperate grasping that leaned her windingly toward the child" (16). LaRose stays with them.

Although the tragic death of Dusty is the starting point of the text and its original motif, the driving force of the narrative is not so much the accident itself as the tough and surprising choice that Landreaux makes after shooting the child. After all, it is immediately made evident that accidental deaths are not unusual in the fictional world of the novel. News of Dusty's death finds tribal policeman Zack Peace overwhelmed by the deadly frontal collision of two vehicles after the bars have closed, and Father Travis is "sick of praying over the car accident victims, sick of adding *buckle your seat belts* to the end of every sermon, sick of so many other early deaths, ready himself to fall down on the floor" (7). In a context where grief over untimely losses is not uncommon, the response to Dusty's death is made exceptional by the literary treatment of the characters' responses to it and of the entangled consequences of Landreaux's decision. Supported by Emmaline—who is, however, never fully convinced of what they are doing—Landreaux makes a conscious but difficult choice, and the consequences will be devastating for both of them, individually and as a couple. As the narrative progresses, Landreaux is presented as having sacrificed himself and his relationships in his attempt to make amends: he gives away LaRose, the child he secretly feels most attached to; his wife—for whom the situation turns out unbearable in spite of "history and tradition, all that, behind what [they] did" (38)—blames Landreaux and falls out of love with him; his other children—Snow, Josette, Coochy, and Hollis, whom the family took in when he was little—also resent his decision. Nonetheless, while it is initially difficult to see any good coming out of all the suffering involved in the giving away of LaRose, this is also the turning point towards a kind of reparation: it indicates the re-creation of the world in terms of the Anishinaabe tradition and the beginning of a process of healing for both the Irons and the Raviches. By allowing the person most clearly affected by this arrangement—a healing boy who is connected to the human and nonhuman world, authorized by his ancestors and taught by his elders—to function at the center of the narrative as a hinge between the two families, Erdrich shifts the emphasis away from the traumatic accident and towards the active choices that we can make while in mourning. She thereby focuses on agency and explores a range of possible responses to traumatic experiences in a text about how to move on after hitting rock bottom, about how to wade overwhelming grief. As I contend, the novel is not merely about pain, but about posttraumatic growth, or what we can do with that pain. In a personal and political process that reflects on the apocalypse (to use Lawrence W. Gross's term [33]) of the traditional Anishinaabe worldview, the characters of *LaRose* move from the necessary acknowledgment of the end of their world to the adaptive reshaping of their traditional beliefs—most notably, the idea of relation—to adapt to their present reality.

Theoretical Threads: Ethics, Politics, and Relationality

As the analysis offered in this essay intends to show, close attention to Erdrich's literary articulation of grief in *LaRose* is illuminating in three key respects: (1) it stresses the ethical potential of its literary representation; (2) it confirms the political implications of the expression of grief; and (3) it contributes to the theorization of relationality or interdependency as an element of Anishinaabe epistemology that can be extrapolated to a non-Native context.

The giving away of LaRose, the novel's central tough choice, can be illuminated by James Phelan's ideas on ethical guidance accounted for in his article on Toni Morrison's *Beloved*. For Phelan, both writing and reading are ethical acts, since a relation of reciprocity is established between author and reader: "Each party both gives and receives. Authors give, among other things, guidance through ethical complexity and expect to receive in return their audiences' interest and attention. Audiences give that interest and attention and expect to receive in return authorial guidance" (321). Phelan emphasizes how, in the writing/reading process, the author articulates certain choices and the reader has to interpret those choices ethically. Hence, it is ethically relevant to admit our position when writing or reading, as is the need to recognize that discussing the values of texts is more important than "getting the text 'right'" (319). This points, in turn, to the communal character of the ethical response to literature. To illustrate this framework, Phelan focuses on the tremendously complicated act that lies at the heart of *Beloved*, that of Sethe's killing of her daughter to prevent her from returning to slavery. Sethe's choice is "beyond the reach of standard ethical judgement—an action at once instinctive and unnatural, motivated by love but destructive to life" (Phelan 329). The way Morrison articulates the narrative, with three different perspectives on the event—Sethe is alternatively seen as an animal, a mother acting on instinct, and a heroic woman—prevents us from finding a fixed or even satisfactory solution for the problem. Most importantly, since our relation to Sethe cannot be unambiguously solved, we automatically put the blame on slavery, the context out of which Sethe's decision arises, so that without having gone through slavery, we can understand it by looking into one of its terrible consequences. To Phelan, what Morrison is intelligently doing, then, in *Beloved*, is transferring the responsibility of interpretation onto readers, calling for their active participation in the construction of meaning, and thus broadening the text's reading possibilities.

This view on the ethics of writing and reading is applicable to Erdrich's *LaRose*, where we are also confronted with a very difficult and unusual ethical choice, which the author does not approve or disapprove of explicitly. Erdrich sustains the novel on a third-person narrator with multiple focalization, giving us access—albeit indirectly—to a wealth of perspectives. New relations between characters and events are constantly unveiled as readers make progress in the narrative, as is the case in Erdrich's oeuvre in general and in the justice trilogy in particular. Any attempt at linearity is bound to fail when accounting for the different relations that bind characters to one another, and we are forced to revise our previous knowledge with every new story or perspective that we read.[1] Not only does this narrative choice contribute to the articulation of an ethics of complexity, requiring readers to take an active role and draw their own conclusions from the aggregation of different points of view; it is also a way to assert culture-specific tenets of Erdrich's Anishinaabe tradition. As Gross puts it, the particular relevance of storytelling as "a method for conveying knowledge about the world" (162)—especially, though not exclusively, for young people—justifies the expectation that listeners will pay close attention. Traditional stories do not necessarily address a topic directly, and they do not usually contain a moral as Western stories often do. "The Anishinaabeg prefer to let the listener figure out the meaning of the story for oneself" (Gross 182), so that stories become "like seeds planted in one's mind that can grow and then be revisited from time to time to harvest the new wisdom they present" (183). Not surprisingly, "one pedagogical practice of the Anishinaabeg is recognition of the complex nature of truth" (196). The wealth of perspectives in Erdrich's narratives together with her nuanced negotiation of opposites refer to the Anishinaabe storytelling tradition and its ceremonial or transformative potential.

The political implications of grief are also explored in *LaRose*. As Leeat Granek observes, although grief—or "the intensely painful experience that results when a meaningful loss has occurred"—is considered a universal phenomenon, "the expression of mourning is culturally, historically, geographically and politically situated" (61). Accordingly, "[t]he expression of grief is always mediated by one's social context and is always political" (61). This becomes particularly relevant for groups whose grief has been disenfranchised, silenced, and invalidated, like the Anishinaabe we encounter in *LaRose*.[2] As Maria Yellow Horse Brave Heart and Lemyra M. DeBruyn offer, because of the devastating processes of colonization for Native Americans, and particularly until the passing of the American Indian Religious Freedom Act in 1978, Natives' right to grieve and capacity to mourn were not recognized (62). One resulting consequence of a people having their grief delegitimized is the inhibition of its expression and subsequent feelings of shame that restrain the mourning process. Moreover, "[g]rief covered by shame negatively impacts relationships with self and others and one's realization of the sacredness within oneself and one's community" (63). Focusing particularly on the consequences of boarding schools and assimilation policies, Brave Heart and DeBruyn investigate the multiple ways in which "unresolved grief and accompanying self-destructive behaviors have been passed from generation to generation" (57); in particular, American Indian historical unresolved grief has been proved to contribute "to the current social pathology of high rates of suicide, homicide, domestic violence, child abuse, alcoholism, and other social problems among American Indians" (56). Similarly, Gross refers to the end of the traditional Native American worlds as an apocalypse, whose effects linger on and continue to be the current-day reality for many Native Americans, who are "faced with having to deal with the consequences of imposed cultural destruction" (33). His theory of postapocalypse stress syndrome (PASS)—which refers to both individual and institutional loss (40–45)—has three parts:

1. the culture suffers personal dysfunctions, the weakening or collapse of social institutions, and a potential crisis in worldview;
2. the above effects will be intergenerational in nature, and;
3. it takes a culture at least 100 to 150 years to fully recover. (34)

Gross's theory significantly acknowledges the devastating effects associated with PASS and also emphasizes the possibility for recovery. This trajectory is borne out in *LaRose*.

LaRose represents the grief of various characters over the death of Dusty and the accompanying dissociative processes they undergo. However, the grief depicted in the novel is not simply individual but also collective and political, for it is directly associated to the effects of settler colonialism. After focusing on the entangled causes and effects of a racist lynching in *The Plague of Doves*, and denouncing unpunished sexual violence against Native women in *The Round House*, Erdrich fills *LaRose* with multifarious effects of PASS, which are deeply embedded in the social tissue. Past and recent experiences like boarding school, death from tuberculosis, sexual violence, or the theft of human remains are the causes of addiction, abandonment, poverty, suicide. In all three texts, Erdrich represents grief strategically in order to make ungrievable lives grievable, to use Judith Butler's account of the "hierarchy of grief" (32). But it is in *LaRose* that she develops the potential of grief for positive transformation most solidly. In Granek's words, "the recognition of everyone's grief and loss is the only solid foundation from which social change can begin" (67). This type of mourning—"the healthy kind that comes with gestation, with new life, and with the process of birthing something new" (Granek 67)—is the healing sort of mourning that we find in *LaRose*, where grief is confronted by the reshaping of a new world based on the recovery and adaptation of the traditional one.

One kind of insight that grief reveals is the capacity to know the self as essentially interconnected to others, as Butler suggests in her account of mourning:

> When we lose certain people, or when we are dispossessed from a place, or a community, we may simply feel that we are undergoing something temporary, that mourning will be over and some restoration of prior order will be achieved. But maybe when we undergo what we do, something about who we are is revealed, something that delineates the ties we have to others, that shows us that these ties constitute what we are, ties or bonds that compose us. (22)

Accordingly, loss comes with a "transformative effect," in such a manner that mourning has to do "with agreeing to undergo a transformation (perhaps one should say *submitting* to a transformation)" (21). It brings to the fore the relational ties that have implications "for theorizing dependency and ethical responsibility" (22). For Butler, grief displays "the thrall in which our relations with others hold us," interrupting "the very notion of ourselves as autonomous and in control" so that "the very 'I' is called into question by its relation to the Other" (23).

Relationality is also an essential motif of the new cultural and philosophical paradigm that is coming to be known as "transmodernity." First introduced by Spanish philosopher Rosa María Rodríguez Magda, the term has a notably ethical and political dimension, and it characterizes the current globalized context as fluid and interconnected (30).[3] Referring to this paradigm, Irena Ateljevic underscores the "new *relational* consciousness" that leads us to "re-participate with the body of nature" and "to accept contradicting realities and multicultural perspectives" (213). Likewise, Christian Moraru's account of "cosmodernism," a literary articulation of transmodernity, argues for "a new togetherness" and "a solidarity across political, ethnic, racial, religious, and other boundaries" (5). Moraru insists that we overcome prevalent egology and think of culture's well-being "in terms of an 'ecological' balance understood as co-presence, co-implication, and co-responsibility of self and his or her 'cultural other,' in short, as ethical relatedness" (50).

The key difference between these Western critical ideas and Native American views is that the former offer relationality as something new or recently rediscovered, whereas Native Americans have variously and consistently shown that the relational value is deeply rooted in their traditions. Shawn Wilson stresses that "[t]he shared aspect of an Indigenous ontology and epistemology is relationality," in such a way that relationships do not merely shape reality—"they *are* reality" (7). Moreover, in correspondence to their inclusive spiritualities, relationality in Native cultures is not limited to human beings, but also encompasses the landscape, other beings, the ancestors, traditions, or ceremonies. In her description of Indigenous resurgence, Leanne Simpson accounts for Anishinaabe relationships in this manner:

> Recognition within Anishinaabeg intelligence is a process of seeing another being's core essence, it is a series of relationships. It is reciprocal, continual, and a way of generating society. It amplifies Anishinaabewin—all of the practices and intelligence that makes us Anishinaabeg. It cognitively reverses the violence of dispossession, because, *what's the opposite of dispossession in Indigenous thought* again? *Not possession* because we are not suppose [*sic*] to be capitalists, *but connection*—a coded layering of intimate interconnection and interdependence that creates an algorithmic network of presence, reciprocity, consent and freedom. (emphasis added)

Thus is relationality vindicated as an Indigenous value that can counter the effects of dispossession by resisting the Western trap of possession. Likewise, Louis Owens urges us to "achieve a transition from egocentrism to ecocentrism," which is, he claims, the only choice for the community we call life to survive (11), to save humanity from itself: "This is a lesson Native Americans and indigenous peoples really do have to teach, and it is time the world began listening carefully" (236). In *LaRose*, Erdrich brings to the fore such a lesson. The remainder of this essay will examine the ethical and political implications of her recognition of disenfranchised grief in this novel, and her account of posttraumatic growth based on an understanding of relationality that places us in the context of Anishinaabe ceremonial transformation.

We Are Chased into This Life: Grief and Dissociation after the Apocalypse

The decision—made by Landreaux with the reluctant acquiescence of Emmaline—of handing LaRose over to the Raviches to make amends for the killing of Dusty may be presented as referring to an old Anishinaabe tradition, but it is still unspeakable, painful, and difficult to come to terms with for characters and readers. Erdrich's call for us to make sense of this act has ethical implications, for it forces us to assume some responsibility as interpreting agents. Thus, the questions that she leaves open—most disturbingly, how could they give their son away?—lead us to look for answers in the context, and when we do, we find such ubiquitous unresolved grief that it is no wonder that "[t]he one psychologist for a hundred miles around was so besieged that she lived on Xanax and knocked herself out every night with vodka shots. Her calendar was full for a year. People who couldn't get on it went to Mass instead, and afterward visited Father Travis in the parish office" (83–84). Landreaux is a representative example of how difficult it is to raise one's head above water: "the years sorting out boarding school, Kuwait, then wild years, through the drinking and after, straightening out through traditional healing, now this" (8). When he tells Randall—a friend who was given ceremonies by elders, runs sweat lodges, and teaches Ojibwe traditions in the tribal high school (50)—about his demons, which he thinks are connected to something that happened to him in childhood but he cannot remember, Randall replies, "it's a whole hell of a lot more complicated": "Going up against demons was Randall's work. Loss, dislocation, disease, addiction, and just feeling like the tattered remnants of a people with a complex history. What was in that history? What sort of knowledge? Who had they been? What were they now? Why so much fucked-upness wherever you turned?" (51).

Indeed, when we look at the antecedents of these people's complications, we see that grief is never merely individual, but historically transmitted and collective. For instance, the sexual assault of Dusty's sister, Maggie, at the hands of some older boys, which leaves her with a "floating grief [that] came over her like a soft veil" (135), can be traced back to 1839, when the first LaRose, aged eleven, was abused by the trader Mackinnon in an isolated Ojibwe trading post (12–13, 63). Back then, LaRose escapes with Wolfred and they kill Mackinnon, whose head will chase them for years, in an "awkward, interminable progress" (132), until LaRose sees it for the last time upon her death (195–96).[4] Tuberculosis—"a disease of infinite cruelty that made a mother pass it to her children before she died" (72), and which finally kills this LaRose—will also chase her descendants, and the second and third LaRoses die from it as well. It is not until the fourth LaRose, who contracts the disease in time for the discovery of a cure in 1952, that this deadly pattern is broken. It takes, however, more time to find a cure against the persecution of another sickness—racism—which sustains the system that allows strangers to keep the remains of the first LaRose. Initially, a doctor invokes the name of science and makes her travel as "an ambassador to the curious" about the progress of tuberculosis (206); then a historical society refuses to give her back and keeps her in a drawer "next to the bones of other Indians" (206), only to lose them after "an unsolved break-in" (206) to declare her "somehow lost" (207). The appropriating structures persist, but so does the fight to recover the bones, beginning with LaRose's husband, Wolfred Roberts, in the 1860s and 1870s and continuing through their descendants all the way to Mrs. Peace, the fourth LaRose and the boy LaRose's grandmother, who will finally succeed.

Racism may develop new forms with the advance of history, but the symbols of evil persecution are similar in different periods. The head of Mackinnon is not the only one chasing runaways, and it later metamorphoses into "the spirit of the boarding schools" (181). Bowl Head is what the children call Mrs. Vrilchyk, a matron in the boarding school where Landreaux and Romeo Puyat meet and become friends in the late 1960s. Romeo was an Indian of unknown origins, found on the same reservation where Landreaux grew up, and he was an outcast before Landreaux befriended him. When the two escape, they see Bowl Head everywhere, and Landreaux "couldn't stop thinking the strange thought that Bowl Head was a spirit, a force, an element set loose by the boarding school to pursue them to the end of time" (173). Mrs. Vrilchyk may intend to help them be good boys, but to her, that means "white boy[s]" (181), reflecting the intentional colonizing process through abusive education based on the racist view of Indians that was still common at the time.

A third chasing head appears in the story, divided into three sections—Old Story 1, 2, and 3—that some willing elders tell LaRose. The narrative, of which Grandma Ignatia remembers "all the pieces" in the middle of the night (263), includes a talking head (described in ways that remind us of Mackinnon's rolling head in the novel) that has been severed from a woman's body by her husband after he kills and feeds her the snake she has taken as a lover (a narrative reminiscent of Marn Wolde in *The Plague of Doves*). The scary "*vicious* rolling head" (*LaRose* 293) chases her children, only to finally become a sturgeon. When LaRose asks about the moral of the story and all he gets is, "Moral? Our stories don't have those!" (293), there is indeed an illuminating conclusion that Ignatia gives him just before passing on:

> It is *about* getting chased, said Ignatia.... We are chased into this life. The Catholics think we are chased by devils, original sin. We are chased by things done to us in this life.
>
> That's called trauma, said Malvern.
>
> Thank *you*, said Ignatia. We are chased by what we do to others and then in turn what they do to us. We're always looking behind us, or worried about what comes next. (294)

This view of the past—one of the dominant motifs in the whole trilogy—is essential in order to apprehend the full implications of the grief caused by Dusty's death and the giving away of LaRose in the narrative present of the novel. One of the consequences of the past chasing characters into their present lives is the discontinuity of traditional views and the corresponding lack of a solid education. At boarding school, Landreaux may have seemed quite self-confident, "cool" in Romeo's eyes (163), but his lapses in knowledge "made Romeo uneasy. Not only that, they just hurt his brain" (163). Landreaux's parents, who "had been alcoholics with short lives" (89), did not instill in him the love for learning that Emmaline inherited from a line of teachers and that they both transmit to their children, including the last LaRose. Instead, they abandoned young Landreaux, sent him to boarding school, and left him with no effective means to respond to the conditions there. The only way for him to survive was to force himself into a kind of stupor: he recalls how, in the bus taking him to school, he fell into a heavy sleep that he may never have woken up from: "He never woke up. He was still sleeping on that bus"

(152). Landreaux's personal history is surely determining for his adult behavior, including his alcohol and substance abuse, which everyone, even himself, assumes could have been behind his fatally misdirected shot. What is certain, in any case, is that at that particular moment—and perhaps in his life more generally—Landreaux is not exactly acting on *bimaadiziwin*, or the Anishinaabe ideal of the good life. As Gross explains it, *bimaadiziwin* allows for continuity from the old world into the new (205) and encompasses the spiritual life of the Anishinaabeg. One of its main tenets is the relation to others and the environment: the Anishinaabeg "recognized the intelligence of animals," and "there were numerous injunctions as to the proper behavior to follow in regard to animals" (Gross 209). When Landreaux recalls the accident a year after it happened, he realizes that "[t]he buck knew": "Of course it knew. Last year it knew. . . . If he had listened, or understood, or cared to know what he understood, he would never have hunted that buck. Never. He would have known the animal was trying to tell him something of the gravest importance. The deer was no ordinary creature, but a bridge to another world" (149). Although sober and clean of drugs for weeks, at that particular moment "[h]e'd not been thinking," and "to Landreaux his crucial lack of attention was as bad as being drunk" (149). The reason he feels so guilty is that he is well aware that he was not following traditional Anishinaabe rules that regulate the proper, balanced, and respectful way of relating to nature.

The accidental death of Dusty is therefore presented as having to do with the disruption of the traditional worldview of the Anishinaabe, the result of which is a process of dissociation. The most painful effects are obviously suffered by Dusty's parents and sister. Nola, the daughter of Marn Wolde and Billy Peace from *The Plague of Doves*, has her own share of the past chasing her. Right after her son's death, Nola feels alienated from Peter: "His lips moved but she couldn't hear the words. He was too calm, she thought, her mind ferocious, too calm" (4). Peter, in turn, is gripped by the worst kind of loneliness: "[t]he kind you feel alongside another person" (79). Because they cannot both go crazy at the same time, Peter becomes adept at maintaining "an inner equilibrium during the screaming, shouting, foul shouting, rage, sorrow, misery, fury, whimper-weeping, fear, frothing, foaming, singing, praying, and then the ordinary harrowing peace that followed" (77). No matter how hard Peter tries to console her, Nola becomes completely isolated, planning her suicide and spreading her pain onto those around her, most notably her daughter, Maggie. Abandoned by her mother, Maggie is furious, devastated. At thirteen, neither a child nor an adult, she wanders in the woods, where she feels more at home than in her house, when she comes across an owl that "she lets into her body" (221). This spirit helper gives Maggie the strength to react when she finds her mother about to hang herself in the barn. From then on, mother and daughter will be tensely united by their terrible secret, although each is completely unable to console the other in her grief. The family of three become strangers to one another, although they will eventually reconnect through the healing presence of LaRose.

Landreaux and Emmaline's loss results in a kind of dissociation that seems more difficult to deal with. When, tormented by guilt, Landreaux sends LaRose to the Raviches, he not only loses his favorite child, but his relationship with his wife inevitably falls apart. They have raised their children well, they are connected to the point where they share the same thoughts (9), but when Emmaline understands what Landreaux intends to do, her reptilian brain resists: "She growled and showed her teeth. I'll kill you first. No" (11). From then on, Emmaline tries to rationalize what they have done, but it is still unbearable in spite of the tradition that supposedly legitimizes it (37–38). She is drawn to the church and has a brief affair with Father Travis, who is in love with her. Her falling out of love with her husband, which Landreaux eventually realizes, is killing him: "When they argued, he turned to air. His atoms, molecules, whatever he was made of, started drifting apart. He could feel himself losing solidity" (255–56). The manner in which Emmaline receives him towards the end of the novel, setting a physical distance between them, and with no emotion in spite of his having returned from a probable death, points to their immense disconnection. Their future as a couple is left open—"Emmaline felt a surge of fear that suddenly contained what might be, could be, identified as possibility" (345)—but for now, they are united in their grief: "She saw a slough thick with reeds, muck bottom, tangled, both deep and shallow. She saw the ducks batter their way across and up. She saw herself, Landreaux beside her. She saw them both wade in together" (345).

The dissociation that these characters experience is the direct consequence of the loss of their children, but it is also indirectly related to the complicated history they have behind them—which is intricate enough in an autonomous reading of *LaRose*, and even more so if we are familiar with *The Plague of Doves* and *The Round House* too. It is, then, no wonder that, as Peter says, "[t]he grief was all mixed up" (18). Erdrich's narrative representation of inherited grief enfranchises people whose suffering has not always been recognized, and this gives a political relevance to her work. Moreover, it is ethically relevant insofar as it confronts us with the pain of others, vindicating a culture-specific way of dealing with that grief. Access to

Anishinaabe worldview may not always be direct or clear, but the truth is that, in spite of all the difficulties and disruptions, Landreaux is acting on a vision, trusting his belief: "Sometimes energy of this nature, chaos, ill luck, goes out in the world and begets and begets. Bad luck rarely stops with one occurrence. All Indians know that. To stop it quickly takes great effort, which is why LaRose was sent" (105). Landreaux's tough choice will work in the end, and after several generations of inherited grief—let us remember Gross's contention that it takes at least 100 to 150 years to recover from PASS—his boy will be the integrating presence that starts the process towards healing. Emmaline thinks that nobody, not even LaRose, can change the story of what Landreaux has done, but he "knew that wasn't exactly true. LaRose had already changed the story" (28).

Resisting the Wedge by Flying to Keep the Self Safe

The dissociation brought on by grief and transmitted throughout various generations is evident in all of the characters in the novel. Nonetheless, there are some who, thanks to their strong connection to traditional worldview and their deliberate agency in preserving it, learn how to resist the persecution of evil and the past that chases them. The LaRoses develop, on the one hand, the ability to fly—a process of dissociation and reassociation that allows them to temporarily disconnect from reality and save themselves—and on the other, the capacity to integrate their traditional Ojibwe knowledge with that acquired in the white men's schools: "You remember what all the elders said? They knew the history. Who killed the mother of the first one, Mink, and what she could do. Then her daughter, her granddaughter, the next one, and Emmaline's mom. Evil tried to catch them all. They fought demons, outwitted them, flew" (51–52).[5] In order to escape from Mackinnon's head, the first LaRose goes to a Presbyterian boarding school for Indians in the newly established state of Michigan. There, everything is taken from her, including her mother's drum—which was "like losing Mink all over again" (145)—and she tries to put her Anishinaabe being to sleep, "[b]ut it never did" (145). She learns how to dissociate parts of herself for safekeeping instead: "It was hard to divide off parts of herself and let them go. At night, she flew up through the ceiling and soared as she had been taught. She stored pieces of her being in the tops of the trees. She'd retrieve them later, when the bells stopped. But the bells would never stop" (145). Reintegration will transcend the individual and take generations, and a fundamental aspect of it is the mother-daughter connection, which remains unbroken in spite of everything. The mission teachers were very aware that, in the process of "eliminating savagery" (189), "[a] wedge should be placed between an Indian mother and daughter. New ways would eliminate all primitive teaching" (189). Despite their efforts, "they hadn't understood the power of sunlight on a woman's throat" (189), so that, as soon as the first LaRose comes back to Wolfred to marry him, once in free contact with nature, she takes off layer after layer of constraining clothing and accessories and recovers her senses. Six years of schooling do not destroy her true self, her attachment with her mother remains unbroken, and she passes her knowledge on to her own children. When tuberculosis finally defeats her, after resisting for years, "[s]he couldn't flee the bed, but she used her mother's teaching. She thrashed out of her body, unsticking her spirit. . . . She broke out of her body and spun up through the rushing air" (196), just in time for Mackinnon's head not to be able to hurt her anymore.

The second LaRose goes to boarding school in Carlisle, Pennsylvania, "because she knew that her mother had gone to a boarding school. It was a way of being like her mother, who had vividly and with desperate insistence taught her daughter everything she knew" (198). At the end of a long list of traditional teachings (198–99) is the ability to dissociate in order to survive: "She taught her how to leave behind her body when half awake or in sleep and fly around to investigate what was happening on the earth. She taught her how to dream, how to return from a dream, change the dream, or stay in the dream in order to save her life" (199). Because of all that the first LaRose taught her, Richard H. Pratt's maxim to *"Kill the Indian in him, and save the man"* (201), the basis of assimilation-era boarding school education, comes too late: "They hadn't started the killing early enough with this LaRose" (201). There is no wedge between the second LaRose and her mother, and since the latter "had taught her to put her spirit away for safekeeping when that was necessary" (201–202), she has the ability to fly and reintegrate: "Out of the treetops, she brought back and absorbed her many selves. She was complete" (202).

The mother-to-daughter transmission of knowledge is not limited to the line of LaRoses but also extends to others, for the second LaRose "was a teacher and the mother of a teacher. Her namesake daughter became the mother of Mrs. Peace. All of them learned two languages, four levels of math, the uses of plants, and to fly above the earth" (202). This way, the bond is integrated with traditional knowledge to counteract the disruptive and alienating effects of colonial education, and the LaRoses' history becomes tied with that of the schools, their names written and rewritten on them (134). When Mrs. Peace—most commonly known by her teacher name and recognized as having saved many people, including Landreaux (23)—receives the visit of her mother, who died when Mrs. Peace was a child, they congratulate themselves on their work. As they say, "It was good we became teachers so we could love those kids" (71). This was their way of countering the exterminating intentions exemplified in the quoted words of Frank Baum, the writer of *Wizard of Oz*, who proposed to *"wipe these untamed and untameable creatures from the face of the earth"* (71). Luckily, this racist view did not succeed, but the resistance continues in different forms. Erdrich completes—for now—her lineage of boarding school experiences by making it Emmaline's mission to be the director of "an on-reservation boarding school for crisis kids" (105), which helps children in families with problems to get an education and thus avoid foster families and outside adoptions.[6] As noted by the third and fourth LaRoses' conversation, all of these women's efforts will be rewarded in the figure of the last LaRose:

> There was good teachers, there was bad teachers. Can't solve that loneliness.
> It sets deep in a person.
> Goes down the generations, they say. Takes four generations.
> Maybe finally worked itself out with the boy.
> LaRose.
> Could be he's finally okay.
> It's possible. (71–72)

The Ethics of Kindness: From Wedge to Hinge

The boy LaRose could be characterized as a whole-brain child, but this characterization entails more than his obvious ability to integrate the different parts of his brain or his notably developed empathy.[7] LaRose is in balance with the whole creation as well as with himself, and he is a healer in the Anishinaabe understanding of the term. He is also the perfect example of the value of kindness, one of the elements of Anishinaabe *bimaadiziwin* that persists in spite of the negative impact of disenfranchised grief and PASS. A manifestation of spiritual growth based on the idea that we need to maintain harmonious relations with others, kindness, in Gross's account, is connected to the possibility of forgiving and offering second chances at the foundation of traditional Anishinaabe justice (225–45). Kindness comes to

LaRose from a set of loving parents and elder siblings, including an adoptive brother. He is close to Dusty, even after Dusty's death and despite their distant mothers, choosing their fathers' friendship as model instead. From Landreaux he learns to sacrifice himself for a larger good, and from the long line of LaRoses he learns how to fly. In fact, it is his mission to recover the "many selves"—the spirits put out on the treetops for safekeeping (201–202) since the first LaRose—integrating them all. The result is a person who facilitates the connections of those around him, establishing an ecology of relations that will be beneficial for the two families and for the whole community.

LaRose is sensitive and open-minded, and he can communicate with animals, with the spirits or transparent people, and with the deceased. Dusty and a dog share with him all the details of the accident. The animals approach LaRose, for he takes care of them. The elders recognize him as the boy who likes them, "[t]he boy who wants the stories" (108). From them, he learns how to accompany the recent dead, how to search for a vision, how to prepare food for the spirits so they feel welcome among the living. In terms that are relevant for the analysis of grief in this essay, and against all odds, LaRose is far from being dissociated. Instead, he has a mind prone to integration, which seems to come naturally to him. He is the child who does not mind being split between two families, connecting them as he does with everything else: living and dead, past and present, even the masculine and the feminine are united in this boy who inherited his name from a woman.

If the previous LaRoses resisted the wedge that colonial education wanted to place between mothers and daughters, LaRose becomes more than a passive connector: he is the conscious hinge uniting the two estranged families. He and Maggie very naturally become brother and sister, protecting and caring for each other. LaRose's going from one house to another draws his sisters, Snow and Josette, towards Maggie, who is welcome to their conversations, mentored, and protected by them. They are all very aware of how this is a step towards normalcy—"Makes it less weird, huh?" (131), says Snow—and Maggie states, frowning, then brightening: "There could be a whole revenge plot going between our families. But now I don't think there ever will," the reason for it being that all of them now share a love for LaRose (131).

Still, the detachment of the two half-sisters is reflected in the very different kinds of houses, and households, they maintain.[8] In Josette's perspective, her house is "more focused on the human side of things—medical, social, humanitarian, and all that" (260), but she admires Nola's garden, her unusual and well-cared-for flowers and vegetables. The Irons' house is more relaxed, spontaneous, but also chaotic, whereas Nola keeps a strict order and cleanliness that she uses as a way to gain "control of herself" (270), but which others find oppressive: "Her house never smelled of people's habits. . . . But nothing has a smell, too" (65–66). This does not seem to be a problem for LaRose, who is capable of accepting opposites, even welcomes them. When Josette wants to grow a lawn like Nola's, LaRose asks her not to. Although the reason he gives her might seem trivial—"I'm not forking dandelions at two places" (352)—in fact, it reflects his understanding that his contribution to each house should not be duplicated, for each family needs and receives something different from him.

Great power comes with great responsibility, and that assigned to LaRose is even heavier than Evelina's trying to come to terms with her relatives' acts in *The Plague of Doves*, or heavier than Joe's trying to save his mother from a white rapist in *The Round House*. LaRose assumes his task to change Nola "from evil . . . into nice" (33), as Maggie—abandoned by her grieving mother—asks him to do. When Nola becomes suicidal, they both take turns watching her (226–27), although to Maggie, it is an "insufferable responsibility" (250). Even if, eventually, Emmaline tries to keep him all the time, LaRose chooses to go back to being shared by the two families: "the change in routine had made LaRose anxious, and restoring the old order was the right thing" (247). He consoles both mothers and assumes that he has two families on his hands: "It was too much to put on him, but there it was" (247).

Thanks to LaRose, Peter thinks Nola is "integrating" (232), and he recognizes that the Irons' "damn unbelievable plan worked its wonder because now I'm better" (234). LaRose also calms Maggie down, protects her, and gives her a second chance to be an elder sister. Nola holds LaRose, cooks for him, and reads to him obsessively. But the most decisive moment in her process towards healing occurs when she listens to LaRose play with Dusty, naturally communicating with him years after his death: "She heard everything. An epic battle between light and darkness. Forms passing through the material of time. Character subverting space. The gathering and regathering. Shapes of beings unknown merging deeply with the known. Worlds fusing. Dimensions collapsing. Two boys playing" (271–72). With this insight on the permeability and interdependency of different realities, Nola finds a new strength to hold onto life: "Something unknown, internal, righted itself. She felt unalone. . . . Because the fabric between realities, living and dead, was porous not only to herself. This pass-between existed. LaRose went there too" (272). After this, Nola burns the chair she was planning to stand on to hang herself, and she starts to reconnect with her husband and daughter: during an evening watching old teenager movies with Maggie, Peter joins them on the couch and sits so that "the three were now connected, sitting there like normal people" (302). Evidently, normalcy should not be underestimated under these circumstances, and it announces some hope for healing.

LaRose's mission is to stop evil, and he succeeds at that, for he is the reason neither Nola nor Peter kills Landreaux. Revenge is a possibility that the two, especially Peter, consider throughout the novel, but the development here is a corrective of what we found in *The Plague of Doves*. Poisoned by Romeo's ill-will and his old-time grudge against Landreaux, Peter actually tries to shoot Landreaux in a climactic scene towards the end of the novel. Luckily, though, LaRose had removed the bullets from the rifle, as he did with everything that could help Nola harm herself. Recognizing LaRose in the resigned way Landreaux walks, Peter then "sees more" (342): he has a vision of the way grief has transformed reality, of the proximity of death, and of how LaRose is saving both his fathers once again:

> Sees all he has kept himself from seeing. Sees the sickness rising out of things. The phosphorus of grief consuming those he loves. A flow of pictures touches swiftly, lightly, through his thinking—all lost things; then all the actual lost things: the aspirin, the knives, the rope, all deadly in Nola's hands. And the bullets deadly in his own hands. LaRose. (342)

The fact that he was capable of shooting his friend—something nobody but Peter will ever know—will accompany him for life, but as he tosses the rifle into the slough he "feels one moment of lightness" (342). His life spared, perhaps feeling himself forgiven, Landreaux feels lighter too, weightless: "He'd got lighter and lighter all the way home until suddenly, at the doorway, he'd lifted off the ground, kicking off his shoes at the door" (344).

These grieving adults can probably not aspire to much more than the "slender threads of okay" (248) that slowly start to accompany Landreaux in his grief. However, as the book progresses, we witness a change in focus from Emmaline and Landreaux, Peter and Nola to members of the younger generation: not only LaRose but Snow, Josette, Maggie, and Hollis gain protagonism and dominate the final parts of the novel, which points to a brighter future. The narrative style becomes lighter too, more humorous, especially in the girls' conversations, which reflect their teenager language and concerns, but also the way they revise tradition to fit their contemporary selves.[9] The children's conversations may be cheerful but are not lacking in depth. Reflecting with Maggie on Nola's obsession with eliminating dandelions, for example, LaRose wonders why adults hate this plant so much. After all, "[d]andelions are cheerful, and they try so hard" (352). Adults may be wrong about dandelions, and children are, in many ways, wiser than they are, capable of relating in a healthier way. This is why when LaRose and Maggie decide to go on strike—"Let's stop being grown-ups, said LaRose" (353)—we take them seriously: they are announcing a restoration of order that feels ethically right, as will be made manifest in the final ceremony.

Normalcy Restored: Ceremonial Feasting and an Ecology of Relations

The final graduation party for Hollis, a ceremonial and restorative ending for the novel and the trilogy, takes place at Emmaline and Landreaux's house. There may not be beautiful flowers or a proper lawn here, but the location itself is a perfect symbol of how the past is encapsulated in the present. Beneath layer after layer of extensions added to it over the years, the house contains "the original cabin from 1846" (87), built by Wolfred for himself and the first LaRose, and which would "eventually be boarded into the center of the house containing the lives of his descendants" (190). Their ancestors "had lived and died in what was now the living room, and there had always been a LaRose" (87). This becomes an illuminating image of the palimpsestic nature of life, where the past is preserved as one of the deepest layers of the self, giving structure to the present.

The children and young adults—especially Josette, on the verge of starting a romantic relationship with Hollis—put their heart into the preparations for the feast. The food, the cakes, the tables are all perfectly organized, and when the people come, they bring their songs, offerings, and prayers. Anishinaabe ceremonies appear throughout the novel, where it is common to have a sweat lodge, a fast, or a pipe-smoking for individual or group healing; where it is believed that beading, handmade moccasins, or the food made by a mother for her son all carry the power and emotions put in them by the maker. On this occasion, LaRose—who first met the spirits of his ancestors accompanying that of Dusty during a vision quest, at the place where his friend died (207–12)—does the smudging, puts out food for the spirits, and decides he will treat the visitors as regular people if they come. As he listens intently to a prayer being said for Hollis in Ojibwemowin, he feels them come out of the woods. Their clothing is less colorful than that of the living people, but their voices can be heard distinctly. They comment on the party guests; Dusty asks for some cake, and only LaRose, the dog, and a perplexed Nola notice that he is there. The first LaRose—from the boy's perspective, "[t]he old-time woman with the feather in her hat" (371)—announces that *"they are going to get a package and it will be my time-polished bones"* (371), the imminent return of her remains offering a hopeful image of restoration and success after several generations' efforts to give her a proper burial.

The dead relatives' message to Ottie, an old man who will very soon join them, sounds like the best possible conclusion for the novel:

> *We love you, don't cry.*
> *Sorrow eats time.*
> *Be patient.*
> *Time eats sorrow.* (371)

This message is a self-reflective comment on the text's main motif: in spite of grief, which can consume our lives, time will also heal a patient sufferer, as will the acknowledgment of his or her relatives' love. Just as relevant as the content of this message is the fact that the transparent people speak "in both languages" (371). As the first LaRose noted, "In English there was a word for every object. In Ojibwe there was a word for every action. English had more shades of personal emotion, but Ojibwe had more shades of family relationships" (191). Her efforts to be educated and understand the worldview transmitted by English as she preserved her traditional knowledge bear fruit in the present: the boy LaRose has a language for expressing both grief and love, as well as the rich shades of relations that accompany those emotions. This way, the two worlds—or rather, many worlds, for reality is described as multilayered—come together in the final ceremony.

Offering further proof of its balancing inclusiveness, the feast has its own miracle in the Christian sense of the word. Hollis's biological father, Romeo Puy-at—a scavenger of drugs and information who has borne a vicious grudge against Landreaux for decades after their failed escape from boarding school—is not only redeemed, but also "cranked around right" (367) in the end. At an AA meeting that he attends alone with Father Travis, he confesses that he has given Peter false evidence pointing to Landreaux's direct, ill-intentioned responsibility in the death of Dusty.[10] It is unclear whether he is moved by a sense of guilt for what he has set in motion—for he intended to trigger a revenge that could have ended like that depicted in *The Plague of Doves*—or by the side effects of some drug he has consumed, but at this crucial moment "a different Romeo . . . an interior Romeo" (331) starts speaking and tells the whole truth. "Romeo tries to take control of Romeo Two, but it's too late to stop. They merge. He keeps talking" (332), confesses everything about how he "fell from grace" and became "a dead person" when he felt disowned by Landreaux (332). Confronted with the wrongfulness of what he has done, "Romeo rounds up all of the scattered bits of who he is, or was, and flings them on the table" (334). He cannot stop talking, cannot see beyond his own revengeful motivation, "because once he finishes he does not know what will happen next" (335). This speaking therapy provides him with a different vision of the reservation town down the hill, whereby "he sees into each heart. Pain is dotted all around, glowing from the deep chest wells of his people" (335). With his new awareness of the pain of the others, Romeo casts himself headlong down the stairs of the church. Turning up at the final ceremony, unharmed, he gives an awkward speech in support of his son, offers him three thousand dollars that may allow him to go to college instead of the National Guard, and feels his own bones, misaligned after a fall he suffered in his childhood, now mysteriously fixed by the fall: "Something shocking—it was as if his bones were slowly shifting, inside of him, back into place. . . . Somehow the fall had not killed him but fixed him, pushing everything back together. That's how it felt. A mysterious inner alignment was occurring. Romeo was increasingly calm right down the center" (367). Respectfully acknowledged by his son, walking by his side, Romeo feels like he is "walking on air," "floating up to the front of the gathering," aligned, "not hunched over. . . . Rooted, he was rooted right there" (368). Romeo's miraculous healing and reintegration in the community is made possible not only by his earlier confession and reconnection with himself and his past, but also by Hollis's open forgiveness and acceptance of his father.

If, in Gross's account of the Anishinaabe ways of knowing and being, "Anishinaabe religion can be seen, in part, as maintaining good family relationships" (259), this final ceremonial scene offers an excellent example of the reconstitution of *bimaadiziwin*. The effects of the apocalypse remain, and the grief that Erdrich details in this and the other novels of the trilogy does not simply go away. But healing is possible, and it will come when we are capable of seeing that "there is room for making mistakes" (Gross 127), that it is worth favoring forgiveness and a second chance (130), and that chaos, like order, is simply a part of life. As Erdrich's novel demonstrates, the process is far from easy. Peter, tense at the party Landreaux has invited him and Nola to attend, wonders about his friend's intentions: "Was it some kind of traditional Landreaux thing or did it just mean that now life should go on?" (366). Nola also attends the party, even if it does not make sense to her (365), although perhaps it does feel right in a more emotional or intuitive way. In any case, she seems to be finally accepting the way things are, a process set in motion when, before the party, at a volleyball match that ends dramatically, Emmaline hugs Nola on impulse, and to Nola, "[i]t hadn't felt bad or good. She didn't know how it had felt. Maybe normal was the way it felt" (310). Normalcy does not mean that life is or ever will be free of grief; it means that grief is accepted as one more part of life. It does not mean that one can go back to being the person they were before their loss; it means that the grieving person can finally submit to the inescapable transformation that loss forces upon them.

Needless to say, in Erdrich's account of the transformation brought on by grief, she is far from suggesting that resignation is the best response. Her careful exploration of the tentacles of the loss derived from colonial injustice and her confidence in the Anishinaabe teachings when dealing with grief are, in this sense, outspoken political vindications. The first two novels of the group that has come to be known as the justice trilogy already dealt with grief in detail. But it is in this final novel that Erdrich offers the most advanced lesson on the defining possibilities of grief. Not only can grief tell us much about who we are as individuals and in relation to others, it also gives us an invaluable opportunity to redefine ourselves by how we choose to respond to it. There is always the option of wading grief independently, seeking strength in isolation, as Dickinson's poem and much of the American individualistic model propound. But the ethical and political possibilities of Erdrich's complex, relational take on grief—which unveils the ties we have to others, our essential relationality—are much more promising and desirable in a world where we have, after all, to live—and die—together with many others. The ecology of relations articulated in this view of grief is one more example of the transition from egocentrism to ecocentrism that, as Louis Owens reminded us, is necessary for the survival of the community we call life. It is up to us to listen carefully.

NOTES

1. While the narrative voices in the three novels vary, the overall emphasis on complexity and relationality does not: *Plague of Doves* starts with a brief chapter with an external narrator, followed by chapters from the intercalated first-person perspectives of Evelina,

Antone Bazil Coutts, Marn Wolde, and Cordelia Lochren; *The Round House* is told from the sole first-person perspective of thirteen-year-old Joe Coutts, an unusual narrative choice for Erdrich, but one that proves particularly effective here; and the external narrator of *LaRose* is sustained on sophisticated focalization, which gives an overall impression of balanced co-responsibility—internal and external—in the interpretation of the main events.

2. For an analysis of grief and its implications for the decolonization of the trauma paradigm in another work by Erdrich, see Martínez-Falquina.

3. See Rodríguez Magda for an account of this term she coined in 1989; some English translations of her work can be found at http://rodriguezmagda.blogspot.com.es/.

4. In her interview with Deborah Treisman, Erdrich has noted that the rolling head is part of a Cree/Ojibwe origin story.

5. As noted by Erdrich in her interview with Treisman, the ability to fly is not to be characterized as fantastical: "The training of spiritual people in many indigenous societies involves learning how to leave one's body. Indeed, it isn't uncommon for people of any culture to experience this during a moment of great trauma, and most people fly in dreams." Although there is not space here to analyze this in detail, flying is also related to evil and trauma for other characters in the novel, including Mrs. Peace (68–72, 94), Romeo Puyat (93–94), Father Travis (111), and of course the boy LaRose (290). Despite their varying circumstances—Romeo's flights, for example, are associated with drug consumption, and Father Travis's is the result of the traumatic haunting of his experience with the Marines—it is clear that Erdrich emphatically connects dissociation to grief in *LaRose*.

6. As Schacht contends in her study of boarding school representations in Erdrich's works before *LaRose*, in spite of the loneliness, alienation, and threat of disease that are associated with boarding schools, there is a wide range of experiences, "from unthinkable abuse to positive support" (62). In *LaRose*, Erdrich goes a step further in covering that complexity and variety. She has recognized that "there is a largely untold story about how vital government education was to Native people's long fight for legal standing," referring specifically to how, thanks to her great-grandfather's sacrifices, her grandfather Patrick Gourneau was educated enough to fight the mid-fifties policy of termination for the Turtle Mountain people (see her interview with Treisman). In fact, Erdrich tells part of that story in her new novel, *The Night Watchman* (published in March 2020), based on the life of her grandfather.

7. As Erdrich describes him, LaRose "is a good kid; nobody ever writes about the good kids, . . . so I let him be as good as he could be" (Kirch 86–87). The good kid at the center is

another element that the three novels have in common: innocent Holy Tracks is killed at thirteen in *The Plague of Doves*, Joe tries to save his mother at the same age in *The Round House*, and LaRose is only five at the start of this novel.

8. Emmaline and Nola are both the daughters of Billy Peace. Although his story is told in *The Plague of Doves*, where Marn Wolde mentioned that he was unfaithful to her, in *LaRose* we get a clearer idea of the effects of his promiscuity: "Nobody really knew how many wives had married Billy, or what had gone on in that cultish compound of his decades ago. Billy's children and now grandchildren kept turning up and were usually added to the tribal rolls" (*LaRose* 24).

9. Their responses to Ignatia Thunder's warning that touching boy's things "might short out the boys' power" (49) as sexist, as well as their conversation with their grandmother about how new rules come up all the time (357–59), are interesting examples of how some traditional Anishinaabe elements are taken into consideration but also transformed as they are adopted by contemporary young women.

10. Erdrich has compared Romeo's false allegations against Landreaux to the deception about weapons of mass destruction that led to the US war with Iraq in 2003; see Kirch 87.

WORKS CITED

Ateljevic, Irena. "Visions of Transmodernity: A New Renaissance of Our Human History?" *Integral Review*, vol. 9, no. 2, 2013, pp. 200–19.

Brave Heart, Maria Yellow Horse, and Lemyra M. DeBruyn. "The American Indian Holocaust: Healing Historical Unresolved Grief." *American Indian and Alaska Native Mental Health Research*, vol. 8, no. 2, 1998, pp. 56–78.

Butler, Judith. *Precarious Life: The Powers of Mourning and Violence*. Verso, 2004.

Dickinson, Emily. "I can wade Grief—" (#252). *The Complete Poems of Emily Dickinson*, edited by Thomas H. Johnson, Little, Brown, 1960, p. 115.

Erdrich, Louise. *LaRose*. HarperCollins, 2016.

———. *The Night Watchman*. HarperCollins, 2020.

———. *The Plague of Doves*. HarperCollins, 2008.

———. *The Round House*. HarperCollins, 2012.

———. "This Week in Fiction: Louise Erdrich." Interview with Deborah Treisman. *New Yorker*, 22 June 2015, www.newyorker.com/books/page-turner/fiction-this-week-louise-erdrich-2015-06-29.

Granek, Leeat. "Mourning Sickness: The Politicizations of Grief." *Review of General Psychology*, vol. 18, no. 2, 2014, pp. 61–68.

Gross, Lawrence W. *Anishinaabe Ways of Knowing and Being*. Routledge, 2014.

Kirch, Claire. "Old Fashioned Justice." *Publishers Weekly*, 18 April 2016, pp. 86–87.

Martínez-Falquina, Silvia. "Re-Mapping the Trauma Paradigm: The Politics of Native American Grief in Louise Erdrich's 'Shamengwa.'" *Memory Frictions in Contemporary Literature*, edited by María Jesús Martínez-Alfaro and Silvia Pellicer-Ortín, Palgrave Macmillan, 2017, pp. 209–30.

Moraru, Christian. *Cosmodernism: American Narrative, Late Globalization, and the New Cultural Imaginary*. U of Michigan P, 2011.

Owens, Louis. *Mixedblood Messages: Literature, Film, Family, Place*. U of Oklahoma P, 2001.

Phelan, James. "Sethe's Choice: *Beloved* and the Ethics of Reading." *Style*, vol. 32, no. 2, 1998, pp. 318–33.

Rodríguez Magda, Rosa María. *Transmodernidad*. Anthropos, 2004.

Schacht, Miriam. "Games of Silence: Indian Boarding Schools in Louise Erdrich's Novels." *Studies in American Indian Literatures*, vol. 27, no. 2, 2015, pp. 62–79.

Simpson, Leanne Betasamosake. "The Misery of Settler Colonialism: Roundtable on Glen Coulthard's *Red Skin, White Masks* and Audra Simpson's *Mohawk Interruptus*," 8 Oct. 2005. www.leannesimpson.ca.

Wilson, Shawn. *Research Is Ceremony: Indigenous Research Methods*. Fernwood, 2008.

Narrative Design in the Justice Trilogy

Nancy J. Peterson

ouise Erdrich is a captivating storyteller, not only because she tells stories of dramatic—sometimes comic and sometimes tragic—events with compassion and humanity, but also because she creates fictional worlds in which stories proliferate, where stories summon other stories into being. Indeed, Erdrich's richly complex narrative strategies have become a hallmark of her fiction, from the publication of her first novel—*Love Medicine*—in 1984 (rev. 1993 and 2009), with its six first-person narrators telling stories dating from 1934 to 1984 (plus a third-person narrator who focuses on various characters throughout), and continuing through the publication of the three novels that make up her justice trilogy. Erdrich's use of multiple narrators for most of her novels is an effective strategy for highlighting the multifarious narrative lines that her novels pursue, but it is an element of her writing that has not always been received well. In fact, several early reviewers were baffled by her complex narrative strategies. Reviewing *Love Medicine* in 1985 for *Newsweek*, for instance, Gene Lyons found the use of multiple narrators, and the mixture of first-person and third-person narratives, to indicate Erdrich's "inexperience as a storyteller" (71). The prevalence of so many narrators and narrative perspectives, for Lyons, means that "No central action unifies the narrative" (71). Needless to say, Erdrich's long and acclaimed career as a novelist and as a storyteller has now put such criticisms to rest, but I would also argue that her narrative strategies continue to be a significant, yet underappreciated element of her fictional world. Why such complexity? Why continually offer so many stories, of so many fascinating characters, that even her most recent novels continue to defy attempts to center the narrative, to discern the main narrative thread?

This is the central question—teasing out the deliberate purposefulness of Erdrich's narrative strategies—that this essay explores by reading the novels of the justice trilogy: *The Plague of Doves* (2008), *The Round House* (2012), and *LaRose* (2016). Of course, given the theme of justice/injustice that runs prominently through all three novels, it could be argued that there is a reverberating action or event, or a prevalent issue, that centers each novel—and the trilogy as a whole. And yet, it is worth noticing that each book also includes many stories that are not necessarily connected to the exploration of justice. For instance, while *The Plague of Doves* focuses on the unsolved story of the Lochren family murders from 1911, followed by a white mob's lynching of three innocent Ojibwe (two men and a boy), it also relates the stories of Evelina's confusing journey into womanhood and her breakdown; of her father's lost stamp collection; of the nineteenth-century survey expedition that founded the town of Pluto; of the kidnapping of Neve Harp engineered by her husband; of the youthful, secret love affair between Antone Bazil Coutts and Cordelia Lochren; and many others. Similarly, while *The Round House* focuses on Geraldine's violent rape and the disappearance of Mayla Wolfskin and her baby—and eventually solves those crimes—it also includes stories of Father Travis as a traumatically wounded former Marine, of Joe's friends and their antics (and their love of *Star Trek: The Next Generation*), of Cappy's love for a young white Christian woman whose family intervenes to cut off any contact between them, of Grandma Ignatia Thunder's bawdy imagination and storytelling, of Sonja and Whitey's sometimes loving and sometimes fighting relationship—and so many other gripping stories. *LaRose*, of all the novels of the trilogy, offers perhaps the most complicated set of stories: the novel focuses on Landreaux's accidental killing of Dusty Ravich while hunting and the overwhelming sense of guilt he feels in the aftermath, followed by Emmaline's and Landreaux's decision to give their son, LaRose, to the Raviches to begin to make amends for Dusty's death. All of this drama is revealed in the first 16 pages of a 372–page novel. What, then, drives the plot of *LaRose* and centers the narrative? As it turns out, there are many other compelling stories that run alongside this central thread—stories of Romeo's and Landreaux's boarding school experiences, and Romeo's deeply rooted desire for revenge against

Landreaux; of the first LaRose, her traumatic experiences, her resilience, and the life she builds with Wolfred; of opioid and alcohol addiction on the reservation; of the teenagers in the Iron and Ravich households trying to come of age and find their source of strength. All of these narrative threads (and more) are given careful attention and draw the reader into close contact with a wide number of characters and their individual lived experiences. No one, it would seem, is unimportant in Erdrich's fictional world.

Erdrich's narrative design shows a purposeful bringing together of peoples, of experiences, of stories. In her acclaimed essay on *Love Medicine* and *The Beet Queen*, published in 1990, Catherine Rainwater calls attention to the narrative complexity of Erdrich's early novels. She describes them as being "rife with narrators . . . bereft of a focal narrative point of view, and replete with characters whose lives are equally emphasized" (415). But rather than situating this multiplicity as too confusing, or the mark of an inexperienced novelist, Rainwater emphasizes the productive effects of Erdrich's narrative diversity. She argues that Erdrich's use of multiple narratives and narrators reorients readers, leaving us "between worlds" (412), between competing frames of reference—Western and Indigenous—so that readers are displaced from "usual positions of theological and epistemological inquiry" (410). By doing so, Erdrich's early novels thus create space for tribally based ways of knowing (kinship networks and Ojibwe spirituality, for instance) to resonate with readers, along with Western epistemologies and assumptions.

Recent scholarship has returned to the issue of Erdrich's narrative complexity.[1] Working from a narratological approach, Corinne Bancroft focuses on *The Plague of Doves*, describing it as a "braided narrative": "braided narratives have distinct narrators who tell different stories that both conflict and intertwine in the same storyworld" (266). As Bancroft notes, Erdrich's novel switches between narrators eight times and thereby involves readers in "a complicated braid where we must recognize a series of different narrators, acknowledge their interdependence and contradictions" (264), and by so doing, readers become aware of being entangled in ethical questions and responsibilities. Although it is illuminating, Bancroft's narratological analysis does not lend itself to a tribally based, culturally informed reading of *The Plague of Doves*, and it is important to recognize that by the time Erdrich crafts the novels of the justice trilogy, Ojibwe culture and epistemology inform her narratives in subtle and significant ways. Lydia Schultz, in a 1991 essay on narrative strategies in *Love Medicine*, anticipated this critical shift as she explores the ways that Erdrich infuses her novel with resonances of Ojibwe storytelling cycles and their oral performance. Erdrich's narrative strategies, as Schultz argues, bring the community together through stories, but also insist that there is no one, singular tribal or Ojibwe viewpoint. Erdrich's use of multiple narrators calls upon the reader's "ability to fit narratives together, building one upon the other, until we begin to see the world through a *collection* of Ojibwe eyes" (Schultz 92).

Indeed, this same sense of entangled narratives and lives preoccupies Erdrich's later novels. In *The Plague of Doves*, Evelina hears the story of the lynch mob from Mooshum, and it reveals a terrible history that is echoed in her own generation of townspeople, descended from those who were killed and those who did the hanging:

> The story Mooshum told us had its repercussions—the first being that I could not look at anyone in quite the same way anymore. I became obsessed with lineage.
> ... I wrote down as much of Mooshum's story as I could remember, and then the relatives of everyone I knew—parents, grandparents, way on back in time. I traced the blood history of the murders through my classmates and friends until I could draw out elaborate spider webs of lines and intersecting circles. (86)

The "elaborate spider webs" and "intersecting circles" of genealogy do not result in a neat alignment that reveals a clear meaning for Evelina; rather, she feels as though "I'd stepped into a clear stream and silt had billowed up around my feet" (86). Muddying the waters sounds like a negative consequence, but for Evelina—and for Erdrich's readers—it is a necessary step. Those who perceive a clear stream perhaps take only one glance to see what lies before them. On the other hand, those who try to look through murky, silt-laden water must draw upon sustained attention, a willingness to sift through the dirt and the chaos to arrive at a profound perspective. The question for Evelina, and by extension for Erdrich's readers, is how to connect the lines of relations, the individual stories, and the complicated conflicts in such a way that, out of the murky chaos, something emerges that is powerful, useful, and beautiful. Or as Peter G. Beidler and Gay Barton observe, "beneath the seeming chaos of story and character in Erdrich's novels lies a series of interlocking patterns, a carefully crafted web of more-than-Faulknerian complexity—as mazelike as life itself, yet ordered by Erdrich's genius" (5).

Devoted readers of Erdrich's fiction learn to create mental story-maps of her novels to draw these kinds of connections and reveal deep understandings.[2] In addition, several of Erdrich's interrelated novels with linked characters include genealogical charts—charts that are designed to help readers readily identify

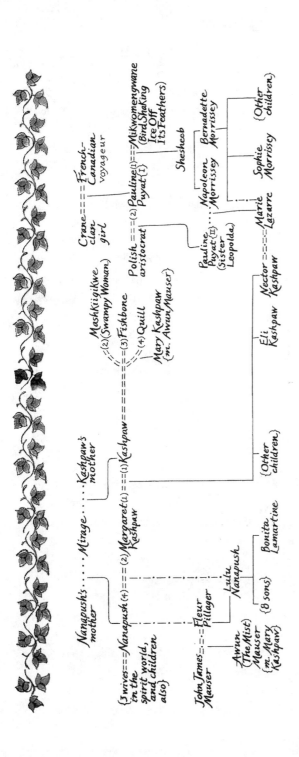

FIGURE 1. Genealogy chart, reproduced on the front and back endpapers of the 2001 hardcover edition of *The Last Report on the Miracles at Little No Horse.*

COPYRIGHT © 2001 BY LOUISE ERDRICH. USED BY PERMISSION OF HARPERCOLLINS PUBLISHERS.

The following text appears within the figure:

Nanapush's....Mirage.....Kashpaw's mother

Crane==== French-Canadian girl

Mashkiigikwe (Swampy Woman)

==(2) ==(3) Fishbone

Kashpaw ====(1) Kashpaw

Polish ===(2) Pauline Puyat(I) ==Mikwomengwane (Bird Shaking Ice Off Its Feathers)

==(4) Quill

aristocrat

Mary Kashpaw (m. Awun Mauser)

Shesheeb

Pauline Puyat (II) (Sister Leopolda)

Napoleon Morrissey

Bernadette Morrissey

{3 wives==Nanapush (4) ====(2) Margaret(1) in the spirit world, and children also}

Marie Lazarre

Sophie Morrissey

{Other children}

Eli Kashpaw

Nector Kashpaw

{Other children}

==(2) Margaret(1) Kashpaw

Nanapush (4) ==== Fleur Pillager

Lulu Nanapush

Bonita Lamartine

{8 sons}

John James Mauser =·= Awun (The Mist) Mauser {m. Mary Kashpaw}

LEGEND

==== Traditional Ojibwe marriage

····· Sexual affair or liaison

=·= Catholic marriage

| Children born from any of the above unions

¦ Adopted children

Marriages and liaisons are numbered in order of any issue.

characters, their families, and various "intersecting circles" (to borrow Evelina's phrase). But even these charts cannot simply follow standard genealogical notations; Erdrich's tangled affiliations have sparked the need for innovative delineations. In *The Last Report on the Miracles at Little No Horse* (2001), for instance, the genealogy chart includes distinct lines for marking a "Traditional Ojibwe marriage" versus a "Catholic marriage" versus a "Sexual affair or liaison." Furthermore, the chart distinguishes between "Children born from any of the above unions" and "Adopted children."

Moreover, the lines of affiliation of this genealogy chart—drawn by hand, using doubled lines, dots, and lines with dots—bear a resemblance to the patterns of stitching found in traditional Ojibwe beadwork (such as the jumping pattern, the ottertail pattern, and so on).[3] Also important to note is that at the top of the page above the genealogy, spanning both the left and right pages, runs a decorative image of a vine with leaves—a design that resembles the floral motifs that recur in Ojibwe beadwork of the nineteenth and twentieth centuries. These parallels—between the design of the genealogy chart in several of Erdrich's novels and the stitching and patterns of Ojibwe beadwork—lead to a productive line of inquiry: How might traditional Ojibwe beadwork and floral design help to reveal the patterns and valences of Erdrich's narrative intricacies?

Ojibwe Beadwork and Narrative Design

Beading is a familiar art form for Erdrich. In fact it forms a central thread in the original and revised versions of *The Antelope Wife* (1998, 2012), as twin sisters who are bringing the world into being through beading try to outdo each other: one uses light-colored beads, the other dark-colored beads, each trying to upset the balance of the world by beading her own colors into the design faster than her twin. In a brief section at the end of the revised version of *The Antelope Wife*, Erdrich directly connects the revisions she made to the novel to traditional Ojibwe beading:

> Revising this book was like repairing an old piece of beadwork. I stitched in new connections and added entirely new chapters. I dropped some chaos but kept some of the mistakes. Ojibwe floral beadwork usually employs one sinuous vine with marvelously inventive offshoots. That became my pattern for the book. The Antelope Woman's narrative would be the vine, the chapters the flowers—some

true to life, some wildly dreamlike, some a mixture of real and surreal. ("About the Revision")

Erdrich's comparison of revising *The Antelope Wife* to "repairing an old piece of beadwork" aligns traditional beadwork with the act of writing and prioritizes stories that meander, like a vine, to explore the truths of dreams and of reality. In fact, threading such stories together may fashion a way to repair the rifts of history and loss by shaping them into a beautiful new pattern.

Erdrich was working on the revisions to *The Antelope Wife* during the same period in which she was writing the novels of the justice trilogy.[4] Significantly, beading is an activity that recurs in the novels of the trilogy. Erdrich's characters who are closest to traditional beliefs are often adorned with beaded items or are dexterous beaders themselves. In *The Plague of Doves*, for instance, Evelina takes a "beaded leather tobacco pouch" from Mooshum with her to college (221). In *The Round House*, Grandma Thunder wears beaded moccasins, LaRose wears a beaded flower hair clip, and Geraldine wears "black-and-pink-beaded earrings" (262) when she rejoins the family. Most important, the powwow regalia for Randall, Suzette, and Josey is adorned with beaded designs, and Randall's "armbands and aprons" are specifically identified as having "beaded floral patterns" on them, which his aunties have created for him (269). Beading is also present in *LaRose*, but in a much more sustained way. Mrs. Peace wears a different pair of beaded earrings every day and has a beading tray on her dresser in her retirement apartment, and she credits beading with helping her to quit smoking (24). Emmaline makes a new pair of moccasins for her children every year, and she is admired for her sewing and beadwork: "Her moccasins sometimes fetched two or three hundred dollars. The family was proud of her work and only wore their moccasins inside the house" (50). This is a skill, an artistry, passed down in her family, as we learn the first LaRose was also a marvelous beader, who teaches her family how to become skillful beaders too (191, 199). Her husband, Wolfred, wears "moccasins beaded with flowers and finished off with colored threads" (189) with pride.

In *The Antelope Wife*, Erdrich includes the Anishinaabemowin word for beads—"manidoominensag"—which she translates as "little spirit seed" (195). "Manidoo" in Anishinaabemowin comes from the word for manitou (*manidoog*), the spirits present in this world and beyond, who are part of Ojibwe traditional stories. In Erdrich's justice trilogy, Ojibwe beadwork is an artistic practice linked to traditional culture.[5] As Michif (Métis) artist Christi Belcourt points out in her how-to book on Indigenous beadwork, oftentimes beadworkers would incorporate "spirit beads"—individual beads of the wrong color—into a design, not as a mistake, but as an important reminder that to be human is to be imperfect (14). In *LaRose*, Snow and Josette echo this teaching when they are beading with their Grandma Peace: "Don't forget to make a mistake," Snow reminds Josette, "you know, to let the spirit out," and Josette responds, "Only the Creator is perfect" (358). As is also clear from this scene, beading brings people—especially women—together. Belcourt observes in her guide to Indigenous beading, "We see women's hands at work when we look at beadwork" (10). In *LaRose*, Emmaline and her mother, Mrs. Peace, make sure the artistry will continue into the contemporary generation, as they teach their skills to Josette and Snow. Indeed, Erdrich draws on this association of Ojibwe women and artistry to craft a meaningful portrait of some of her most resilient and memorable Ojibwe women characters, such as the first LaRose, Mrs. Peace, Emmaline, Snow, and Josette in *LaRose*.

Returning once again to Erdrich's comments comparing her revisions to *The Antelope Wife* to traditional Ojibwe beading, we may also notice that she mentions specifically the curvilinear-floral designs that Ojibwe women developed in spot-stitched beadwork of the late nineteenth century. Erdrich highlights, for instance, the "sinuous vine" that links leaves and flowers and allows for "marvelously inventive offshoots" in floral beadwork designs. Some of these leaves and flowers correspond to plants and trees found in traditional Ojibwe homelands, while others are more abstract—or as Erdrich describes them, "dreamlike" or "surreal." Erdrich's description suggests that her narrative designs are akin to traditional Ojibwe beadwork in creating beauty out of chaos, in tracing vines that sometimes run wild with startling offshoots but also incorporate beautiful leaves and flowers.

To develop this connection further, it is helpful to have in mind a brief overview of the development of floral beadwork among Ojibwe women in the Great Lakes region. Ojibwe curvilinear-floral beading designs adorned many kinds of objects and articles of clothing in the late nineteenth century. Moccasins, leggings, collars, vests, yokes, tobacco pouches, pipe bags, and other items were handmade by Ojibwe women, who made even utilitarian objects beautiful by adding beaded designs. Indeed, floral designs became prevalent among many Native peoples in the nineteenth century as trade relations made glass beads and other materials readily available, as colonialism in the form of residential schools taught sewing arts to Native girls, and as Native women worked to support their families by creating handcrafted objects and designs that could be sold or bartered with

FIGURE 2. Ojibwe bandolier bag decorated with spot-stitch floral beadwork with a deer in the mid-panel, ca. 1890.

white traders and collectors.[6] Ojibwe women became particularly noted for their beaded bandolier bags (*gashkibidaaganag*, plural, in Ojibwemowin) embellished with curvilinear-floral designs.[7] These bags may originally have been developed for everyday use (to carry or store things), but they soon became items of adornment—used to complement ceremonial regalia, gifted to honor a notable person, or sold as a means to support the family. A close examination of one particularly striking bandolier bag, crafted circa the 1890s and now housed in the collections of the Minnesota Historical Society, exemplifies several of the essential elements associated with this art form.

Bandolier bags, no matter what their design, have several common elements: a front panel for the bag, a pocket opening, a band above the pocket, a strap, and bottom fringe.[8] As Marcia G. Anderson notes in *A Bag Worth a Pony*, her illuminating work on Ojibwe bandolier bags, "the Ojibwe bags documented in Minnesota and parts of Wisconsin feature an interest in asymmetry, use of contrast rather than co-ordination of motifs, and the creative use of unmatched motifs" (57). The bandolier in figure 2 is marked by the asymmetrical, curvy designs that Ojibwe women were noted for—not only on the pocket and the band above it, but also on the strap. The berries, leaves, flowers, vines, and tendrils beaded on this bag are common motifs found on bandolier bags from a variety of Ojibwe communities. The deer on the flap above the pocket opening could perhaps have been an element designed to capture the interest of white traders and collectors; indeed a note included in the Minnesota Historical Society record for this item suggests that this bag was "reportedly obtained through William F. 'Buffalo Bill' Cody." But the deer is also an interesting element to focus on for another reason: it is centered on the flap above the pocket, and the "weight" of the design to the left and right of it seems equal, but in fact the flowers and leaves on each side are notably different. In other words, this element of the bag exemplifies the asymmetrical design preferences of Ojibwe women from Minnesota communities, but also an asymmetrical design that is carefully balanced. As curator Lois S. Dubin observes in the catalog for *Floral Journey*, based on a 2014 special exhibit organized by the Autry Center in Los Angeles, "The pairing of opposites within the layered universe signified cosmological unity. . . . Woodlands artisans' tendency toward bilateral asymmetry—seen in most flower beadwork designs and colors—likely signifies an attempt to create balance by uniting opposing (as well as complementary) realms and beings" (67). Significantly, then, a design preference for carefully balanced asymmetries reflects Ojibwe cultural and spiritual beliefs that emphasize a balance of opposites throughout the universe.

In a similar fashion, the straps of the bag feature balanced asymmetry: the strap includes a plethora of different kinds of flowers (some having three or four petals, others five or six), leaves, as well as berries linked by a meandering vine. In nature, we would not find this kind of variation on one plant or vine. And yet, the design here beautifully links naturalistic elements (prairie roses, blueberries, maple leaves with accented veins) in an unexpected, innovative way: strung along one vine, they are brought into proximity along the strap and become a kinship community. The pocket panel on the front of the bag also revels in an asymmetrical design: anchored by a flower and leaf cluster in the lower left corner, the design features a curvilinear vine that incorporates other kinds of leaves and flowers (as well as berries and a glimpse of something that looks like a stylized pinecone)—none of which, of course, would be found on the same vine in nature. Anderson memorably describes the floral motifs that distinguish Ojibwe bags: "the floral-based motifs are artistically successful because they create a symphony of space and movement between a cacophony of leaves, stems, vines, fruits, and flowers" (57). In other words, out of the infinitely diverse and colorful natural world of flowers, plants, and vines, Ojibwe women beaded bandolier bags, creating designs emphasizing beauty, balance, and harmony. Anderson also sees a dynamic sense of movement as important to the floral design of these bags, which "represent rhythmic, flowing, eclectic, asymmetrical designs from the natural world" (57). Indeed, as we will see below, an aesthetic emphasizing equally weighted, flowing asymmetry is a vibrant aspect of Erdrich's intricate narrative design.

Roses are one of the flowers most frequently included on bandolier bags. Wild roses in Minnesota, Anderson points out, have five petals, and bandolier bags often include five-petaled roses that closely resemble prairie roses (69). Other roses on bandolier bags feature heart-shaped petals (found at the anchor point of the pocket panel in figure 2), and even roses with simple round petals may combine different shades of a color for artistic and naturalistic purposes (as found in the flowers on the straps of the bag in figure 2).

Perhaps inspired by the Ojibwe propensity for floral designs featuring roses, Erdrich's lineage of LaRose characters brings to mind the rose as a powerful symbol of Ojibwe culture and female strength. How the first LaRose comes to be called by that name is a small but fascinating moment in the novel. When Wolfred asks the girl for her name, she draws a flower—hence, he assumes that she is named "flower" (or "LaRose," through French voyageur influences on him). She does not tell him her Anishinaabe name because she does not want him "to own her" (*LaRose*

145). But the novel, through the use of third-person omniscient narration, goes on to reveal her Anishinaabe name and her inner convictions: "Her whole being was Anishinaabe. She was Illusion. She was Mirage. Ombanitemagad" (145).

The first LaRose is taken aback when Wolfred begins referring to her as LaRose, or "flower"—"That he called her Flower made her uneasy. Girls were not named for flowers, as flowers died so quickly" (146)—but the name becomes engrained in their family, as the first LaRose bestows the same name on one of her daughters, who passes the name down to her own daughter, and so on. The first four LaRoses are women, followed by the young boy LaRose in Erdrich's novel. They become known for their powers—of flying and healing. Before the first LaRose succumbs to tuberculosis, she passes down essential knowledge to her namesake daughter:

> Before the first LaRose died, she had taught her daughter how to find guardian spirits in each place they walked, how to heal people with songs, with plants, what lichens to eat in an extremity of hunger, how to set snares, jig fish, tie nets, net fish, create fire out of sticks and curls of birchbark. How to sew, how to boil food with hot stones, how to weave reed mats and make birchbark pots. She taught her how to poison fish with plants, how to make arrows, a bow, shoot a rifle, how to use the wind when hunting, make a digging stick, dig certain roots, carve a flute, play it, bead a bandolier bag. She taught her how to tell from the calls of birds what animal had entered the woods, how to tell from the calls of birds which direction and what type of weather was approaching, how to tell from the calls of birds if you were going to die or if an enemy was on your trail. (198–99)

The list continues, impressively cataloging the skill, wisdom, and resilience passed down from the first LaRose to her daughter, culminating in important knowledge concerning survival: "She taught her how to leave behind her body when half awake or in sleep and fly around to investigate what was happening on the earth. She taught her how to dream, how to return from a dream, change the dream, or stay in the dream in order to save her life" (199). The name "LaRose" signifies a powerful presence: it is a name bestowed upon those who preserve traditional Ojibwe knowledges, artistry, and "survivance"[9] and who then pass those teachings on to the next generation.

One of the essential skills LaRose teaches her daughter is how to select medicinal plants and use them to heal people. Linking leaf, floral, and plant motifs to healing is also a significant aspect of the floral designs found on bandolier bags.

Art historian Ruth B. Phillips observes that in Algonkian and Iroquoian traditions, "Plant life is a potential locus of medicine power for healing and also, of course, an integral link in the chain of life, transforming the energy of the greatest *manito*, the sun, into food for animals and humans." She also notes that, "[f]or many Woodlands peoples[,] plants supply the names of spring and summer months when specific foods and medicine can be gathered" (195). Ojibwe women enacted healing rituals—and survivance—in the late nineteenth and early twentieth centuries as they used sales of their beadwork to support themselves and their families at a time of hardship and oppression inflicted by US settler colonialism; they also encoded healing knowledges via beading by highlighting plants that have medicinal properties and are found in their traditional homelands. The emphasis on finding beauty amidst chaos, of locating healing properties in the aftermath of settler colonialism, is visualized in Ojibwe bandolier bags and resonates in the narrative arcs of Erdrich's justice novels.

Narrative Design and Narrative Perspective

The mixture of various real and surreal flowers and leaves in traditional Ojibwe floral beadwork illuminates another significant aspect of Erdrich's narrative design in the justice trilogy: the possibility of viewing the diverse, manifold stories told in each novel as constituting one big book.[10] Indeed Seema Kurup observes, "When read as individual novels, as opposed to viewing the books as part of a trilogy, the fullness of her message may be lost" (114). From my perspective, the novels of the trilogy are linked together by a sinuous vine—formed out of questions of injustice and justice, trauma and healing—with individual characters, events, and chapters rendered sometimes in realistic modes, particularly when Ojibwe history and legal precedents are foregrounded (as when the Judge and Joe discuss specific legal cases in the moldy casserole scene in *The Round House*, for instance). And yet, alongside these textured scenes of material reality, we find many other stories and incidents that take a more "dreamlike" shape—such as when the rolling head pursues Wolfred and the first LaRose throughout *LaRose*, or when the violin mysteriously appears to Shamengwa in a canoe on the lake twenty years after Henri and Lafayette Peace have held their fatal competition in *The Plague of Doves*, or when Mooshum relates the story of Akii, a woman wrongfully accused of being a wiindigoo in *The Round House*, who is saved by her son's actions and devotion.[11]

Like the abundant flora depicted in Ojibwe beaded designs, Erdrich's trilogy employs diverse, distinctive narrative perspectives to convey the main story line and accompanying stories in each novel. *The Plague of Doves* uses the multiple narrators and multiple narrative focal points that have long been associated with Erdrich's novels. There are several characters who are identified by name at the beginning of the key sections of the novel they narrate: Evelina Harp, Judge Antone Bazil Coutts, Marn Wolde, and Doctor Cordelia Lochren. Along with their first-person accounts, Erdrich includes stories told to them and remembered in detail, and so this complex and at times meandering mode of storytelling broadens the scope and reach of the novel. It is Evelina, for instance, who listens carefully to Mooshum's story of finding the murdered Lochren family, followed by the angry lynch mob's pursuit of four innocent Ojibwe men, culminating in the hanging of Asiginak, Holy Track, and Cuthbert. She augments this story by talking to her mother, by visiting Sister Mary Anita, and by confronting Mooshum with the part of the story he left untold. Erdrich's narrative is richly layered, and the depth of color and detail Erdrich includes echoes the flowers and leaves in Ojibwe beaded designs that are outlined and shaded in complementary colors of beads.

Although several key characters carry over from *The Plague of Doves* to *The Round House*, Erdrich employs a strikingly different narrative perspective in the second novel of the trilogy. In *The Round House*, the story is told from one perspective—that of Joe Coutts, a thirteen-year-old boy coming of age and seeking first to understand and then to avenge his mother's rape and attempted murder. Joe tells us the story as a first-person narrator—indeed, as the only first-person narrator in the novel. Erdrich makes a fascinating choice of narrative perspective for this novel: she uses Joe's thirteen-year-old-teenage-boy perspective to narrate the brutal details of the attack on his mother (and on Mayla Wolfskin), and to expose the vagaries and inequalities of the US legal justice system (both as it pertains to the rape and more broadly as it pertains to tribal sovereignty). In other words, the subject matter of the novel seems well beyond the capacity of a typical teenager to be interested in or fully understand. Indeed, for much of the novel, Erdrich allows the teenage-boy aspects of Joe and his buddies to spark the narrative—as when they share their passion for sci-fi, for instance, or as they ride their bikes all over the reservation, or as they share stories of their awakening sexuality. Occasional comments, however, clue readers into the fact that an older Joe—one who has become a lawyer and has married a woman named Margaret (whose grandmother's last name suggestively is Nanapush)—is the voice relating the story. For instance, the opening chapter—which starts out as an ordinary Sunday afternoon but then quickly turns into a tragic scene when Geraldine arrives home beaten, bruised, and bloody and is rushed to the hospital—clearly identifies Joe as having "just turned thirteen" (3). The thirteen-year-old Joe, understandably, does not know how to react to his mother's attack, and it seems that for the first time he is learning what the word "rape" signifies; his reactions are a blend of love, anger, fear, and bewilderment—exactly what we would expect from a teenage boy. However, the flow of Joe's thirteen-year-old consciousness is interrupted by comments that come from Joe as an adult, as when we are told: "Much later, after I had gone into law and gone back and examined every document I could find, every statement, relived every moment of that day and the days that followed, I understood that this was when my father had learned from Dr. Egge the details and extent of my mother's injuries" (14).

As it turns out, the narrative perspective of the novel is a unique presentation of the older Joe's return to the traumatic events of the summer of 1988 in an effort to understand what happened; in his search for meaning, and perhaps to come to some kind of peace with everything, he vividly relives the events, speaking for most of the novel as the thirteen-year-old Joe. Because of the turmoil around him, because his mother continues to be vulnerable, because he is asked to take on huge responsibilities all of a sudden, the teenage Joe comes of age quickly. We might say that the narrative arc of *The Round House* follows Joe as his teenage self and voice are forced to grow up over the course of a few weeks. Joe is deeply sensitive, even as a boy: he listens to everyone (as when he stays awake at night listening to Mooshum's stories of Akii, Old Buffalo Woman, Nanapush, and the building of the round house), he tries to see from other people's perspectives, and so he becomes someone people talk to—Sonja, for instance, or Linda Wishkob. As he adds these other stories to his own experiences as a boy and as an older, wiser adult, Joe brings together a network of stories that offer profound insight into tribal law, violence against Indigenous women, as well as Ojibwe traditions and spirituality. The emotional and intellectual depths of the novel depend upon Joe's richly textured narrative perspective. In this way, Erdrich's narrative design for the novel parallels Ojibwe beadwork designs with their penchant for bringing together many different kinds of colors, flowers, and leaves all connected by a sinuous, meandering vine.

After crafting *The Plague of Doves* using multiple first-person narrators, and then giving over the narrative voice of *The Round House* to one first-person narrator, Erdrich extends her own narrative design by crafting *LaRose* using a third-person omniscient narrator, a narrator who typically follows one character at a time to tell a story from their interior perspective (using what narratologists would call "focalization"). As the novel unfolds, readers also begin to understand that this narrator has the capacity to reveal the spirit world. The boy LaRose often chooses to visit the tree that Dusty liked to climb, the tree Dusty was sitting in when Landreaux accidentally shot him. In a remarkable scene that stands almost at the center of the novel, LaRose spends the night alone beneath that tree, attentively waiting for "the manidoog, the spirits that lived in everything, especially the woods" (209), a teaching that Emmaline and Landreaux have instilled in him. In the morning, as he awakens, he sees a group of people around him: "Half were Indians and half were maybe Indians, some so pale he could see light shining through them" (210). At first the group does not acknowledge his presence, and they talk about him as though he were not there, until one of them points at LaRose and then everyone "acted like relatives who suddenly notice you" (210). And so LaRose learns that the ancestors will be ready to teach him the things he needs to know at the proper time. Indeed, one older woman tells him directly, *"You'll fly like me"* (211). LaRose takes this marvelous encounter all in stride, and he is especially happy to see that Dusty is among the group, and they begin to play together. If only for a few brief pages, the third-person narrator allows readers to vicariously experience LaRose's restorative encounter with the spirits.

The narrative perspective of *LaRose* also sets the stage for the final scene of the novel, which features a graduation party for Hollis. In a 2016 interview with Erdrich, Emily Gray Tedrowe commented that the narrative point of view for *LaRose* is quite different from the novels preceding it. Erdrich did not address Tedrowe's question about point of view directly; rather, she started talking about the importance of community in the novel, noting that "the community . . . is another member of the cast of characters" (Erdrich, "Sunday *Rumpus* Interview")—thus suggesting that she purposefully chose third-person omniscient narrative perspective as a sustained narrative technique that can interconnect diverse peoples, stories, and perspectives. Moreover, Erdrich's use of this narrative perspective leads up to the final scene of *LaRose* in which the community is literally gathered together at the graduation celebration.

As described previously, the striking beauty of Ojibwe beadwork based on floral curvilinear patterns is connected to Ojibwe women's preference for balanced asymmetry, and this is what we find when we read Erdrich's justice trilogy as one big book: a strategic use of multiple narrative perspectives, chosen deliberately to suit the narrative arc of each novel—novels that are related but are not entirely the same, working together to create a beautiful design out of diverse and vibrant perspectives and stories.

Narrative Design, Trauma, and Healing

The range of narrative perspectives in the trilogy builds an artful complexity and a layering of voices and stories. So many of these stories are traumatic. But by viewing the three novels as one big book, readers see the design come together and detect a healing pattern that emerges out of the oppression, violence, and dispossession narrated in each novel. As Kurup suggests: "Though the enactment of restorative justice is not an easy or uncomplicated course, in fact it may be more wrenching and fraught [than] the knee-jerk reaction of violent retribution, it is more compatible with traditional Ojibwe wisdom, cultural values, and norms" (114). This mixture of loss, injustice, and oppression is a striking part of the pattern, but just as the Ojibwe bandolier bag has many individual elements that contribute to its stunning design, so too should the tragic stories and actions of Erdrich's justice novels be linked to an overall design that includes the possibility of reparation, healing, and forgiveness.

In *The Plague of Doves*, Mooshum laments (in his Michif-inflected speech), "there is no justice here on eart" (55), and the novels of Erdrich's justice trilogy depict the absence of justice and the cruelty of injustice time and again. History impinges on the lives of Erdrich's characters in the form of land loss, plagues and epidemics, settler colonialism, laws that diminish sovereignty, intergenerational trauma manifested in alcoholism and drug abuse, as well as in psychological and emotional instability. This is a terrible legacy passed down from generation to generation, as Evelina comes to understand in *The Plague of Doves*:

> But when Neve Harp said that she was going back to the beginning of things and wanted to talk about how the town of Pluto came to be and why it was inside the original reservation boundaries, even though hardly any Indians lived in Pluto, well, both of the old men's faces became like Mama's—quiet, with an elaborate reserve, and something else that has stuck in my heart ever since. I saw that the loss of their land was lodged inside of them forever. This loss would enter me, too. Over time, I came to know that the sorrow was a thing that each of them covered up according to their character—my old uncle through his passionate discipline,

my mother through strict kindness and cleanly order. As for my grandfather, he used the patient art of ridicule.

"What you are asking," said Mooshum that afternoon, opening his hands and his mouth into a muddy, gaping grin, "is how was it stolen? How has this great thievery become acceptable? How do we live right here beside you, knowing what we lost and how you took it?" (84)

This is one of the great scenes of reckoning in Erdrich's justice trilogy: Mooshum bluntly speaks of Ojibwe peoples being swindled out of their lands to Neve—the sister to his nephew-in-law, and the woman he otherwise adores and tries to woo. No matter, the harsh truth is spoken in this scene, and Evelina as a sensitive, perceptive observer also registers that this is her historical legacy—to have "loss" "lodged inside," "forever."

Throughout *The Plague of Doves*, a history of colonialism, genocide, and land loss continues to impact tribal nations in the contemporary moment; the novel also shows how oppression can become internalized and passed down from one generation to the next. In fact, the novels of the justice trilogy reverberate with several key elements of Maria Yellow Horse Brave Heart's (Hunkpapa/Oglala Lakota) theory of historical trauma and unresolved grief. Land loss, violence against Native peoples, the punitive and soul-wounding effects of boarding schools, the relocation of Ojibwe peoples from their homes and tribal communities, the struggle to practice or follow traditional medicine teachings in the contemporary world—all these agonies are present in Erdrich's justice trilogy and they correspond to Brave Heart's historical trauma theory.[12]

Given the historical and legal injustices that plague the novel, one might wonder how *The Plague of Doves* can manage to come to any satisfying or fair resolution. After all, the novel opens with "Solo," the section that narrates the murders of the members of the Lochren family, which sets in motion the actions of the lynch mob, creating ripple effects that come to haunt the living. There is no adequate way—even in the present day—to repair the social and communal fabric torn apart by the lynching of Asiginak, Cuthbert, and Holy Track in *The Plague of Doves* (though the demise of the town of Pluto alluded to in the final pages offers some measure of restoring the land to tribal governance and sovereignty). And yet, the story of the lynch mob eventually is told, which leads to Holy Track's boots being given by Sister Mary Anita to Evelina to Mooshum, which subsequently leads to the full story being revealed, including Mooshum's guilty role. When Evelina and

Mooshum make a trip to the hanging tree to pay their respects, they find the tree has become a resonant site for active remembrance: "Alone in the field, catching light from each direction, the tree had grown its branches out like the graceful arms of a candelabra. New prayer flags hung down—red, green, blue, white. The sun was flaring low, gold on the branches, and the finest of new leaves was showing" (253). They are there to add the boots to the tree, an act Evelina questions when she remarks, "This is sentiment instead of justice" (253). At the same time, the fact that the tree has new growth, that prayer flags are still being added decades after the terrifying event, that the sun flares "gold" at this very moment also indicates the possibility of healing.

Similarly, *The Round House* has a dramatic opening chapter, revealing Geraldine's rape and the way it affects her husband, son, and family. The opening chapter triggers haunting questions of whether the law and the justice system have any resources adequate for solving the crime and punishing the perpetrator. Much of the novel is marked by lingering traumatic repercussions, and the struggle toward healing is especially difficult given that there will be no adequate official legal response to Geraldine's rape or Mayla's murder. In *The Round House*, the legal justice system fails to hold Linden Lark accountable, and so Joe's (and Cappy's) eventual decision to shoot and kill Lark—an act the Judge suggests is in line with old-time "wiindigoo" law (306)—is the only way to protect Geraldine and the community. As the Judge explains, "Lark's killing is a wrong thing which serves an ideal justice. It settles a legal enigma. It threads that unfair maze of land title law by which Lark could not be prosecuted" (306). But to carry out justice in this way is also to create another force that needs to be balanced. In fact, Joe has to learn to live with the consequences of killing another human being, an act that we know from his retrospective narration continues to haunt him into adulthood. The novel too has its own scales of justice that require balancing: after Joe kills Lark, he loses his best friend in a car accident—a means of punishment and atonement for taking a human life.

Real justice continues to be elusive at the end of *The Plague of Doves* and *The Round House*, and yet there is a fragile peace that emerges in the wake of violence and devastation in the novels of the justice trilogy. Erdrich's narrative design, following the striking balanced asymmetries of Ojibwe floral-designed beadwork, relies on the balance of opposing forces, not on ideal justice, to create the sense of an ending, where most crimes have been solved, if not appropriately punished; where the main characters survive with greater insight into the fragility of community, safety, and life. As Joe observes in the last paragraph of *The Round House*, "The sentence was to endure" (317).

The fragile peace at the end of *The Plague of Doves* and *The Round House*, however, shifts toward genuine reparation in *LaRose*. To be sure, the accidental shooting of Dusty Ravich, which opens *LaRose*, sets in motion undercurrents of resentment between Landreaux and Peter, between Nola and Emmaline, despite the compensatory act of sending the boy LaRose to the Raviches to take Dusty's place. Even an accidental shooting can unleash rifts and bitterness, and create forces of unrest in the world: like Mackinnon's rolling head, which terrifyingly pursues the first LaRose and Wolfred through much of their lifetimes, Landreaux's shooting of Dusty creates the stark possibility that Romeo will hatch a successful revenge plot against him, or that Peter's feeling of friendship for Landreaux will be overcome by his desire to avenge his son's death. Even LaRose's adoption into the Ravich family, an act meant to assuage the shooting of Dusty, is not adequate reparation by itself. The loss of LaRose creates a sense of ungovernable grief for Emmaline, and she comes to resent Landreaux's insistence on this act of atonement, creating a rift between them that for a while draws her toward another man, Father Travis. Neither does the gifting of LaRose to the Raviches bridge the rift that has remained steadily in place between the two half-sisters, Emmaline and Nola. Nola's spirit comes back to life in the presence of LaRose, and yet his presence is not enough to prevent her from trying to kill herself. The novel includes so many stories of relationships that have been torn and frayed it would seem almost beyond belief that the novel could end in anything other than the fragile peace that marks the ending of the two justice novels that precede it.

But in *LaRose*, not only is tragedy averted, the community is brought together in the end. The final section of the novel, fittingly entitled "The Gathering," restores community in a beautiful way. Hollis's graduation celebration at Landreaux and Emmaline's house brings people together, even those who have serious reasons to consider staying away, such as Peter and Nola, or Romeo. Even the dog is a vibrant part of the scene. And interpersonal connections are emphasized: Romeo finally tells Hollis who his mother is and how they met; Josette reveals her love for Hollis; Nola understands that Maggie and Waylon are a couple. LaRose is a key figure in the scene: he blesses the food with an eagle feather and burning sage. Most important, he invites the ancestors and offers them food, leading to the moment when they offer their love and wisdom to everyone in both English and Ojibwemowin:

We love you, don't cry.

Sorrow eats time.
Be patient.
Time eats sorrow. (371)

This final scene of Ojibwe community restored is the culmination of the justice trilogy, and it reveals a narrative design that Erdrich has created one character, one scene, one story, one novel at a time. As a writer/beadworker, Erdrich incorporates dark, somber hues of the stories involving injustices, violence, and loss, but her palette also includes dazzling colors for stories that are marked by healing, forgiveness, humor, and compassion. Through her intricate and multihued design, Erdrich repairs rifts in community and in spirit in every novel.

The potential for deep wounds and losses to eventually lead toward healing is one of the great narrative impulses of Erdrich's fictional world. More often than not, Ojibwe traditions and medicine lead to restorative acts and events in Erdrich's justice trilogy. This is one reason why Ojibwe beadwork and traditional floral designs are thematically present in each of the novels. Erdrich's narrative design creates order and kinship in a world that has been riven by injustice, trauma, and malice. The justice novels, read as one big book, gather multifarious narrative strands to hold all of these stories, all of these voices, next to each other—they function as individual beads, ranging widely in color and tone, sewn together to reveal a stunning design. Like the marvelous beaded floral patterns on Ojibwe bandolier bags, Erdrich's novels create beauty amidst chaos, strike restorative balance out of reeling asymmetries, honor Ojibwe traditions while healing the contemporary world so that the wisdom and teachings of the elders can become, once again, a vibrant part of the design.

NOTES

1. See, for example, Jean Wyatt's 2011 essay for an especially insightful analysis of narrative structure in *The Painted Drum*.
2. Beidler and Barton's meticulous work in *A Reader's Guide to the Novels of Louise Erdrich* (rev. ed. 2006), as well as their chapters on the novels in the justice trilogy included in this collection, have helped readers of Erdrich's novels tremendously in this regard.
3. See plates 79 and 81 of Densmore's *Chippewa Customs* for illustrations of some of the traditional geometric patterns found in the beadwork of Ojibwe women. On pp. 183–84, Densmore identifies the most typically used as the "jumping pattern," the "block pattern,"

and the "ottertail pattern."

4. The revised edition of *The Antelope Wife* was published in 2012, the same year that *The Round House* appeared. The retitled version of the novel, *Antelope Woman*, was published in 2016, the same year as *LaRose*.

5. Janet Dean's recent essay on *The Painted Drum* analyzes the ways in which sacred objects—such as the painted drum of the title—are linked to an ethical, Ojibwe way of looking at the world and kinship relations. Her essay also includes an insightful discussion of "beadwork's realignment of relations" in that novel (220).

6. Lois S. Dubin's *Floral Journey* details the history of beading among various Native nations across North America and traces lines of influence on the distinct patterns each Indigenous community developed and became known for; see especially pp. 31–63.

7. Ojibwe women were skilled in two different methods of beading: loom-woven patterns, typically geometric, appeared first; then spot-stitch beading, which allowed for curves, vines, flowers, and leaves to become part of the design, became more prominent.

8. As bandoliers became more frequently designed for regalia or for honoring someone, the pocket became more decorative and less functional. Anderson's book includes images of *gashkibidaaganag* where the slit for the pocket has become so small that the pocket is inaccessible, bags where the slit has been rendered as a line of beads without any opening whatsoever, and bags where there is no visible reminder of the pocket at all (see pp. 36, 53–54, 56, 152).

9. "Survivance" is a term used extensively by Gerald Vizenor (White Earth Anishinaabe) to indicate something "more than survival, more than endurance or mere response; the stories of survivance are an active presence" (15).

10. My phrase "one big book" echoes an exchange between Erdrich and interviewer Lisa Halliday in a 2010 *Paris Review* interview. Halliday asks: "Do you ever feel like you're writing one long novel?" To which Erdrich responds: "All of the books will be connected somehow—by history and blood and by something I have no control over, which is the writing itself. The writing is going to connect where it wants to, and I will have to try and follow along" ("Art of Fiction" 149–50).

11. In an interview with Deborah Treisman of the *New Yorker* (published online in 2015 the same week that Erdrich's story "The Flower" appeared in the print magazine), Erdrich resists making firm distinctions between everyday reality and what Treisman calls "supernatural" elements. Erdrich acknowledges multiple sources for the stories she includes in the novel she was then working on (*LaRose*)—such as Brenda Childs's analysis of the effects of US boarding schools on Native children, trading-era journals and records (including one account that mentions a child being sold by her mother), Cree/

Ojibwe origin stories, spiritual teachings from Ojibwe elders, and so on. Responding to Treisman's query about whether extraordinary events such as flying should be read as "supernatural" or "allegorical," Erdrich says: "These situations are based on such well-known stories and skills that I didn't think them fantastical while I was writing" (Erdrich, "This Week in Fiction").

12. See Brave Heart's 1998 article, coauthored with Lemyra M. DeBruyn, for an analysis of the ways in which devastating moments in Native history may be passed down as intergenerational trauma and unresolved grief. Another widely cited article from 1998 (E. Duran, B. Doran, M. Y. H. Brave Heart, and S. Yellow Horse-Davis) outlines stages of historical trauma that have adversely impacted Native peoples and communities, beginning with contact, colonization, and genocide, and including various epochs of US-Native history such as the establishment of reservations and the loss of land and sustenance, the boarding school period and the loss of Indigenous languages, the relocation era and the loss of religious freedom.

WORKS CITED

Anderson, Marcia G. *A Bag Worth a Pony: The Art of the Ojibwe Bandolier Bag*. Minnesota Historical Society Press, 2017.

Bancroft, Corinne. "The Braided Narrative." *Narrative*, vol. 26, no. 3, 2018, pp. 262–81.

Beidler, Peter G., and Gay Barton. *A Reader's Guide to the Novels of Louise Erdrich*. Revised ed., U of Missouri P, 2006.

Belcourt, Christi. *Beadwork*. Saugeen (Ontario), Ningwakwe Learning Press, 2010.

Brave Heart, Maria Yellow Horse, and Lemyra M. DeBruyn. "The American Indian Holocaust: Healing Historical Unresolved Grief." *American Indian and Alaska Native Mental Health Research*, vol. 8, no. 2, 1998, pp. 56–78.

Dean, Janet. "Getting on with Things: Ontology and the Material in Louse Erdrich's *The Painted Drum*." *Studies in American Indian Literatures*, vol. 32, nos. 1–2, 2020, pp. 209–30.

Densmore, Frances. "Chippewa Customs." *Bureau of American Ethnology Bulletin 86*, 1929, pp. 1–204. [Digitized facsimile available online at https://repository.si.edu/handle/10088/15553.]

Dubin, Lois S. *Floral Journey: Native North American Beadwork*. Autry National Center of the American West, 2014.

Duran, Eduardo, Bonnie Duran, Maria Yellow Horse Brave Heart, and Susan Yellow Horse-Davis. "Healing the American Indian Soul Wound." *International Handbook of Multigenerational Legacies of Trauma*, edited by Yael Danieli, Plenum Press, 1998, pp.

341–54.

Erdrich, Louise. "About the Revision." Included in the P.S. section at the end of *The Antelope Wife*, revised ed., HarperPerennial, 2012, p. 15.

———. *The Antelope Wife*. 1998. Revised ed. HarperPerennial, 2012.

———. "The Art of Fiction No. 208: Louise Erdrich." Interview by Lisa Halliday. *Paris Review*, no. 195, Winter 2010, pp. 133–66.

———. *LaRose*. HarperCollins, 2016.

———. *The Last Report on the Miracles at Little No Horse*. HarperCollins, 2001.

———. *Love Medicine*. Newly revised ed. HarperPerennial, 2009.

———. *The Plague of Doves*. HarperCollins, 2008.

———. *The Round House*. HarperCollins, 2012.

———. "The Sunday *Rumpus* Interview: Louise Erdrich." Interview by Emily Gray Tedrowe, 29 May 2016, http://therumpus.net/2016/05/the-sunday-rumpus-interview-louise-erdrich/.

———. "This Week in Fiction: Louise Erdrich." Interview by Deborah Treisman. *New Yorker*, 22 June 2015, www.newyorker.com/books/page-turner/fiction-this-week-louise-erdrich-2015-06-29.

Kurup, Seema. "From Revenge to Restorative Justice in Louise Erdrich's *The Plague of Doves*, *The Round House*, and *LaRose*." *American Revenge Narratives,* edited by Kyle Wiggins, Springer International, 2018, pp. 99–117. doi.org/10.1007/978-3-319-93746-5.

Lyons, Gene. "In Indian Territory." Review of *Love Medicine*, by Louise Erdrich. *Newsweek*, 11 Feb. 1985, pp. 70–71.

Ojibwe bandolier bag, ca. 1890. Minnesota Historical Society, St. Paul, Accession No. 8701.1. [Full-color digital image available online at http://collections.mnhs.org/cms/display?irn=10084199&return=brand%3Dcms%26q%3D8701.1]

Phillips, Ruth B. *Trading Identities: The Souvenir in Native North American Art from the Northeast, 1700–1900*. U of Washington P, 1998.

Rainwater, Catherine. "Reading between Worlds: Narrativity in the Fiction of Louise Erdrich." *American Literature*, vol. 62, no. 3, 1990, pp. 405–22.

Schultz, Lydia A. "Fragments and Ojibwe Stories: Narrative Strategies in Louise Erdrich's *Love Medicine*." *College Literature*, vol. 18, no. 3, Oct. 1991, pp. 80–95.

Vizenor, Gerald. *Fugitive Poses: Native American Indian Scenes of Absence and Presence*. Lincoln: U of Nebraska P, 1998.

Wyatt, Jean. "Storytelling, Melancholia, and Narrative Structure in Louise Erdrich's *The Painted Drum*." *MELUS*, vol. 36, no. 1, Spring 2011, pp. 13–36.

Debwe, Onaakonige gaye Nanaandawi'iwe

Finding Justice in the Language of Louise Erdrich's Novels

Margaret Noodin

> "Never forget that justice is what love looks like in public."
> —Cornel West, online post

> "Justice is prey to unknown dreams."
> —Judge Antone Bazil Coutts, *The Plague of Doves*

Across time and through tangled histories, Louise Erdrich tells stories of justice, love, and dreaming. She writes in response to civil concerns and savage reality. Her characters want to believe in the combination of order and empathy Cornel West describes as love in public, but they find justice to be a fragile ideal. The dreams and denials they experience illustrate the many ways justice is, and often is not, manifest in society. Erdrich's novels interrogate the way humans understand and embody truth, righteousness, morality, and the many other philosophical ideas related to justice. She asks whether balanced equity is possible for imperfect beings to maintain and whether the scales of justice represent a separation of opposites or a recognition of complex, overlapping dependencies. To construct the most holistic representation possible of justice, Erdrich reaches beyond English and incorporates other languages fluidly. Defining a community through language, for Erdrich, is a sound methodology for constructing the most holistic representation possible of justice in modern Anishinaabe society. Although the most common non-English language added to Erdrich's novels is Ojibwemowin, there are traces of other voices that shape the overall reading of her work. Peter Beidler and Gay Barton have offered a summary of the Ojibwemowin used in previous novels, and it is a continuation of their close reading that inspires this essay. By examining the non-English words and phrases Erdrich adds to novels written in English, the limits she places on translation, her use of the English word "justice," and the way Erdrich's ideas of justice might be expressed in Ojibwemowin, readers will find a complex and nuanced view of Anishinaabe society that offers paradigms for understanding human nature more broadly.

Arguably, all of Erdrich's novels deal with justice. *The Future Home of the Living God* reveals what might happen when social justice is deconstructed, and *The Painted Drum* seeks historic justice for a living artifact as it returns home. *The Antelope Wife*, in its original and revised form, and the stories of Fleur Pillager, especially in *Four Souls* and *Tracks*, show how justice, or the lack of it, can shape a personality and can be either stolen or given freely. However, three of Erdrich's novels focus more specifically on the theme of justice. *The Plague of Doves* illustrates how the truth of intergenerational injustice casts a long shadow not often recognized and rarely removed by those who live beneath it. In *The Round House* the modern system designed to uphold legal justice fails and more ancient constructs are resurrected. In *LaRose*, one life is taken, and one life is given, posing the question of whether justice can be found in a binary equation and how the living can be healed by those no longer alive.

Language is a meager vessel for human ideas and experience, but it is the soul and substance of storytelling. Words are the seeds of parables, oaths, dialogue, and record-keeping. Throughout her novels Erdrich uses the English word "justice" sparingly and never offers a direct translation for the concept in any language. To describe events and outcomes in the fictional multicultural communities she creates, Erdrich typically includes an average of fifty non-English words in each novel.[1] The most common language she uses is Ojibwemowin, which shares a confederated history with Odawa and Potawatomi, which is why all three of these languages are also known collectively as Anishinaabemowin. Ojibwemowin, Odawa, and Potawatomi are three of thirty-two related Algonquian languages that have been spoken in the North American Great Lakes and woodland region for several thousand years. The fact that Erdrich includes endangered languages in her modern novels is a form of decolonizing justice. These languages were once presumed to be inferior and were outlawed in the United States until the Native Languages Act of 1990. By asking readers to remember and seek meaning in these languages, she changes the linguistic landscape of American literature.

Connected to Ojibwemowin by history and economy, French is the second most common non-English language used in Erdrich's justice novels. French came to the continent when New France extended from the northeastern tip of North America along the waterways south of Hudson's Bay, past Lake Winnipeg into the Great Lakes region, continuing south along the banks of the Mississippi to the Gulf of Mexico. Many names of people and places mark its presence, and French is still one of the official languages of Canada today. French is used in *The Round House* and *LaRose* but appears most often in *The Plague of Doves*, where it connects two generations to their undocumented past and imagined future. Evelina strives for a bilingual identity as she practices saying "la nord, le sud, l'ouest, et l'est sont les quatre points cardinaux," and readers are directed to consider the importance of the four cardinal directions as Erdrich again demonstrates the way symbols ripple across cultures (*Plague* 191).

When Anishinaabe and Cree people encountered French traders and Jesuit missionaries in the seventeenth century, they moved between languages as needed, but as families and fates were blended, the Michif language was created by the French, Cree, and Ojibwe people. Michif became one of the common languages in the Red River Valley and Great Lakes region, where it also serves as a reminder of old alliances, the injustice suffered by Louis Riel, and the ongoing anti-colonial efforts of the Métis people. Mooshum's name is the Michif variation of the Ojibwe word *mishomis* (grandfather), and the phrases he uses illustrate how he keeps the Métis language alive, just as his brother kept Métis music alive. Most often he simply uses a Michif interjection as a reply, and frequently these interjections are cognates to Ojibwemowin. For example, *tapway* echoes the Ojibwemowin *debwe*, meaning correct, and appears several times in *The Plague of Doves* (24, 42, 59, 243). It is also a marker of truth, a verb used to account for reality and seek justice through an alternate cultural perspective.

Erdrich's justice novels also trace the layers of America's immigrant past and present. As characters use German, Italian, Korean, Polish, Spanish words and exclamations, they reflect the complex identity of the United States. There was a time when *ya vole*, used in *The Plague of Doves*, would have been cause for discrimination, but today it is only one of many phrases woven into the fabric of American

English (72). Spanish and Italian were languages of conquest, which became the dialects of immigrants. While the phrase *la vida loca* used in *LaRose* is reminiscent of a popular twentieth-century song, it is also a reminder of unavoidable diversity (101). Less recognizable are the older layers of linguistic history that were formed when the old world (which some thought was new) exceeded anything a colonial language could describe, and so words from Indigenous languages slipped into the American English vernacular as place names, nouns, and events. Many have now been fully adopted into English. Erdrich uses *chinook* and *toboggan* in this way in *The Round House* (181, 186).

To truly expand the idea of language and intelligibility, Erdrich includes mention of characters "speaking in tongues" in *The Plague of Doves* and a small sample of the completely fictional Klingon language in *The Round House*. The Klingon phrase "*Heghlu meh qaq jajvam*," which means "this is a good day to die" (197), is a typical warrior sentiment and draws a comparison between real Lakota and imagined Klingon societies. The statement is commonly attributed to Lakota warriors (although it has only been recorded as such by non-Native editors), but it has now taken on significance in pan-tribal modern culture. The overall message, like the parable of Babel, demonstrates how linguistic diversity, while serving to divide communities, also allows people to preserve and protect individual perspectives, creating circles of communication and innovation that add to, rather than detract from, the whole. By creating justice through a multilingual landscape, Erdrich's characters maintain or assert their individual and collective identities as they survive varying political storms, philosophical seasons, and spiritual crises. Her characters are the original inhabitants, immigrants, martyrs, murderers, heroes, fools, lawyers, sinners, victims, and innocents who narrate their own lives, the lives of their ancestors, their children, and the gods and demons at the edge of perception. Their words are attempts to both preserve the past and control the present, seeking justice for all while grappling with the seeming impossibility of that desire.

The majority of the non-English words in the justice novels are Ojibwemowin, which Erdrich uses for a wide range of reasons as she tells each story of justice. Perhaps the most basic use is the insertion of exclamations that destabilize the soundscape. Just when a reader might know what to expect, Mooshum's hiss of "saah" serves as a reminder that his instincts and exasperation are grounded in Michif and Ojibwemowin (*Round House* 215, 218). *Howah*, used as an equivalent to "wow," serves the same purpose and is found in each of the justice novels (*Plague* 35, 39, 77; *Round House* 204, 273; *LaRose* 81). Yet another example, *mii'iw*, creates space in a sentence and signals that the story is about to continue (*LaRose* 89). The modern and pan-tribal "eyyyy" is used in *The Round House* as a pointer to solidarity and survivance in times of golf courses, gas stations, powwows, and continued injustice (203, 205, 273). These are some of the words often used even by those who cannot speak the language of their ancestors. They are markers of community that sound foreign but are familiar in a way that marks English as the "foreign" language in some places.

Beyond shifting the overall soundscape of the text, Erdrich acknowledges the verb-based nature of Ojibwemowin and the action-based worldview of the Anishinaabe people. Where English typically focuses on the subject and then what happens, Ojibwemowin focuses on the action and who or what is connected to it. Some of the verbs she uses, including *biindige* (come in), *miigwech* (thanks), *wiisini* (to eat), *boogid* (to fart), *maajaa* (to leave) and *weweni* (take care), are so common they are part of the shared vernacular in Anishinaabe communities (*Round House* 62, 72, 102, 215; *LaRose* 101, 108). In a few instances she uses verbs not easily translated into English and allows them to represent the ways cultures differ. For instance, with connections to *giiwanaadingwaan* (to have a bad dream) and *giiwanaadizi* (to be mentally unstable), when *giiwanimo* is used in *LaRose*, it means much more than simply "to lie" (264).

As much as Erdrich might wish to reflect Anishinaabe linguistic structure in her novels, because they are written in English, nouns unavoidably dominate. But her use of nouns, as names and objects, often brings readers back to the basic verb. Many of the names in her novels are intransitive verbs that describe natural phenomena. For example, *ombaanitemigad*, the verb used to express the occurrence of a mirage, is particularly significant because it is the name carried by each person named LaRose. Related to *ombaangeni* (to raise up) and *ombaashi* (to be lifted on wind), the word evokes power and transformation, an ability to maintain a core identity despite what others see. When the youngest LaRose is sent away from his parents, they speak his name, Ombaanitemigad, because they believe "[t]hat name would protect him from the unknown, from what had been let loose with the accident" (*LaRose* 105). Other names in *LaRose* reflect the atmosphere and landscape: Awan (fog), Anakwad (cloud), Mashkiig (swamp), and Shingobii (balsam). One name is simply humorous, as some names are. Mrs. Webid, an old friend of Mrs. Peace, laughs and teases young Romeo, making him uncomfortable, which is particularly funny if the reader knows the definition of *webid* is "tooth" in Ojibwemowin.

In *The Round House* Erdrich uses eighteen different Ojibwemowin names, most of them remembered during a visit to the cemetery. Multiple cultures are woven among the memories with a first name in Ojibwemowin, a Catholic name in the middle, and the translation of the first name used as the newly required last name. Through these names and languages, Erdrich illustrates the process of cultural erasure and the struggle to maintain Indigenous identity. The names appear on gravestones "covered by fine gray lichen" with the Midewijig and Christians beside one another in the family plot.

- *Shawanobinesiik*, Elizabeth, Southern Thunderbird.
- *Adik*, Michael, Caribou.
- *Kwiingwa'aage*, Joseph, Wolverine.
- *Mashkiki*, Mary, The Medicine.
- *Ombaashi*, Albert, Lifted by Wind.
- *Makoons*, The Bearling and
- Bird Shaking Ice Off Its Wings. (*Round House* 100; emphasis added)

The list ends with two names that defy the new format; presumably they were not christened or counted by the Indian agent. *Makoons* is simply The Bearling, and Bird Shaking Ice Off Its Wings is recorded without the Ojibwemowin version, *Bipawaangeni-Bineshi-Gii-Agwanamikwamiigaazo*. One other name included in *The Round House*, within an older embedded story, is Akiikwe, whose name means Earth Woman, and "like her namesake she was solid" (179).

The Plague of Doves has only two Ojibwemowin names: *Shamengwa*, an uncommon name meaning "monarch butterfly," and *Asiginak*, which is a common and historically significant name meaning "blackbird." For members of the Anishinaabe diaspora, *Asiginak* connotes omens and treaty signings, while *Shamengwa* represents the elegance and artistry of dancers and performers. The non-English name uttered most often in the justice novels is the Michif name Mooshum. Like other children who know their elders first as branches on the family tree, Evelina looks to Mooshum for stories and explanations. Grandfathers are teachers. What they teach and how clear the lessons will be may vary. Erdrich's use of Ojibwemowin shows how names can be individual talismans or mimetic connections to ancestors or nature. They can serve to uphold or change a single or shared identity, and they are used by Erdrich to map the multicultural histories of her characters.

Using Ojibwemowin within English sentences causes more nouns to appear in the text, but the story they tell is one of geography and genealogy. Relationships between people are fixed within an Anishinaabe cultural context through language. Consider the intimacy created by the following words:

- *niiji*—friend (*LaRose* 32)
- *gwiiwisens*—little boy or son (*LaRose* 109)
- *kookum*—your/our grandma (*LaRose* 23, *Round House* 73)
- *nokomis*—my grandma (*LaRose* 357)
- *nimoshe*—sweetheart (*Plague* 104)

Not only are these nouns able to preserve family relationship terms, they also preserve the connections between concepts. *Niiji* is very close to the verb *wiijiw*, to be with someone. *Gwiiwis*, son, is very close to the idea of making a bundle, *wiiwegan*, and having a wife, *wiiwi*. *Nimoshe*, also spelled *niinimoshenh*, is a reference to which branch of cousins are available for marriage in the complex kinship system. When all else falls away and is no longer allowed, terms of endearment endure.

Beyond terms for family and personal relationships, Erdrich uses Ojibwemowin to indicate social roles. *Ogemakwe* is a term for the "traditional head woman" or "female chief" (*LaRose* 234). The word is also sometimes translated as "queen" or any woman in a position of power or strength. Knowing the Ojibwemowin terms *ogi*, which is to raise someone, and *ogimaakandaw*, which is to govern others, shapes the way the word is used and understood. Another community role is *akiwenzi*, which is simply an elder man or one who has lived on the earth a long time, and is a term used in *LaRose* (234). Erdrich also includes a variation on this term with an added ending, *akiwenzhiish*, to indicate the way old men can become tricksters, fools, and troublemakers; this playful variation is found in *The Round House* (183).

Many of the other nouns Erdrich includes are also verbs at their core, which emphasizes the Anishinaabe tendency of focusing on the action of an object as the reason for its existence. Several of these words illustrate the way Anishinaabe words are constructed. For example, *mashkiki*, meaning medicine (*Round House* 100), combines the verb *mashkawizi*, to be strong, with *aki*, the earth, to communicate the concept of the earth as sustainable source of support for stamina, health, and healing. Adding the prefix *makade-*, meaning the color black, and the suffix *-waboo* to indicate a liquid, the word for coffee, *makademashkikiwaboo*, is easily understood as black medicine water (*LaRose* 81). Similarly, Erdrich uses the word *bashkizigan* (a gun), which is literally translated as something that can *baashkide* or explode (*Round House* 183). She also includes several of the Ojibwemowin words adopted into English, including "moccasin" (*LaRose* 70, 63, 199) and "toboggan" (*Round House* 186). "Toboggan" comes from the older verbs *odaabaadan*, meaning "to haul," and *odaabaa'ige*, meaning "to drag," and has now been applied to such Ojibwemowin terms for modern vehicles as *odaabaan* (car) and *gichidaabaan* (bus) today. As she does in many other books, most notably in the *Birchbark House* series, Erdrich threads lessons about the language in her prose.

Other nouns add dimension to the setting, marking it as Anishinaabe territory, by naming the co-inhabitants of the space. Knowing the range and habitat of plants and animals can clarify community space and mark the parameters of an ecosphere without the use of contemporary geopolitical boundaries. Naming the familiar nonhumans is a way to invoke other ways of knowing and other ways of seeking justice. All of the following are familiar to Anishinaabe people:

- *wiikenh*—sweet flag (*Round House* 39)
- *kinnikinnick*—red willow (*Round House* 39, *LaRose* 23)
- *waaboose*—rabbit (*LaRose* 30)
- *opichi*—a robin (*Round House* 41)
- *ma'iingan*—wolf (*Round House* 48)
- *adik*—caribou (*Round House* 107)
- *ajijaak*—crane (*Round House* 133, 142)
- *bizhew*—lynx (*Round House* 73)
- *shigag*—skunk (*Round House* 48)
- *miikinaak*—box turtle (*Round House* 154)
- *mishikenh*—snapping turtle (*Round House* 154)

Over time, the presence of these plants and animals has changed, which has impacted both the ecosystem and the social system in the region. Many of these beings are connected to the *doodemag*, or clan system, mentioned several times in *The Round House* (133, 134, 147). Erdrich does not address these changes, but by inserting the older Ojibwemowin words for these nonhuman characters she reminds readers of a time before the existence of the United States, Canada, treaties, and reservation boundaries.

One category of beings in Anishinaabe country never received English names. If Erdrich wants to include the original identity of these nonhuman characters, she is required to use their Anishinaabe names. For instance, she refers to the *aadizookaanag* in *LaRose* (11). Ojibwemowin has a specific word, *dibaajimowinan*, for stories, news, theater, and literature; by contrast, *aadizookaanag* are the living, complex narratives who take the same verb forms as animals and people. This is not to say these narratives should be personified, only that when speaking of them, the relationship they have to things and beings is more layered. Sometimes they are described as teaching tales, fables, or legends, but these are terms with limitations. *Aadizookaanag* are messengers we both create and are created by. They are set in absolute time, which is beyond the relative time we perceive in our lives, and they mark the beginning of Anishinaabe history, humor, ritual, and law. By referring to them as *aadizookaanag*, Erdrich shows that her characters understand the difference between literary traditions and maintain important distinctions within their own tradition.

Erdrich also mentions *animikiig* (*LaRose* 121), *gizhe-manido* (*LaRose* 359), *manidoog* (*LaRose* 209), *Nanabozho* and *Wishketchahk* (*LaRose* 293, *Round House* 181). Not one of these can be easily translated. The *animikiig* are often called "thunder beings" and described as giant raptors. They are inhabitants of a realm beyond earth, and their voices mark the end of winter when seasons change and new life begins with a rush of water. They are closely associated with the electrical discharge that causes lightning, followed by the waves of sound we know as thunder. In many stories they provide protection, but also teach humility. Young LaRose is not afraid of a storm that scares his adoptive sister because "[h]is father had put an eagle feather up in the lodge for him and talked to the Animikiig; he had explained to the thunder beings where LaRose lived so that they wouldn't shoot lightning and hit him or anyone else in that house" (*LaRose* 121).

Gizhe-manido is similarly complex, and once again Erdrich includes the Ojibwemowin as a sign that her characters know these words and their meanings. In fact, late in the novel when Josette and Snow mention *Gizhe-manido*, it is with syncretic irony and humor, including a hand sign for best friends and a background soundscape from the movie *Terminator*. The girls are beading with their grandmother, while also watching the movie, when Snow says, "Don't forget to make a mistake . . . you know, to let the spirit out," to which Josette automatically replies, "Only the Creator is perfect" (*LaRose* 358). They don't dwell on the fact that Anishinaabe cosmology and spiritual tradition include a central essence responsible for creation. The girls are young, and it is enough to know that mistakes happen and are part of a greater design. As the author, Erdrich may be emphasizing intentional imperfection and human entropy, but she works around the idea rather than addressing it directly. The *manido*—which is either given a superlative prefix (*gichi-*) or a dynamic centralizing prefix (*gizhe-*)—is one of several *manidoog* mentioned in the justice novels. LaRose takes comfort in knowing "the manidoog, the spirits that lived in everything, especially the woods" (*LaRose* 209). By using both *gizhe-manido* and *manidoog*, Erdrich makes clear there are roles among the spirits relative to nature and the universe, a perspective that is quite different from the contrasting Christian tradition of the settlers who spoke of a personified dominant male in heaven with winged warriors at his command (as in Psalm 103, for instance).

Not least of all are the references to Nanabozho and Wishketchahk, who are both real and imagined on several levels in the work of Erdrich. The Anishinaabe Nanabozho and the Cree Wishketchahk are part of the third old story Ignatia tells LaRose. In the story Ignatia explains this figure as "a being who could do many things," who is "kind of foolish, but also very wise," and has many other names (*LaRose* 293). By using his Anishinaabe and Cree names, Erdrich connects the two literary traditions and acknowledges both as part of contemporary culture. Stories of Nanabozho are typically classified as *aadizookaanag* and are constantly rewriting themselves. Erdrich has included allusions to Nanabozho in many of her poems and stories, perhaps most infamously as the Ojibwe man Nanapush, who held onto traditional Anishinaabe belief systems and came to be known as a source of both knowledge and protection but also lust and irreverence in *Tracks* and other novels. His father, who also carried the name Mirage, told him: "Nanapush. That's what you'll be called. Because it's got to do with trickery and living in the bush. Because it's got to do with something a girl can't resist. The first Nanapush stole fire. You will steal hearts" (*Tracks* 33). The name of the fictional Nanapush's mother was Akiikwe, which is mentioned in *The Round House* during Mooshum's nighttime storytelling. Her nickname was Akii, Earth, and one winter her husband accused her of becoming wiindigoo (*Round House* 180).

Wiindigoo is the most frequently used Ojibwemowin word in *The Round House* (180, 182, 184, 187, 213, 214, 236, 248, 306). As the facts of the brutal crime are revealed, Joe learns from Mooshum's stories about creatures who represent an alternate form of justice. The basic etymology ties the word to the prefix *wiin-*, used to indicate something dark or opaque, but branches beyond the simple *wiinibiig* of silty Lake Winnebago and Lake Winnipeg to the idea of *wiini'iwe*, being responsible for defiling or polluting something, or *wiindigoowi*, to become a *wiindigoo* who preys on others. Mooshum explains, "A wiindigoo could cast its spirit inside of a person. That person would become an animal, and see fellow humans as prey meat" (*Round House* 180). This becomes an archetype for sociopathic behavior in the eyes of young Joe Coutts.

Erdrich's use of individual words in Ojibwemowin, as well as full phrases and sentences, is strategic throughout the justice trilogy. Erdrich places individual words into English sentences to help readers make connections not possible in English. Sometimes Erdrich includes full phrases that offer more than alternate definitions. Full sentences in languages other than English allow readers to see when and why characters might express themselves in a language other than the one that has become the dominant mode of expression. Often, these actions and relationships appear to be a single word, but they are verbs with pronoun prefixes and suffixes extending their meaning to equal a full sentence in English.

In *LaRose* Wolfred uses Ojibwemowin when he tells LaRose "giimiikawaadiz" (you are beautiful) first in the dismal trade cabin and again when she returns, elegant and educated after attending school in the east (20, 189). In the first instance it might be assumed that Ojibwemowin was the only language the first LaRose knew as a child of only eleven years, but by the time she returned from boarding school his use of the phrase would be an exception, a choice, not necessary but intentional. To use the word similar in Ojibwemowin to *miikwenimo*, meaning confidence, says a great deal about the way he loves her and recognizes her ability to love herself. Another word sentence is used when the first LaRose reflects on the power of language and identity.

> Her whole being was Anishinaabe. She was Illusion. She was Mirage. Omban-itemagad. Or what they called her now—Indian. As in, *Do not speak Indian*, when she had been speaking her own language. It was hard to divide off parts of herself and let them go. . . . My thoughts are all tangled up, she said out loud to herself, Inbiimiskwendam. (*LaRose* 145)

Using a single word, "Inbiimiskwendam," she conveys a loss of self by using the first-person prefix *in-* with a morpheme indicating a twisted line, *biimasko-*, and the root verb for consciousness, *endamo*. Although the rough equivalent in English—"my thoughts are all tangled up"—could serve as a translation, "in-biimiskwendam" reveals the intimacy of interior unraveling. Through LaRose's use of Ojibwemowin, Erdrich deconstructs, decolonizes, and unsettles settler stereotypes and assumptions about language and culture that led to the creation of an ethnocidal education system.

Confronting a tangle of another sort in *The Plague of Doves*, Erdrich uses phrases to show the ways languages and identity can mix without dissolution.

Sometimes characters combine languages, as Henri Peace does when he says "Gaawiin ojidaa, ma frère" combining Ojibwemowin and French, followed by "I am sorry to have insulted you" in English. He is described as speaking "the French-Chippewa patois as well as either English or pure Chippewa or Cree" (*Plague* 101). Through Henri, Erdrich reminds readers of Indigenous polyglottal traditions. Sometimes characters use only untranslated Ojibwemowin: "Aniin ezhinikaazoyan? (*Plague* 78); "Minopogoziwag ingiw zaasakok waanag" (*Round House* 73). At other times characters use only untranslated French, as Evelina does to prove she knows the language: "*Je vais à Paris, je vais à Paris. Je n'ai jamais visité la belle capitale de la France*" (*Plague* 183). Her comment reveals that her connection to France is limited, but she uses French because it is the language of literature, of Camus, and the University. She never considers studying Métis, although she easily translated Mooshum's sentence for Marn Wolde, to whom it is completely foreign. Furthermore, the sentence she translates, "La michiinn li doctoer ka-ashtow ita la koulayr kawkeetuhkwawkayt," which means "the *Michif* doctor your bites from snakes he will treat," is proof of both her linguistic capabilities and the value of Métis traditional medicine (*Plague* 192).

What readers will not find in Erdrich's justice novels is a translation of the word "justice," although it appears in English in each novel. Instead, we find in these novels multiple Anishinaabe concepts relating to justice that require more than a single word. This is perhaps the reason Erdrich does not attempt to move the term from one language to another. What she does instead is offer three views of justice that could be categorized as actions centering on *debwe* (truth), *onaakonige* (decision-making), and *nanaadawi'iwe* (healing). This multidimensional view of justice is one that originates in Anishinaabe language, praxis, and philosophy but can be applied beyond Ojibwe, Odawa, and Potawatomi communities.

Debwemigad mizwe. Truth is universal. The challenge lies in verification and interpretation. In *The Round House*, Erdrich writes about the connection between justice, violence, and the way humans organize their own perceptions of reality. For the Anishinaabeg the network of *doodemag*, a noun derived from the words *doodam* (to do something) and *doodaw* (to do something for others), is the original system of law and order. "An Ojibwe person's clan meant everything at one time and no one didn't have a clan, thus you knew your place in the world and your relationship to all other beings" (*Round House* 153). Judge Coutts tells his son: "The clan system punished and rewarded; it dictated marriages and regulated commerce; it told which animals a person could hunt and which to appease, which would have pity on the doodem or a fellow being of that clan, which would carry messages up to the Creator" (*Round House* 154). Elsewhere, he speaks about responsibilities across generations, saying, "These sorts of complications are simply part of tribal justice" (*Plague* 209). And he illustrates his point about connections between animals and humans with two stories, one about his aunt who was saved by a turtle, and another, from Greek historian Herodotus, about Arion of Methymna, who was saved by a dolphin (*Round House* 155).

Judge Coutts and his son, Joe, speak of justice as the responsibility of someone with a clan role and community context to recognize truth. Truth has been weighed, measured, and represented in many languages and on many continents by Bear and Ajijaak clan leaders, Egyptian Anubis, Roman goddess Justitia, and Greek Themis with her daughter Dice. As the end of the Roman Empire drew near, Cicero was busy translating Greek philosophy into Latin and among other things wrote, "Fundamentum autem est iustitiae fides, id est dictorum conventorumque constantia et veritas" (24).[2] Cicero believed the foundation of justice is faith and fidelity to promises and agreements. Meanwhile on another continent, the Anishinaabeg were developing sustainable ecological practices, gardening, and creating food caches (see Howey). As they managed their resources collectively, it is likely they were perfecting the oral arguments of their own traditional justice systems. While there are no direct quotations from the Anishinaabe orators of the time, Ojibwemowin, unlike Latin, is still in use and, unlike English, has not evolved to include vocabulary and grammar from other languages. Contained in the morphology of the words and the semiotics of the clan system are the philosophies of the people. The following verbs show some of the connections between various concepts:

- *debwe*—to be correct
- *debwetaw*—to believe, trust, or obey
- *diba'ige*—to measure or determine payment
- *debise*—to be enough
- *dibendaagwad* or *dibendaagozi*—to belong or be a member

Anishinaabe justice perceived through this lens is based on accountability and the need to enact the truth through *dibaajimo*, telling stories or sharing the news.

After seeking universal truth, there is the implication in Erdrich's novels that justice requires an active response. Seeking justice involves making decisions. Her novels contain violence, confusion, and disintegration, which leads Mooshum to say "there is no justice here on eart" (*Plague* 55) and Judge Coutts to claim "justice is prey to unknown dreams" (*Plague* 117). At Shamengwa's funeral Father Cassidy declares, *"The Metis believed in a merciful God, you see, but it is my sorry duty to report that God is also just"* (*Plague* 211). At the end of *The Plague of Doves*, Evelina offers a view of justice through contrast when she tosses Holy Track's boots into the branches of a tree and muses, "this is sentiment instead of justice," which can only mean that acts of justice require a lack of sentiment (253). The best description of a just and equitable act in Ojibwemowin is *onaakonige*, which is often translated as "to decide," but is used in the context of voting and treaty making to represent a social decision with consequences. The words with *onaakon* as a root morpheme relate to the framework of justice in society:

- *onaakon*—decide on, judge, sentence someone
- *onaakonan*—decide about, plan something
- *onaakonige*—decide, plan, judge something; to be in court
- *onaakonigewin*—a decision, a policy, a law or treaty
- *onaakosidoon*—to set something up as frame

In *The Round House* Bazil tells his injured wife, "there will be justice" (156), which leads their son, Joe, to believe in "murder, for justice" (280). They seek judgment without mercy. In *LaRose* Romeo saw life as a movie where "revenge was justice" (322) because he also seeks actions he believes will compensate for his experience. Each of these examples involve decisions, *onaakonigewinan*, with outcomes. Erdrich's stories describe justice as taking action, but an additional element is required to make the modern form of Anishinaabe justice echo the older ancient version. According to this set of novels, Anishinaabe justice is more than truth followed by an active response. There is an implication that the response should lead to healing, *nanaandawi'iwe*. When Emmaline and Landreaux give their son to Peter and Nola, it is described as "an old form of justice," an act of balance and restoration (*LaRose* 36).

Across the relatively short arc of human existence on earth, many individual thinkers, alone or as representatives of various cultures and communities, have attempted to define justice because it is a volatile concept able to destroy or repair social organisms. Confucian concepts of relational and restorative justice, in addition to distributive justice, were recorded by his followers in *The Analects* and spread throughout the world around 500 BC (Confucius 123). The concept that has come to be known as "the Golden Rule" has been part of civic decision-making and religious foundations in many cultures and has been advocated by the Greek philosophers, Jesus Christ, and the Prophet Mohammad, to name only a few (Braithwaite and Yan Zhang 24). Clearly, global political philosophy has strands of continuity across continents, but these ideas are also slightly changed in each situation and nation. Applying this ideal to the colonization that set the backdrop for Erdrich's justice novels, we find that although George Washington said "law can never make just [that] which in its nature is unjust" (qtd. in Allen 107), he was speaking of injustice toward members of his own community and not of national values applied to others or carried forward in time, which is why Frederick Douglass had to remind Americans in an 1886 speech he delivered in Washington, DC, "The American people have this lesson to learn: That where justice is denied, where poverty is enforced, where ignorance prevails, and where any one class is made to feel that society is an organized conspiracy to oppress, rob, and degrade them, neither persons nor property will be safe" (434). One year earlier, in 1885, Métis leader and elected president of the Provisional Government of Saskatchewan, Louis Riel, was executed by the Canadian government. At his trial he declared: "What you will do in justice to me, in justice to my family, in justice to my friends, in justice to the North-West, will be rendered a hundred times to you in this world, and to use a sacred expression, life everlasting in the other" (Riel 154).

Erdrich's novels are the legacy of these men who strove to understand justice. In each case, they sought justice for themselves and those counted as members of their own communities, but failed to find a sustainable solution that could heal the pain of previous injustices. The characters of Erdrich's novels, using many languages, attempt to carry on the search for justice that is both equalizing and sustainable. In *LaRose*, elder storyteller Ignatia Thunder is correct, *debwe*, when she says, "we are chased into this life." We begin our lives as part of a complex relational network of stories, beliefs, and historical precedents. For the Anishinaabeg this landscape of human and nonhuman participants includes rolling heads, transformational snakes, dangerous escapes, love affairs, prayers, songs for all occasions, and lessons learned in and out of school. Erdrich's characters are constantly making choices, *onaakonigewag*, as they write the stories of their own lives. Against the social expectation to choose a life of tradition or assimilation, they are constantly fusing realities. Ultimately, the language of Erdrich's novels, the words she uses and does not use, suggests that they are in search of ways to heal, *nanaandawi'iwewag*, to move through time in balance with the universe and one another. At the end of the novel *LaRose*, which is arguably barely the beginning of his life, young LaRose is gifted with a chorus from his ancestors who "spoke in both languages" (371):

> *We love you, don't cry.*
> *Sorrow eats time.*
> *Be patient.*
> *Time eats sorrow.*

Their words remind us that communities continuing to seek justice must trust in time as a source of the strength needed to evolve. I find hope in taking time to translate the novel's final words into Anishinaabemowin:

> *Gizaagigo, gego mawiken.*
> *Apii osidaawendamoyan beji-diba'igane.*
> *Akawaabin.*
> *Gegaa-apii jiikendamoyan mii dash gizhii-diba'igane.*

Glossary for Erdrich's Recent Novels

Please note that this glossary matches the orthography of the novels and does not conform with a specific dictionary.

KEY TO ABBREVIATIONS OF NOVELS
- PD—*The Painted Drum*
- PL—*The Plague of Doves*
- RH—*The Round House*
- LR—*LaRose*

Part One: Anishinaabe Words and Phrases

WORD / PHRASE	ENGLISH EQUIVALENT	PART OF SPEECH	NOVEL AND PAGE
aadizookaanag	living stories	noun	LR 11
aaniin	hi	greeting	RH 224
aniin ezhinikaazoyan	what are you called	phrase	PD 124; PL 78
adik	caribou	noun (name)	RH 100

WORD / PHRASE	ENGLISH EQUIVALENT	PART OF SPEECH	NOVEL AND PAGE
ahau	ok	exclamation	PD 182
ajijaak	crane	noun	RH 133, 142
akii	earth	noun (name)	RH 179 (ff.)
akiikwe	earth woman	noun (name)	RH 179 (ff.)
akiwenzhiish	naughty old man	noun	RH 183
akiwenzii	old man	noun (name)	PD 164; RH 74
amanisowin	haunting	noun	PD 111
ambe	come in	verb	PD 113
anakwad	cloud	noun (name)	PD 108 (ff.); LR 121, 187
animikiig	thunder	noun	LR 121
anishaaindinaa	just kidding	phrase	RH 205, 206
anishinaabeg	Anishinaabe people	noun (people)	PD 108; PL 78; RH 182; LR 293
anishinaabe	anishinaabe	adjective	RH 273
anishinaabemowin	anishinaabe language	noun	LR 51
apijigo miigwech	very much thanks	phrase	RH 73
apitchi	robin	noun (name)	PD 189
asiginak	blackbird	noun (name)	PL 61 (ff.); RH 53
awan	fog	verb (name)	LR 7
awee	oh	exclamation	RH 203
awegonen	who	phrase	PD 125
bashkizigan	shotgun	noun	RH 183
bashkwegin	leather	noun	PD 126
bezhig	one	number	PD 132
biindigeg	come in you all	verb	LR 108
bijiu	lynx	noun (name)	RH 73
bineshi	bird	noun (name)	RH 100
boogid	s/he farts	verb	RH 67, 275
boozhoo	hello	greeting	PD 224, 231
buganogiizhig	"hole in the day," eclipse	noun (name)	PD 32
bwaanag	Lakota people	noun	PL 75
chi miigwech	big thanks	verb	PD 209, 244
chiboy	big boy	noun (name)	RH 39
chimookamaan	"long knife," American	noun	PL 191; LR 63
deydey	daddy	noun	PD 176; PL 78
doodemag	clans	noun	RH 133, 134, 147
dodooshag	breasts	noun	PL 61
eyah	yes	exclamation	RH 73
gaawiin memwech	not so, not exactly	phrase	LR 264

WORD / PHRASE	ENGLISH EQUIVALENT	PART OF SPEECH	NOVEL AND PAGE
geezhik	sky	noun	PD 157
gegaa	already	particle	PD 210
gego	don't	verb	PD 109
giimiikawaadiz	you are beautiful	phrase	LR 20, 189
giin	you	pronoun	LR 264
giin igo	you then	phrase	PD 171
giiwanimo	lie	verb	LR 264
ginimoshe	your sweetheart	noun	PL 104
ginitam	your turn	phrase	LR 51
gisina	cold	verb	PD 208
giwii minikwen anibishaabo ina	will you drink some tea	phrase	PD 126
gizhe-manido	god, creator	noun	LR 359
gwiiwisens	boy	noun	LR 109
hiyn	no	exclamation	PL 24
howah	wow	exclamation	PL 35, 39, 77; RH 204, 273; LR 81
-iban	deceased	past preterite suffix	LR 11, 358
inbiimiskwendam	I am tangled	phrase	LR 145
ishkode wabo	fire water, alcohol, liquor	noun	PD 112, 173
jiimaanan	canoes	noun	PD 164
jiisikid	perform shake ceremony	verb	LR 291
kakageeshikok	forever sky	noun (name)	PD 157
kinnikinnick	red willow smoking mixture	noun	RH 39; LR 23
kookum	(my/your) grandma	noun	RH 73; LR 23
kwiingwa'aage	wolverine	noun (name)	RH 100; LR 10
maaja	leave	verb	RH 102, 215
madwesin	it makes a noise	verb (name)	RH 12, 53
ma'iingan izhinikaazo	wolf is my name	phrase	PD 204
ma'ingan	wolf	noun (name)	RH 48
makade-mashkikiwaaboo	coffee	noun	LR 81
makak	box	noun	PD 165
makazinan	shoes	noun	PD 123, 182; LR 63, 70, 199
makoons	little bear	noun (name)	RH 100
manaa	intercourse	verb	RH 203

WORD / PHRASE	ENGLISH EQUIVALENT	PART OF SPEECH	NOVEL AND PAGE
manidoog	spirits	noun	PD 110; LR 11, 209
manidoominensag	beads	noun	PD 182
mashkiig	swamp	noun (name)	LR 12
mashkiki	medicine	noun (name)	RH 100
mewinzha	long ago	phrase	LR 283
migwan	feather	noun (name)	RH 172
mikinaak	snapping turtle	noun	RH 154
minopogoziwag ingiw zaasakok waanag	they taste good these fried wieners	phrase	RH 73
mishiikenh	mud turtle	noun	RH 154
miigwayak	that's correct	phrase	RH 202
miigwech	to give thanks	verb	LR 101, 357
mii'iw	that's it	adverb	LR 89
mii'sago iw	that's really it	adverb	PL 217
namadabin	sit	verb	PD 123
nanabozho, nanapush	cultural character, trickster	noun (name)	PD 69; RH 181 (ff.); LR 293
naanan	five	number	PD 132; LR 263
n'dawnis	my daughter	noun	PD 167
n'deydey	my daddy	noun	PD 117, 167
ningabianong	west	noun (name)	PD 164
ninimoshe	sweetheart	noun	PD 210
niswi	three	number (name)	PD 132, RH 65
niibin'aage	summer one	noun (name)	PD 145
niiji	friend	noun	PD 203; LR 32
niinimoshenh	my dear	adjective	RH 216
niiwin	four	number	PD 132
niizh	two	number	PD 132
nokomis	(my) grandmother	noun	LR 357
ogema-ikwe	head woman	noun (name)	LR 234
ogichidaa	leader	noun	PD 123
ombaashi	breeze	noun (name)	RH 100
ombanitemagad	mirage	noun (name)	LR 105
opichi	robin	noun (name)	RH 41
piindegen	come in	verb	PD 102
puckoons	little nuts	noun	PD 178
saaah	frustration	exclamation	RH 215, 218
shamengwa	monarch butterfly	noun (name)	PL 22 (ff.), RH 99

WORD / PHRASE	ENGLISH EQUIVALENT	PART OF SPEECH	NOVEL AND PAGE
shawanobinesiik	southern bird	noun (name)	RH 100
shaawano	south	noun (name)	PD 68 (ff.)
shigaag	skunk	noun (name)	RH 48
shingobii	balsam fir	noun (name)	LR 12
shkwebii	drunk	adjective	PD 113
tikinagaan	cradleboard	noun	PD 123, 127
toboggan (odaabaa'igan)	something used to drag or move items or beings from place to place	noun	PD 130, 146; RH 186
waboose	rabbit	noun	LR 30
webid	tooth	noun (name)	LR 114
weweni	careful	verb	LR 114
wiigwaasi-jiimaan	birch canoe	noun	PD 164
wiikenh	sweet flag	noun	RH 39
wiinag	penis	noun	PD 198; RH 70, 204
wiindigoo(g)	evil greedy being, cannibal(s)	noun	PD 198; RH 180, 213, 214, 236, 248, 306
wiisinig	you all eat	verb	RH 72
wishkob	sweet	adjective (name)	RH 50 (ff.)
zagimeg	mosquitoes	noun	PD 168
zashi manoomin	slippery grain, oatmeal	noun	PD 163
zhaaginaash	English	adjective	PD 202
ziigwan'aage	wolverine	noun (name)	PD 134 (ff.)

Part Two: Words and Phrases in Other Languages

LANGUAGE	WORD / PHRASE	ENGLISH EQUIVALENT	PART OF SPEECH	NOVEL AND PAGE
Anish/ French	gawiin ojidaa, ma frère	I'm sorry my brother	phrase	PL 101
Chinook	chinook	warm winds	noun	RH 181
Cree	wishketchahk	cultural character, trickster	noun	LR 293
Cree/ French	payhtik, mon frère	careful my brother	phrase	PL 41
English	moon of the little spirit	anishinaabe term for December	noun	RH 180
French	mon dieu	my lord	exclamation	PL 24
French	courage, mon père	courage, my father	phrase	PL 22

LANGUAGE	WORD / PHRASE	ENGLISH EQUIVALENT	PART OF SPEECH	NOVEL AND PAGE
French	père	father	noun	PL 23
French	frère	brother	noun	PL 24, 101
French	bois brûlé(s)	woodland Indians	noun	PL 98, 107
French	très jolie	very pretty	phrase	PL 111
French	je vais à Paris, je vais à Paris	I am going to Paris	phrase	PL 183
French	je n'ai jamais visité la belle capitale de la France	I have never visited the beautiful capital of France	phrase	PL 183
French	voilà	here it is!	exclamation	PL 187
French	qu'est-çe que c'est	what it is	phrase	PL 189
French	la nord, le sud, l'ouest, et l'est sont les quatre points cardinaux	the north, the south, the west and the east are the four cardinal points	phrase	PL 191
French	je parle français	I speak French	phrase	PL 191
French	chanson	song	noun	PL 213
French	pièce de résistance	best	adjective	RH 34
French	ma chère	my dear	adjective	RH 216
French	mon père	my father	noun	RH 133
French	eau sauvage	wild water	phrase	LR 41
German	ya vole	for sure	exclamation	PL 72
Italian	omerta	code of silence	noun	LR 37
Klingon	heghlu meh qaq jajvam	this is a good day to die	phrase	RH 197
Korean	dojo	classroom	noun	LR 244
Korean	tae kwon do	defense way of life—jump hand way	noun	LR 311
Kutenai	kootenai	band of people	noun	PL 163
Latin	ergo sum	I exist	phrase	LR 217
Latin	thamnophis radix	garter snake	noun	PL 39
Michif	awee	hey	exclamation	PL 42
Michif	mooshum	grandfather	noun	PL 6 (ff.), RH 4 (ff.)
Michif	tawnshi	hello	greeting	PL 23
Michif	tawnshi ta sawnee	hello and to your health	phrase	PL 23
Michif	tawpway	s/he is correct—from Anishinaabemowin "debwe"	verb	PL 24, 42, 59, 253

LANGUAGE	WORD / PHRASE	ENGLISH EQUIVALENT	PART OF SPEECH	NOVEL AND PAGE
Michif	gewehn	go home	verb	PL 60
Michif	owehzhee	neaten, fix up	verb	PL 195
Michif	la zhem feey katawashishiew	the young girl is pretty	phrase	PL 191
Michif	lee Kenayaen	the Canadiennes (French Canadians)	noun	PL 191
Michif	la michiinn li doctoer ka-ashtow ita la koulayr kawkeetuhkwawkayt	the michif doctor your bites from snakes he will treat	phrase	PL 192
Pan-tribal	eyyyyy	you know what I mean	exclamation	RH 203, 205, 273
Polish	pierogi	Polish dumpling	noun	LR 277
Spanish	la vida loca	the crazy life	phrase	LR 101
Spanish	caca	poop	noun	RH 184
Wyandotte	wyandotte	nation/chicken breed	noun	LR 272

NOTES

1. This average is based on the following number of instances when a non-English word appears in the English text: 61 in *The Plague of Doves*, 50 in *The Round House*, and 55 in *LaRose*. For further details, see the glossary included with this essay.

2. The full sentence translated into English reads, "The foundation of justice, moreover, is good faith—that is, truth and fidelity to promises and agreements" (Cicero 25).

WORKS CITED

Allen, William B. "Washington and the Standing Oak." *Patriot Sage: George Washington and the American Political Tradition*, edited by Gary L. Gregg and Matthew Spalding, ISI Books, 1999, pp. 99–122.

Beidler, Peter C., and Gay Barton. *A Reader's Guide to the Novels of Louise Erdrich*, revised and expanded ed., U of Missouri P, 2006.

Braithwaite, John, and Yan Zhang. "Persia to China: The Silk Road of Restorative Justice I." *Asian Journal of Criminology*, vol. 12, no. 1, 2017, pp. 23–38.

Cicero, Marcus Tullius. *De Officiis*. Vol. 21 of *Cicero in 28 Volumes*. Translated by Walter Miller, Harvard UP, 1956.

Confucius. *The Philosophy of Confucius*. Translated by James Legge, Crescent Books, 1974.

Douglass, Frederick. "Southern Barbarism." 1886. *The Life and Writings of Frederick Douglass*, vol. 4, edited by Philip S. Foner, International Publishers, 1955, pp. 430–42.

Erdrich, Louise. *Future Home of the Living God: A Novel.* Harper Collins, 2017.

———. *LaRose.* Harper Collins, 2016.

———. *The Painted Drum.* Harper Collins, 2005.

———. *The Plague of Doves.* Harper Collins, 2008.

———. *The Round House.* Harper Collins, 2012.

———. *Tracks.* Henry Holt and Company, 1988.

Howey, Meghan C. L., et al. "Detecting Precontact Anthropogenic Microtopographic Features in a Forested Landscape with Lidar: A Case Study from the Upper Great Lakes Region, AD 1000–1600." *PLOS One*, vol. 11, no. 9, 2016. doi.org/10.1371/journal.pone.0162062.

Riel, Louis. *The Queen vs. Louis Riel, Accused and Convicted of the Crime of High Treason: Report of Trial at Regina.* Ottawa, The Queen's Printer, 1886.

Honoring Our Relatives

Gwen Nell Westerman

Dakota language is an integral part of my writing. I often begin a new piece with phrases from Dakota songs that inspire a connection to the landscape of my father's family, the place where I have now lived longer than anywhere else in my life. In 1995, I learned to say "Dakota iwaye śni k'a caŋte maśice," which means "I don't speak Dakota and I am sad." Ten years later, my Dakota language teacher told me to stop saying that because I *did* speak it. Today, it is important to me that people know our language is alive and being spoken and written—in poetry and in prose.

In 2006, I went to the Turtle Mountain Writers Workshop with a blank journal. Sitting outside of the Queen of Peace Inn, I wrote three new poems that afternoon in preparation for my first meeting with mentor Louise Erdrich. She read them, and said, "Is that all you have?" Alarmed that the poems had not met her expectations, I apologized for not having more and explained that my plan was to write new work during the week. She replied, "These are wonderful!" and encouraged me to come back the next year with thirty completed poems.

I did what she said, and those poems became the core of *Follow the Blackbirds*. She made suggestions on organization, additional poems to write, and a revision strategy. A few years later, with excellent editing guidance from James Cihlar, I submitted the manuscript to the American Indian Studies Series at Michigan State University Press, edited by Gordon Henry. The book was published in 2013 and includes untranslated Dakota language throughout with the exception of one poem, "Dakota Odowaŋ." Knowing that many of our people are learning the language, I included a glossary and pronunciation guide at the back of the volume to encourage their use of those words and phrases.

Here is one of the poems in that collection that honors Dakota as a living language.

GENETIC CODE

On the edge of a dream,
the songs came.
Condensed from the fog,
like dewdrops on cattails,
they formed perfectly clear.
Whispering through leaves,
heavy voices rise up,
drift beyond night
toward the silent dawn,
and sing.

> *Hekta ehaŋna ded uŋṭipi.*
> *Heuŋ he ohiŋni uŋkiksuyapi kte.*
> *Aŋpetu dena ded uŋṭipi.*
> *Heca ohiŋni uŋdowaŋpi kte.*

Always on still morning air,
they come,
connected by
memories and
song.

The lines of the song in Dakota translate as follows:

Long ago, we lived here.
We will always remember that.
Today we live here.
So, we will always sing.

These days, I have to remember to forgive myself for not knowing more, for making mistakes when I speak the language, for forgetting the stories my grandparents told me. That is why I love the line "on the edge of a dream." It is in stillness that we acknowledge the power beyond us. It is in silence that we know the meaning beyond words. It is Louise Erdrich, through her invocation of songs and dreams—*nagamonan*—who has helped open our eyes to the power of story to reclaim history and challenge injustice. Through her encouragement I have become an authentic poet anchored in my homeland. Like her, I am a woman who cherishes my language, who continues to try harder to be a good human being and a good writer, and who does what she can to resist the erasure of our stories. And, now and then, I will use Anishinabemowin to strengthen the historical bonds between our peoples. *Indinawemaaganidog*. For we truly are all related. Mitakuyapi, dena hecetu.

A Reader's Guide to the Novels of the Justice Trilogy

Peter G. Beidler and Gay Barton

Editors' Note: In 1999, the University of Missouri Press published the first edition of Peter Beidler and Gay Barton's *A Reader's Guide to the Novels of Louise Erdrich*, a guide that became indispensable for avid readers of Erdrich's fiction as the author continued to interweave characters and genealogies throughout her novels. The first edition sold out its print run, and Erdrich continued publishing novels, so in 2006, a revised and expanded edition of *A Reader's Guide to the Novels of Louise Erdrich* was published by the University of Missouri Press. The expanded edition includes sections on *The Last Report on the Miracles at Little No Horse, The Master Butchers Singing Club, Four Souls*, and *The Painted Drum*—novels that appeared after the first edition of the guide was published. After the revised and expanded edition came out, Erdrich wrote the novels of the justice trilogy, and what follows are individual chapters on each novel designed to update and continue the work Beidler and Barton accomplished in the previous editions of their reader's guide. Each chapter begins with an overview, followed by a list of chapters, a chronology of events, genealogical charts for key families, and a dictionary of characters.

The Plague of Doves

Louise Erdrich's 2008 novel is based loosely on an actual event—the murder in February 1897 of the Spicer family near Winona, North Dakota. Five Dakota Indians from the Standing Rock Reservation were arrested for the murders, and three of those were hanged by a vigilante mob in November 1897. The murder and the lynching were widely reported. There is no question that Erdrich knew about the Spicer murders. Indeed, she names one of her characters Holy Track, the name of one of the lynched Dakota Indians. She made so many changes, however, that the original Spicer murders are barely recognizable in *The Plague of Doves*. Erdrich's murdered family is named Lochren, not Spicer; the Indians are Ojibwe, not Dakota; the location is north-central North Dakota, not south-central. Unlike those in the factual account, the accused Indians in the novel are neither jailed nor given trials. A more important change is that while at least two of the accused Spicer murderers almost certainly were guilty—indeed, they confessed to their part in the murders—the accused Lochren murderers were innocent. Another major change is that while none of the Spicers survived the attack, one of the Lochrens did—the seven-month-old Cordelia, who lives to old age and plays an important role in Erdrich's novel.

Many of the chapters in *The Plague of Doves* had been previously published as short stories and were reframed for the novel, a common practice in Erdrich's work. Characters, events, and rich details from the stories are woven into the central story line to create a complex, interlocking narrative web. We find unusually complicated family relationships in this novel, as the lives of the descendants of the lynchers and the victims become entangled. Judge Antone Bazil Coutts puts it this way when he speaks of the various interconnected families: "We can't seem to keep our hands off one another, it is true, and every attempt to foil our lusts through laws and religious dictums seems bound instead to excite transgression" (116). The relationships are especially difficult to unravel because the events of the novel encompass two time periods separated by decades: an early period around the turn of the twentieth century (Lochren murders, lynching) and a later period encompassing the 1950s through the 1980s (the descendants trying to make sense of what happened). Only a few characters have important roles in both parts. One is Seraph Milk ("Mooshum"). Early in his life, Mooshum narrowly escapes lynching twice. As a teenager, he runs away with his future wife Junesse to the Badlands, where the two are taken in by Mustache Maude; a group of angry ranchers assumes that he is responsible for the murder of a white woman and come after him, but Maude and her husband drive the men away and send the couple back to the reservation. After his return home, Mooshum is directly involved in the discovery of the Lochren murders and is hanged a few days later but is cut down before he dies. Many years later, as an old man, he tells his grandchildren about these events. Warren Wolde, the white man who actually murdered the Lochren family, also reappears as an old man in the later narrative. A nonhuman character that bridges the early and later parts of the story is the violin belonging to Henri and Lafayette Peace, which connects several characters across the two time periods.

Many of the events in the novel take place in or near the town of Pluto, which is close to an unnamed reservation in northern North Dakota. Though Erdrich does not identify the reservation by name, it is probably based in some ways on the Turtle Mountain Reservation near the Canadian border. She seems to locate the reservation in *The Plague of Doves* further east, however. Pluto citizen Cordelia Lochren mentions the development of an interstate highway that pulled commerce away from the town. This may refer to Interstate 29, which runs north and south just inside the eastern border of North Dakota. Cordelia's statement that the nearest shopping mall is a precise "sixty-eight miles south" of Pluto (295) suggests that the town may be somewhere near Pembina in the northeast corner of the state. If so, then the shopping mall may be in Grand Forks, where Evelina Harp attends college. As usual, however, Erdrich is careful not to locate her imaginary reservation too precisely. She insists in her acknowledgments section that "the reservation, towns, and people depicted are imagined places and characters" (313).

A controlling theme in *The Plague of Doves* is the theme of guilt and the various ways that guilt plays out in the lives of the characters. Henri Peace feels guilty for sabotaging his brother's canoe and thus causing his death. Warren Wolde feels guilty for murdering the Lochren family and tries to assuage his guilt by secretly giving money to the survivor, Cordelia. Mooshum feels guilty for having drunk so much one night that he revealed that he and his three friends had been at the Lochren farm. He feels guilty both for causing their deaths and for not having died with them. Some of the lynchers come to feel guilty for killing innocent men. Cordelia feels guilty for turning away Indian patients and saving the life of the man who murdered her family. Evelina Harp feels guilty for insulting Sister Mary Anita Buckendorf, who in turn feels guilty knowing that one of her ancestors had participated in the lynching.

A related theme is European settler entitlement. The town of Pluto, after all, exists only because some Euro-American surveyors platted it out and named it. With a few exceptions, like Mustache Maude and Sister Mary Anita, non-Natives treat Indians as savages. On no evidence whatsoever, the lynchers in the novel assume that when settlers are murdered, Indians must have murdered them. The white man who actually murdered his neighbors can quietly go about his business, knowing that no one will think to accuse him. Warren Wolde thus gets to live out his life unaccused and unpunished. The men in the lynch mobs, confident in their self-righteous demand for supposed justice, feel that it is their right and duty, without benefit of a trial, to retaliate by murdering the nearest Indians. Cordelia establishes a medical practice in Pluto, but assuming that Indians killed her parents and siblings, she refuses to treat them. She has a long affair with a young Indian man, Antone Bazil Coutts, yet she refuses his repeated offers of marriage.

Euro-American settler greed may be reflected in the title of *The Plague of Doves*. Though the doves are described as "brown" (8), they may on one level represent a plague of white people. The doves come uninvited, swarm over the land, and cannot be driven off because there are too many of them: "The doves ate the wheat seedlings and the rye and started on the corn. They ate the sprouts of new flowers and the buds of apples and the tough leaves of oak trees and even last year's chaff. . . . [O]ne could wring the necks of hundreds or thousands and effect no visible diminishment of their number" (5). Like the doves, settlers swarm in uninvited, take what they want, and ignore the Indians who seek, without noticeable effect, to drive them out.

The Plague of Doves has four different narrators, but Evelina Harp and Judge Antone Bazil Coutts do most of the telling. Marn Wolde describes her life with the fanatical Billy Peace, and in the last chapter Cordelia Lochren describes what she knows about the history of Pluto. The last chapter also solves the mystery of the Lochren family murders and brings the narrative full circle.

Chapters in *The Plague of Doves* (2008)

NOTE: Erdrich does not provide a table of contents for *The Plague of Doves*. We have provided one here. We have also included bracketed chapter numbers for ease of reference in the "Dictionary of Characters" that follows. The half-page introductory narrative, "Solo," we call a prologue rather than a chapter.

[Prologue] Solo   1
EVELINA
    [1] The Plague of Doves   5

[2] A Little Nip   21

[3] Sister Godzilla   43

[4] Holy Track   54

[5] Bitter Tea   80

JUDGE ANTONE BAZIL COUTTS

[6] The Way Things Are   89

[7] Town Fever   96

[8] The Wolf   114

[9] Come In   118

MARN WOLDE

[10] Satan: Hijacker of a Planet   137

[11] The Daniels   147

[12] The Kindred   158

EVELINA

[13] The 4-B's   183

JUDGE ANTONE BAZIL COUTTS

[14] Shamengwa   195

EVELINA

[15] The Reptile Garden   221

[16] All Souls' Day   255

[17] Road in the Sky   267

JUDGE ANTONE BAZIL COUTTS

[18] The Veil   271

[19] Demolition   274

DOCTOR CORDELIA LOCHREN

[20] Disaster Stamps of Pluto   295

Chronology of Events in *The Plague of Doves*

1880s—Louis Riel makes his last stand at Batoche, Saskatchewan. His defeat forces the Milk family to flee Canada and take up residency in the Dakota Territory. A group of speculating adventurers attempts to lay claim to land they hope will make them rich. In 1888, one of the guides on this expedition, Henri Peace, writes a letter about the violin that he and his brother, Lafayette Peace, had both wanted for themselves. [Historical event—in 1889 North Dakota becomes a state.]

1890s—A plague of doves swarms into the area near Pluto (1896). Mooshum and Junesse run off together to the Badlands of western North Dakota. Mustache Maude and Ott Black give them a place to live until they are old enough to marry at age seventeen.

1900s—Mooshum and Junesse marry. To escape a mob of white ranchers who assume Mooshum murdered a white woman, the newlyweds return to the reservation and take up an allotment of land. Shamengwa's father takes away the violin that Shamengwa has taught himself to play, and Shamengwa receives a spirit-message directing him to wait by the shore of a lake, where he will find the Peace brothers' violin. The town of Pluto is officially named (1906).

1910s—Five members of the Lochren family, all except baby Cordelia, are murdered (1911). A day or so later, Mooshum, Holy Track, Asiginak, and Cuthbert Peace come to the farm and find the dead bodies and the living baby. After learning that the Indians were there, a mob of white men seize them and murder all of them except Mooshum, who is the son-in-law of one of the lynching party.

1920s—Octave Harp, owner of Pluto's only bank, tries to run off to Brazil (1928) with the town's money and his stamp collection. His brother, Murdo, brings him back, together with most of the money. Octave has a breakdown, ultimately drowns himself, and Murdo takes over as president of the bank.

1930s—Cordelia Lochren goes to an Eastern college. After finishing medical school, she returns and sets up a practice in Pluto. She renovates the house in which her family had been murdered and moves her practice into it.

1950s—John Wildstrand has an affair with Maggie Peace, and she becomes pregnant. Maggie's brother, Billy, kidnaps Neve, John's wife. Maggie gives birth to Corwin Peace. Evelina is born to Clemence and Edward Milk. Billy Peace joins the army and is sent to Korea. On his return he becomes a charismatic preacher, and the sixteen-year-old Marn Wolde becomes involved with him. Marn and Billy move to her family's farm with their two babies, Judah and Lilith. They eventually place Marn's uncle Warren in a mental institution.

1960s—Evelina Harp has a schoolgirl crush on Corwin Peace. Father "Hop Along" Cassidy comes to take up his duties as the reservation priest. Sister Mary Anita Buckendorf is Evelina's sixth-grade teacher. From hearing Mooshum's stories about the murder of the Lochren family and the lynching, Evelina learns that her beloved teacher is a member of a family that had helped lynch the three Indians in 1911. She also learns that her grandfather Seraph (Mooshum) had been cut down from the hanging tree at the last moment because his wife,

Junesse, was the daughter of one of the lynchers, Eugene Wildstrand. Corwin Peace steals a violin from Shamengwa and is sentenced by Judge Antone Bazil Coutts to take lessons from him. Corwin and Shamengwa bond. Corwin plays the violin at the old man's funeral, then smashes it and places it in the coffin.

1970s—Evelina Harp goes to college in Grand Forks. She gets a temporary position as a psychiatric aide in the state mental hospital, the same hospital to which Warren Wolde has been committed. She has a brief affair with Nonette, one of the patients. After Nonette leaves, Evelina has a breakdown and is herself committed to the hospital. Then, encouraged by Corwin Peace, she walks out of the hospital and goes home. Judge Antone Coutts's long-term affair with Cordelia Lochren ends, and he begins to court Geraldine Milk and eventually marries her.

1980s—The town of Pluto, long in decline, is now virtually abandoned. Two of the last residents, Neve Harp and Cordelia Lochren, now old women, become self-appointed historians of the dying town. As they try to put the various stories together, Cordelia reveals the truth about who had murdered her family.

Family Trees for *The Plague of Doves*

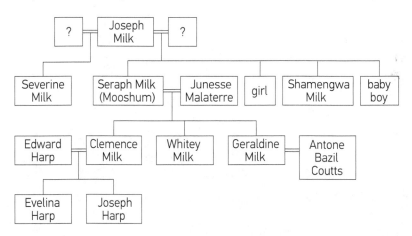

CHART 1. Milk family in *The Plague of Doves*. Courtesy of Peter G. Beidler and Gay Barton.

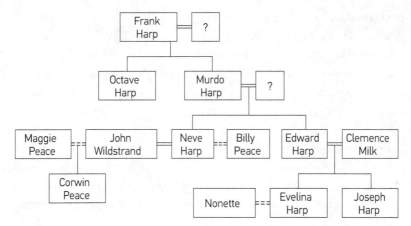

CHART 2. Harp family in *The Plague of Doves*. Courtesy of Peter G. Beidler and Gay Barton.

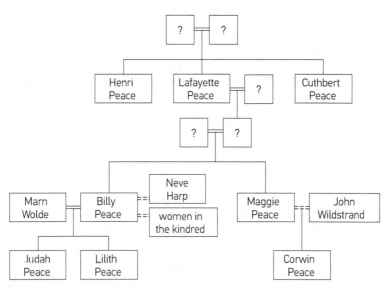

CHART 3. Peace family in *The Plague of Doves*. Courtesy of Peter G. Beidler and Gay Barton.

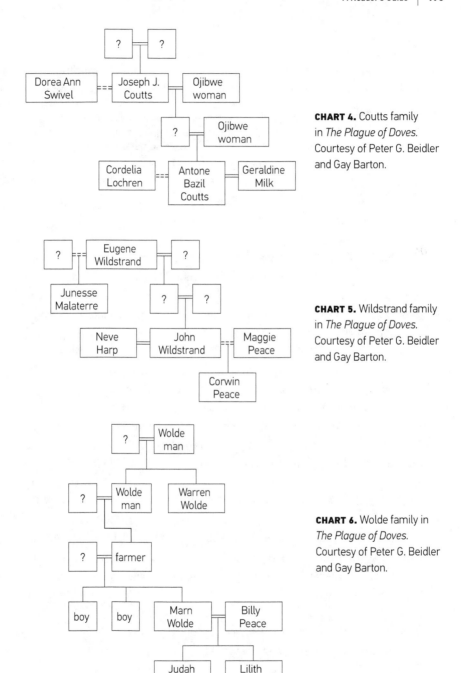

CHART 4. Coutts family in *The Plague of Doves.* Courtesy of Peter G. Beidler and Gay Barton.

CHART 5. Wildstrand family in *The Plague of Doves.* Courtesy of Peter G. Beidler and Gay Barton.

CHART 6. Wolde family in *The Plague of Doves.* Courtesy of Peter G. Beidler and Gay Barton.

Dictionary of Characters for *The Plague of Doves*

Anguish. Caretaker of the children in Billy Peace's religious community. All of Anguish's own children died in a burning trailer house from which Anguish escaped [chap. 12].

Antone Bazil Coutts. Lawyer and tribal judge, son and grandson of lawyers. As a teenager Antone works at the Pluto cemetery. He also begins a long affair with an older woman, Cordelia Lochren, whom he refers to as simply "C" [chap. 19]. She will not marry him because of their age difference and eventually tries to end the relationship by marrying the contractor Ted Bursap. Frustrated, Antone begins to study law and finds that he enjoys it. After a year, the affair resumes.

When Antone's mother needs to go into the Pluto nursing home, he sells his beloved family home to Bursap, who demolishes it. Antone and Cordelia end their relationship. After completing his law degree, he moves to the reservation and begins courting Geraldine Milk, whom he meets at the tribal offices [chap. 6].

Antone and Geraldine's first outing is a fishing trip where they catch a snapping turtle with initials carved into its shell [chap. 6]. They eventually marry and are devoted partners [chap. 17, 18]. Before the marriage, Judge Coutts is asked to sentence Corwin Peace for stealing old Shamengwa's violin. Antone sentences Corwin to take violin lessons from Shamengwa. The sentence is redemptive. Corwin both learns to play the violin and becomes attached to the old man. After Shamengwa's death, Antone and Geraldine take Corwin in and help him turn his life around. (See also the entry for him in the Dictionary of Characters for *The Round House*.)

Antone's mother. An unnamed Ojibwe woman. She and Antone live in their family home, but by the time he is twenty-five, she has become frail. To afford a nursing home, they would need to sell the house. She wants to leave it to Antone, so she is trying to die. After she falls down the stairs, Antone puts her into the nursing home and sells the house. When he and Geraldine marry, they ask her to live with them on the reservation, but she refuses [chap. 19].

Asiginak. Great-uncle of Holy Track. When Holy Track's mother dies, the boy comes to live with Asiginak far out in the bush [chap. 4]. Asiginak teaches Holy Track to make baskets, which they sell. On one of their sales trips, they meet Mooshum and Cuthbert Peace, and the four happen upon the Lochren farm where the whole family except the baby has been murdered. They milk the cows, feed the baby, and leave a note in the sheriff's box. Asiginak insists they must not reveal they were at the farm, but the white farmers find out and come for them. The next day a lynching party hangs them as Asiginak and Cuthbert sing their death song.

Benton Lungsford. The retired colonel who tries to stop the mob from lynching the accused Indians [chap. 4].

Billy Peace. Brother of Maggie Peace, husband of Marn Wolde, father of Judah and Lilith. When Maggie becomes pregnant by John Wildstrand, seventeen-year-old Billy confronts him with a gun, demanding money to take care of Maggie and the baby. Wildstrand concocts a plan for transferring the money without raising his wife Neve's suspicions: Billy will kidnap Neve and demand a ransom [chap. 9]. The kidnapping goes awry, Neve thinks she knows his identity, and Billy flees and joins the army. While in Korea he begins having visions. He returns a decorated hero [chap. 9, 20].

After coming home, he begins to speak at revival meetings. When teenager Marn Wolde attends one of these meetings, she is captivated by his charisma [chap. 10]. Marn begins traveling with Billy, and they have two children, Judah and Lilith. After three migrant years, Marn wants to return home, so Billy brings his new congregation of eight to live on the Wolde farm. Once there, he takes charge of the farm, has it declared a tax-exempt religious organization, becomes increasingly controlling, and grows fat. One day as the congregation is praying for rain, a thunderstorm moves in, and Billy is hit by lightning [chap. 11].

After the storm, Billy grows more fanatical and develops his own religion, whose community is called "the kindred." He becomes increasingly harsh with his family, while also having sex with other women in the congregation. After returning from a fundraising trip, Marn, who has become a snake handler, milks the venom from her snakes, and one night after an intense bout of sex, injects it into Billy's heart [chap. 12]. (See him mentioned in the Dictionary of Characters for *LaRose* as the father of both **Emmaline Peace Iron** and **Nola Peace Ravich.**)

B. J. Bolt. Man who is scheduled to bring supplies to the starving scouting party. He begins with four men and three pack ponies but arrives alone with few supplies [chap. 7].

Bliss. Treasurer of Billy Peace's religious organization. Marn Wolde invites Bliss to join "the kindred" but comes to hate her. Bliss gives herself insulin injections for diabetes. Marn steals one of her needles to murder Billy by injecting him with snake venom [chap. 12]. After his death, Bliss attacks Marn in a Pluto cafe, and Marn wounds her with a steak knife [chap. 13].

Buckendorf family. See **Emil Buckendorf** and **Mary Anita Buckendorf.**

Bull. See **Reginald Bull.**

C. Antone Bazil Coutts's shortened form of the name of Cordelia Lochren, with whom he has an affair [chap. 18, 19].

Cassidy, Father. Ineffectual and affected Catholic priest sent to the reservation in *The Plague of Doves*. Traditional Indians like Shamengwa and Mooshum ridicule him, nicknaming him "Hop Along." Even Clemence, who goes to mass regularly, doesn't like him, though he frequently stops by her family's house [chap. 2]. At Shamengwa's funeral, the foolish Cassidy begins preaching a funeral for his brother Seraph Milk. Everyone is shocked, but it is Clemence who silences and humiliates him by marching up and opening Shamengwa's coffin, while Seraph (Mooshum) waves from his pew [chap. 14]. When Mooshum is injured on Halloween and goes to the hospital, Father Cassidy shows up hoping to perform his last rites. Mooshum disappoints him by rising and going home. A year later, Cassidy gives up the priesthood and becomes an entrepreneur, selling Montana beef on billboards and TV ads [chap. 16].

Clemence Milk Harp. Daughter of Seraph Milk and Junesse Malaterre, sister of Whitey and Geraldine, wife of Edward Harp, and mother of Joseph and Evelina [chap. 1]. She faithfully attends Mass, but she ignores the Church's prohibition of birth control, because another pregnancy would kill her [chap. 2]. She disapproves of her father's flirtation with Neve Harp and is especially unhappy about Geraldine's affair with Judge Coutts. She doesn't want Mooshum to tell the children about the lynching, but she is distracted by her argument with Geraldine and doesn't stop him [chap. 4, 5].

When at Shamengwa's funeral Father Cassidy preaches a funeral for Seraph, it is Clemence who silences him [chap. 14]. When she and Edward take Evelina off to college, Evelina notes how totally unselfish her mother is [chap. 15]. (See also the entry for her in the Dictionary of Characters for *The Round House*.)

Cordelia Lochren, Doctor. Sole survivor of the Lochren family massacre. Cordelia is seven months old when her family is murdered, and she is raised by Electa and Oric Hoag [chap. 20]. She has a happy childhood, and the Hoags send her to an expensive Eastern college, where she gets a medical degree. She returns home, restores her family's house, and uses income from leasing the farmland to finance her medical practice. She will not treat Indians because she believes Indians murdered her family [chap. 19, 20].

Cordelia has a long, passionate affair with young Antone Bazil Coutts, whom she will not marry both because of their age difference and because he is Native [chap. 5, 19, 20]. In an attempt to end the affair, she marries contractor Ted Bursap, but after surviving a bee swarm, he later dies from a single sting. Cordelia does not remarry [chap. 19].

When she is in her fifties, Cordelia treats Warren Wolde after his leg is gored by a bull and becomes infected, saving him from a leg amputation. In her seventies, she has a close friendship with Neve Harp and joins her friend's efforts to record the history of the town of Pluto. In the closing chapter, Cordelia reveals that it was Warren Wolde who murdered her family [chap. 20].

Corwin Peace. Out-of-wedlock son of John Wildstrand and Maggie Peace [chap. 9]. In grade school, Evelina Harp has a crush on Corwin until he makes fun of her new braces. The Tuesday after Easter, they kiss on the school playground [chap. 1]. But when Corwin tells the other boys about the kiss, Evelina is furious. That summer, she does everything she can to torment and humiliate him, but Corwin continues to be in love with her. The war continues into sixth grade and reaches its peak when Corwin lets loose a wind-up Godzilla toy to mock their teacher. He thinks he is taking Evelina's side, but the incident hurts her deeply [chap. 3].

His mother, Maggie, develops a drinking problem, and Corwin becomes a drug addict and a dealer. One night he breaks into Shamengwa's house, ties him to the bed, and steals his violin. He ends up in a Fargo mall, where he takes in money pretending to play the fiddle. After he is picked up, he is brought to Judge Coutts, who sentences him to take violin lessons from Shamengwa. The lessons outlast the sentence, and Corwin both bonds with the old man and learns to play. At Shamengwa's funeral, when Geraldine gives the violin to Corwin, he plays it, then smashes it and puts the pieces back into the coffin [chap. 14].

After Judge Coutts and Geraldine Milk marry, they take in Corwin, and he begins to play with a traveling band [chap. 14]. While Evelina is at college, Corwin gives her blotter acid, and she has hallucinations for several days. When she is admitted to the mental hospital where she had been working, Corwin visits and plays his new violin. That gives Evelina the courage to walk out, and he takes her home [chap. 15]. (See also the entry for him in the Dictionary of Characters for *The Round House.*)

Coutts family. See **Antone Bazil Coutts, Geraldine Milk Coutts,** and **Joseph J. Coutts.**

Cuthbert Peace. Younger brother of Henri and Lafayette Peace. As young men, Cuthbert and Seraph Milk are drinking buddies. Cuthbert's nose had grown abnormally and looked like a potato, giving him the nickname Opin (Ojibwe for potato). One summer day in 1911, Cuthbert and Mooshum run into Asiginak and Holy Track. The four happen upon the Lochren farm where they find the family murdered. Hearing a baby's cry, Cuthbert goes into the house, brings out the baby girl, takes her to the barn where the cows are moaning, and feeds her from a teat. He wants to take her to the sheriff, but Asiginak warns against it, so they leave a note in the sheriff's box. But white neighbors learn that the Indians were at the farm and decide to lynch them. Cuthbert pleads their innocence but is lynched anyway and dies singing his death song [chap. 4]. Years later, reservation people remember his unjust hanging [chap. 6, 15].

Deborah. Secretary of Billy Peace's religious organization. Deborah is the only one of the kindred whom Marn Wolde Peace considers a friend, though she assumes that Deborah is one of the many women with whom Billy has sex. Deborah's children are close in age to Marn's, and some afternoons when they share cooking duty, their children are with them [chap. 12].

Dorea Ann Swivel. A large, widowed woman who owns a boarding house in St. Anthony, Minnesota. She has an affair with boarder Joseph J. Coutts. He will later recall her sexual skill and facility with bad words. When he tells her about his plans to join a town-platting expedition, she is excited and gives him a locket with a photograph of her plain face. When Joseph returns to St. Anthony months later, he is greeted at the door by her new husband, to whom he gives the locket [chap. 7].

Earl. Short-tempered owner of the 4-B's café. Evelina Harp and Whitey Milk work for him, but after Whitey marries Earl's sister, he can get away with insulting him. Earl has a crush on former employee Marn Wolde and tries to get her to return to the job [chap. 13].

Edward Harp. Son of banker Murdo Harp, brother of Neve Harp, husband of Clemence Milk, and father of Joseph and Evelina. A soldier in World War II, Edward is sustained though the conflict by thoughts of his sweetheart Clemence [chap. 1]. Fascinated by the natural world, he becomes a high school science teacher. He shares this interest with his son, and the two engage in a long-term field study of black salamanders [chap. 2]. The other fascination the two share is stamp collecting [chap. 2, 4]. When his sister, Neve, takes all their inheritance, their father approves because he has never forgiven Edward for not becoming a banker. Edward doesn't fight Neve, just asks for his uncle Octave's stamp collection [chap. 5].

Edward knows how valuable the stamps are. When Mooshum steals some of them, Edward is desperate to get them back and tells Evelina that they are "our family's future." But only a few months later, driving to Fargo with the collection, Edward spins off an icy road. He is unconscious when the ambulance arrives, so the stamps are left behind. His children search for them but find them soaked. Edward tries to dry them out and restore them, but they crumble to dust [chap. 16]. Neve later realizes that the stamps were valuable [chap. 20].

When Edward and Clemence take Evelina to college, she retains an image of them standing by the car in parting, their faces "naked with love." This look sums up for her all the loving care with which they had raised her [chap. 15]. (See also the entry for him in the Dictionary of Characters for *The Round House*.)

Electa Hess Hoag. Older sister of Tobek Hess and wife of Oric Hoag. She and Oric take in the seven-month-old Cordelia Lochren after her family is murdered [chap. 4, 20]. After Electa hears about the murders, she decides not to reveal that the seventeen-year-old Tobek ran off after the murders, lest he be suspected [chap. 4]. The Hoags are good parents to Cordelia, even sending her to an expensive Eastern college where she gets her medical degree [chap. 20].

In 1949 the town of Pluto creates a monument to its heroes from both World Wars. Electa insists that Tobek's name be added, since he died in WWI, but townspeople who suspect him of the Lochren murders chip his name away [chap. 20].

Emil Buckendorf. Participant in the expedition to plat a new town site and in a lynching mob. As a young man, Emil and his three brothers are ox-team drivers for the ill-fated expedition into what was to become North Dakota [chap. 7]. When fellow adventurer Joseph Coutts becomes a lawyer and secures his ownership of the platted land, the Buckendorfs benefit [chap. 8]. Several years later, in 1911, Emil is the wagon driver for a mob that lynches three Indians. He finds the tree and fits the nooses [chap. 4].

Eugene Wildstrand. A leader of the lynching party. Wildstrand's own daughter Junesse Malaterre has a French-Chippewa mother [chap. 5], but he hates

Indians. A neighbor to the murdered Lochren family, he helps lynch the Indians wrongly accused of the murders, even though one is just a boy. When the sheriff tries to intervene, he shoots the sheriff's horse [chap. 4]. In the lynching, Seraph Milk's life is spared because he is Junesse's husband [chap. 5].

Evelina Harp. Granddaughter of Mooshum, daughter of Edward and Clemence Harp, sister of Joseph. Evelina grows up hearing stories told by her Mooshum, who lives with her family—stories about the plague of doves, about a murder and a lynching, and about the romantic adventures of numerous family members [chap. 1, 2].

In grade school, Evelina has a crush on Corwin Peace, but their interactions are fraught with adolescent conflict [chap. 1, 3]. Their teacher in sixth grade is Sister Mary Anita Buckendorf. At first Evelina mocks the teacher's ugliness, creating the class's nickname for her, "Sister Godzilla." But she ends up developing a crush on the nun, so when Corwin insults the teacher by setting loose a wind-up Godzilla toy dressed as a nun, Evelina is distraught [chap. 3].

As a teen, Evelina becomes enamored with everything French. She is learning the language, reads Camus, and wants to go to Paris [chap. 13, 15, 16]. She also works in the 4-B's café, saving money for college. One day, Marn Wolde Peace comes in with her two children. When they order dessert, Evelina creates large servings with lots of whipped cream. The manager Earl is angry with her and threatens to fire her, but her Uncle Whitey and Marn defend her [chap. 13].

In 1972, Evelina's parents take her to college in Grand Forks. Her second year she lives off campus with a group of poets and hippies. Corwin visits occasionally, still deals drugs, and gives Evelina some blotter acid that causes reptile hallucinations for several days. Her psychology professor helps her find work at a mental hospital for one term, where she takes care of patients, including Warren Wolde and a young woman named Nonette. She and Nonette have an intense affair, and when Nonette leaves, Evelina becomes deeply depressed and commits herself to the hospital [chap. 15].

One day, Corwin comes to visit with his new violin, which he plays for an entranced gathering. In response, Warren collapses and Evelina gains the strength to walk out. On the ride home, Corwin tells Evelina that he has given up drugs, and she tells him she is a lesbian. Back on the reservation, Evelina visits Sister Mary Anita, who gives her Holy Track's boots. She shows them to

Mooshum, and he takes her to the hanging tree [chap. 15]. When her Aunt Geraldine marries Judge Coutts, Evelina sees clouds that look like a road in the sky [chap. 17]. (See also the entry for her in the Dictionary of Characters for *The Round House*.)

Expedition members. These men go off on an expedition to lay claim to a large piece of land: Joseph J. Coutts, Reginald Bull, Emil Buckendorf and his three brothers, the cook English Bill, and two Métis French-Indian guides, Henri and Lafayette Peace. The financiers of the project are Odin Merrimack and Colonel LeVinne P. Poolcaugh [chap. 7].

Frank Harp. Speculator who came with the second, successful expedition to plat the site of towns along the Great Northern rail tracks. It was he who proposed the name for the future town of Pluto. He is the grandfather of Neve Harp [chap. 20].

Frederic Vogeli. Participant in the lynching. When his wife becomes ill, he beats her, and after her death he uses pages from her diary to roll cigarettes. When the Buckendorfs arrive with Indians to lynch, he goes with them and forces his son Johann to come along. When Johann begins to sob, Frederic strikes him across the face, and Johann lunges at him, knocks him off his horse, and begins to beat him [chap. 4].

Frenchie. A member of Billy Peace's religious community. He picks up Billy's wife Marn at the train station after a fundraising trip and is uncomfortable when they stop at the 4-B's for lunch [chap. 12].

Geraldine Milk Coutts. Daughter of Mooshum and Junesse, sister of Clemence and Whitey, and aunt of Evelina and Joseph. Her first romance begins when she is picking berries and waves at a young man who smiles at her from a passing train. She waits there all night and another whole day until the boy walks back the sixty miles to her [chap. 1]. His name is Roman. They go fishing, catch a small turtle, carve their initials on its back, and turn it loose. After Roman dies, Geraldine stays unattached for a long time [chap. 6].

Geraldine lives in the old family house out on reservation land, keeps horses that Evelina and Joseph ride, and is Evelina's source for information about sex [chap. 2]. She becomes a tribal enrollment officer and meets Judge Antone Coutts in the tribal office. Their first outing is a fishing trip where Geraldine hooks a large turtle. When they reel it in, she sees and points out the initials G. R. carved on its shell [chap. 6]. The day Mooshum tells the children about the events of 1911, Geraldine comes to their house to talk to her sister about her relationship with Judge Coutts. Clemence becomes angry, and the sisters continue their argument all the way to their uncle Shamengwa's house, ignoring the onset of a rainstorm [chap. 4, 5].

Geraldine helps Shamengwa regularly, driving him to fiddling contests and trimming his hair. One morning, she finds him tied to his bedposts, his precious violin stolen. Much later, after the violin is recovered, she arrives one morning to find him dead. After a long affair, Geraldine finally marries Antone Coutts [chap. 17, 18]. A month later, she makes clear that she knows about Antone's relationship with Cordelia Lochren [chap. 19]. (See also the entry for her in the Dictionary of Characters for *The Round House*.)

Gottschalk. The man in charge of the Pluto cemetery. When seventeen-year-old Antone Coutts gets a job at the cemetery, Gottschalk has been working there most of his life and knows the history of everyone buried there. When he dies three years later, Coutts carefully prepares his grave and becomes the cemetery manager [chap. 19].

Harp family. See **Clemence Milk Harp, Edward Harp, Evelina Harp, Frank Harp, Joseph Harp, Neve Harp, Murdo Harp,** and **Octave Harp.**

Henri Peace. Brother of Lafayette and Cuthbert Peace. Both Henri and Lafayette are Métis guides on the town-platting expedition. The trip is brutal, but the Peace brothers save the group through their expert hunting skills, comfort them with the violin they bring along, and bury their dead [chap. 7]. Antone Coutts recalls years later that the Peace brothers saved his grandfather Joseph Coutts's life [chap. 6, 14].

Henri and Lafayette have inherited the violin from their father, who willed that if they could not decide who should own it, they should race for it. Each brother tries to sabotage the other's canoe, but Henri survives and Lafayette does not. So in 1888 Henri writes a letter, puts it into the violin, and sends it out into the lake in his canoe. Years later, sometime after the plague of doves, Shamengwa Milk is led to the violin by a dream, and later still, after Shamengwa's death, Antone Coutts finds and reads Henri's letter [chap. 14].

Holy Track. Boy who has crosses nailed to the bottom of his shoes. The boy's mother is wasting away from tuberculosis, so she has Mooshum nail the crosses to her son's boots so that the illness will not follow him. After she leaves for a sanatorium, Holy Track goes to live with his great-uncle Asiginak. One summer day in 1911, Asiginak, Holy Track, Cuthbert Peace, and Seraph Milk happen upon the Lochren farm, where they find the family murdered. Although they erase

Holy Track's boot prints as they leave, the settlers learn the Natives were there and plan to lynch them. They hide in the church, but when Asiginak is captured and cries out that he doesn't want to die alone, Holy Track shows himself. They and Cuthbert are hanged. Death comes hardest for the boy, since he is so light. But in his fear, he hears his mother's voice tell him to open his eyes, and he dies looking into the sky [chap. 4]. (See also the entry for him in the Dictionary of Characters for *The Round House*.)

"Hop Along." See **Cassidy, Father.**

Jasprine, Father. One of the original Catholic missionaries to the Ojibwe. He brings with him a violin, which he leaves to his altar boy, who becomes the father of Henri and Lafayette Peace and who, in turn, leaves the violin to his sons [chap. 14].

Johann Vogeli. Son of Frederic Vogeli; his mother is deceased. Johann's mother liked to write letters and keep a diary. When she became ill, her husband beat her, and after her death he began to destroy the diary, so Johann hides it. In the following months, he grows in height and strength. When his father joins the lynching party, he forces Johann to come with him, and when the young man begins sobbing, Frederic strikes him across the face. Johann then lunges at his father, knocks him from his horse, and begins to beat him [chap. 14].

John Wildstrand. Grandson of Eugene Wildstrand, husband of Neve Harp, and president of the Pluto bank. He has an affair with Maggie Peace and is the father of her child (Corwin Peace). When Maggie's brother, Billy, confronts him and demands support for Maggie and the baby, Wildstrand concocts a plan for Billy to kidnap Neve and demand ransom. After visiting Maggie one day, he decides to leave Neve, but when Corwin is born, Maggie rejects Wildstrand. Neve subsequently confronts him about the affair, he confesses to the kidnapping scheme, and she calls the police [chap. 9]. The law catches up with him in Florida, and he is tried, convicted, and sentenced to prison. Neve apparently has not stopped loving him, since she visits him in prison [chap. 8].

Joseph J. Coutts. Grandfather of Antone Bazil Coutts. He is a schoolteacher in St. Anthony, Minnesota, and has an affair with his landlady, Dorea Ann Swivel, before going on an ill-fated land expedition. He returns to St. Anthony the next spring more broke than he began, with only a deed for acres of seemingly worthless land. He finds that Dorea has married another man, and he is ill for a long time. He visits the woman that Bull, his deceased traveling companion, was in love with. Cured of town fever, he decides to become a lawyer [chap. 7].

In this capacity, Joseph gets back the land the railroad tried to steal from him. He sets up a law practice in Pluto. Both he and his son marry Ojibwe women. His son is also a lawyer, inherits the land from Joseph, and builds a large house on it. Antone Bazil Coutts grows up in this house [chap. 8].

Joseph Harp. Son of Edward and Clemence Harp, brother of Evelina. At school, it is hard on Joseph to be a teacher's son and to be smart and studious himself. He is especially interested in science and gets his father to join him on a year-long observation of a certain local black salamander [chap. 2]. One day at home, he and Evelina listen entranced to Mooshum's story of the 1911 murders and lynching [chap. 4]. After high school, Joseph attends the University of Minnesota and majors in biology [chap. 13, 15]. He occasionally writes his sister and visits her in the mental hospital [chap. 15]. Characteristic of his family's tendency to display impulsive emotional responses, at some point Joseph joins a commune, but ultimately settles down to married life as a science teacher [chap. 1].

Joseph Milk. Father of Severine by one wife and of Seraph, Shamengwa, and two other children by a second wife. He, his wife, Severine, and toddler Seraph live in Saskatchewan and support Louis Riel, but after Riel is defeated, their farm is burned and the family flees across the border [chap. 2]. In the Dakotas, they have a daughter, a son Shamengwa, and a baby boy who dies of diphtheria. The mother's unshakable grief destroys the family's joy. The daughter leaves for boarding school, and Joseph permanently puts away his violin. Years later they discover that Shamengwa has secretly been learning to play the violin. Reminded of his own love for the instrument, Joseph leaves, taking the violin with him [chap. 14].

Judah Peace. Son of Billy Peace and Marn Wolde, brother of Lilith. When the children are babies, Marn convinces Billy to move back home to the Wolde land, where Marn's parents see the children for the first time [chap. 11]. As Billy becomes increasingly fanatical, he grows harsher in his treatment of Judah [chap. 12]. When Marn takes the children and leaves, their first stop is the 4-B's café in Pluto, where Judah and Lilith experience an abundance of food for the first time in their lives [chap. 13].

Junesse Malaterre Milk. Daughter of a French-Ojibwe woman and Eugene Wildstrand, wife of Seraph Milk, and mother of Geraldine, Whitey, and Clemence. Her father leaves her, and she is raised by her aunt [chap. 5]. In 1896, when Junesse takes part in the procession to pray away the doves, she sees the fallen, unconscious candelabra bearer (Seraph) and stops to care for him. When he rouses, it is love at first sight. They run away together and encounter Mustache Maude. Maude takes them in, makes them wait until they are seventeen to marry, and sends them back home to the reservation on her best horses, where they receive their land allotments and raise their five children [chap. 1]. These horses become a source of income, since Junesse's mare is a racer and Seraph collects stud fees from his horse [chap. 4].

Junesse helps to care for a tubercular cousin who lives on their land and who is the mother of Holy Track [chap. 4]. She teaches her daughters to make special foods that Seraph still loves as an old man [chap. 2].

Kindred. Religious group formed by Billy Peace. See **Billy Peace, Bliss, Deborah,** and **Marn Wolde Peace.**

Lafayette Peace. Brother of Henri and Cuthbert Peace, grandfather of Maggie and Billy Peace. His father was an altar boy for the priest Jasprine, who gave him a violin. The father plays it and bequeaths it to Lafayette and Henri [chap. 14]. The two are guides for the ill-fated land expedition, on which they take the violin. Lafayette's hunting skill often saves the group from starvation, and, a devout Catholic, he gives his crucifix to the despondent Joseph Coutts [chap. 7]. Lafayette also fights for Louis Riel [chap. 9]. Since Lafayette and Henri both want to own the violin, they follow their father's instructions to race for it. Each sabotages the other's canoe, but Henri survives and Lafayette does not [chap. 14].

Lilith Peace. Daughter of Billy Peace and Marn Wolde, sister of Judah. Lilith is a baby when her parents move to the Wolde farm [chap. 11]. When Marn and the children leave the kindred, their first stop is the 4-B's café in Pluto, where they eat abundantly for the first time in their lives [chap. 13]. (See also the entry for **Nola Peace Ravich** in the Dictionary of Characters for *LaRose*.)

Liver-Eating Johnson. Mythical white trapper who hates Indians, chases down his victims, and cuts out and eats their livers. Mooshum tells a story of his race and battle with Johnson [chap. 2, 13]. (See also the entry for him in the Dictionary of Characters for *The Round House*.)

Louisa Bird. An early lady friend of Joseph J. Coutts. She rejects Coutts in favor of a Presbyterian minister with a fine beard [chap. 7].

Louis Riel. Defeated Michif political and folk hero supported by the Milk family. After Riel is defeated, the farm of Joseph Milk is burned, and the family flees south across the border. In both Mooshum's and Clemence's generations, the

Milk family continues to honor him [chap. 2, 14]. Clemence even names Evelina after Riel's first love [chap. 16].

Lynching mob. The men who take part in the lynching of Holy Track, Asiginak, Cuthbert Peace, and Seraph Milk (Mooshum). See **Emil Buckendorf, Eugene Wildstrand, Frederic Vogeli,** and **William Hotchkiss.** Other men who participate are Jabez Woods, Henric Gostlin, and Emery Mantle [chap. 4].

Maggie Peace. Sister of Billy Peace. Maggie and Billy are close to the same age, but when their mother dies, Maggie raises him in their grandparents' house. As a teenager, Maggie has an affair with banker John Wildstrand and becomes pregnant. She tells Billy about the pregnancy, and without her knowledge he demands money from Wildstrand. The affair continues until Billy suddenly joins the army. Inconsolable, Maggie becomes cold with Wildstrand. After giving birth to baby Corwin and realizing that Wildstrand is responsible for Billy's leaving, she rejects him entirely [chap. 9]. Over time, Maggie stops being family for Billy [chap. 11]. She develops a drinking problem and seems to have a bad influence on her son [chap. 14]. (See her mentioned in the entry for **Maggie Ravich** in the Dictionary of Characters for *LaRose*.)

Marn Wolde Peace. Daughter of a farmer, great-niece of Warren Wolde, and wife of Billy Peace. From childhood on, Marn has visions. The summer she is sixteen, she attends a tent revival, hears Billy preach, and falls in love with him [chap. 10]. After traveling with him over the next three years and bearing his children, Judah and Lilith, Marn tells him she wants to go home. With Billy's eight disciples, they move to her parents' farm, where he takes charge of everything. One hot August day, praying for rain in the backyard, Billy is struck by lightning [chap. 11]. Billy becomes increasingly controlling, Marn's parents die, and Uncle Warren predicts that Marn will kill. Traveling to raise money for Billy's new religion, Marn meets snake handlers and becomes one herself. On one long fundraising trip, Marn's plans crystallize. After Billy puts Judah on "schedule" and Marn takes the punishment for him, she milks the venom from her snakes, puts it into a syringe, and when the time is right injects it into Billy's heart [chap. 12]. After she leaves the compound with her children, their first stop is the 4-B's café. When Bliss, the kindred's treasurer, comes in and accosts her, Marn fights her off with a knife and a hammer. Marn says she needs to see Judge Coutts to get her land back to start a snake ranch [chap. 13]. (See her mentioned in the Dictionary of Characters for *LaRose* in the entry for **Nola Peace Ravich,** Marn's daughter "Lilith," who is renamed when Marn flees with her two children after she kills Billy Peace. In Fargo, Marn starts a new life and makes her children "go by their second names because of certain people" [*LaRose* 77].)

Mary Anita Buckendorf. The nun who is Evelina Harp's sixth-grade teacher. Mary Anita is descended from the Buckendorfs, who years earlier participated in the lynchings after the Lochren murders. The younger of those Buckendorfs had a projecting jaw like the nun [chap. 4]. Because Sister Mary Anita is so unattractive, Evelina privately nicknames her Sister Godzilla. But she has beautiful hands and is a gifted athlete. When Sister Mary Anita sees Evelina drawing a dinosaur in a nun's habit, she has her stay after school and explains how hurtful such mocking is, and Evelina promises never to hurt her again. When Corwin Peace names "Godzilla" as an example of a reptile from a different part of the world, the nun simply laughs. But when he turns loose a wind-up Godzilla toy dressed in a nun's habit, she destroys it with a kick. Because Evelina tries to grab the toy just before the nun sees it, she thinks Evelina is responsible and has thus broken her promise [chap. 3]. Years later, Evelina pays her a surprise visit at the convent. When they talk about the lynching, Evelina reveals that she knows the nun's ancestors had taken part in the violence, and Mary Anita reveals that Evelina's grandfather's loose tongue precipitated the event. As Evelina leaves, the nun gives her Holy Track's boots in a paper bag [chap. 15].

Milk family. See **Clemence Milk Harp, Geraldine Milk Coutts, Joseph Milk, Junesse Malaterre Milk, Seraph Milk (Mooshum), Severine Milk, Shamengwa Milk**, and **Whitey Milk.**

Mooshum. Ojibwe word for grandfather, primary name used for **Seraph Milk.**

Mrs. L. Polish nurse at the state mental hospital. When Evelina Harp is on the staff, Mrs. L. is her day-shift supervisor, and when she becomes mentally disturbed, Mrs. L. admits her to a patient room [chap. 15].

Murdo Harp. Cutthroat president of the Pluto bank, brother of Octave Harp, and father of Edward and Neve Harp. When Octave steals money from the bank and heads off for Brazil, Murdo is the one who retrieves him, catching up with him in New York City. After Octave commits suicide, Murdo takes over the bank [chap. 20]. Murdo expects his son, Edward, to take over the bank after him and never forgives him for becoming a teacher instead [chap. 5, 15]. As an old man, Murdo moves into the Pluto Nursing Home, where his son-in-law John Wildstrand, now bank president, visits him. But Murdo knows that Wildstrand is seeing another woman and tells his daughter, Neve [chap. 9].

Mustache Maude Black. Rancher with a reputation for stealing her neighbors' livestock, married to Ott Black. On horseback one day, Maude comes across the teenage runaways Seraph Milk and Junesse Malaterre, takes them in, and insists they wait until they are seventeen to marry. At their wedding, she throws a huge feast. When a lynching party comes for Seraph, Maude and Ott turn them away, shooting one of them. The next morning she sends the couple home on her two best horses [chap. 1].

Neve Harp. Daughter of Murdo Harp and sister of Edward Harp. After her bachelor uncle Octave dies and Murdo takes over the bank, Neve manages to keep the family inheritance to herself, not sharing it with her brother, who gets only his uncle's stamp collection [chap. 5, 20].

Neve is married to John Wildstrand, who has taken over as president of the Pluto bank when old Murdo goes into the nursing home. Neve is a 51% shareholder [chap. 9]. One evening, a masked man (Billy Peace) comes to the door and kidnaps Neve. Wildstrand uses their savings to pay the ransom, and she is released just outside of town. But a blizzard comes up as she walks home, and she almost freezes to death. The trauma affects her physical and emotional health. One afternoon Wildstrand tells her he is leaving and packs up his things. Neve is losing the bank because a competitor is opening a new one next to it. She also learns from her father that Wildstrand is seeing another woman. Later on, when Wildstrand comes to the house, she confronts him, he confesses that he arranged the kidnapping, and she calls the police [chap. 9]. Wildstrand goes to prison, but Neve apparently still loves him, since she visits him in prison for several years [chap. 8]. Neve's niece and a friend speak of two other husbands whom the novel does not name; Neve's last husband has children, and as an older woman she visits her stepchildren and grandchildren [chap. 2, 20].

Neve's primary interest is creating a historical record for Pluto. In efforts to get information, she often pays unwelcome visits to her brother's family. Edward's father-in-law Mooshum, who lives with them, is infatuated with Neve, flirts with her, and writes letters to her [chap. 2, 5]. Neve generally ignores these attentions, but one November evening when Mooshum gets a ride to her house, she lets him stay the night. Mooshum suggests to Evelina the next day that they slept together [chap. 16].

When Neve is in her seventies, she and her friend Cordelia Lochren take daily walks around the town's perimeter. The café where they stop to eat is housed in the elegant building that was once her bank. One evening Neve phones her friend, upset. She has realized that the stamp collection Edward inherited was worth more than the money and bank shares she had received [chap. 20].

Nonette. Young patient in the state mental hospital where Evelina Harp is an aide. She seeks out Evelina because she wants to talk to someone her own age and tells her about being molested as a child. The next morning, she kisses Evelina, and shortly thereafter they begin a series of sexual encounters. Nonette's parents come to visit her in the evenings when Evelina is not on duty, and one day she tells Evelina that she is going home the next week. Evelina is so devastated by Nonette's departure that she herself becomes a mental patient and is placed in Nonette's bed [chap. 15].

Octave Harp. Bachelor president of the National Bank of Pluto and brother of Murdo Harp. Octave's primary passion is stamp collecting. He attempts to collect increasingly exotic stamps, and when it appears that an ancient stamp he wants may be available in Brazil, he steals the town's money and tries to go there. Murdo catches up with him in New York City, where Octave has had a breakdown and is paralyzed. After returning to Pluto, Octave begins drinking heavily and eventually kills himself by drowning. After his death, Murdo takes over the bank, and Murdo's children inherit Octave's fortune and stamp collection. When the bank closes, its elegant building is used to house the 4-B's café [chap. 1, 5, 13, 20].

Oric Hoag. The man who with his wife, Electa, raises the orphaned baby, Cordelia Lochren. When the Lochren murders are discovered, the sheriff and Colonel Lungsford summon Oric. He takes the baby back to Electa, then catches up with the lynching party. When one of the men suggests they hang the Indians from Oric's beef windlass, Oric refuses and dismounts to help the injured Sheriff Fells [chap. 4].

Ott Black. Husband of Mustache Maude. He stands with his wife against a lynching party, shooting one man in the leg [chap. 1].

Peace family. See **Billy Peace, Corwin Peace, Cuthbert Peace, Henri Peace, Judah Peace, Lafayette Peace, Lilith Peace, Maggie Peace,** and **Marn Wolde Peace.**

Quintus Fells. Sheriff. After finding a note in his mailbox, Sheriff Fells goes with Colonel Benton Lungsford to the Lochren farm and finds the family murdered. He and the colonel try to stop a mob from lynching the Natives they assume are guilty, but when a Wildstrand shoots the sheriff's horse in the head, it falls on his legs [chap. 4]. The incident cripples him [chap. 5].

Reginald Bull. Man who organizes the town-site expedition. Bull convinces Joseph

Coutts to join the group because it will be well outfitted and the Peace brothers will be the guides [chap. 7].

Roman. First boyfriend of Geraldine Milk. From the window of a passing train, Roman smiles at a girl picking berries in the adjacent ditch. When his train stops sixty miles away, he walks back to where he saw her, arriving the next day, and finds her waiting [chap. 1]. One day he and Geraldine catch a young turtle. He carves their initials in its shell and throws it back. After Roman dies in a car accident, Geraldine stays unattached for a number of years. She speaks of him when she and Antone Coutts catch the same turtle [chap. 6].

Seraph Milk (Mooshum). Older brother of Shamengwa; father of Geraldine, Whitey, and Clemence; grandfather of Joseph and Evelina Harp. Seraph is a toddler when his parents and half-brother (Severine) flee their home in Saskatchewan and settle in the Dakotas [chap. 2]. His father, Joseph, has a fiddle, which brings joy to the whole family. A sister is born, then his brother Shamengwa, then another brother who dies as a baby. Their mother's lingering grief destroys the family's joy. When Seraph is a teenager, his half-brother Severine, a priest, takes him from home and has him help with Mass [chap. 14]. In 1896, when Severine gathers his parishioners to march through the fields to pray away the doves, Seraph carries the candelabra. But instead of going home, he runs away with Junesse Malaterre. They are taken in by Mustache Maude, who insists they wait till they are seventeen to marry. When Seraph's life is threatened by a mob, Maude sends them home on her two best horses. Back on the reservation, they receive the allotments where they will raise their five children [chap. 1]. The horses become a source of income. Seraph races Junesse's mare and profits from the stud services of his horse [chap. 4].

One summer day Seraph, Cuthbert Peace, Asiginak, and Holy Track come across the murdered Lochren family. A mob of settlers captures and hangs the Indians [chap. 4] but cuts Seraph down because his wife is kin to one of the lynchers [chap. 5].

As a grandfather, Mooshum keeps Joseph and Evelina entertained with his stories [chap. 1, 2, 4]. He has a variety of stories for why part of his ear is missing—it was pecked off by doves [chap. 1], bitten off by Liver-Eating Johnson [chap. 1, 2], or shot off by Shamengwa [chap. 16]. Mooshum also amuses himself by baiting priests, first the old, retired priest and then the ridiculous Father Cassidy [chap. 2]. Mooshum is infatuated with Edward's sister, Neve Harp. On her visits to the house, he flirts, and when he can't see her, he writes letters [chap. 2, 5], sometimes stealing stamps from Edward's stamp collection [chap. 16]. One Halloween, Mooshum smears bread dough on his head to frighten the trick-or-treaters, but when he is hit by a stone, he winds up in the hospital. A few days later he gets a ride to Neve's house, and she lets him stay the night [chap. 16]. He is uncharacteristically subdued when he goes to Shamengwa's funeral. But when Father Cassidy mistakenly preaches the service for Seraph, he is delighted [chap. 14]. (See also the entry for him in the Dictionary of Characters for *The Round House*.)

Severine Milk. Older half-brother of Seraph and Shamengwa Milk. Severine is born in Saskatchewan to the first wife of Joseph Milk. After the family moves to a reservation in the Dakotas, Severine becomes a priest [chap. 2]. Severine brings the teenaged Seraph to the church to assist in the Mass. In 1896 Severine calls his flock together to walk the fields and pray away the plague of doves [chap. 1]. When Seraph and Junesse return to the reservation, Severine prevents the tribal police from confiscating their horses [chap. 4]. A few years later when Holy Track hides in the church from a lynching party, Father feeds him and tries unsuccessfully to protect him [chap. 4].

Shamengwa Milk. Younger brother of Seraph Milk. When Shamengwa is born, his family includes his parents, half-brother Severine, brother Seraph, and a sister. It is a lively household until Shamengwa is four, when his baby brother dies. His mother becomes rigid with grief, and his father puts away his fiddle. Shamengwa misses the music, and for seven years, whenever he is alone, he takes the fiddle out and learns to play it. Once during milking, the cow kicks him and breaks his arm. Shamengwa ties it up so that he can still hold the fiddle. But one day the family catches him playing. By the next morning, his father has left, taking the fiddle with him. Shamengwa is stricken with grief, but a dream leads him to a second fiddle, which he cherishes and plays beautifully all his life [chap. 14].

As an old man, Shamengwa often visits Seraph (Mooshum) at the Harp home, where he plays his music and shares stories and drinks with his brother. They especially enjoy harassing the Catholic priest together, first the old, retired priest and then Father Cassidy [chap. 2, 5].

Shamengwa is as neat and dignified as Seraph is disheveled [chap. 2]. His niece Geraldine is like a daughter to him, often coming to his house to trim his hair. One morning she finds him tied to the bedposts and the fiddle gone. (Shamengwa says he slept through the whole incident.) Corwin Peace is caught, and his sentence is to take violin lessons from Shamengwa. The two bond, and

Corwin learns to play, not with Shamengwa's skill but with some of his fire. When the old man dies, the fiddle is placed in his coffin. His nieces remove it and give it to Corwin, who plays a chanson. He then smashes it and puts the pieces back in the coffin. It is buried with the old man [chap. 14].

Ted Bursap. General contractor in Pluto. Bursap buys graceful old properties, strips them of everything of value, tears them down, and replaces them with cheaply built structures. When his first wife dies, he buries her in a cheap pine coffin. He later marries Doctor Cordelia Lochren. Their relationship lacks passion, but he treats her kindly. Bursap buys Antone Coutts's elegant family home and, as always, strips its finery in preparation for the demolition. But this time, as his equipment rips out the back wall, he is covered by a swarm of bees. He survives this attack, but a year later dies from a single bee sting [chap. 19].

Tobek Hess. Younger brother of Electa Hess Hoag. As a teen he is in love with the Lochren daughter and gives her a valentine, which she keeps in her pocket [chap. 20]. In 1911, the night after the Lochren family is murdered, seventeen-year-old Tobek runs away [chap. 4, 6]. Years later his beloved's surviving sister speculates that he fled out of grief. He goes to Canada and enlists in the First World War, where he dies. Many townspeople think Tobek was the murderer of the Lochren family, and though his sister insists that his name be added to a war memorial, some community members later chip it out of the stone [chap. 20].

Vogeli family. See **Frederic Vogeli** and **Johann Vogeli.**

Warren Wolde. Uncle of Marn Wolde's father. The Wolde farm was originally bought by Warren's father. Marn's father farms the land and takes care of Warren, who flies into disorderly rages and periodically goes missing, wandering the countryside until his nephew finds him. He stares disconcertingly at people, especially at Marn, who thinks he is having visions like hers [chap. 10]. He once even takes an ax to a cow [chap. 11]. One day the farm's bull tramples him, severely injuring his leg. He refuses to see a doctor, the wound becomes necrotic, and Doctor Cordelia Lochren makes twice daily visits to save his leg. He initially reacts with horror when he sees her [chap. 20]. Sometime after Marn and her husband, Billy Peace, move to the farm, Warren begins to tell Marn that he can see it, she is going to kill. She and Billy admit him to a state mental hospital [chap. 12].

While Evelina is working as an aide at the hospital, Warren gets up early, is carefully groomed and obsessively active, walking up and down the halls saying to everyone he meets, "I'll slaughter them all." When she asks about the voices he hears, he tries to give her one of his folded-up dollar bills and begins, "Please . . . I did it because they told me . . . ," and then goes rigid, caught in a waking dream. The day Corwin Peace gives a violin concert at the hospital, Warren collapses [chap. 15]. After his death, his lawyer fulfills his request of sending to Cordelia Lochren a package containing hundreds of folded bills. When she speaks with the nurse who found him dead, the nurse says it was the music that killed him. At that point Cordelia realizes that it was Warren who murdered her family [chap. 20]. Thus, by the novel's end, the pieces come together—Warren's history of madness and violence, the image of a murderer cleaning a gun while listening to violin music ("Solo"), and the folded bills that Cordelia receives and Evelina is offered [chap. 15, 20].

Whitey Milk. Son of Seraph and Junesse Milk, brother of Clemence and Geraldine. Whitey dates the Haskell Indian Princess, who cuts off her braids and gives them to him the night before she dies of tuberculosis. In her memory, he remains a bachelor until his fifties. He is a short-order cook and fights in the Golden Gloves [chap. 1, 3]. On visits to Clemence's family, he tries to teach Evelina and Joseph how to defend themselves [chap. 5]. When Evelina works at the 4-B's café, Whitey is a cook there, and because he is now married to Earl's (the owner's) sister, he can get away with insulting Earl. He is there when Marn Wolde Peace has the knife fight with Bliss [chap. 13]. Whitey is drunk when he goes to his uncle Shamengwa's funeral [chap. 14]. (See also the entries for him in the Dictionary of Characters for *The Round House* and for *LaRose*.)

Wildstrand family. See **Eugene Wildstrand** and **John Wildstrand**.

William Hotchkiss. One of the members of the 1911 lynching party. Hotchkiss threatens Colonel Lungsford with his rifle and slams its butt into Cuthbert Peace's head [chap. 4].

Wolde family. See **Marn Wolde Peace** and **Warren Wolde**.

The Round House

Louise Erdrich's 2012 novel is the second in a three-novel trilogy starting with *The Plague of Doves* (2008). The first of these novels deals with the injustice of Euro-American men stealing Indian land and lynching Indians for crimes they did not commit. The second novel in the trilogy, *The Round House*, deals with the injustice of Euro-American men raping and murdering Indian women and going free because of a maze of laws that unfairly protect whites who commit crimes on Indian land.

The chronology of the two novels is consistent. The events described in *The Round House* take place in 1988, just after Joe Coutts, the son of Antone Bazil Coutts and Geraldine Milk Coutts, turns thirteen. Because Geraldine becomes pregnant shortly after the wedding that takes place at the end of *The Plague of Doves*, this wedding would have happened in 1974 or 1975. We know from the earlier novel that Bazil and Geraldine are not young when they marry, and Joe says in *The Round House*, "I was born late, into the aging tier of the family, and to parents who would often be mistaken for my grandparents" (25). He adds that "My cousins Joseph and Evelina were in college when I was born" (25). At the beginning of "The Reptile Garden" in *The Plague of Doves*, Evelina's parents drive her to college in the fall of 1972. Her brother, Joseph, is already in college by then. *The Plague of Doves* also reveals that Mooshum is twelve in 1896, so he would have been born around 1884, which would make him about 104 in 1988. That is unusually old, but is consistent with his frailty, foolishness, and confusion in *The Round House*, and it comes close to his claim to be around 111 years old.

In other ways, the chronology of the two novels is quite different. The narrative of *The Plague of Doves* moves backward and forward in time over nearly a century, while the sequence of *The Round House* is almost entirely linear, and its present-time action spans only three months. Also, while *The Plague of Doves* features four narrators, *The Round House* has only one, Joe Coutts, who is thirteen at the time of the story. Other characters tell their stories—Linda Wishkob's story of her parents' abandonment of her at birth, and Mooshum's story of Nanapush's stalking the Buffalo Woman—but these are woven into the novel as stories that thirteen-year-old Joe hears and repeats. The narrative voice, however, is not only that of a boy, but also that of a grown man looking back on earlier experiences, and he often draws attention to the fact that he is looking back. In the second chapter, for example, he says, "Cappy walked me home. It is unusual to see people walking places on the reservation now, except on the special walking paths created to promote fitness. But in the late eighties young people still walked places" (20–21).

The three months' span of *The Round House* encapsulates a crucial time in Joe's young life. It begins when a white man brutally attacks two Indian women just three weeks before school lets out in late spring. It ends when that man is dealt justice by the son of one of his victims and the son's best friend shortly before school resumes in the fall. In the intervening three months, the boy Joe becomes a man. Indeed, *The*

Round House can be described as a coming-of-age novel about a thirteen-year-old boy who in the course of the summer of 1988 learns about life and death, lust and love, murder and justice. Because of this condensation of narrative voice and time, *The Round House* reads more like a single narrative than many of Erdrich's earlier novels, which often contain previously published stand-alone short stories.

Erdrich takes great care in *The Round House* to tie the novel accurately to specific verifiable events. Father Travis, for example, says he was wounded in Lebanon while guarding the US embassy. That is a direct reference to the terrorist attack that blew up the Marine barracks in Beirut in October 1983, in which 220 Marines were killed. And while sitting in the hospital waiting room during his mother's surgery, Joe sees a woman pick up an "old *People* magazine" (8) with a picture of Cher on the cover and a headline about how she had made *Moonstruck* a hit movie. The January 25, 1988, issue of *People* magazine did in fact have Cher on the cover, and it did say exactly what Joe reads on the cover: "*She's made* Moonstruck *a megahit, her lover is 23 and she's tough enough to say 'mess with me and I'll kill you'*" (*Round House* 8–9).

The reservation on which most of the action takes place seems to be the same unidentified Ojibwe reservation that appears in Erdrich's earlier novels. The town of Hoopdance is close by. Some characters from earlier novels show up with familiar names like Nanapush, Napoleon, Lulu and Lyman Lamartine, and Mrs. Bijiu. The reservation is never named, but as in earlier novels, it has a senior citizens center and a large lake. In *The Round House* the lake is called Reservation Lake rather than Matchimanito.

The novel emphasizes the complexity of interwoven families as narrator Joe tries to figure out his relationships: "I now realized that Angus was some kind of cousin to me, as Star was a Morrissey and her sister, mother to Angus, was once married to Alvin's younger brother, Vance, and yet as Vance had a different father from Alvin the connection had weakened. . . . If Alvin is my half-uncle and Star's sister was married to Vance and they had Angus what does that make Angus to me?" (205). Related to this interweaving of families is the connection of living men and women to events long past. The man who attacked Joe's mother is a blood relation of a member of the 1911 lynching party from *The Plague of Doves*. Referring to this fact in *The Round House*, the Judge tells Joe: "We know the families of the men who were hanged. We know the families of the men who hanged them" (211).

The symbolism of the round house is set forth in a dream-story that Joe overhears Mooshum telling. In this story, the Old Buffalo Woman, whose carcass protected Nanapush from the bitter cold, instructs him to build the round house:

"Your people were brought together by us buffalo once. . . . Now we are gone, but as you have once sheltered in my body, so now you understand. The round house will be my body, the poles my ribs, the fire my heart" (214).

Because Joe tells his story in the order in which the events occurred, or at least in which he learned about them, the chapters are in chronological sequence. The titles of virtually all of the chapters are episode names from Joe's favorite television show, *Star Trek: The Next Generation*. Another popular genre that contributes to the shape of the novel is the crime/murder mystery narrative: Erdrich's novel follows that plot line by revealing a horrific crime in the first chapter, which is then solved and avenged by the final chapter.

Chapters in *The Round House* (2012)

NOTE: Erdrich does not provide a table of contents for *The Round House*. We have provided one here for ease of reference.

[1] 1988	1
[2] Lonely Among Us	17
[3] Justice	47
[4] Loud as a Whisper	57
[5] The Naked Now	85
[6] Datalore	109
[7] Angel One	129
[8] Hide and Q	149
[9] The Big Good-bye	201
[10] Skin of Evil	241
[11] The Child	285

Chronology of Events in *The Round House*

Sunday, May 15, 1988—When Geraldine does not come home, Bazil and Joe go looking for her. She returns home beaten, bleeding, and in shock. They take her to the emergency room, where she undergoes surgery and is interviewed by three policemen—state, local, and tribal. She has been brutally raped.

Five days later—Geraldine comes home from the hospital, and Joe goes back to school.

Just before the next-to-last week of school—Once home, Geraldine stays in bed and Clemence makes casseroles for them. Saturday afternoon Bazil cooks an intentionally disgusting supper to induce her to get up and start cooking again. Bazil's scheme works, since Geraldine cooks for the whole week—until Friday. When Bazil comes home on Friday, he startles Geraldine in the kitchen. The experience creates a traumatic flashback to the rape, and she retreats to her room. Cappy and Joe assist Randall in a sweat-lodge ceremony.

Last week of school—Geraldine remains in bed the entire week. During that time, Bazil and Joe go through old case files that may hold clues to the attacker's identity. The name Linden Lark emerges in these files, as does a reference to the round house.

June—Joe bicycles to the round house and visualizes what happened there. He retrieves a gas can from the lake, his three friends join him, and they find a cooler of beer and a mound of stinking clothes. On the way home, they stop by Grandma Thunder's house for a meal. When Joe gets home, he finds his uncle Edward talking with his dad. He overhears their conversation about Father Travis. That night, alerted by Pearl, Joe sees a ghost in the backyard. The next day, he helps his dad put in a garden for his mom. Afterward, he asks his mom about the file she went to get on the day of the attack. Deeply upset, she insists that Joe not become involved. Joe and Angus go to an afternoon Mass, then slip out and smoke in the churchyard. Cappy joins them, and they go spy on the priest at his house. He catches them and is angry but ends up explaining how he got his scars.

Some days later—Bazil and Joe begin a casual conversation with Linda Lark Wishkob. Linda comes over twice to visit with Geraldine. After the second visit, Joe and his dad engage her in a long conversation in which she tells them the story of her abandonment, her adoption by the Wishkobs, and her giving a kidney to her twin brother, Linden.

June 17—Mooshum tells Joe to find his totem animal (the heron) to get his luck. Joe goes to the slough near town, sees a heron, and finds a doll stuffed with money. He shows it to Sonja, who helps him open savings accounts in various banks with Sonja as cosigner. Taking their direction from the sun, they bury the passbooks fifty paces from the hanging tree. Joe takes a job at Whitey and Sonja's gas station. That evening FBI agent Bjerke is at Joe's house talking with Bazil, and Joe tells them about the file his mother had gone to find on the day of the attack.

The next morning—Bazil, Bjerke, and Joe ask Geraldine to tell them about the file. She refuses. That evening, Bazil sets up a card table in her room so they can have supper together.

The following several days—Night after night, Bazil attempts conversation by telling stories. Geraldine remains silent until the night he mentions the Indian baby whom the white governor of South Dakota wants to adopt. Realizing that this is Mayla Wolfskin's baby, Geraldine vomits and begins to blurt out the story—Mayla's enrolling the baby, her call asking Geraldine to bring the enrollment file to the round house, the attack, Mayla and the baby's presence in the round house, the man's dousing them with gasoline and attempting to strike a match, his threat to kill Mayla and the baby if Geraldine talks, his leaving to get another match, and her escape. She will not talk about the file or the identity of the rapist until she is sure Mayla and the baby are safe.

When Bazil takes Geraldine to the hospital in Minot for a few days, Joe stays with Whitey and Sonja. One day several bad things happen. Whitey angrily notices Sonja's new diamond earrings, Joe notices other new things she has bought (apparently with his money), and he realizes he has sold gas to Linden Lark. That night Whitey strikes Sonja, assuming her new earrings are from a lover, and she hits him over the head with a bottle. The next day, Joe quits his job and moves in with Clemence. Sleeping in the same room as Mooshum, he overhears his grandfather talking in his sleep, telling the story of Nanapush and his mother, and Old Buffalo Woman.

The next day, Joe learns that the rapist is in jail, and Geraldine is trying to return to normal. Joe and his three friends bike down to the beach, where they encounter the members of Father Travis's youth encampment. When Cappy meets Zelia, from Montana, they fall hopelessly in love. On another day, the boys watch as police pull Mayla's car out of the lake, and Joe realizes that the doll stuffed with money had been hers.

Some days later—Clemence organizes a community birthday party for Mooshum. Cappy is not there because he and Zelia have a tryst at the cemetery.

The next several days—When Bazil shows Geraldine a photo of the Indian baby the governor wants to adopt, she identifies it as Mayla's baby. A few days later, she begins working regular hours at the tribal office and tells Bazil where the missing file is hidden. It contains a photo of Linden Lark, which Bazil shows to Joe. When Bazil and Geraldine go to Bismarck, Joe again stays with Clemence and Edward. Mooshum continues to sleep-talk, and Joe hears the end of the

Nanapush–Buffalo Woman story. One day when the Harps are out, Sonja comes over to give Mooshum her promised birthday present. Joe refuses to leave, so he watches while Sonja does her old striptease act in the old man's bedroom.

Some days later—Cappy tells Joe what he and Zelia did at the graveyard and then in the catechism room at the church. When Joe nears his house that night, he hears his mother scream. Linden Lark has been released. Joe scornfully asks his father why he even bothers with being a tribal judge, and Bazil answers by building a structure on the table out of a moldy casserole and various kitchen utensils. Each layer he labels with a decision from Cohen's *Handbook of Federal Indian Law*. His answer is that he, like all tribal judges, is trying to push away the boundaries restricting Indian justice, to build a case for sovereignty.

Another day—Cappy tells Joe that he and Zelia have exchanged letters. When Cappy goes to confession and reveals that he and Zelia made love in the church building, Father Travis angrily chases him all around town in a highly comic scene that becomes an often retold story in the novel.

Some days later—At Clemence's house, Joe learns that Sonja has left Whitey. He thinks about the buried passbooks, and he and Cappy dig up the tin box. Sonja has left him some cash and one of the passbooks but has taken the rest.

Some time later—Learning that Linden Lark is back in town, Bazil and Joe do the grocery shopping for Geraldine. At the store they spot Lark. Bazil lunges, knocks him down, and begins beating him. Lark breaks loose and flees, and Bazil has a heart attack. The week he is in the hospital in Fargo, Joe and his mom stay in a hotel. One night they get a call telling them that friends and family have beaten up Lark and then another call telling them of Lark's revenge and threats. Eating a burger after the calls, Geraldine suddenly says, "I will be the one to stop him."

Coming home from Fargo—As Geraldine drives them home from the hospital, Joe realizes that he must kill Lark. His first idea is to take catechism class, hoping the priest will teach him to shoot. The priest instead gives him an unsatisfying explanation for why God allows people to do evil things.

Midsummer—Joe tells Cappy why he is going to catechism class. Cappy understands that Joe wants to kill Lark and, using his dad's deer rifle, he helps Joe practice. Joe decides to ask Linda about Linden's golf schedule. While they eat lunch together one day, Linda tells Joe she is sorry she saved her brother's life and wishes he were dead. Joe sees the drunken Bugger Pourier riding Joe's bike and tries to get it back. Bugger says he needs to go see if something he saw was a dream or was real.

Cappy tells Joe he should break in and steal Doe's rifle and helps him map out a plan. During the annual summer powwow, Joe follows the plan and hides the rifle in a hole on the rise overlooking the golf course.

Several mornings the next week Joe goes through his planned routine, but Lark does not show up. On Thursday, he comes. At the right time, Joe carefully aims for Lark's heart, but is off target and gut-shoots him. Lark is down but still moving and screaming. Joe tries again and, on the third try, can't pull the trigger. Cappy, who has been there all along, takes the rifle and kills Lark. They walk back to Cappy's house, jump-start an old car, and take the gun to Linda Wishkob's place, where they shove it under her porch. Afterward, they agree to meet at Whitey's gas station, where they hope to get drunk. Whitey tells Joe the news of Lark's shooting and also that Sonja is coming home. Joe says he has the stomach flu and, when Cappy shows up, asks for whiskey. Whitey gives it to them on the condition that they drink it out back and tell no one. When Joe gets home, his father tells him about Lark's death and asks if he knows anything about it.

Last weeks of summer—Joe is ill with the flu. When he gets well, he goes to the post office to see Linda. Not finding her there, he bikes to her house. He asks her why Linden did it, and Linda talks about the monster inside Linden. Joe then asks her to hide the rifle, and she tells him she already found it and took it to her brother Cedric, who disassembled it, and she then scattered the pieces on a zigzag path coming home. She gives Joe the one remaining screw.

The four friends get drunk again. When Joe finally gets home that night, his father raises the question of what he would do if he had information about Lark's murder. The answer—he would do nothing, based on the principle in tribal law that it is right to kill a wiindigoo. Joe is not entirely comforted because Lark haunts him and Cappy in their dreams.

Joe goes to see Bugger in the hospital to ask about the "dream" the old drunk mentioned when he took Joe's bike. From his answer Joe realizes that Bugger had seen Mayla's body buried in the construction site. If only he had pursued Bugger's dream back then, Lark would have been jailed for Mayla's murder, and Joe would not have had to kill him. He goes to see Cappy, who has received a letter from Zelia's parents telling him to never contact her again and that they are moving so he can't find her. Cappy gets the money Joe had given him, puts gas in Randall's car, and with Joe, Zack, and Angus sets out for Montana to find Zelia. There is an accident on the trip. Cappy dies, and Joe's parents come to get him in Havre and take him home.

Years later—Joe becomes a lawyer and marries Margaret, a girl he met at a powwow.

Family Trees for *The Round House*

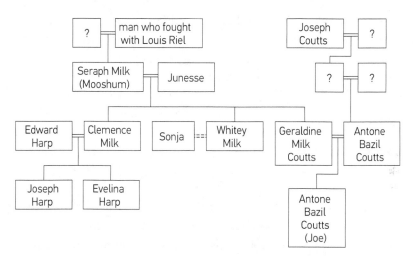

CHART 7. Joe Coutts's family in *The Round House*. Courtesy of Peter G. Beidler and Gay Barton.

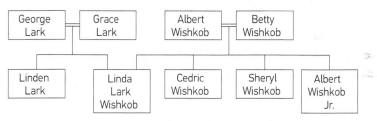

CHART 8. Linda Lark Wishkob's families in *The Round House*. Courtesy of Peter G. Beidler and Gay Barton.

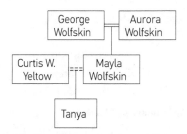

CHART 9. Wolfskin family in *The Round House*. Courtesy of Peter G. Beidler and Gay Barton.

Dictionary of Characters for *The Round House*

Albert Wishkob. Husband of Betty and adoptive father of Linda Lark Wishkob. In "Justice," we learn the Wishkobs and their three children—Sheryl, Cedric, and Albert Jr.—are enrolled in the Chippewa tribe. After bringing baby Linda home from the hospital, Albert and Betty spend years trying to reshape her deformed head and body, as described in "Datalore."

Angus Kashpaw. One of Joe Coutts's close friends. He is a roundabout cousin to Joe (see "The Big Goodbye"). Angus and his two brothers live with his Aunt Star and various other family members in the housing project just outside of town, as described in "Lonely Among Us." In "Loud as a Whisper," we learn Angus is always hungry, and his nickname is Starboy. He is with Joe, Cappy, and Zack on the excursion to the round house, where they find a cooler of beer by the lake and afterwards go to Grandma Thunder's house for a meal.

One day when Joe comes over, Angus has a swollen lip. His aunt or her boyfriend has slugged him again. The boys go to an afternoon Mass. That night they and Cappy go to the priest's house to spy on him, and he catches Angus and makes the boys come inside (see "The Naked Now"). Angus is with his friends at the lake when they run into the Youth Encounter Christ group in "Hide and Q," and the next day they watch police pull Mayla Wolfskin's car from the water. Angus also witnesses Father Travis's wild chase of Cappy in "The Big Good-bye." When Cappy decides to drive to Montana to find his beloved Zelia, Angus and the others tag along. Angus and Zack are injured in the accident that takes Cappy's life (see "The Child").

Antone Bazil Coutts. Lawyer and tribal judge; married to Geraldine Milk Coutts; father of Joe Coutts. Bazil's story from *The Plague of Doves* resumes fourteen years later in *The Round House*. In *The Plague of Doves*, he is most often referred to as Judge Coutts, and it is not clear whether he is called Antone or Bazil familiarly; in *The Round House* Geraldine calls him Bazil (see "Hide and Q"). Shortly after their wedding, Geraldine becomes pregnant, a surprise to both of them. They name their son Antone Bazil, but he calls himself "Joe."

Just after Joe's thirteenth birthday, on Sunday, May 15, 1988, Geraldine does not come home, so Bazil and Joe go looking for her in Clemence's car. They see her driving home, staring grimly ahead, and think she has tried to go to the grocery store. But when they get home, they find her in her car, battered, bleeding, and in shock. They take her to the emergency room, where she has surgery. Bazil learns that she has been brutally raped. He brings her home five days later. At first, she just stays in her bed, so one night, Bazil deliberately cooks an appalling meal so she will decide to get up and start cooking again. That works for several days. But the following Friday, Bazil accidentally startles her in the kitchen, and her trauma returns. She refuses to leave her room or eat for the entire week. Meanwhile, Bazil and Joe go through a stack of court case files that Bazil thinks may contain clues about her attacker. The name of Linden Lark emerges, and Bazil tells Joe that family's story in "Justice."

The Judge is deeply frustrated that the tribal courts do not have jurisdiction over non-Native men who abuse Indian women. At one point in "Hide and Q" he tells Joe that he wishes he were one of the old movie Western hanging judges, because then he could hang Linden Lark. In "The Big Good-bye" he learns that Linden Lark has been released from custody and now runs free. Warned by Linda Wishkob that her brother is in the vicinity, the Judge goes grocery shopping for Geraldine and encounters Linden Lark in the store. He attacks him, but the stress of fighting brings on a heart attack. The Judge has to spend a week in a hospital in Fargo. When he learns that Linden Lark has been shot, he quickly comes to understand that his son, Joe, was probably the killer. In a talk with his son in "The Child" he tells Joe that the killing of Linden Lark was justified by an old Indian law about putting to death people who were wiindigoo.

In "Lonely Among Us," Joe mentions that his father would eventually die of a heart attack. (See also the entry for him in the Dictionary of Characters for *The Plague of Doves*.)

Asiginak. Not the same Asiginak who is lynched by the mob in *The Plague of Doves*. In *The Round House*, Asiginak is the leader of an Ojibwe Shaking Tent ceremony in 1973 and the defendant in a lawsuit, as described in "Justice." At the Shaking Tent ceremony, Asiginak sees that Horace Whiteboy and others are drinking alcohol, and so he asks tribal police officer Vince Madwesin to remove them. Horace Whiteboy stumbles and falls, and dies after choking on his own vomit. Asiginak is sued by Horace's brother for negligence, but the tribal court rules in favor of Asiginak and the other defendants.

Aurora Wolfskin. Mother of Mayla Wolfskin, mentioned briefly in "The Big Good-bye." When Mayla disappears, her infant daughter is sent to live with Aurora and her husband, George, who are the grandparents.

Betty Wishkob. Enrolled Chippewa tribal member, wife of Albert, mother of Cedric, Sheryl, and Albert Jr., and adoptive mother of Linda Lark Wishkob. When a deformed second twin is born to white parents George and Grace Lark in 1938, a nurse saves her life, and Betty, a janitor at the hospital, nurses her and takes her home. She and Albert unofficially adopt Linda, and over the next several years, they work to correct her deformed head and body. They raise her as an equal with their own children.

Bijiu, Mrs. One of the women who live in the senior center. She comes in to talk with Joe, Zack, Cappy, and Angus in "Loud as a Whisper."

Bineshi. The old woman who lives near the cemetery. Her dogs attack Joe and his friends in "The Naked Now."

Bugger Pourier. A minor character in *The Round House*. We learn in "Angel One" that he had left the cooler, two six-packs of Hamm's beer, and some old clothes down by the lake. Joe finds out that, by sneaking in to take the beer, he and his friends interfered with the FBI probe of the crime scene. Bugger shows up again in "Skin of Evil" when he "borrows" Joe's bike to investigate a dream. We find out in "The Child" that Bugger had dreamed—accurately, it turns out—that Mayla Wolfskin's body had been buried in a construction site. (Or perhaps he actually saw the body but was too drunk to remember clearly.)

Cappy Lafournais. Joe Coutts's best friend. His given name is Virgil, but no one calls him that. He has a brother named Randall and two aunts named Suzette and Josey. In "Lonely Among Us" after Geraldine is raped, he gives Joe a black stone that he calls a thunderbird egg, a very meaningful gift because the thunderbird is one of the most important Anishinaabe manitous and serves as a powerful guardian spirit. Cappy is with Joe and Angus when they spy on Father Travis in "The Naked Now." Cappy has several adventures that Joe retells. In "Hide and Q" Cappy meets, falls in love with, and eventually has sex with Zelia, a young woman of Mexican ancestry visiting the reservation from Montana, who takes part in Father Travis's Youth Encounter Christ camp. In "The Big Good-bye" Cappy and Zelia make love in the church. When Cappy later goes to confession and tells Father Travis about that, the priest gets angry and chases Cappy all around the reservation. In "Skin of Evil" Cappy helps Joe plan the killing of Linden Lark, helps him practice shooting, and on the morning of the attack at the golf course, shows up and, when Joe misses, delivers the killing shot. In "The Child" Cappy gets a letter from Zelia's parents telling him that he may never see Zelia again. He takes his brother Randall's car to Montana to rescue her. Joe, Angus, and Zack go along. Cappy falls asleep at the wheel and dies in the resulting car crash. His friends survive.

Carleen Thunder. Mother of Zack Peace. We learn in "Lonely Among Us" that Zack's father, Corwin Peace, has mostly abandoned the family so that he can go on his musical tours. After a second divorce from him, Carleen has married Vince Madwesin, the tribal policeman. She runs the tribal newspaper. Her mother is Grandma Thunder, who feeds Zack and his friends when they come for visits at the senior citizens center.

Cedric Wishkob. Adoptive brother to Linda Lark Wishkob. Even though Linda is white and Cedric is Chippewa, the two become trusted siblings, according to Linda's story in "Datalore." Later in the novel, per Linda's request, Cedric disassembles the rifle that Joe and Cappy use to shoot Linden Lark so that she can dispose of it (see "The Child").

Cheryl Wishkob. Wife of Cedric Wishkob. She is not to be confused with Sheryl Wishkob, Cedric's sister.

Clemence Milk Harp. Clemence, whom we first encounter in *The Plague of Doves*, appears again in *The Round House*. She and her husband, Edward, live just down the hill from the house where her sister, Geraldine, lives with her husband. Clemence comes to the hospital where Geraldine is taken after the rape and comforts Joe. In "The Big Good-bye," Clemence plans a community birthday party for Mooshum, her father, and makes him a sheet cake iced with whisky-laced frosting and topped with a hundred or so candles. Because of all the lit candles (and the traces of whisky), the cake bursts into flames. (See also the entry for her in the Dictionary of Characters for *The Plague of Doves*.)

Corwin Peace. Corwin Peace appears again in *The Round House*, this time as a traveling musician and the mostly absent father of Zack Peace, one of Joe Coutts's special friends. (See also the entry for him in the Dictionary of Characters for *The Plague of Doves*.)

Court case names. In *The Round House*, Judge Coutts and Joe look through various files of court cases in "Justice," and we find the following names as plaintiffs, defendants, or legal counsels: Asiginak, Albert Wishkob, Betty Wishkob, Cedric Wishkob, Durlin Peace, Francis Whiteboy, George Lark, Grace Lark, Horace Whiteboy, Johanna Coeur de Bois, Linda Lark Wishkob, Linden Lark, Lyman Lamartine, Sheryl Wishkob Martin, Tommy Thomas, Vince Madwesin, William Sterne.

Coutts family. See **Antone Bazil Coutts, Geraldine Milk Coutts, Joe Coutts,** and **Joseph J. Coutts.**

Curtis W. Yeltow. The corrupt governor of South Dakota. He is mentioned in "Justice," "Hide and Q," and again in "The Child." He invites a pretty Indian high school girl named Mayla Wolfskin to be an intern in the governor's office. The governor then apparently seduces her and becomes the father of her baby, then buys her a car and gives her some money to go away. Linden Lark, who is also enamored of Mayla, is jealous of him.

Damien, Father. Former Catholic priest on the reservation who is a notable character in Erdrich's earlier novels (such as *Tracks*). He is mentioned only briefly in *The Round House*.

Doe Lafournais. Father of Cappy and Randall, brother of Josey and Suzette. A widower, Doe works as a janitor in the tribal offices and, from time to time, is elected chairman of the tribe. His sons have a lot of freedom since their mother is dead and their father is busy with his work. He performs a sweat-lodge ceremony for Linda Wishkob after she becomes ill after donating a kidney to her twin brother, Linden. In "Skin of Evil," Doe unwittingly provides the deer rifle that is used to kill Linden Lark.

Edward Harp. Husband of Clemence, father of Evelina and Joseph. He is mentioned several times in *The Round House*, but never prominently. (See also the entry for him in the Dictionary of Characters for *The Plague of Doves*.)

Egge, Dr. The doctor who treats Geraldine Coutts in the hospital in the first chapter of *The Round House*. We do not learn his first name.

Elwin. Live-in boyfriend of Angus Kashpaw's aunt Star. In "The Naked Now" we find out that Elwin often beats Angus.

Evelina Harp. A prominent narrator in *The Plague of Doves*, Evelina is scarcely mentioned in *The Round House*. She has apparently left home, because her mother tells Joe in "Hide and Q" that he can sleep in Evelina's room. She and her brother, Joseph, return for Mooshum's birthday party in "The Big Good-bye." (See also the entry for her in the Dictionary of Characters for *The Plague of Doves*.)

Gabir Olson. A lawyer and an old friend of Antone Coutts. In "Lonely Among Us" Antone drives to Bismarck for a consultation with him. He is mentioned again in "The Big Good-bye."

George Lark. The biological father of the twins Linden Lark and Linda Lark Wishkob. In "Datalore" we learn from Linda's account to Joe and the Judge that George and Grace Lark had rejected her at birth because of her deformity.

George Wolfskin. Father of Mayla Wolfskin, mentioned briefly in "The Big

Good-bye." When Mayla disappears, her infant daughter is placed in custody of George and his wife, Aurora, the grandparents.

Geraldine Milk Coutts. The mother of Joe Coutts and the wife of Judge Antone Bazil Coutts. Geraldine plays a larger role in *The Round House* than she does in *The Plague of Doves*. She is attacked and beaten in "1988," the first chapter of *The Round House*. She manages to escape her attacker and drive home. Her husband and son take her to the hospital. Dr. Egge fixes the physical wounds, but the emotional ones continue to devastate her. In "Lonely Among Us" she is frightened by her husband's quiet entrance into the kitchen. She drops a casserole and disappears into her bedroom. She refuses to come out or eat, even when, in "The Naked Now," Joe begs her to. In "Hide and Q" she eventually does come out of her shell and tells what happened in the round house. She begins to take an interest in cooking and gardening, especially when she finds out that Linden Lark has been arrested, but in "The Big Good-bye," when she learns that he has been released, she has a relapse into terror. In the end she comes to understand that her son has murdered her attacker. (See also the entry for her in the Dictionary of Characters for *The Plague of Doves*.)

Ghost. The shadowy figure that Joe sees in his yard in "Loud as a Whisper." In "The Child" Joe dreams about that ghost, and after Cappy's death, he sees the ghost again at the scene of the accident. It was "The same ghost Randall saw in the sweat lodge" (307).

Grace Lark. The biological mother of the twins Linden Lark and Linda Lark Wishkob. In "Datalore," Linda tells Joe and the Judge the story of her day-of-birth rejection by her biological parents and her adoption by Betty and Albert Wishkob. Grace has no contact with Linda until she asks her to donate a kidney to save the life of her twin brother. In "Justice," when Linda becomes sick from an infection contracted during the operation, Grace tries to have herself named Linda's legal guardian so that she can take control of the Wishkob family land that Linda lives on after Betty and Albert have died.

Harp family. See **Edward Harp, Evelina Harp, Frank Harp, Joseph Harp, Neve Harp, Clemence Milk Harp, Murdo Harp,** and **Octave Harp.**

Holy Track. Holy Track is mentioned briefly in *The Round House* as the only one of the three lynched Indians to be buried in the Catholic cemetery. (See also the entry for him in the Dictionary of Characters for *The Plague of Doves*.)

Ignatia Thunder, Grandma. Zack Peace's grandmother. She lives in the senior center, and in "Loud as a Whisper" she cooks Indian tacos for Joe, Cappy,

Angus, and Zack. In "The Big Good-bye" she comes to Mooshum's birthday party and engages in risqué banter with him. Joe thinks of going to her for spiritual medicine in "The Child." (See also the entry for her in the Dictionary of Characters for *LaRose*.)

Iranian doctor. The doctor who tells Linda Lark Wishkob that her kidney is a match for that of her birth-brother, Linden (see "Datalore"). She also cautions Linda against the donation, telling her that Linden damaged his own kidney through various addictions and a suicide attempt.

Joe Coutts. Son of Antone Bazil Coutts and Geraldine Milk Coutts. His real name is, like his father's, Antone Bazil Coutts, but he picks Joe as the name he wants people to call him. He realizes later that this is his paternal great-grandfather's name (Joseph J. Coutts). It is also the name of his maternal great-grandfather (Joseph Milk). Because his mother and Clemence are sisters, Evelina and Joseph Harp are his cousins. His grandfather, Mooshum, sometimes calls him Oops because Geraldine was thought to be too old to have children, so her pregnancy and successful delivery of a son were a surprise. Joe is the narrator of *The Round House*; he appears in every chapter, on every page. In the course of one summer Joe learns about sex, love, betrayal, murder, the traditions of his people, death, dying, guilt, sacrifice. We find out in "The Big Good-bye" that he eventually becomes a lawyer and marries a linguistics major named Margaret, who has done research about why Indians pronounce certain English words one way on the reservation, but differently off it.

Joe Coutts's ancestors. In "The Naked Now," Joe gives a list of some of his ancestors who are buried in the church cemetery. In listing the names he gives them in triples: the Ojibwe name, an English name, and an English translation of the Ojibwe: "Shawanobinesiik, Elizabeth, Southern Thunderbird. Adik, Michael, Caribou. Kwiingwa'aage, Joseph, Wolverine. Mashkiki, Mary, The Medicine. Ombaashi, Albert, Lifted By Wind. Makoons, The Bearling, and Bird Shaking Ice Off Its Wings."

Joseph J. Coutts. Joseph J. Coutts is mentioned briefly in *The Round House*. In "1988" he is said to be Joe's great-grandfather and to have been the original owner of some of the family's law books. (See also the entry for him in the Dictionary of Characters for *The Plague of Doves*.)

Josey. One of Cappy's aunts. She and Suzette, another aunt, provide the food for participants in Randall's sweat-lodge ceremony in "Lonely Among Us," and they organize the family camp at the summer powwow in "Skin of Evil."

LaRose Migwan. An old boarding school friend of Geraldine Milk Coutts and a cousin of Mayla Wolfskin in *The Round House.* She is mentioned briefly in "Loud as a Whisper," "Hide and Q," and elsewhere. She has had so many husbands that people just call her by her first name. She tells Joe some of Mayla's history: that she went to a boarding school in South Dakota, was selected for an internship in the governor's office, and so on. (See also the entry for **LaRose 3** in the Dictionary of Characters for *LaRose.*)

Lark family. See **George Lark, Grace Lark, Linda Lark Wishkob,** and **Linden Lark.**

Linda Lark Wishkob. White postal worker, born physically deformed and raised by adoptive parents. In "Datalore" she tells her story to Antone and Joe Coutts. She was the second twin born to George and Grace Lark in 1938. Because she was badly deformed, the parents had asked the doctor to let her die. A nurse, however, saved her life. A janitor named Betty Wishkob and her husband, both Indians, raised Linda as their own. Biologically white, she becomes culturally Indian. She is given the nickname Tuffy by her Wishkob brother Cedric. Linda's birth mother, Grace Lark, does not bother to come see her, though they live not far apart. Finally, after almost fifty years, Grace does call. Linda is devastated to learn that Grace called only because she wanted to ask Linda to donate a kidney to her birth-twin, Linden. Even though the Larks continue to ignore her, Linda does donate one of her kidneys to Linden. Linda gets an infection during the operation and almost dies. Despite her donation, Linden returns to the life of irresponsible profligacy that had caused him to ruin his own kidney in the first place. Linda visits the Judge in "Skin of Evil" to warn him and Geraldine that her brother Linden is in the vicinity. Later Joe tricks her into telling him when Linden likes to play golf. In the end she lets Joe know that she understands, and approves of, his murdering her twin brother. In "The Child," by destroying the murder weapon, Linda even makes herself an accomplice in the murder.

Linda Lark Wishkob's spirit visitor. The spirit that sometimes visits Linda. She describes it as a "doppelganger" in "Datalore." In "The Child," Joe visits Linda at her home and discovers that everything there has a double, and she explains that, in a sweat-lodge ceremony, Doe Lafournais told Linda that she has a "double spirit" that she should welcome. This double can be interpreted as the other half of herself, her absent twin.

Linden Lark. Son of George and Grace Lark, twin brother of Linda Lark Wishkob. We learn in "Datalore" that because Linda is deformed, her birth parents abandoned her to be raised by an Indian family, the Wishkobs. The Larks then raise Linden as an only child. After a life of crime, profligacy, failed romantic and marital relationships, and even attempted suicide, Linden winds up on kidney dialysis. Linda generously donates one of her kidneys, but during the operation she contracts a life-threatening infection. Far from showing gratitude, however, Linden and his mother attempt to claim that Linda is incompetent to manage her own affairs—a ploy that would allow them to gain title to the Wishkob family land that Linda lives on after her adoptive parents have died. When his family's gas station fails because of their dishonest business practices, Linden spends much of his time pursuing questionable actions and political connections in South Dakota. He becomes a suspect in the attack against Geraldine Coutts. He apparently murders Mayla Wolfskin and hides her body in an excavation site. In "Hide and Q" he comes to Whitey's gas station, where Joe is temporarily employed. Not long after that, in "The Big Good-bye," he is released from jail. In "Skin of Evil" he is murdered on the golf links by Joe and Cappy.

Liver-Eating Johnson. In "The Big Good-bye," Mooshum tells another tall tale about Liver-Eating Johnson. (See also the entry for him in the Dictionary of Characters for *The Plague of Doves*.)

London. See **Murphy**.

Lulu Lamartine. Lulu Lamartine, who is a memorable character in Erdrich's earlier novels such as *Love Medicine* and *Tracks*, is mentioned only briefly in *The Round House*. In "The Big Good-bye" she is said to have had two sons, Alvin and Vance, and Alvin's father is identified as Mooshum. Joe Coutts discovers that, because he is a grandson of Mooshum, he is related to some of Lulu's many progeny, including his friend Angus.

Margaret Coutts. Mentioned as the future wife of Joe Coutts in *The Round House*. We are told in "The Child" that she conducted a linguistic study on the reservation. We are not told what her maiden name was, but her grandmother is named Margaret Nanapush, so perhaps that is her family name also.

Margaret Nanapush. Mentioned briefly in "The Child" as the grandmother of the Margaret that Joe Coutts eventually marries.

Mayla Wolfskin. Young Indian woman who asks Geraldine Coutts for help filling out enrollment papers for her baby; she then asks Geraldine to meet her at the round house, where both women are attacked in the opening chapter of the novel. We find out about Mayla's past in "Hide and Q." As an intern, Mayla apparently had an affair with Curtis W. Yeltow, the corrupt governor of South Dakota, who now wants to adopt the baby. Mayla has apparently incurred the jealous wrath of Linden Lark, who wants to claim her as his girlfriend and is incensed that she will not give him the money Yeltow has paid Mayla to keep silent about their affair. It turns out that Mayla stuffed the money—$40,000— into a doll that Joe later finds in the lake. In the final chapter, "The Child," Joe learns from Bugger Pourier that Mayla's body has been buried in a construction site by her murderer, Linden Lark.

Mayla Wolfskin's baby. The infant who is with her mother during the attack in the round house. We learn in "The Big Good-bye" that a baby in a car seat is abandoned at a Goodwill store and that the governor of South Dakota has been trying to adopt the baby, of whom he is the father. The baby is eventually placed with her grandparents, George and Aurora Wolfskin, who presumably do not allow her to be adopted by the governor of South Dakota. We learn the baby's name is Tanya in the last chapter of the novel.

Mooshum. See **Seraph Milk.**

Murphy. Sonja's estranged daughter. We find out in "Hide and Q" that Murphy changed her name to London and refused to go to college.

Nanapush. Nanapush is a prominent character in Erdrich's earlier novels but makes a brief appearance in *The Round House*. He is said to be the son of Mirage and Akii in the story that Mooshum tells in his sleep in "Hide and Q." Mirage tells Nanapush to kill his mother because she is accused of being a wiindigoo, but Nanapush refuses. Instead, he rescues her. The next morning Mooshum tells Joe that Nanapush had given him advice about how to please a woman sexually. The next night during his sleep, Mooshum continues the story about Nanapush's stalking and killing of an old buffalo cow to feed his family, and about Nanapush's mother then rescuing him from the snow-covered buffalo hide he has been frozen into. In "The Big Good-bye" Mooshum finishes his dream story about Nanapush and relates it to the design and building of the round house.

Napoleon. A man named Napoleon is mentioned briefly in "Loud as a Whisper." He is said to be a man who does not drink and so has more sexual ability and durability. It is not clear whether he is related to Napoleon Morrissey from Erdrich's earlier novels.

Neil. The pimply Youth Encounter Christ boy on the beach with Zelia in "Hide and Q."

Niswi. The old man with three balls mentioned briefly, perhaps in jest, in "Loud as a Whisper."

Oops. See **Joe Coutts.**

Opichi Wold. Judge Coutts's legal secretary. In "Lonely Among Us" we learn that Judge Coutts relies on Opichi (whose name means robin) for trustworthy information about what is going on around the reservation. In "Skin of Evil" she gives Geraldine information about the brutal behavior of Linden Lark.

Pearl. The large, part-wolf guard dog Sonja and Whitey loan to the Coutts family after Geraldine is raped. Pearl sees the ghostly presence in Joe's backyard and alerts him to possible danger. Pearl watches over and protects Joe and his parents throughout the novel. In "The Big Good-bye," the adult Joe remarks that he has always had a dog named Pearl.

Randall Lafournais. Older brother of Cappy. In "Lonely Among Us" Randall, who has acquired the nickname Birkenstock, conducts a sweat-lodge ceremony for his friends that ends with a surprising explosion of hot pepper. We are told in "Datalore" that Randall and his family help to heal Linda Lark Wishkob after she donates a kidney to Linden and is afflicted by a "spiritual infection." Randall participates eagerly in the summer powwow in "Skin of Evil" and in "The Child." (See also the entry for him in the Dictionary of Characters for *LaRose*.)

Ruby Smoke. One of the participants in Father Travis's Youth Encounter Christ group in "Hide and Q." She claims to have been delivered of a snake.

Seraph Milk (Mooshum). Mooshum is mentioned as being very old in the first chapter, "1988," in *The Round House*. Later, in "Angel One," he is said to claim to be almost 112 years old. He lives with his daughter Clemence (and her husband, Edward Harp), not far from his other daughter Geraldine (and her husband, Antone Bazil Coutts) and his son, Whitey (and Whitey's sexy girlfriend Sonja). In "Angel One" he answers his grandson Joe's questions about the ghost he has seen and sends him on the quest for his "luck"—which turns out to be a submerged plastic doll full of hundred-dollar bills. In "Hide and Q" Joe listens as Mooshum tells a story in his sleep about the conflict between Mirage and his wife, Akii. Mooshum continues his dream story for the next couple of nights. The story is mostly about Nanapush's hunting of a buffalo woman and his crawling into her belly, his deliverance from it, and his design of the round house. In "The Big Good-bye" Mooshum celebrates his birthday with a party and cake. Several days later Sonja gives him (and Joe) a private strip show so effective that Mooshum almost dies of excitement. (See also the entry for him in the Dictionary of Characters for *The Plague of Doves*.)

Shamengwa. Mooshum's brother Shamengwa is mentioned briefly in "Lonely Among Us" and in "The Naked Now" in *The Round House*. We learn that his name means monarch butterfly. (See also the entry for him in the Dictionary of Characters for *The Plague of Doves*.)

Sheryl Wishkob. Adoptive sister of Linda Lark Wishkob. In "Datalore" Linda describes her special friendship with Sheryl. They are true sisters, even though they have different biological parents and even though Sheryl is Indian and Linda is not. In "Justice" we learn that Sheryl had been instrumental in boycotting Linden Lark's gas station and helping Whitey Harp, Joe Coutts's uncle, to establish his own rival gas station. Lark's gas station failed as the people from the reservation now gladly took all their business to Whitey's station.

Skippy. One of Randall Lafournais's friends in the sweat-lodge scene in "Lonely Among Us."

Sonja. An ex-stripper, girlfriend of Whitey Milk. We learn in "Lonely Among Us" that Sonja has a daughter named London from a previous relationship, but they do not get along well. In "Angel One" Sonja helps Joe Coutts set up a series of savings accounts with the money he has found in a plastic doll in the lake. She also steals some of his money to buy herself some expensive jewelry. She knows that young Joe Coutts has a crush on her and will not tell Whitey. In "Hide and Q" she gets into an argument with Whitey, who, seeing the jewelry, accuses her of having a lover. Joe takes her side and lies by telling Whitey that he has given Sonja the jewelry as a birthday present. In "The Big Good-bye" Sonja comes to give Mooshum (with Joe watching) a birthday strip show. She then tells Joe about her sordid childhood. She says that she is not Whitey's wife because he refused to marry her. She then packs up and leaves Whitey, taking with her most of Joe's money.

Soren Bjerke. The FBI agent assigned to investigate Geraldine's assault. In "Angel One" he talks with Joe Coutts about his and his friends' interference with the cooler and the two six-packs of beer. Soren Bjerke is mentioned again in "The Big Good-bye" and "The Child."

Star. The sister of Angus's mother and the de facto parent of her nephew, Angus Kashpaw, and his brothers. In "Lonely Among Us" we learn that she lives with her lover Elwin and with assorted relatives in a derelict house in a poor section of the reservation. In "The Naked Now" we learn that she sometimes hits Angus. She comes to Mooshum's birthday party in "The Big Good-bye."

Suzette. One of Cappy's aunts. She and Josey, another aunt, provide the food for participants in Randall's sweat-lodge ceremony in "Lonely Among Us," and they organize the family camp at the summer powwow in "Skin of Evil."

Toast. Boyfriend of Ruby Smoke, mentioned briefly in "Hide and Q."

Travis Wozniak, Father. The new priest on the reservation. He is first mentioned in "Loud as a Whisper," but we find out more about him in "The Naked Now" when Joe and his friends spy on him. They see him naked and see the scars that have unmanned him. At first he is angry, but then he decides to tell them about his time in the Marines and the almost-fatal wounds he received defending the US Embassy in Lebanon in 1983. The incident he speaks of is an actual event: on October 23, 1983, a suicide bomber set off a truck bomb at a Marine compound in Beirut, killing 220 Marines and 21 other service personnel. In the novel, Travis is one of the few survivors of this attack. Later, in "Hide and Q," Father Travis runs a Youth Encounter Christ group that Joe, Zack, Cappy, and Angus join, or pretend to join so they can get acquainted with pretty girls like Zelia. In "The Big Good-bye" he hears Cappy's confession about having sex with Zelia in the church and angrily chases him around the countryside in a great comic scene. (See also the entry for him in the Dictionary of Characters for *LaRose*.)

Tuffy. See **Linda Lark Wishkob.**

Vince Madwesin. Stepfather of Zack Peace, married to Zack's mother, Carleen Thunder. Vince is the tribal police officer who comes to the hospital in "1988" to find out from Geraldine Coutts what had happened to her. He is mentioned briefly in "Justice." In "The Child" he returns a pickle jar to Joe's mother that Joe had inadvertently left near the crime scene, and makes veiled remarks that indicate he suspects that Joe is the murderer, but that he will not interfere with the justice that has been done.

Virgil Lafournais. See **Cappy.**

Whitey Milk. Brother of Geraldine and Clemence, Whitey operates a gas station that becomes a central meeting place on the reservation. We find out in "Lonely Among Us" that he lives with an attractive ex-stripper named Sonja and that he has sons from his first marriage. We find out in "Justice" that he got his start in the gas station business because Sheryl Wishkob organized a boycott against the predatory prices of the gas station owned by the Lark family. He and Sonja quarrel in "The Big Good-bye" about how she acquired some diamond jewelry. By the end of the novel she has left him. We learn in "The Child," however, that she will come back and that he will welcome her. (See also the entries for him in the Dictionary of Characters for *The Plague of Doves* and for *LaRose*.)

Wiindigoo. In Anishinaabe tradition, a cannibal monster with a heart of ice whose origins lie in the fear of starvation during freezing northern winters. In "Hide and Q," Mooshum tells a story during his sleep about Nanapush and his mother Akii, who was accused of being wiindigoo, and explains that a "wiindigoo could cast its spirit inside a person. That person would become an animal and see fellow humans as prey meat" (180). For the safety of the community, a wiindigoo must be put to death. In "Skin of Evil," Geraldine Coutts identifies her rapist, Linden Lark, as a wiindigoo, and her son, Joe, uses this belief as part of his justification for killing Lark. In "The Child," Joe's father, Judge Coutts, reasons that Lark "met the definition of a wiindigoo" and therefore his killing "fulfilled the requirements of a very old law" (306).

Wishkob family. See **Albert Wishkob, Betty Wishkob, Cedric Wishkob, Cheryl Wishkob, Linda Lark Wishkob,** and **Sheryl Wishkob.**

Wolfskin family. See **Aurora Wolfskin, George Wolfskin, Mayla Wolfskin,** and **Mayla Wolfskin's baby.**

Zack Peace. A friend of Joe Coutts. We learn in "Lonely Among Us" that he is the son of Corwin Peace and Carleen Thunder. Corwin, however, is a musician who is almost always on tour, and so he has mostly abandoned his family. Zack's mother has remarried, so Vince Madwesin is his stepfather. (See also the entry for him in the Dictionary of Characters for *LaRose*.)

Zelia. The pretty girl of Mexican ancestry on the beach in "Hide and Q." She has come from Montana to work with Father Travis's Youth Encounter Christ group. She accompanies the pimply Neil to the beach, but quickly becomes attracted to Cappy, whom she sees come out of the water naked. She and Cappy become lovers, but soon she has to go home to Montana, leaving him distraught. In "The Child," her parents find Cappy's love letters and write to Cappy that he may not see Zelia ever again. On his way to rescue her, Cappy dies in a car wreck.

LaRose

Louise Erdrich's 2016 novel is the last novel in what has been referred to as the "justice trilogy," starting with *The Plague of Doves* (2008) and continued in *The Round House* (2012). *LaRose* has many narrative threads: a white fur trader purchases an eleven-year-old Ojibwe girl from her mother; the girl poisons the trader and runs off with her white accomplice, whom she later marries; Indian boys and girls are sent away to various boarding schools; an Ojibwe man accidentally shoots his neighbor's son and in reparation gives his own son to the bereaved parents; another Native man abandons his son and permits him to be raised by a man he later tries to have murdered; a teenage girl deals with bullying and sexual abuse and prevents her mother's suicide; a priest falls in love with one of his parishioners; a boy is able to communicate with his dead relatives in the spirit world.

The action shifts from place to place and from decade to decade, which requires readers' diligence to follow the story line. Most of the important action, however, takes place in the early twenty-first century on and near a North Dakota reservation. The reservation is not named and is not specifically located, but the towns near it are familiar to us from other novels. Readers are told that one of the characters drives off the reservation to Hoopdance (9), which is to the west. To the south is the dying little town of Pluto, also off the reservation (22, 77). The reservation is apparently west of Pembina, to judge by the mention of Wolfred Roberts and his wife's journey to "Pembina, then farther out" (188), where he built a cabin and made his farm: "The land would become reservation land, but Wolfred had homesteaded it and the agents and priest left them alone" (191).

The novel invokes a large cast of characters, including five with the first name LaRose; assorted spirit characters, mostly unnamed; as well as talking disembodied heads. A few of the minor characters repeat from earlier novels in the trilogy, but they are a generation older now. Marn Wolde Peace, one of the wives of Billy Peace in *The Plague of Doves*, is mentioned as the Polish grandmother of Dusty, the boy who is accidentally shot. The two children—Judah and Lilith—that Marn had by Billy before she murdered him in *The Plague of Doves* are not mentioned by their biblical names in *LaRose*, but Nola is presumed to be Lilith, now taking her second name (see *Plague* 167 and *LaRose* 77). Judah doesn't reappear. Whitey and his gas station, fairly important in *The Round House*, are referred to in passing in *LaRose*, but not Joe or his parents, Geraldine and Bazil Coutts, the pivotal characters of *The Round House*. One of the five characters named LaRose was mentioned briefly in *The Round House* as a close boarding-school friend of Geraldine, but she plays a similarly minor role in *LaRose* (see the entry for **LaRose 3** in the Dictionary of Characters that follows). Other characters from *The Round House* who make an appearance include Grandma Ignatia Thunder, Star, and Randall. The most important repeating character is Father Travis Wozniak, who played a fairly significant role in *The Round House*.

LaRose in no way depends on the earlier novels. Readers who find it confusing because of its broad scope, its large cast of characters, and its nonlinear narrative will not be aided much by reading the two previous justice narratives. The only way to discover the unifying elements in *LaRose* is to read it—and reread it—carefully. Some of these elements are:

The continuity of the name LaRose. LaRose is the first name of five different characters in the story. Four are women, one a boy. They are all blood-related and all said to be traditional healers. In the Dictionary of Characters, we have listed them in chronological order as LaRose 1, LaRose 2, and so on. It turns out that only three of them are important characters in this novel: LaRose 1, the eleven-year-old girl whose mother sells her to a trader; LaRose 4, referred to as Mrs. Peace, the great-granddaughter of LaRose 1; and LaRose 5, the grandson of LaRose 4. He is the boy who is given to the bereaved parents of the boy who is killed.

Substance abuse. Mink sells her daughter for a small supply of alcohol. Landreaux Iron has abused alcohol and pills in the past. His reaction to his killing of Dusty and then giving up his own son, LaRose, is to buy a bottle of whiskey, though he does not drink it and turns instead to traditional healing. Romeo Puyat steals painkillers from people who really need them. High school students have easy access to marijuana. Beer is readily available. We are never far in *LaRose* from the danger of substance abuse.

Giving up children. LaRose 1 is sold by her mother for the trader Mackinnon's "milk," his homemade rum mixture. LaRose 5 is given by his parents to another family in reparation for the accidental shooting of their own son. Another child, Hollis, is abandoned first by his mother, who goes off to get a PhD, and then by his father (Romeo), who allows Hollis to be raised by Landreaux Iron, a former classmate. While many readers might assume that under most circumstances it is not good to give up one's children, surely LaRose 1 was better off away from her alcoholic mother and murderous father. And surely the best thing that ever happened to Hollis was being raised by stable parents like Landreaux and Emmaline Iron rather than by the irresponsible and vindictive Romeo Puyat, his biological father.

Education of children. LaRose challenges the stereotypes that white schools are better than Indian schools and that boarding schools are necessarily always bad for students. Mrs. Peace (LaRose 4), who taught Landreaux Iron and Romeo Puyat at their boarding school, was an amazingly fine and loving teacher, the best teacher that they would ever know. And the on-reservation boarding school for children in crisis, headed by Emmaline Iron, serves as a place of refuge and stability for Native children.

The spirit world. Otherworldly events occur in *LaRose*. The talking rolling head of the poisoned Mackinnon chases LaRose 1 and Wolfred Roberts through the woods. LaRose 1 plays her mother's sacred drum to help cure Wolfred. When he asks her where she got the drum, she replies, "It flew to me" (143). She herself flies as well. LaRose 5 is joined one night in the woods by the spirits of his deceased relatives, including his great-great-great-grandmother LaRose 1. He plays games with his dead cousin Dusty-iban. Randall, who conducts traditional sweat-lodge ceremonies, insists that such doings are not magic. They are, he says, "beyond ordinary understanding now, but not magic" (52).

Justice. The novel quotes Frank Baum, who appallingly wrote in 1888 that "The Whites by law of conquest, by justice of civilization" (70), have earned the right to annihilate the Indians. Wolfred Roberts speaks of finding a way to murder Mackinnon in which "there might be justice" (118). Father Travis is surprised to learn that Landreaux and Emmaline Iron give their son to the parents of Dusty, the boy Landreaux accidentally killed, but he reflects that it is "an old form of justice" (36). Maggie Ravich exacts her own kind of justice when she learns that Dougie Veddar bullied her adopted brother, LaRose 5: she kicks Dougie in the crotch and jams a candy bar down his throat.

Home and land. All of the characters named LaRose occupy, at least for a time, the house built by Wolfred Roberts, the husband of LaRose 1, on the land his descendants still occupy. That home on that land gives the family an enduring stability and continuity.

Forgiveness. People do injurious things in *LaRose*. A young girl poisons a man who has been abusing her. A man accidently shoots his wife's half-sister's little boy. A mother gives up her child. Another takes a child from her sister. A man abandons his son. A priest has a romance with one of his married parishioners, who willingly accepts him. A man breaks into confidential hospital files to build a fraudulent case against one of the few people ever to befriend him. Another man, not questioning the evidence, sets out to kill an innocent man. A group of boys grope a girl. Much is forgiven in *LaRose*. The mostly happy ending of the novel is made convincing by that forgiveness. Peter and Nola Ravich forgive Landreaux for killing their son, Dusty. Landreaux and Emmaline forgive them for trying to keep their son, LaRose 5, from them. Everyone seems to be convinced that observing this particular form of traditional justice is a good thing, even for the boy LaRose 5, who benefits from having two sets of loving parents and an extra, loving sister. Hollis invites his selfish absentee father to his graduation celebration, and everyone seems willing to forgive Romeo for trying to have Peter kill Landreaux. *LaRose* offers no easy answers, but forgiveness is surely an important element in the healing that brings together these hurting people.

Love. Love is triumphant in *LaRose*. We find fraternal love in the Iron and Ravich families, romantic love between LaRose 1 and Wolfred Roberts, sexual love between Maggie and Waylon, mature love between husbands and wives, forbidden love between a priest and one of his parishioners, adoring love of a very young man for his favorite teacher and her daughter. Near the end of the novel, Mrs. Peace (LaRose 4), noticing that Josette pricks her finger while making a beaded medallion for Hollis, says, "Ooooo. Old-time love medicine" (357), thus invoking the title of Erdrich's first novel, *Love Medicine* (1984). Thirty-two years later, love is still the most effective, the most healing, medicine.

Chapters in *LaRose* (2016)

NOTE: There are five large sections in *LaRose*, identified in a table of contents in the novel. Each section has at least one chapter. We have included the title of each chapter below, and we have for convenience given bracketed numbers to these chapters. Some of the chapters have subchapters with titles (not shown here). There are two more kinds of divisions in the novels: some are marked by small, centered icons; some by a line of white space. We also do not show those below.

TWO HOUSES, 1999–2001
    [1] The Door — 3
    [2] The Gate — 17
    [3] The Passage — 63
    [4] Hello, beauty — 95
    [5] The Crossbeams — 100
    [6] Almond Joy — 120
    [7] The Pain Chart — 133
TAKE IT ALL, 1967–1970 — 153
    [8] Romeo and Landreaux — 155
WOLFRED AND LAROSE — 185
    [9] The Old One — 187
1,000 KILLS, 2002–2003 — 203
    [10] The Letters — 205
    [11] The Green Chair — 220

THE GATHERING   347

    [12] You Go   349

Chronology of Events in *LaRose*

LaRose covers some 164 years, from 1839 to 2003, with much shifting back and forth in time. Most of the action takes place from 1999, when Landreaux accidentally shoots Dusty Ravich, to 2003, when Hollis graduates from high school. A few specific dates, listed below, are given. Some others can be inferred from the historical context, as in the reference to the March 2003 invasion of Iraq: "In March there was the war. Father Travis started to watch the shock and awe, then switched it off" (316). The reference to "shock and awe" is an unmistakable reference to George W. Bush's invasion of Iraq.

1839—The fur trader Mackinnon reluctantly buys an Ojibwe Indian girl, LaRose 1, from Mink, her mother. Mackinnon's young assistant, Wolfred Roberts, realizes the girl has unique traditional skills. Together they poison Mackinnon, who has been abusing LaRose, and run away, but Mackinnon's rolling head follows them. Taken in by missionaries, the girl is sent off to a mission school. Wolfred returns to Mackinnon's trading post to take over Mackinnon's job as trader.

1846—LaRose 1 returns from the mission school and marries Wolfred Roberts. They head west of Pembina (a trading center in the northeast corner of what is now North Dakota) to land Wolfred is homesteading. That land would eventually be declared part of a reservation, but Wolfred and his wife and their descendants retain ownership of it. The cabin he built, variously enlarged and modernized in the 1950s, 1970s, and 1980s, is home to all five LaRoses down through the generations.

1912—Date given by the old, nearly blind farm woman who aids Landreaux and Romeo in their escape from boarding school as the year her husband acquired their rich farmland from an Indian family who were unable to pay their land taxes [chap. 8]. This was one of many ways that Indians lost their land to Europeans, a land loss that is a central theme in Erdrich's work.

1953—Father Travis Wozniak is born.

1959—Fort Totten Boarding School closes.

1967—Landreaux Iron and his friend Romeo Puyat are sent off the reservation to attend an unnamed Bureau of Indian Affairs boarding school.

1970—Landreaux Iron and Romeo Puyat run away from boarding school by hiding in the undercarriage of a school bus. They are befriended by an old, nearly blind farm woman who gives them food and money. They take a bus to Minneapolis, where they fall in with a group of railroad bums. They watch lots of movies, all of which came out in 1970. One night they fall off a railroad piling. Romeo is injured when Landreaux lands on him. A doctor saves Romeo's leg from being amputated, but Romeo has a permanent limp and—so he says—enduring pain.

1983—Father Travis Wozniak, then a Marine in Beirut, survives a barracks bombing.

1989—Maggie Ravich is born.

1994—LaRose 5 Iron and Dusty Ravich are born.

1999—Landreaux Iron, aiming to shoot a deer, accidentally kills his wife's half-sister's son, Dusty Ravich. Landreaux and his wife, Emmaline, heartbreakingly deliver their son, LaRose 5, as recompense for the loss of his dead cousin, to the grieving parents—Peter and Nola Ravich—and their preteen daughter, Maggie. Both families celebrate a somber Christmas in the aftermath of the killing of Dusty.

2000—Dougie Veddar stabs LaRose 5 with a pencil. Maggie punishes Dougie with a crotch kick. She is later, in retaliation, groped by Dougie's older brother and his friends, but she successfully defends herself and leaves. LaRose 5 then unsuccessfully tries to retaliate against the older boys.

2002–2003—Nola Ravich tries to hang herself but is prevented from doing so by her daughter, Maggie, and the mongrel dog who alerts Maggie to the danger. Emmaline Iron decides that she wants her son LaRose 5 back, and the two families work out a plan for sharing him. Meanwhile, he sneaks off one night to be in the place where his cousin Dusty was killed. The spirits of some of his dead relatives, as well as Dusty's spirit, come to him and assure LaRose that they will provide help and guidance to him. Romeo Puyat, having convinced himself that Landreaux was responsible for his damaged arm and leg, takes a job in the hospital, where he finds evidence that he thinks proves that Landreaux could have saved Dusty's life. He shares this (erroneous) information with Peter Ravich, who then goes to find Landreaux in order to kill him. Father Travis learns of Peter's intentions and, having fallen in love with Emmaline and had a clandestine rendezvous with her in Grand Forks, still desperately tries to intervene. Peter's shots are ineffective because LaRose 5, to keep Nola from committing suicide, had earlier emptied the bullets from Peter's deer rifle. Meanwhile, Maggie Ravich triumphantly helps her volleyball team, the

Warriors, defeat the Pluto Lady Planets. Jason "Buggy" Wildstrand attacks Hollis, Waylon, and Coochy, but hurts only himself. These and other plot lines are brought to conclusion in a celebration for Hollis Puyat's high school graduation. The party brings the various families, and their spirit ancestors, together in an atmosphere of love and forgiveness.

Family Tree for *LaRose*

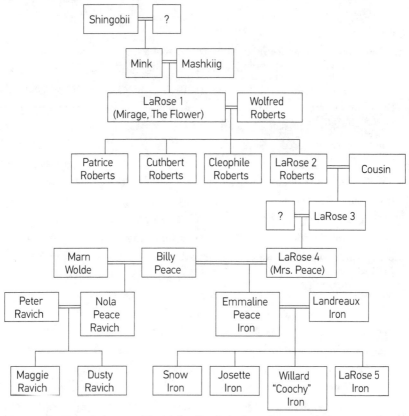

CHART 10. The Roberts, Iron, and Ravich families in *LaRose.* Courtesy of Peter G. Beidler and Gay Barton.

Dictionary of Characters for *LaRose*

Alice Anakwad. Classmate of LaRose 1 in the mission school. She gets tuberculosis and probably passes it on to several of her classmates, including LaRose 1 [chap. 9].

Awan. An old man mentioned briefly as one of the patients Landreaux Iron takes care of [chap. 1, 3]. (Although the spelling is slightly different, Awan's love of cards is similar to the card-playing skills of Fleur Pillager's son, Awun, in *The Bingo Palace* and *Four Souls*.)

Baptiste "Bap" Plume. Wife of Ottie Plume, usually called "Bap." She is Emmaline's cousin.

Behring, Miss. Teacher in the Pluto school that Maggie attends. She tries (not very successfully) to punish Maggie for calling her "Miss Boring" [chap. 6].

Billy Peace. Prominent character in *The Plague of Doves*. In *LaRose*, he is referred to as the father of both Emmaline Iron and Nola Ravich [chap. 2] though he does not actually appear in the novel. (See also the entry for him in the Dictionary of Characters for *The Plague of Doves*.)

Bowl Head. Students' name for Mrs. Vrilchyk, matron at the boarding school Landreaux and Romeo attend. She tells Landreaux and Romeo that there will be dire consequences if they try to escape. Later, when they do escape, they see—or imagine that they see—her pursuing them. She takes them back to school [chap. 8].

Brad Morrissey. One of the "Fearsome Four" boys who abuse Maggie [chap. 7]. (He is presumably related to the Morrisseys from *Love Medicine*, but no connection is specified in *LaRose*.)

Braelyn Wildstrand. Star player on the Pluto Lady Planets volleyball team. She is the sister of Jason "Buggy" Wildstrand, one of the boys who groped Maggie Ravich [chap. 11].

Buggy Wildstrand. See **Jason "Buggy" Wildstrand.**

Ceel. Son of the old, nearly blind farm woman who befriends runaways Landreaux Iron and Romeo Puyat. We are not told his last name [chap. 8].

Cleophile Roberts. One of four children born to LaRose 1 and Wolfred Roberts, older sibling of LaRose 2.

Coochy. See **Willard Iron.**

Curtains Peace. One of the "Fearsome Four" boys who abuse Maggie [chap. 7].

Cuthbert Roberts. One of four children born to LaRose 1 and Wolfred Roberts, older brother of LaRose 2.

Diamond. Captain of the girls' volleyball team (the Warriors) that Snow and Josette Iron, and Maggie Ravich, play on [chap. 11].

Dick Bohner, Father. Priest who arrives to replace Father Travis at the end of *LaRose*. He does not seem to realize that his name is an obscene pun [chap. 12].

Dog. Unnamed. The stray, rusty mongrel originally hangs around the Iron house, then follows LaRose 5 when he goes to live with the Ravich family. Maggie has dreamed that Dusty had a stuffed animal that looked just like the stray dog, and Peter recognizes that the stray is not an ordinary dog. The dog "mind-talks" to Peter with the comforting news that "I carry a piece of his [Dusty's] soul in me" (64). The dog alerts Maggie to Nola's attempted hanging and provides emotional support to both Nola and Peter [chap. 11]. He assists La Rose 5 in healing the grieving Ravich family.

Dougie Veddar. Schoolyard kindergarten bully who stabs Maggie Ravich's adoptive brother LaRose's shoulder with a pencil. Maggie later punishes Dougie, and then Dougie's big brother Tyler and his gang of friends try to get their revenge by abusing her [chap. 6, 7].

Duke, Coach. Coach of the Warriors, the volleyball team that Snow and Josette Iron, and Maggie Ravich, play on. He welcomes Maggie to the team even though she is inexperienced and trains her as a secret weapon who is good at diving for spikes from the opposing team [chap. 11].

Dusty Ravich. Son of Nola and Peter Ravich, brother of Maggie. At age five he is accidentally shot by Landreaux Iron [chap. 1]. One night, with other spirit people, he visits young LaRose 5, his replacement in the Ravich household, who is sleeping under the tree where Dusty was killed, and they play with their favorite action figures [chap. 10]. He shows up again with the spirit people at Hollis Puyat's graduation party at the end of the novel [chap. 12].

Eddieboy. Emmaline's uncle. Landreaux Iron says that it was at Eddieboy's funeral that he first met Emmaline [chap. 11], though that does not match a previous statement that he had met her much earlier at Fort Totten when she was "a little girl" [chap. 8].

Emmaline Peace Iron. Daughter of Billy Peace and LaRose 4; wife of Landreaux Iron; mother of Willard, Snow, Josette, and the boy LaRose 5; and foster mother of Hollis Puyat. When she reluctantly gives her youngest and favorite child, LaRose 5, to Nola and Peter Ravich [chap. 1], she misses him fiercely. It almost breaks her heart when she sees him in the supermarket with Peter Ravich. She seeks help from Father Travis, who tells her she can ask that her son be returned to her [chap. 2]. She eventually does demand him back, but when LaRose 5 objects and tells her that that would endanger Nola, she relents and agrees to continue to share the boy with the Raviches [chap. 11]. After Maggie's volleyball game, which is attended by both sets of parents, Emmaline gives her half-sister, whom she has barely spoken to for three years, a loving hug [chap. 11]. Emmaline feels romantically drawn to Father Travis and meets him for a lover's rendezvous in Grand Forks.

Florian Soreno, Bishop. Father Travis's supervisor and superior in the Catholic Church hierarchy.

Flower. See **LaRose 1.**

Georgie Mighty. The eighty-two-year-old retired nurse who serves as coroner after the shooting of Dusty Ravich [chap. 1].

Haniford Ames, Dr. The doctor who treats LaRose 1 for tuberculosis. When LaRose 1 dies, Ames takes ownership of her bones for research purposes and puts them on museum display [chap. 9, 10].

Hollis Puyat. Abandoned son of Romeo Puyat, raised by Landreaux and Emmaline Iron. He turns out to be a good person, even buys his freeloading father a beer on his (Hollis's) eighteenth birthday [chap. 10]. Hollis joins the National Guard [chap. 11]. He has a crush on Josette Iron but is afraid to tell her his feelings. He is honored by the whole family at a massive graduation party at the end of the novel. He invites his father to the party and finally finds out who his mother was, a woman named Karisma Li [chap. 12].

Hossel, Mr. Maggie Ravich's science teacher in the reservation school. He praises Maggie's excellent work in his class [chap. 11].

Ignatia Thunder, Grandma. An older Ojibwe woman who lives in the Elders Lodge and is known for her storytelling abilities. She tells three old-time stories to La Rose 5 in order to instruct him on the devastation of revenge and on the wisdom found in traditional ways. She concludes her story sequence by relating how a man, whose wife has been unfaithful, feeds his wife a soup made of the meat of her lover and then beheads her. The woman's talking, rolling head then chases her two terrified sons, one of whom becomes the cultural hero/trickster Wishketchahk, or Nanabozho, and his brother, his trusted companion, turns into a wolf/dog. As she finishes that story, Ignatia dies [chap. 11]. (See also the entry for her in the Dictionary of Characters for *The Round House*.)

Iron family. See **Emmaline Peace Iron, Hollis Puyat, Josette Iron, Landreaux Iron, LaRose 5, Snow Iron,** and **Willard (Coochy) Iron.**

Jason "Buggy" Wildstrand. One of the "Fearsome Four" boys who abuse Maggie [chap. 7]. He later attacks Coochy, Waylon, and Hollis when they come to find him in an abandoned shack in the woods [chap. 11]. Buggy and his equally bullying sister, Braelyn Wildstrand, are apparently related to the Wildstrands in *The Plague of Doves*, but the exact connection is not specified.

Josette Iron. Daughter of Landreaux and Emmaline Iron. She likes Hollis Puyat but is shy about telling him so. She and her sister, Snow, call themselves "The Iron Maidens" [chap. 2] and welcome their cousin Maggie Ravich as a sister [chap. 11, 12].

Karisma Li. The mother of Hollis Puyat. Hollis's father, Romeo Puyat, does not say much about her except that he lost her to a PhD program at the University of Michigan [chap. 12].

Landreaux Iron. Ojibwe man; husband of Emmaline; father of Willard, Snow, Josette, and LaRose 5; and foster father of Hollis Puyat. Landreaux works as a physical therapy assistant, or personal care assistant, and is training to be a dialysis technician. Landreaux accidentally shoots young Dusty Ravich in the opening chapter. He then buys but does not drink a bottle of whiskey. He follows a traditional way of justice by giving the Raviches his own son, LaRose 5. He is said to have gone hunting at age seven with his grandfather [chap. 1], who is not identified by name. It is not entirely clear who Landreaux's parents are. We know that they sent him at age nine to a BIA boarding school and then presumably moved to Minneapolis. They never came to visit Landreaux at boarding school [chap. 7]. While at boarding school, Landreaux is befriended by one of his teachers, Mrs. Peace (LaRose 4), and her young daughter, Emmaline, whom he later marries. Landreaux runs off from the school three years later to try to find his parents in Minneapolis. Romeo Puyat, a fellow student at their boarding school, runs off with him. They escape by concealing themselves in the undercarriage of a school bus (reminiscent of Lulu Lamartine's escape from school, which occurs in *Tracks* and is detailed in *The Last Report on the Miracles at Little No Horse*). With the help of a lonely, nearly blind old farm woman, who mistakes Landreaux and Romeo for boys she knew in the past, they make their escape. She feeds them, gives them a bed to sleep in, and gives them money, more than a thousand dollars. They buy bus tickets to Minneapolis but seem not to succeed in finding Landreaux's parents. There they fall in among some homeless Natives. Romeo is injured in a fall from a railroad-trestle support piling and blames Landreaux for his damaged arm and leg [chap. 8]. Landreaux joins the military and serves in Desert Storm. When Romeo convinces Peter Ravich that Landreaux passed up a chance to save the life of Dusty immediately after the shooting, Landreaux, riddled with guilt, makes it easy for Peter to get his revenge by murdering him. Peter's rifle is empty, however, and in the end, Landreaux is exonerated and rejoins his wife, Emmaline [chap. 11].

LaRose. See **LaRose 1, LaRose 2, LaRose 3, LaRose 4, LaRose 5.** (For hints about their relationships see pages 23, 51, 134, 191, 202, 290 of the novel.)

LaRose 1. The original LaRose. Also known as Illusion, Mirage, Ombanitemagad, and Flower [chap. 7], she is the daughter of Mink and Mashkiig. When LaRose 1 is eleven, Mink sells her to the trader Mackinnon in exchange for the trader's cheap homemade liquor [chap. 1]. She and Wolfred Roberts poison Mackinnon, who has been abusing LaRose, and they run off together [chap. 5]. LaRose 1 has traditional healing powers. For example, she takes Wolfred out of his body to protect him and flies with him, and she also calls her mother's sacred drum to fly to her [chap. 7]. She is taken in by missionaries, who arrange for her to attend a Presbyterian boarding school in Michigan. While there she gets tuberculosis, a disease that troubles her off and on for the rest of her life [chap. 9]. When she graduates from boarding school, she returns, sheds her fashionable clothing, and marries Wolfred Roberts. They have four children: Patrice, Cuthbert, Cleophile, and LaRose 2. Wolfred takes her to a sanitarium in St. Paul to be treated for tuberculosis by Dr. Haniford Ames. At first she responds well to his treatments, but then Mackinnon's rolling head begins to appear to her, and not long after that she dies [chap. 9]. Her husband is not given her body to bury in a traditional way. It turns out that Dr. Ames keeps her bones for "research" and to display in a museum [chap. 10]. Wolfred petitions to have his wife's bones returned to him, but Dr. Ames refuses. His daughter LaRose 2 and later Mrs. Peace (LaRose 4, her great-granddaughter) continue to try to get the bones back through vigorous and persistent letter-writing [chap. 10]. LaRose 1 shows up as one of the spirit people the night LaRose 5 goes into the woods [chap. 10] and later at the graduation party for Hollis Puyat [chap. 12].

LaRose 2. Daughter of the first LaRose and her husband, Wolfred Roberts. She is sent off to Carlisle Indian Industrial School, a boarding school in Pennsylvania run by Richard H. Pratt [chap. 9]. There she is taught to dress like a white woman and to do servant work in the homes of white women. Like her mother before her, she contracts tuberculosis. She eventually marries her cousin (not further

identified) and has a daughter (LaRose 3) who becomes a teacher and the
mother of a teacher (LaRose 4, Mrs. Peace).

LaRose 3. Daughter of LaRose 2. She goes to the Fort Totten boarding school and
eventually has a daughter, LaRose 4 (Mrs. Peace). She also contracts tuberculosis, which had killed her mother and grandmother [chap. 3]. (This is apparently
the LaRose mentioned in *The Round House* as a close boarding-school friend
of Geraldine Coutts. See the entry for **LaRose Migwan** in the Dictionary of
Characters for *The Round House*.)

LaRose 4. Daughter of LaRose 3. She "marries" Billy Peace and has a daughter named
Emmaline. (Note: even though Billy Peace is an important character in *The
Plague of Doves*, and he is said there to have had many wives, no one named
LaRose is mentioned in that novel.) LaRose 4 is usually identified in the novel
as "Mrs. Peace." She becomes a teacher at an Indian boarding school [chap. 3]
where she teaches Landreaux Iron and Romeo Puyat [chap. 8]. Her daughter,
Emmaline, eventually marries Landreaux, so she becomes the grandmother of
LaRose 5, the boy who is given to the Raviches to raise. In retirement she lives in
the Elders Lodge, and her son-in-law, Landreaux, looks after her when she grows
sick [chap. 2]. She continues her great-grandfather Wolfred Roberts's petitions
to have the bones of the original LaRose, her great-grandmother, returned to
the family [chap. 10], and she eventually succeeds [chap. 12].

LaRose 5. The boy given by Landreaux and Emmaline Iron to Peter and Nola Ravich
as a replacement for their accidentally killed son, Dusty [chap. 1]. At first he cries
often when he is taken in by his strange new family, but gradually he begins to
fit in. His first Christmas in his new home is a somber affair [chap. 2], but he
is happier when the two sets of parents agree to share him. He becomes good
friends with all of his siblings, wrestling with them and teasing them [chap.
5]. When a kindergarten bully named Dougie Veddar stabs him with a pencil,
LaRose's cousin Maggie punishes the bully with a crotch kick and a candy bar
stuffed down his throat. This fifth LaRose, the only male with that name, is able
to communicate with spirit people, most of whom he seems to be related to.
Among the spirit people is Dusty Ravich, his friend and cousin, with whom he
plays their favorite games [chap. 10]. LaRose 5 is quick to learn from both his
birth parents and his adoptive parents. He helps his new sister, Maggie, keep
watch to prevent Nola Ravich from committing suicide. To that end he hides
sharp knives, ropes, and poisons away from Nola and removes the bullets from
Peter's rifles [chap. 11]. He learns the basics of the martial art tae kwon do from

Father Travis Wozniak and vows to get revenge on the Fearsome Four boys, who live in Pluto and who earlier had abused his adoptive sister, Maggie. He bravely tries, but, at age eight, he is too small to punish them much. One of them knocks him out, almost killing him. Another drives him home and pays him the compliment of suggesting that he try out for football someday [chap. 11].

Mackinnon. Fur trader who buys Mink's daughter, LaRose 1, and sexually abuses her. She and Wolfred poison him [chap. 5], but Mackinnon's rolling head pursues them as they make their escape [chap. 6]. His dead body is torn apart by his dogs [chap. 7].

Maggie Ravich. Daughter of Nola and Peter Ravich, sister of Dusty. One of her grandmothers, Marn Wolde, is Polish, and she is named after her great-aunt Maggie Peace, the sister of Billy Peace and mother of Corwin Peace [chap. 1]. (See the entry for **Maggie Peace** in the Dictionary of Characters for *The Plague of Doves*.) When LaRose 5 becomes her brother (replacing her real brother, Dusty), she is at first mean to him [chap. 2], but she soon grows to like him. She punishes Dougie Veddar for bullying LaRose 5, and then in turn she is abused by several junior-high boys who call themselves the Fearsome Four. She capably defends herself [chap. 6, 7]. When she is thirteen, she climbs a tree, and she feels a spirit-owl enter her body. Shortly after that she finds her mother, Nola, about to hang herself in the barn. Maggie saves her with the help of the mongrel dog who alerted her [chap. 11]. When her adoptive brother, LaRose 5, goes to the reservation school, she enrolls also. Her mother is part Ojibwe, so she has a right to go there. She makes friends easily and even tries out for the volleyball team. She grows to like and respect a husky football player named Waylon. She invites him to come home and help her weed the garden and that day gives up her virginity to him [chap. 11]. By the end of the novel, she has become close to the Iron family members, especially her new "sisters," Snow and Josette, who give her friendly advice about cosmetics and birth control [chap. 12].

Malvern Sangrait. An old woman who lives in the Elders Lodge. She is sometimes nasty to Ignatia Thunder, whom she accuses of seducing her husbands. When the old storyteller dies, however, Malvern helps start her on her journey to the spirit world. Malvern tells LaRose 5 to listen to what she says, because someday it will be his job to start the dead on their journey west [chap. 11].

Marn. Mother of Nola Ravich. She is said to have murdered her husband Billy Peace [chap. 2]. (Note: She is the Marn Wolde Peace of *The Plague of Doves* where she has two children named Judah and Lilith with her husband, Billy

Peace. In *LaRose* only one child is mentioned, Nola, who is presumably Lilith. See the entry for **Marn Wolde Peace** in the Dictionary of Characters for *The Plague of Doves*.)

Mashkiig. Husband of Mink, father of LaRose 1. He is a brutal man who mutilates and eventually kills his wife, Mink, and others [chap. 4]. He is said to be a conjurer who taught his daughter to fly.

Meyer Buell, Dr. The Polish doctor who helps the injured Romeo. Because of his skill, Romeo's leg is not amputated [chap. 8].

Mightie George. The nurse who examines the body of Dusty Ravich, after Landreaux accidentally shoots him [chap. 1, 11].

Milbert Good Road. An Indian boy who drowned and whose ghost greets Landreaux Iron and Romeo Puyat when they arrive at Indian boarding school [chap. 8].

Mink. Ojibwe woman in *LaRose*, the daughter of Shingobii, wife of Mashkiig, mother of LaRose 1. Mink is an alcoholic: she sells her daughter to the fur trader Mackinnon for homemade liquor. She is defaced and eventually killed by Mashkiig [chap. 1, 4].

Mirage. English translation of the Ojibwe word Ombanitemagad, the name given to all of the characters named LaRose.

Nola Peace Ravich. Daughter of Marn and Billy Peace. Presumably called Lilith in *The Plague of Doves*—after Billy Peace's death, Marn moved to Fargo with her two children, where Marn "[m]ade them go by their second names because of certain people" (*LaRose* 77). Nola is the half-sister of Emmaline Iron, wife of Peter Ravich, mother of Maggie and Dusty, adoptive mother of LaRose 5 in *LaRose*. She is at first reluctant to accept LaRose [chap. 1], but she grows fond of the substitute son. In her confused state of shock and depression, she makes cake after cake that no one eats [chap. 2]. She is prone to fits of anger; for example, during a church service she smacks her daughter, Maggie. Later, in a chat with Father Travis she hints that she will harm herself if LaRose 5 is taken from her. When Father Travis mentions the smacking of Maggie and threatens to report her to Social Services, Nola falsely accuses him of touching her bosom [chap. 3]. In a later conference with Father Travis, she admits that she has thought of hanging herself. She almost does hang herself in the barn by kicking away a green chair she stands on. Her daughter, Maggie, talks her out of it, but she is still an emotional wreck [chap. 11]. Slowly she comes out of her depression: she lands a job in a convenience store and makes plans for running a farm on her land. She is comforted when she hears LaRose 5, her adoptive son, playing imaginary games with his old friend Dusty, her deceased son [chap. 11]. She gradually warms to her husband, Peter. A final step in Nola's recovery is her triumphant burning of the green chair—the one she had tried to use to commit suicide [chap. 11].

Oberjerk, Mr. A teacher who rescues Dougie Veddar after Maggie Ravich attacks him.

Old, nearly blind farm woman. An elderly woman whose eyesight is diminished by cataracts. She, along with her dog, Pepperboy, welcomes the runaways Landreaux Iron and Romeo Puyat. She gives them food, lets them sleep in her bed, and then lies about it to her son, Ceel. She talks to Landreaux as though she knew his parents and grandparents. As Landreaux and Romeo leave her house, she gives them food and more than a thousand dollars [chap. 8]. We are not told her name.

Ombanitemagad. One of the original names of LaRose 1, and a name shared by all those who are called LaRose. LaRose 5 is referred to by this name before Landreaux and Emmaline take him to the Raviches to become their adoptive son [chap. 5].

Ottie Plume. A diabetic man whom Landreaux drives to dialysis treatments [chap. 2, 11]. Ottie's wife's name is Baptiste "Bap" Plume.

Patrice Roberts. One of four children born to LaRose 1 and Wolfred Roberts, older sibling of LaRose 2.

Peace, Mrs. See **LaRose 4.**

Peter Ravich. The husband of Nola, and the father of Maggie and Dusty. He is said to be from a family of Russian-German immigrants [chap. 3]. When his friend Landreaux Iron accidentally shoots Dusty, he agrees to take LaRose 5 as a replacement son [chap. 1]. He convinces himself that there will be a terrible catastrophe when the year 2000 arrives and a new century approaches, and he goes deeply into debt to stockpile food and other provisions in preparation for Y2K [chap. 2]. The death of Dusty severely strains his relationship with his wife, Nola, but over the course of the novel, they gradually grow closer together. For the sake of LaRose 5, Peter suggests to Landreaux that the two families should share the boy, letting him alternate between the two houses. That arrangement works well [chap. 3]. Later in the novel, when he learns from Romeo that Landreaux had been negligent in not saving Dusty (according to Romeo's misreading of various documents), Peter gets his rifle and vows to kill Landreaux. He picks up Landreaux and takes him to the woods, intending to shoot him. He would have succeeded if LaRose 5 had not earlier unloaded the rifle to prevent Nola from harming herself with it [chap. 11].

Pits. The male "matron" at the B.I.A. Indian boarding school who helps Bowl Head capture the runaways Landreaux Iron and Romeo Puyat. On the way back he urinates on Landreaux [chap. 8].

Randall. Healer who holds a sweat-lodge ceremony for Landreaux Iron [chap. 1, 2]. He makes ceremonial pipes from pipestone [chap. 11] and sings a song at Hollis Puyat's graduation party [chap. 12]. (He is apparently the same person as Randall Lafournais in *The Round House*, though no last name is given for him in *LaRose*. See the entry for **Randall Lafournais** in the Dictionary of Characters for *The Round House*.)

Ravich family. See **Dusty Ravich, Maggie Ravich, Nola Peace Ravich,** and **Peter Ravich.**

Rolling Heads. Also known as "Cannibal Heads"; found in Midwestern and Plains Indian legends. They come into being as the victim of a vengeful crime (usually involving an unfaithful wife) and, in their desire for revenge, haunt their murderer and their descendants and disrupt the balance of a community. In *LaRose*, the trader Mackinnon's head follows LaRose 1 throughout her life. The heads symbolize how the pursuit of revenge ultimately must be averted through magic or it will continue to sow evil wherever it goes. The three old stories Ignatia Thunder tells LaRose 5 include a rolling head, and they warn him of the consequences of revenge and its lasting destructive power to injure not only people and their families but also communities as a whole [chap. 11]. When Landreaux and Romeo run away from boarding school, they spend days hiding in a movie theater, where they think they see the disembodied head of Mrs. Vrilchyk (Bowl Head), the matron at the boarding school where Landreaux and Romeo are students and who is pursing them: "Landreaux . . . thought that Bowl Head was a spirit, a force, an element set in motion by the boarding school to pursue them to the end of time" (173).

Romeo Puyat. Ojibwe freeloader and drug/alcohol addict. His origins are obscure. He was found as a child of four or five wandering around on the reservation in a deplorable state: he was "burned, bruised, starved" (156) and scarred (159). He is clearly an Indian, but his origins are unknown. (He shares the same last name as Pauline Puyat from the novel *Tracks*, but no familial connection is made explicit in *LaRose*.) Romeo winds up at a B.I.A. boarding school where he is befriended by Landreaux Iron and gets to know Mrs. Peace and her daughter, Emmaline [chap. 8]. He is found to be very intelligent. Romeo abandons his son,

Hollis, at age five, to be raised by his former schoolmate, Landreaux Iron, and his wife, Emmaline. Over the years, he becomes deeply resentful and distrusting. He convinces himself that Landreaux has stolen both his girlfriend Emmaline [chap. 2] and the affections of his son, Hollis [chap. 10]. To get even, he steals gas from people's gas tanks and robs patients of their painkillers. At one point he takes pills from medicine cabinets in the Elders Lodge, thinking they are painkillers, but they are actually "psychotropic laxative erection pills," and the results are painful, comic, and the deliberate consequence of the elders taking their revenge on him [chap. 11]. Romeo convinces himself that the injuries he received while running away from boarding school were caused by Landreaux [chap. 8]. Instead of buying his son, Hollis, a beer on his eighteenth birthday, he lets Hollis buy him several beers [chap. 10].

Romeo eventually charms his way into janitorial jobs at the tribal college and at the Indian Health Service. He uses these jobs as a source of narcotics and information about patients, their medical histories, their medicines. He picks the lock on a confidential file cabinet and steals documents that he takes to be evidence that Landreaux had been negligent three years earlier when he had accidently shot Dusty Ravich [chap. 11]. He convinces himself that the documents prove that the boy would have lived if Landreaux had given him immediate aid and not run instead to inform Nola. He reports his findings to Peter Ravich, hoping that Peter will kill Landreaux in revenge. At an AA meeting run by Father Travis, Romeo, high on drugs, blurts out the "evidence" he has found against Landreaux and inadvertently goes deeper and deeper into all of his past misdeeds. Then in remorse, Romeo flings himself down the twenty stone steps leading up to the church. He gets up and walks away, amazed that his tumble has readjusted his bones so that he can live henceforth almost pain-free again. At his son Hollis's graduation party, Romeo gives his son a gift of more than three thousand dollars, and he finally tells his son who his biological mother was, a woman named Karisma Li, who went into a PhD program at the University of Michigan [chap. 12].

Sam Eagleboy. Resident of the Elders Lodge and a respected elder who is helping LaRose 5 to step into his role as a traditional healer. He is also the boyfriend of Malvern Sangrait. He gives LaRose 5 advice about how to face problems with an open mind, and he sings a song at Hollis Puyat's graduation party [chap. 11, 12].

Snow Iron. Older daughter of Landreaux and Emmaline Iron. She and her younger sister, Josette, shop for cosmetics and for a gift for their mother, while the store clerk eyes them with suspicion [chap. 2]. She and Josette welcome their cousin Maggie Ravich as a sister and teach her to play volleyball [chap. 11].

Star. Old woman in the Elders Lodge. She was a kind of foster mother to Romeo Puyat [chap. 5]. (Apparently she is the same Star who appears in *The Round House*. See the entry for her in the Dictionary of Characters for *The Round House*.)

Sterling Chance. Hospital administrator (head of maintenance) who gives a job to Romeo.

Sweit, Mrs. Maggie Ravich's kindergarten teacher—"the only teacher she'd loved" [chap. 11].

Travis Wozniak, Father. Catholic priest. An important character in *The Round House*, he is also a key character in *LaRose*. (See also the entry for him in the Dictionary of Characters for *The Round House*.) He consoles Emmaline and Landreaux Iron after the killing of Dusty Ravich and the relinquishment of their own son, LaRose 5 [chap. 1]. He chose to give up drinking liquor after it threatened to develop into a serious habit or addiction [chap. 3]. He remembers being wounded as a Marine [chap. 5]. He encourages physical fitness on the reservation and later teaches tae kwon do to LaRose 5. He falls in love with Emmaline Iron, mother of LaRose 5, and meets her for a lover's tryst in Grand Forks [chap. 11]. When he learns from Romeo Puyat that Landreaux Iron's life is in danger, he drives off to try to save him. A part of him, however, thinks he wants to let Landreaux die so that the way would be clear for him to marry Emmaline. At the end, Father Travis, after making sure that Peter understands that Romeo had falsely accused Landreaux of negligence in the aftermath of his accidental killing of Dusty, leaves the reservation. He is replaced by the new priest Father Dick Bohner [chap. 12].

Trucker Hat and Mrs. Trucker Hat. A term used to refer to Mr. and Mrs. John Wildstrand, parents of Braelyn Wildstrand and Jason "Buggy" Wildstrand. The Wildstrand parents sit behind Peter and Nola Ravich at the intensely fought girls' volleyball game between the Pluto Lady Planets and the reservation team, the Warriors. Peter punches John but later apologizes [chap. 11].

Tyler Veddar. One of the Fearsome Four boys who abuse Maggie [chap. 7].

Vrilchyk, Mrs. See **Bowl Head.**

Waylon. A football player at the reservation school who has a crush on Maggie Ravich. She meets him on her first day at the new school, introduced to him by her cousin/sister Snow Iron. Near the end of the novel he has consensual sex with Maggie [chap. 11].

Webid, Mrs. A woman who lives in the Elders Lodge and appears in comedic scenes in the novel [chap. 5].

Whitey Milk. Whitey himself does not play a role in *LaRose*, but his gas station and store still function as an important meeting place and source of food, drink, and gas on the reservation. Now referred to as "Old Whitey," he runs the place with London, the daughter of his former girlfriend Sonja, and Josette and Snow Iron work for him part-time. (See also the entries for him in the Dictionary of Characters for *The Plague of Doves* and for *The Round House*.)

Willard Iron. Nicknamed Coochy, son of Landreaux and Emmaline Iron. He joins Hollis Puyat and Waylon in challenging the brutal Jason "Buggy" Wildstrand, one of the abusers of Maggie Ravich [chap. 11].

Wolfred Roberts. Young assistant to the trader Mackinnon. Originally from New Hampshire, he falls in love with an eleven-year-old Ojibwe girl, LaRose 1 [chap. 1, 2]. When he sees how lovely she is and realizes that Mackinnon has been molesting her, he poisons Mackinnon with her help and runs off with her [chap. 4, 5], but Mackinnon's rolling head chases them. While LaRose 1 is off at the Presbyterian mission school, Wolfred returns to take up Mackinnon's duties as fur trader. During this time of separation, their roles reverse: "He was turning into an Indian while she was turning into a white woman" (147). Wolfred and LaRose 1 marry when she returns from the mission school, and he builds a rustic cabin for them and their four children to live in. That cabin, remodeled and added to over the years, stays in the family and is occupied by LaRose 5 as the novel opens. When his wife dies of tuberculosis, Wolfred tries repeatedly to have her bones returned to him, but he fails [chap. 10].

Zack Peace. Cousin to Emmaline Iron, coroner, and acting chief of reservation police. He investigates the death of Dusty Ravich [chap. 1]. (This apparently is the same character as the Zack Peace in *The Round House*, though he was only a young teenager there.) He is the grandson of Ignatia Thunder.

The Art of Fiction No. 208

Louise Erdrich

An interview conducted by Lisa Halliday

O nly one passenger train per day makes the Empire Builder journey from Chicago to Seattle, and when it stops in Fargo, North Dakota, at 3:35 in the morning, one senses how, as Louise Erdrich has written, the "earth and sky touch everywhere and nowhere, like sex between two strangers." Erdrich lives in Minneapolis, but we met in the Fargo Econo Lodge parking lot. From there, with Erdrich's eight-year-old daughter, Kiizh, we drove five hours up to the Turtle Mountain Chippewa reservation, on the Manitoba border. Every August, when tick season has subsided, Erdrich and her sister Heid spend a week in a former monastery here to attend the Little Shell Powwow and to conduct a writing workshop at the Turtle Mountain Community College. One afternoon, participants took turns reciting poetry under a basswood tree beside the single-room house where Erdrich's mother grew up. Another day, they ate homemade enchiladas and sang "Desperado" and "Me and Bobby McGee," accompanied by a fellow workshopper on the guitar. In class, the writing is personal, the criticism charitable. It helps that Erdrich does the exercises, too—reading out the results

Originally published in *The Paris Review*, Issue No. 195, Winter 2010 (pp. 133–66). Copyright © 2010 by The Paris Review Foundation Inc., used by permission of The Wylie Agency LLC.

in her mellifluous, often mischievous voice. In tidy fulfillment of an assignment entitled "very short fiction," she wrote, "You went out for the afternoon and came back with your dress on inside out."

Karen Louise Erdrich, born June 7, 1954, in Little Falls, Minnesota, was the first of seven children raised in Wahpeton, North Dakota, by a German American father and a mother who is half French, half Ojibwe—Ojibwe, also known as Chippewa, being one of six Native American tribes comprised by the Anishinaabe ("Original People"). Both of Erdrich's parents taught at a Bureau of Indian Affairs boarding school. For many years, her grandfather Patrick Gourneau was the Turtle Mountain Chippewa tribal chair.

Erdrich was in the first coed class to attend Dartmouth, where she studied English and met her eventual husband, Michael Dorris, another writer and the founder of the college's new Native American Studies program. Shortly after receiving an M.F.A. in creative writing from Johns Hopkins, Erdrich wrote "The World's Greatest Fishermen," a story about the hypothermia death of June Kashpaw, an Ojibwe divorcée whose funeral summons relatives home to a fictional North Dakota Indian reservation. "Fishermen" won the Nelson Algren short-fiction prize and became the first chapter of *Love Medicine*, Erdrich's debut novel and winner of a 1984 National Book Critics Circle Award. Since then, she has written twelve more novels (including *The Crown of Columbus*, coauthored by Dorris), three books of poetry, three books of nonfiction, dozens of short stories, and five children's books. Four of these books she illustrated herself. With Dorris, who was also her first literary agent, she raised three adopted and three biological children before the couple separated in 1995; two years later, Dorris committed suicide.

Erdrich returned to Dartmouth in June of 2009 to receive an honorary doctorate of letters and deliver the main commencement address; the same year, her novel *The Plague of Doves*, which centers on the lynching of four Indians wrongly accused of murdering a white family (and which Philip Roth has called "her dazzling masterpiece"), was named a finalist for the Pulitzer Prize. After invariably classifying Erdrich as a Native American writer, many reviewers proceed to compare her work to that of William Faulkner or Gabriel García Márquez: Faulkner for her tangled family trees, her ventriloquist skill, and her expansive use of a fictional province no less fully imagined than Yoknapatawpha County; García Márquez for her flirtations with magical realism. But so strange are Erdrich's narrative rhythms, and so bonded is her language to its subject matter, that it seems just as accurate to call hers a genre of one.

When the workshop was over, Erdrich drove us back to Fargo for walleye cakes at the Hotel Donaldson, and then to visit her parents, who still live in the modest house in Wahpeton where Erdrich grew up. The next day, while Erdrich attended a wedding in Flandreau, South Dakota, her sister took me the remaining two hundred miles to Minneapolis, where, three days later, Erdrich and I reconvened at her bookstore and Native American arts shop, Birchbark Books. Here, Erdrich's eldest daughter, Persia, decides which children's books to stock. Taped to most of the shelves are detailed recommendations handwritten by Erdrich herself. An upside-down canoe hangs from the ceiling, suspended between a birch-bark reading loft and a Roman Catholic confessional decorated with sweetgrass rosaries. We linger at the store, but not until we make the long walk to Erdrich's house do we finally sit down on the back porch and turn the tape recorder on.

Erdrich was wearing her driving clothes: jeans, sandals, and an untucked button-down shirt. A Belgian shepherd named Maki dozed at our feet, and Erdrich's youngest daughter came out a couple of times—once to ask whether we wanted Play-Doh ice-cream cones, later to report that a Mr. Sparky was on the phone. Then a neighboring buzz saw started up, and we moved inside: up to a small attic room pleasantly cluttered with photographs, artifacts, and many more Catholic and Ojibwe totems, including moccasins, shells, bells, dice, bitterroot, a bone breastplate, an abalone shell for burning sage, a turtle stool, a Huichol mask with a scorpion across its mouth and a double-headed eagle on its brow, and a small army of Virgin statuettes. Crowded into a bookshelf beside a worn armchair in the center of the room are the hardbound spiral notebooks in which, in a deeply slanted longhand, Erdrich still writes most of her books—sitting in the chair with a wooden board laid across its arms as a desk.

—Lisa Halliday

INTERVIEWER: In *The Beet Queen*, Dot Adare's first-grade teacher puts Dot into the "naughty box." Was there a naughty box in your own childhood?

ERDRICH: Do I have to talk about this? It is a primal wound. Yes, I was put into the naughty box.

INTERVIEWER: What had you done?

ERDRICH: Nothing. I was a model child. It was the teacher's mistake I am sure. The box was drawn on the blackboard and the names of misbehaving children were written in it. As I adored my teacher, Miss Smith, I was destroyed to see my name appear. This was just the first of the many humiliations of my youth that I've tried to revenge through my writing. I have never fully exorcised shames that struck me to the heart as a child except through written violence, shadowy caricature, and dark jokes.

INTERVIEWER: Was your teacher anything like the one in your story "Sister Godzilla"?

ERDRICH: No, but I had Franciscan Sisters for teachers later. Some were celestial, others were disturbed. My sixth-grade teacher, Sister Dominica, hit home runs at recess and I loved her, but there was no exact Sister Godzilla. As for Miss Smith, I still have her photograph. She had cat's-eye glasses, a blond bouffant do, and wore a chiffon scarf tied at the tip of her chin. I'd been reading for a while before Miss Smith, but I'd never thought about how there's a presence inside of words. The Ojibwe say that each word has a spirit. Miss Smith drew eyelashes on the *o*'s in *look*, and irises in the middle of the *o*'s, and suddenly *look* contained the act of looking. I had a flash of pure joy.

INTERVIEWER: Is it true your father paid you a nickel for every story you wrote as a child?

ERDRICH: Yes, he did, and he's sick of hearing about it. It's also true that, about a year ago, he gave me a roll of antique nickels and said, I owe you.

INTERVIEWER: What were the stories about?

ERDRICH: Lonely girls with hidden talents. At a family white-elephant sale we auctioned off one of my early stories for eight bucks—someone else got it. I've been trying to buy it back.

My father is my biggest literary influence. Recently I've been looking through his letters. He was in the National Guard when I was a child and whenever he left, he would write to me. He wrote letters to me all through college, and we still correspond. His letters, and my mother's, are one of my life's treasures.

INTERVIEWER: What are they about?

ERDRICH: Mushroom hunting. Roman Stoics. American Indian Movement politics. Longfellow. Stamp collecting. Apples. He and my mother have an orchard. He used to talk about how close together meadowlarks sit on fence posts—every seventh fence post. Now, of course, they are rare. When I went off to college, he wrote about the family, but in highly inflated terms, so that whatever my sisters and brothers were doing seemed outrageously funny or tragic. If my mother bought something it would be a cumbersome, dramatic addition to the household, but of course unnecessary. If the dog got into the neighbor's garbage it would be a saga of canine effort and exertion—and if the police caught the dog it would be a case of grand injustice.

INTERVIEWER: How did your parents meet?

ERDRICH: My mother is Turtle Mountain Chippewa, and she lived on her home reservation. My father taught there. He had just been discharged from the Air Force. He went to school on the GI Bill and got his teaching credentials. He is adventurous—he worked his way through Alaska at age seventeen and paid for his living expenses by winning at the poker table. He saved the money he made as a cook's flunky and helped out his parents. After he got his credentials, I guess he thought it would be interesting to work on a reservation. He assumed there would actually be mountains in the Turtle Mountains, so he brought his skis. In fact, on the way there, he looked north and saw cloud formations on the horizon and thought they were mountains. But when he arrived he found that the Turtle Mountains are low hills—no skiing. He met my grandfather before he met my mother.

INTERVIEWER: Your mother's father.

ERDRICH: Patrick Gourneau. Aunishinaubay was his Ojibwe name. He had an eighth-grade education, but he was a fascinating storyteller, wrote in exquisite script, and was the tribal chairman during the treacherous fifties termination era (when the U.S. Congress decided to abrogate all Indian treaties and declare Indian Nations nonexistent). My grandfather was a persuasive man who made friends with people at every level of influence. In order to fight against our tribe's termination, he went to newspapers and politicians and urged them to advocate for our tribe in Washington. He also supported his family through the Depression as a truck farmer. My father, himself a great talker, got to know Pat Gourneau as another interesting person who loved to converse. Then he saw Pat's daughter Rita and apparently she knocked his socks off. My mother has always been the reserved beauty to his smitten schoolteacher. I was born when she was nineteen and I've always loved having a young mother—she is often mistaken for my sister.

INTERVIEWER: Did she speak Ojibwemowin when you were growing up?

ERDRICH: My grandfather spoke the Red Lake dialect of the language as his family had originated there, but he also spoke and wrote an exquisite English. My mother learned words here and there, but you have to be immersed in a language as a child to pick it up.

INTERVIEWER: Why?

ERDRICH: We are wired to have a period of language opportunity. It is harder to learn languages after the age of eight or ten. In addition, Ojibwe is one of the most difficult languages to learn because its verbs take on an unusual array of forms. There's no masculine or feminine designation to the nouns, but instead they're qualified as animate or inanimate. The verb form changes according to its status as animate or inanimate as well as in regard to human relationships. The verbs go on and on. Often when I'm trying to speak Ojibwe my brain freezes. But my daughter is learning to speak it, and that has given me new resolve. Of course, English is a very powerful language, a colonizer's language and a gift to a writer. English has destroyed and sucked up the languages of other cultures—its cruelty is its vitality. Ojibwe is taught in colleges, increasingly in immersion programs, but when my grandfather went to government boarding school he wasn't allowed to speak Ojibwe. Nor were Indian students in Catholic boarding schools, where my mother went, as so many of our family were Catholic.

INTERVIEWER: Were you raised to be devout?

ERDRICH: Every Catholic is raised to be devout and love the Gospels, but I was spoiled by the Old Testament. I was very young when I started reading, and the Old Testament sucked me in. I was at the age of magical thinking and believed sticks could change to serpents, a voice might speak from a burning bush, angels wrestled with people. After I went to school and started catechism I realized that religion was about rules. I remember staring at a neighbor's bridal-wreath bush. It bloomed every year but was voiceless. No angels, no parting of the Red River. It all seemed so dull once I realized that nothing spectacular was going to happen.

I've come to love the traditional Ojibwe ceremonies, and some rituals, but I hate religious rules. They are usually about controlling women. On Sundays when other people go to wood-and-stone churches, I like to take my daughters into the woods. Or at least work in the garden and be outside. Any god we have is out there. I'd hate to be certain that there was nothing. When it comes to God, I cherish doubt.

INTERVIEWER: What was it like to leave Wahpeton for Dartmouth?

ERDRICH: My father, rightly, picked out a paragraph in *The Plague of Doves* as a somewhat autobiographical piece of the book. Evelina leaves for college and at their parting her parents give her a love-filled stare that is devastating and sustaining. It is an emotion they've never before been able to express without great awkwardness and pain. Now that she's leaving, that love beams out in an intense form.

As the eldest child, I often felt that I belonged more to my parents' generation than to my own. In the beginning of the book, Evelina is always scheming to watch television. My parents didn't let us watch much television. Dad had us cover our eyes when the commercials came on. He didn't want us to nurse any unnecessary desires and succumb to capitalism. Shakespeare's history plays and *The Three Stooges* were major influences.

INTERVIEWER: What was Dartmouth like?

ERDRICH: For one thing, the ratio of men to women was nine to one. And I was quite shy, so meeting people was painful. I'd be at a party and because I was so quiet, someone would say, You're stoned, aren't you, Karen? (My name was Karen then.) But I was only rarely stoned, just shy.

Recently I read a book by Charles Eastman, one of the first Native American physicians in Dakota, about going to Dartmouth. He described exactly how I felt: like I was being torn away. And yet, I wanted to go, I wanted to get away. Sinclair Lewis knew about the crazed feeling that you get when people think you're a pleasant person. You get all this praise for your good behavior but inside you're seething. I was fairly dutiful, and I felt that way. I've always loved that line from Flannery O'Connor's "Revelation": "Go back to hell where you came from, you old wart hog." In Wahpeton I was a graveyard-shift waitress who wanted to destroy my customers.

At Dartmouth, I was awkward and suspicious. I was in the first year of the Native American program. I felt comfortable with Chippewas and people from the Turtle Mountains, and I felt comfortable with Dakotas because Wahpeton is part of the Dakota reservation and I knew many Dakota people. It took me a while to get to know people from other tribes. People assume there is just one sort of Native experience. No. Do the Irish immediately feel comfortable with the Chinese? I was intimidated by the mighty Mohawks; it took me a long time to get to know my serene and beautiful Navajo roommate. Certainly I didn't understand the non-Indians, the people who came from East Coast backgrounds. Until then, I had met three African American people in my entire life. I had never met an East Indian person, a Jew, a Baptist, a Muslim. I hadn't left Wahpeton so I only knew a peculiar Wahpeton mixture of people, all smashed and molded into a similar shape by small-town life. I don't have a thick skin, and I especially didn't then. I obsessed over everything people said, ran it over forever in my mind. I still do that, but it's better now.

INTERVIEWER: Why did you decide to change your name to Louise?

ERDRICH: There were so many Karens when I was born. It was the 1954 name of the year. I think there was a Mouseketeer named Karen. I was happier when I was called Louise. My grandfather was named Louis. I thought it had a good, lucky sort of writerliness to it. There were lots of Louises who were artists and writers: Louise Bogan, Louise Bourgeois, Louise Glück. The only Karen writer I knew and liked was Karen Blixen and she changed her name, so I did too.

INTERVIEWER: Were you a good literature student?

ERDRICH: I worked hard to catch up with people. I didn't know any of the writers other Dartmouth freshmen had read. I knew the Old Testament, of course, and read indiscriminately from the local library—Leon Uris and James Michener and Ayn Rand and Herman Wouk—but nobody at Dartmouth was reading *Marjorie Morningstar*. They were reading Joyce. Who was that? I did have some Shakespeare, because in Wahpeton we'd bought a wonderful record player with green stamps, and my father brought home recordings of the plays—the tragedies, of course. And I liked James Welch, the Blackfeet writer. But otherwise, it was the Dune trilogy and Isaac Asimov and *The Prophet*.

Before coming to Dartmouth, I won a scholarship to an American Legion summer camp and was trapped with the John Birch Society. So I had a strange, brief flirtation with the right. I voted for Richard Nixon. But then Nixon was a hero to a lot of Native people. Despite everything else, he was one of the first presidents to understand anything about American Indians. He effectively ended the policy of termination and set our Nations on the course of self-determination. That had a galvanizing effect in Indian country. So I voted for Nixon and my boyfriend wanted to kill me and I didn't know why. Why was this so important? Nixon was even running against a South Dakota boy, George McGovern. But McGovern had no understanding of treaty rights, and I also thought I was voting in accordance with my father, because he kept saying George this, George that, what a demagogue. Then about a year ago, I said, Dad, I thought we were both against George in that election. And he said, I was talking about George Wallace.

INTERVIEWER: How does your father feel about your books?

ERDRICH: He gave me those nickels, remember? It didn't occur to me that my books would be widely read at all, and that enabled me to write anything I wanted to. And even once I realized that they were being read, I still wrote as if I were writing in secret. That's how one has to write anyway—in secret. At a certain point, you have to not please your parents, although for me that's painful because I'm close to my parents and of course I want them to be happy.

INTERVIEWER: When did you start writing *Love Medicine*?

ERDRICH: I went back to North Dakota after college and became a visiting poet in a program called Poets in the Schools. It was a marvelous gig. I went all around the state in my Chevy Nova, teaching, until I contracted hepatitis at the old Rudolf Hotel in Valley City. What did I expect for eight dollars a night? I was in my smoking, brooding phase, and I was mostly writing poetry. In time, the poems became more storylike—prose, really—then the stories began to connect. Before the hepatitis I also drank, much more than I do now, so I spent a lot of time in bars and had a number of crazy conversations that went into *Love Medicine*. I also used to go to tent revivals up in the Turtle Mountains—that experience eventually became part of *The Plague of Doves*.

INTERVIEWER: A tent revival?

ERDRICH: Where the revivalists pitch a tent and you sit under it and listen to preachers who try to convert you—bring you to Jesus right in the tent. It's like a traveling church. I went to hear that biblical language. Maybe I thought at last I'd witness a miracle. I used to listen to Jimmy Swaggart and Jack Van Impe, who are televangelists. I don't listen to TV preachers anymore because they lost their music and became political, but I used to love it. The formality of Mass was gone—it was just you and some crazy, powerful version of God. As a child, I couldn't get up in the middle of Holy Mass and shout, Come down on me! Come Spirit, Spirit! The closest version was a charismatic Catholic group I joined called the God Squad—I was still a teenager then—mainly I'd heard you could go on retreats and make out.

I started writing *Love Medicine* after I realized that narrative was invading the poetry. In the beginning, I was trying to write a spare kind of poetry, like James Wright or Robert Creeley, I suppose, but it was terrible. Then I started writing poems with inner rhymes but as they became more complex they turned into narrative. I started telling stories in the poems. But the poems I could write jumping up from my desk or lying on the bed. Anywhere. At last, I had this epiphany. I wanted to write prose, and I understood that my real problem with writing was not that I couldn't do it mentally. I couldn't do it physically. I could not sit still. Literally, could not sit still. So I had to solve that. I used some long scarves to tie myself into my chair. I tied myself in with a pack of cigarettes on one side and coffee on the other, and when I instinctively bolted upright after a few minutes, I'd say, Oh, shit. I'm tied down. I've got to keep writing.

INTERVIEWER: Where were you when you wrote *Love Medicine*?

ERDRICH: I had come back to Fargo again and was living downtown. I worked in a little office space with a great arched window on the top floor. It was seventy bucks a month. It was heaven to have my own quiet, beautiful office with a great window and green linoleum floors and a little desk and a view that carried to the outskirts of Fargo. The apartment I lived in over Frederick's Flowers belonged to my brother and had no windows, only a central air shaft that was gloomy and gray. That apartment also got into the book. It was a peculiar apartment—you couldn't stay in it all day or you'd go nuts. It cost fifty dollars a month, so all I had to pay every month was one hundred and twenty bucks in rent. I had a bicycle. I ate at the Dutch Maid café. I was living well.

INTERVIEWER: What did you do for money?

ERDRICH: My best job was working for a man named Joe Richardson who had a small-press outfit called Plains Distribution. He managed to get funding for a fancy traveling RV stuffed with small-press books. We distributed work by writers like Ted Kooser, Linda Hasselstrom, Mark Vinz, Tom McGrath. In the middle of all of this I found myself at the trial of Leonard Peltier. It was all taking place right near the sinister apartment I lived in. I was surprised to see neighbors from Wahpeton and a lot of other people I'd grown up with. They were passionate about the American Indian Movement. They got me into the courtroom every day. After listening to all that was said, I was astounded when Peltier was convicted. There was simply no evidence that convicted him. He was convicted out of fear. We know how that goes.

At last, I ran out of money. I applied to the Yaddo and MacDowell writers' residencies. I got some time there, and I was able to finish "Scales." Then I thought I'd better write a real novel. So I left everything else and wrote a book called *Tracks*. I started it at Johns Hopkins, where I received a teaching stipend. I got a lot of encouragement there from John Barth, a genius, a superb teacher, and Edmund White, whom I adored—a man of tender intelligence, and a daring writer. I also got to study with Richard Howard. What luck. He would set one of my poems aside and say, "This one we'll allow to leech away into the sands of discourse." So some of my poems leeched away into the sands of discourse. Then Richard looked at other poems and responded from his sublime knowledge, but he always spoke with a natural sort of kindness. I also met C. Michael Curtis at Johns Hopkins, but he wouldn't have remembered me. Later, he was the first person who accepted a story of mine—"Saint Marie"—into a glossy magazine. That was a huge moment for me. I still have his acceptance letter. I stared at it for hours and days. After the story was published I got two letters. One from an outraged priest who said I'd written nauseating phantasms of convent life. The other was from Philip Roth. He sent me a letter out of the blue just to say that he liked the story. I stared at his letter for a long time as well. I think I was too shy to answer it, but I wrote the rest of the book.

INTERVIEWER: What happened with *Tracks*?

ERDRICH: It continued to be rejected. It was rejected all over the place. And thank God for that—it was the kind of first novel where the writer tries to take a high tone while loads of mysterious things happen, and there was way too much Faulkner in there. People would find themselves suddenly in cornfields with desperate, aching anguish over the weight of history. I kept it though, the way people keep a car on blocks out in the yard—for spare parts.

INTERVIEWER: The *Tracks* I've read is a short book.

ERDRICH: That's because all of the spare parts got used in other vehicles. And of course I rewrote *Tracks* entirely by 1989, but before that I had withdrawn it from consideration by publishers and started again on *Love Medicine*.

INTERVIEWER: One of the characters in *Love Medicine* says, "You know Lulu Lamartine if you know life is made up of three kinds of people—those who live it, those afraid to, those in between. My mother is the first." Which category is yours?

ERDRICH: I suppose I've always wanted to be the first, but really I'm the last. By writing I can live in ways that I could not survive. I've only had children with two fathers. Lulu's had children by what, eight? People sometimes ask me, Did you really have these experiences? I laugh, Are you crazy? I'd be dead. I'd be dead fifty times. I don't write directly from my own experience so much as an emotional understanding of it.

I suppose one develops a number of personas and hides them away, then they pop up during writing. The exertion of control comes later. I take great pleasure in writing when I get a real voice going and I'm able to follow the voice and the character. It's like being in a trance state. Once that had happened a few times, I knew I needed to write for the rest of my life. I began to crave the trance state. I would be able to return to the story anytime, and it would play out in front of me, almost effortlessly. Not many of my stories work out that way. Most of my work is simple persistence. I've had some stories for twenty years. I keep adding to them word by word.

But if the trance happens, even though it's been wonderful, I'm suspicious. It's like an ecstatic love affair or fling that makes you think, It can't be this good, it can't be! And it never is. I always need to go back and reconfigure parts of the voice. So the control is working with the piece after it's written, finding the end. The title's always there, the beginning's always there, sometimes I have to wait for the middle, and then I always write way past the end and wind up cutting off two pages.

INTERVIEWER: Why do you do that?

ERDRICH: When I can't end a story, I usually find that I've actually written past the ending. The trick of course is to go back and decide where the last line hits.

INTERVIEWER: How do you keep all your characters straight?

ERDRICH: I used to try to keep them straight in my head, but I didn't really care if they got messed up. It didn't mean a lot to me if I got them wrong. I'd like to say it was out of some sense of aesthetics, or adherence to some tradition, but really I just didn't care. I wanted to get on with the story. If it weren't for Trent Duffy, the best copy editor in New York, everything would be inconsistent and I still wouldn't be worried about it. And, you know, there still are inconsistencies.

INTERVIEWER: But they're not deliberate?

ERDRICH: You mean are they there so that English and Native American literature scholars have something to work on? No.

INTERVIEWER: Why did you decide to add family trees to your books?

ERDRICH: I resisted for a long time, but then at readings people began to come up and show me their painfully drawn out family trees, so finally I was overcome by guilt. Delightfully, my dear Trent had kept track of the relationships. Now people come up to me and say how grateful they are that they don't have to write out the family trees themselves. It never seemed particularly important to me. In the Turtle Mountains, everybody is related because there are only so many families. Nobody sits down and picks apart their ancestry. Unless you want to date somebody.

INTERVIEWER: How do your books come into being? Where do they start?

ERDRICH: I have little pieces of writing that sit around collecting dust, or whatever they're collecting. They are drawn to other bits of narrative like iron filings. I hate looking for something to write about. I try to have several things going before I end a book. Sometimes I don't have something immediately and I suffer for it.

INTERVIEWER: Why?

ERDRICH: I feel certain that I'm never going to write again. I'm positive that it's over. The world seems boring. I can't enjoy anything. My family knows I'm moping. I'm not nice to live around, and I'm not a stellar cook. Nothing seems right. The worst times are ending a book tour and not having a book to return to. It's sheer emptiness.

But I guess that's an essential part of this entire process: You feel your mortality and there's nowhere to go. I walk more, which is good. Then I start rummaging around, thinking, It's all over, so what's there to lose? I go to our bookstore, and others, used bookstores, I talk to the booksellers and look around. I go back to things I didn't finish, but then, if I didn't finish it in the first place, it probably isn't really worth going back to. I go to a historical society and leaf through things. I'll take a drive in the car. Eventually something turns up. That's where I am now. I haven't really engaged with the next book in the same way that I engaged with *Shadow Tag*. I suppose I could go back to my eternal science-fiction novel, though it is a failure.

INTERVIEWER: Then why do you go back to it?

ERDRICH: It's irresistible, especially when I'm in free fall. Maybe in a decade I'll have finished it.

INTERVIEWER: Is it set in North Dakota?

ERDRICH: Yes. The North Dakota of the future!

INTERVIEWER: Do you ever feel like you're writing one long novel?

ERDRICH: All of the books will be connected somehow—by history and blood and by something I have no control over, which is the writing itself. The writing is going to connect where it wants to, and I will have to try and follow along.

INTERVIEWER: Is it true that you have control over the cover designs of your books? Writers aren't always afforded that privilege.

ERDRICH: That's because the most clichéd Native images used to be suggested for the cover design, so I fought to have some say. On a foreign copy of *Tracks* there was a pair of massive breasts with an amulet hanging between them. Often, a Southwestern landscape appears. Or an Indian princess or two. A publisher once sent me a design for *Master Butchers Singing Club* that was all huge loops of phallic sausages. They were of every shape and all different textures, colors, sizes. I showed it to my daughter and we looked at it in stunned silence, then we said, Yes! This is a great cover! I have twenty copies left of that edition, and I'm going to keep them. Sometimes I'll show one to a man and ask what he thinks of it. He'll put it in his lap and look at it for a while and the strangest look will cross his face. He'll look sideways at the women in the room, and he'll point and say, I think I see myself in that one.

INTERVIEWER: Do you revise already-published work?

ERDRICH: At every opportunity. Usually, I add chapters that I have written too late to include in the original. Or I try to improve the Ojibwe language used in the book. As I learn more or I consult my teachers, I learn how much I don't know. Ojibwe is something I'll be a lifelong failure at—it is my windmill. I've changed *Love Medicine* quite a lot, and I wanted to revise *The Blue Jay's Dance*. For one thing I wanted to take out the recipes. Don't try the lemon-meringue pie, it doesn't work. I've received letters. I can't wait to change *Four Souls*. There are some big mistakes in that.

INTERVIEWER: Like what?

ERDRICH: I'm not saying; it is absurd and filthy—and this is a family publication. But I also feel the ending is too self-consciously poetic, maybe sentimental. I wouldn't end it that way now. I am engaged these days in rewriting *The Antelope Wife* substantially—I always had a feeling it began well and got hijacked.

INTERVIEWER: Many of the books are hijacked by a child in trouble.

ERDRICH: When I had to go on my first book tour—those are the lowest points in my life, the times just before a book tour, when I have to leave my children—I was sitting on a plane next to a psychiatrist. I said to her, "I've just written this book and it has another abandoned child in it. Another loveless person abandons another child in the beginning. What is it about abandonment?" This psychiatrist, who had a deep, scratchy voice, said, "My dear, we are all abandoned."

Abandonment is in all the books: the terror of having a bad mother or being a bad mother, or just a neglectful mother; letting your child run around in a T-shirt longer than her shorts.

INTERVIEWER: Every summer you drive several hours north to visit the Turtle Mountains, sometimes also Lake of the Woods. Why?

ERDRICH: Actually, I do this all year. These places are home for me. And I like to travel. Driving takes hold of the left brain and then the right brain is freed—that's what some writer friends and I have theorized. But I can't always stop when I get an idea. It depends on the road—North Dakota, no traffic. When I'm driving on a very empty stretch of road I do write with one hand. It's hardly legible, but still, you don't want to have to stop every time.

Of course, if you have a child along, then you do have to stop. By having children, I've both sabotaged and saved myself as a writer. I hate to pigeonhole myself as a writer, but being a female and a mother and a Native American are important aspects of my work, and even more than being mixed blood or Native, it's difficult to be a mother and a writer.

INTERVIEWER: Because of the demands on your time?

ERDRICH: No, and it's not because of hormones or pregnancies. It's because you're always fighting sentiment. You're fighting sentimentality all of the time because being a mother alerts you in such a primal way. You are alerted to any danger to your child, and by extension you become afraid of anybody getting hurt. This becomes the most powerful thing to you; it's instinctual. Either you end up writing about terrible things happening to children—as if you could ward them off simply by writing about them—or you tie things up in easily opened packages, or you pull your punches as a writer. All deadfalls to watch for.

Having children also makes it difficult to get out of the house. With a child you certainly can't be a Bruce Chatwin or a Hemingway, living the adventurer-writer life. No running with the bulls at Pamplona. If you value your relationships with your children, you can't write about them. You have to make up other, less convincing children. There is also one's inclination to be charming instead of presenting a grittier truth about the world. But then, having children has also made me this particular writer. Without my children, I'd have written with less fervor; I wouldn't understand life in the same way. I'd write fewer comic scenes, which are the most challenging. I'd probably have become obsessively self-absorbed, or slacked off. Maybe I'd have become an alcoholic. Many of the writers I love most were alcoholics. I've made my choice, I sometimes think: Wonderful children instead of hard liquor.

INTERVIEWER: Were you ever in danger of becoming a drunk?

ERDRICH: Likely, but for the gift of the Rudolf Hotel. I got hepatitis. That saved me.

INTERVIEWER: On your journeys do you visit with members of the reservation and hear their stories?

ERDRICH: You'd think so. That would make sense. But I never hear stories that go into my work, although place description might. Just germs of stories, and most of those I hear from my father. I've internalized my father to such a degree that sometimes he has only to start a few sentences and my mind races off. Same with my mother. She once told me a story about a boy secretly playing a violin and it was only a few sentences, but it became "Shamengwa." Bits of narrative always cling to a title, like magnetism. I love titles. I have lists of titles that I haven't gotten to. *Tales of Burning Love* and *Shadow Tag* were there for the longest time.

The closest thing to a complete story that went into my work was a bank robbery. My dad's great on bank robberies. He was telling me a story about a woman taken hostage during a holdup. She was being used as a hostage shield, and a deputy shot her in the hip. She became "Naked Woman Playing Chopin."

INTERVIEWER: Some people refer to your writing as magical realism. Is that another pigeonhole?

ERDRICH: I have six brothers and sisters, and nearly all of them work with Ojibwe or Dakota or other Native people. My youngest brother, youngest sister, and brother-in-law have worked with the Indian Health Service for a total of more than forty years. My second-oldest brother works in northern Minnesota sorting out the environmental issues for all of the Ojibwe Nations throughout the entire Midwest. Their experiences make magical realism seem ho-hum. It's too bad I can't use their experiences because everyone would know who they are, but believe me, my writing comes from ordinary life.

INTERVIEWER: A man nursing a baby in *The Antelope Wife*?

ERDRICH: What's strange about that? There are several documented cases of male lactation. It's sometimes uncomfortable for me to read that scene in front of mixed audiences. Men get upset. But I think it's a great idea. It would solve about half of the world's problems.

INTERVIEWER: A violin washing ashore in an empty canoe in *The Plague of Doves*?

ERDRICH: It made the story.

INTERVIEWER: When you're writing and a character or situation starts to approach the supernatural, do you think twice about writing it?

ERDRICH: I'm not aware of the supernatural in the same way, so I can't tell when it starts to approach. Maybe it goes back to childhood, still spoiled by the Old Testament. Maybe it's Catholic after all, this conviction that there are miracles and things like violins appearing in a canoe. To me that was possible. I love it when a story begins to write itself, and that particular story did. The piece in *The Plague of Doves* where the men are taking on a surreal journey—there's nothing magical in the least about it. "Town Fever" is based on a historical trip that ended up in Wahpeton. There is now a stone that commemorates their near starvation. It fascinated me that they began right down at the river here in what became Minneapolis, where I go every week or so. With their ox-pulled sleighs, they traveled what is now Interstate 94. So I knew the exact route they took, and my description was based on reality. Daniel Johnston, who wrote the account, recorded that the party had bowel troubles and so took "a remedy." Then it only remained for me to look up what remedy there was at the time, and it was laudanum. They were high on opium the whole time. Then I read *The Pursuit of Oblivion* and became interested in what it is like to be high all the time. And last week you saw me reading *Methland*. You must think I'm obsessed with drugs.

INTERVIEWER: Do you discuss your books with other writers?

ERDRICH: I talked to Gail Caldwell quite a bit about *Shadow Tag* and *Last Report*. She describes this wonderful state when there's "fire in the room." When there's a fire burning in the room, and it's illuminated and warm, you can't stop reading. With *Shadow Tag*, she told me when the fire was in the room. And she was kind when the fire went out, which a number of times it did.

INTERVIEWER: At what point do you show a manuscript to your editor?

ERDRICH: Terry Karten has been my editor since *The Last Report on the Miracles at Little No Horse*. I have no rule about when to show her something; I trust her, and often we talk about books I'm thinking about before I do show the work to her. She is ruthlessly honest, has superb instincts, and is a true book person. There are probably very few relationships like this left in the publishing world. I have also worked with Jane Beirn all of my writing life—another person of the highest caliber. I don't know what I would do without her.

INTERVIEWER: What do you do when you can't make something work?

ERDRICH: I walk—I usually have a little pen and some note cards with me. But one day I didn't and I was halfway around the lake when the words started to appear, the end of *Shadow Tag*. The words rained into my mind. I looked up and saw my sister Heid's car on the road around the lake, and I ran over to her, flagged down her car, and said, "Give me a pencil and paper! Quick, quick, quick! Please." I still have the piece of paper that she gave me taped into my notebook.

INTERVIEWER: If not with a title, how did you begin working on what you're working on now?

ERDRICH: That began with digging shoots and saplings out of the foundation of my parents' house. I was quite aware that this was the beginning of something. Driving from Wahpeton to Minneapolis, I started writing it in my head and I had to pull over and start writing. I pulled over because I had my youngest child in the car.

I figured I was all washed-up when I learned I was going to have another baby at forty-six. I thought, Oh, the hell with it. I'm never going to get out of this. But before she was born, I had all of this pent-up desperation and I wrote *The Master Butchers Singing Club*. I'd always wanted to write that book. I wrote the first part of the book by hand, but because I was pregnant I started writing my first draft on the computer. My baby was getting bigger and bigger, and my arms were stretching farther and farther to reach over her to the keyboard.

INTERVIEWER: Were you concerned that the quality of your writing would suffer?

ERDRICH: It's a touchstone for me to have everything written down by hand.

INTERVIEWER: Do you transfer your writing to the computer yourself?

ERDRICH: I don't let anybody touch my writing.

INTERVIEWER: And do you revise at that point?

ERDRICH: I revise as I type, and I write a lot by hand on the printouts so they feel repossessed. I have always kept notebooks—I have an obsessive devotion to them—and I go back to them over and over. They are my compost pile of ideas. Any scrap goes in, and after a number of years I'll get a handful of earth. I am working right now out of a notebook I used when I wrote *The Blue Jay's Dance*.

INTERVIEWER: You wrote in that book about moments in which suicide was appealing.

ERDRICH: Postpartum depression, but I beat that thought down. Certainly after Michael's death it became clear that I wouldn't kill myself to save my life. At that point I realized that the main thing a parent has to do is stay alive. It doesn't matter how rotten you are, or if you fail. A failed parent is better than a dead parent. A failed parent at least gives you someone to rail against. A former army psychiatrist said something that struck me. He said that there are people who will kill themselves no matter what, and there are people who won't do it no matter what. There are people who can go through an endless level of psychological pain, and still they will not kill themselves. I want to be that last person.

INTERVIEWER: You wrote *The Crown of Columbus* with your husband, Michael. How was that different from the experience of writing your other books?

ERDRICH: I've not spoken much about what it was like to work with Michael, partly because I feel that there's something unfair about it. He can't tell his side of the story. I have everything that we once had together. It touches me that he left me as his literary executor. I think he trusted that I would be good to his words, and I have tried to do that. So it's difficult to set the record straight because it would be my view, the way I see it. Still, he controlled our narrative when he was living. I am weary of all of the old leftover assumptions, and what else, really, do people have to go on?

I would have loved for Michael to have had his own life as a writer and not covet my life as a writer. But he couldn't help himself. So in agreeing to write *The Crown of Columbus* I really made a deal, at least in my thoughts, that if we wrote this one book together, then we could openly work separately—as we always did in truth, of course. I wanted to make him happy, you know. He was the kind of person whom people want to make happy. People did this all the time, they tried to make him happy, but there was a deep impossibility within him and he couldn't really be happy. Or he couldn't be happy alone. So I'd had the idea for *The Crown of Columbus*; I'd done the research and I said, This is the project. We can do it together because you can write your part and I can write mine and both of our names will be on the cover.

I haven't ever read the published book. I've never watched the movie of *The Broken Cord* either. There are just certain things that I've never been able to get close to again. I haven't been able to revisit most of the year 1997. I hoped that *The Crown of Columbus* would be what Michael needed in order to say, Now it is enough, we truly collaborated. Instead, it became the beginning of what he wanted for every book. When he told me he wanted both of our names on every book now, something in me—the writer, I guess—couldn't bear it any longer and that was the beginning of the long ending. We're talking only of our writing relationship, as distinct from the tangle of our family.

INTERVIEWER: Why do you think he wanted and needed so badly to see himself as a writer?

ERDRICH: Perhaps because I loved writing so much and he loved me. Perhaps because he was a very good writer. Or perhaps—I don't say this in a negative or judgmental way, because this is the case with writers whether they admit it or not—Michael also adored everything that went with the identity. He adored meeting other writers, adored being part of a literary world. He would answer everyone who wrote to him, beautiful letters, every single person. I don't take much pleasure in being "the writer." That's what my bookstore is for. So that people can visit a version of the writer, and incidentally, visit a real bookstore. I can't talk to people, so—

INTERVIEWER: You can't talk to people?

ERDRICH: Still socially awkward. Once I was in a bookstore in New York and a very short man reached up and patted me on the top of my head and said, "I think you're a good little writer." So I patted him on the head and said, "Thank you. You're a good little reader." Then I thought, I can't take this anymore. It's just what I tried to get away from in Wahpeton, being a good little anything.

INTERVIEWER: How did the relationship with Michael break down?

ERDRICH: There were signs from the beginning, but I ignored them or even exhaust-
edly encouraged them. He took over as the agent for *Love Medicine*. After it
won an award and *The Beet Queen* was published, we went to New York for
an interview with *The New York Times*. I was walking out the door to meet the
interviewer, and I noticed that he was dressed up, too. So I asked him where
he was going. He said, "I'm going to be in the interview." And I said, "No, they
asked me." And he said, "What do you mean—I can't come?" So it was both of
us from then on. As long as he was content with being in on the interview and
saying what he needed to say, I wasn't that unhappy. Actually, I was tired. *Love
Medicine* and *Jacklight* were published in 1984, and I had a baby. *The Beet Queen*
was published in 1985, and I bore my second daughter in that year. What kind
of woman can do that? A tired woman who lets her husband do the talking
because she has the two best things—the babies and the writing. Yet at some
point the talking infected the writing. I looked into the mirror and I saw Michael.
I began to write again in secret and put together a novel that I didn't show him.

INTERVIEWER: Was he a good agent?

ERDRICH: He was a terrific agent. He had the energy for it, and the excitement about
the book world. He was a very good and generous editor, too. Not to mention
a teacher.

INTERVIEWER: A journalist once asked you what advice you would give someone
trying to write a novel. You said, "Don't take the project too seriously." Is that
what you would say today?

ERDRICH: I think I meant that grand ideas kill first efforts. Begin with something in
your range. Then write it as a secret. I'd be paralyzed if I thought I had to write
a great novel, and no matter how good I think a book is on one day, I know now
that a time will come when I will look upon it as a failure. The gratification has
to come from the effort itself. I try not to look back. I approach the work as
though, in truth, I'm nothing and the words are everything. Then I write to save
my life. If you are a writer, that will be true. Writing has saved my life.

INTERVIEWER: How?

ERDRICH: I needed a way to go at life. I needed meaning. I might have chosen
something more self-destructive had I not found writing.

INTERVIEWER: Do your daughters help you when you write your books for children?

ERDRICH: They are great editors—they read and react. When my older daughters
were little, I used to tell them the story of a little girl marooned alone on an
island; everyone else had died. My daughters wanted that story over and over, so

finally I wrote it down and showed it to a friend who said, This is the anti–"Little House on the Prairie"! Of course, "Little House on the Prairie" is foundational literature. Everyone refers to it. But the series has an appalling view of how the American settlers went into an empty world: There was no one there, so Pa set out his claim. The Indians are always slinking off and Ma's holding her nose. But I do love the parts about making sausage.

I thought I would write about the other side, the people who were in that "empty" space, the people who were forced ahead of the settlers and what happened to them. The path taken by these people in the Birchbark books roughly mirrors the path the Ojibwe side of my family took crossing from Madeline Island, over what is now Minnesota, up to Lake of the Woods and over to the Turtle Mountains. So far in the series, I've reached Lake of the Woods.

INTERVIEWER: How is writing novels for children different from writing them for adults?

ERDRICH: One of the jobs I had in the old days was writing for children's textbooks. I followed a mathematical formula to choose big words and little words in combination to make each sentence. A maddening challenge for a young writer. Writing for children now, I pare back description, stick to action, humor, trouble, triumph. Of course there also has to be death, but not too much. I have to watch that. I can't become Cormac McCarthy for the middle reader.

INTERVIEWER: Do you ever fall into the wonderful writing trance when you're working on nonfiction?

ERDRICH: Nonfiction is always a grind for me. A great deal of research goes into the fiction, but when the research is for nonfiction all the pleasure is dulled. And no, I never fall into a trance.

INTERVIEWER: Are you still writing poetry?

ERDRICH: I stopped thinking like a poet back when I started writing narrative poems. Occasionally I get some poetry, and I'll write poetry for as long as I can. But it is as though I've been temporarily excused by the novel, and it wants me back. So I usually put whatever poetry I would have written into the novel. I only keep a few of my poems as poems.

INTERVIEWER: Why?

ERDRICH: It usually turns out that the poem was connected to the prose in a subterranean way. If I am writing a novel, it casts an aura around me and I get ideas for it, descriptions, words, phrases, at all times. I'm always jotting in notebooks I keep with me. That delight of immersion in a book is as good as a trance. For a while, the book is so powerful that I can follow the thread even through my chaotic daily existence, with children at all hours, school, dinner, long calls to my daughters, my ever-demanding house, barking dogs, and the bookstore.

INTERVIEWER: You said before that your bookstore is a way you have of meeting with other people. Is the business still working?

ERDRICH: Birchbark Books is still here! In fact, doing well. But I'm not a business person. At first I looked at the bookstore as a work of art that would survive on its own artfulness. Now I get that it's a business, but it is also much more. Any good business is about its people. Marvelous people work at Birchbark Books. That's why it's still alive. Walking into a huge bookstore feels a bit like walking into Amazon.com. But walking into a small bookstore, you immediately feel the presence of the mind that has chosen the books on the shelves. You communicate intellectually with the buyer. Then, if you're lucky, you meet another great reader in person—our manager, Susan White, ready with ideas for you. People need bookstores and need other readers. We need the intimate communication with others who love books. We don't really think we do, because of the ease that the Internet has introduced, but we still need the physical world more than we know. Little bookstores are community services, not profitable business enterprises. Books are just too inexpensive online and there are too many of them, so a physical bookstore has to offer something different. Perhaps little bookstores will attain nonprofit status. Maybe one fine day the government will subsidize them, so they can thrive as nonprofit entities. Some very clever bookstore, probably not us, is going to manage to do that and become the paradigm for the rest.

INTERVIEWER: What do you do to differentiate your store?

ERDRICH: We attract writers, especially Native writers, and we host literary events, which means, again, the bookstore is more than a business—it is an arts organization. We support a number of Native artists: basket makers and jewelers and painters. We sell medicines grown by a Dakota family: sage, sweetgrass, bear root. My sister Heid and I launched an affiliated nonprofit press that will publish in the Ojibwe and Dakota languages. With a small bookstore, you get to encourage your eccentricities. It's quite a wonderful thing, this bookstore. I thought it would be a project for my daughters and me, some work we could do together, and that has happened. Each daughter has worked in the store.

There's something very wrong in our country—and not just in the book business. We now see what barely fettered capitalism looks like. We are killing the small and the intimate. We all feel it and we don't know quite why everything is beginning to look the same. The central cores of large cities can still sustain interesting places. But all across our country we are intent on developing chain after chain with no character and employees who work for barely livable wages. We are losing our individuality. Killing the soul of our landscape. Yet we're supposed to be the most individualistic of countries. I feel the sadness of it every time I go through cities like Fargo and Minneapolis and walk the wonderful old Main Streets and then go out to the edges and wander through acres of concrete boxes. Our country is starting to look like Legoland.

INTERVIEWER: Do you find any shortage of good books being published these days?

ERDRICH: Writing is better than ever. As for the book as an object, it's like bread. It is such a perfectly evolved piece of technology that it will be hard to top. A hardcover book is a beautiful and durable piece of work. The paperback—so low-tech and high-tech at the same time—is also a great piece of technology because you don't mind passing it along. It is inexpensive. Even if you drop it in the bathtub, you haven't really lost much. You can leave a paperback somewhere and buy a used one for the price of a loaf of bread. You can't pass on an electronic reader, you can't page back in the same way, you can't write in it; you've lost the tactile sense of being able to fold it over, rip it up, feel its weight. I also like that you can throw books across the room, as people have done with mine. Plus, you don't need a power source. The whole absence of touching and feeling a book would be a loss, though I think there are a number of readers who really only want the text, so they'll adopt electronic books. Ultimately it's just another form of publishing, so I'm not against it. I don't feel that sense of alarm and threat that some writers seem to feel about e-books.

INTERVIEWER: Is writing a lonely life for you?

ERDRICH: Strangely, I think it is. I am surrounded by an abundance of family and friends, and yet I am alone with the writing. And that is perfect.

SELECTED BIBLIOGRAPHY

Louise Erdrich is a prolific author, and her works have been studied widely. What follows is a selective bibliography listing major primary works and scholarly resources pertaining to Erdrich's fiction and prose, offered as a starting place to encourage further reading and understanding of her works.

Novels by Louise Erdrich

Erdrich, Louise. *The Antelope Wife*. 1998. Revised ed. HarperPerennial, 2012, 2014. Re-revised and retitled as *Antelope Woman*. HarperPerennial, 2016.

———. *The Beet Queen*. Holt, 1986.

———. *The Bingo Palace*. HarperCollins, 1994.

———. *Four Souls*. HarperCollins, 2004.

———. *Future Home of the Living God*. HarperCollins, 2017.

———. *LaRose*. HarperCollins, 2016.

———. *The Last Report on the Miracles at Little No Horse*. HarperCollins, 2001.

———. *Love Medicine*. 1984, 1993. Newly revised ed. HarperPerennial, 2009.

———. *The Master Butchers Singing Club*. HarperCollins, 2002.

———. *The Night Watchman*. HarperCollins, 2020.

———. *The Painted Drum*. HarperCollins, 2005.

————. *The Plague of Doves*. HarperCollins, 2008.

————. *The Round House*. HarperCollins, 2012.

————. *Shadow Tag*. HarperCollins, 2010.

————. *Tales of Burning Love*. HarperCollins, 1996.

————. *Tracks*. Holt, 1988.

Nonfiction by Louise Erdrich

Erdrich, Louise. *The Blue Jay's Dance: A Birth Year*. HarperCollins, 1995.

————. *Books and Islands in Ojibwe Country*. National Geographic Society, 2003.

————. "Rape on the Reservation." *New York Times*, 27 Feb. 2013, p. A25.

————. "Two Languages in Mind, But Just One in the Heart." *New York Times*, 22 May 2000, pp. E1–2.

————. "Where I Ought to Be: A Writer's Sense of Place." *New York Times Book Review*, 28 July 1985, pp. 1, 23–24.

Scholarly Books Discussing Erdrich's Novels

Beidler, Peter G. *Murdering Indians: A Documentary History of the 1897 Killings That Inspired Louise Erdrich's* The Plague of Doves. McFarland, 2014.

Beidler, Peter G., and Gay Barton. *A Reader's Guide to the Novels of Louise Erdrich*. Revised ed., U of Missouri P, 2006.

Chavkin, Allan. *The Chippewa Landscape of Louise Erdrich*. U of Alabama P, 1999.

Chavkin, Allan, and Nancy Fehl Chavkin, eds. *Conversations with Louise Erdrich and Michael Dorris*. UP of Mississippi, 1994.

Fitzgerald, Stephanie J. *Native Women and Land: Narratives of Dispossession and Resurgence*. U of New Mexico P, 2015.

Furlan, Laura M. *Indigenous Cities: Urban Indian Fiction and the Histories of Relocation*. U of Nebraska P, 2017.

Hafen, P. Jane, ed. *Louise Erdrich*. Ipswich, Mass.: Salem Press, 2013.

Hollrah, Patrice. *"The Old Lady Trill, the Victory Yell": The Power of Women in Native American Literature*. Routledge, 2004.

Jacobs, Connie A. *The Novels of Louise Erdrich: Stories of Her People*. Peter Lang, 2001.

Kurup, Seema. *Understanding Louise Erdrich*. U of South Carolina P, 2016.

Madsen, Deborah L., ed. *Louise Erdrich: Tracks, The Last Report on the Miracles at Little No Horse, The Plague of Doves*. Continuum Intl., 2011.

McHugh, Susan. *Love in a Time of Slaughters: Human-Animal Stories against Genocide and Extinction*. Pennsylvania State UP, 2019.

Noodin, Margaret. *Bawaajimo: A Dialect of Dreams in Anishinaabe Language and Literature.* Michigan State UP, 2014.

Owens, Louis. *Mixedblood Messages: Literature, Film, Family, Place.* U of Oklahoma P, 2001.

———. *Other Destinies: Understanding the American Indian Novel.* U of Oklahoma P, 1992.

Peterson, Nancy J. *Against Amnesia: Contemporary Women Writers and the Crises of Historical Memory.* U of Pennsylvania P, 2001.

Rainwater, Catherine. *Dreams of Fiery Stars: The Transformations of Native American Fiction.* U of Pennsylvania P, 1999.

Sarris, Greg, Connie A. Jacobs, and James R. Giles, eds. *Approaches to Teaching the Works of Louise Erdrich.* Modern Language Association of America, 2004.

Sawhney, Brajesh, ed. *Studies in the Literary Achievement of Louise Erdrich, Native American Writer: Fifteen Critical Essays.* Mellen, 2009.

Stirrup, David. *Louise Erdrich.* Manchester UP, 2014.

———. *Picturing Worlds: Visuality and Visual Sovereignty in Contemporary Anishinaabe Literature.* Michigan State UP, 2020.

Stookey, Lorena L. *Louise Erdrich: A Critical Companion.* Greenwood, 1999.

Suzack, Cheryl. *Indigenous Women's Writing and the Cultural Study of Law.* U of Toronto P, 2017.

Tillett, Rebecca. *Contemporary Native American Literature.* Edinburgh UP, 2007.

Washburn, Frances. *Tracks on the Page: Louise Erdrich, Her Life and Works.* Women Writers of Color Series. Praeger, 2013.

Wilson, Michael D. *Writing Home: Indigenous Narratives of Resistance.* Michigan State UP, 2008.

Wong, Hertha D., ed. *Louise Erdrich's* Love Medicine: *A Casebook.* Oxford UP, 2000.

Scholarly Articles on the Novels of the Justice Trilogy

Bancroft, Corinne. "The Braided Narrative." *Narrative*, vol. 26, no. 3, 2018, pp. 262–81.

Bender, Jacob, and Lydia Maunz-Breese. "Louise Erdrich's *The Round House*, the Wiindigoo, and *Star Trek: The Next Generation*." *American Indian Quarterly*, vol. 42, no. 2, 2018, pp. 141–61.

Carden, Mary Paniccia. "'The Unkillable Mother': Sovereignty and Survivance in Louise Erdrich's *The Round House*." *Studies in American Indian Literatures*, vol. 30, no. 1, 2018, pp. 94–116.

Cheyfitz, Eric, and Shari M. Huhndorf. "Genocide by Other Means: US Federal Indian Law and Violence against Native Women in Louise Erdrich's *The Round House*." *New Directions in Law and Literature*, edited by Elizabeth S. Anker and Bernadette Meyler, Oxford UP, 2017, pp. 264–78.

Däwes, Birgit. "'Pain Kept the Room Clear for Spirit': Facets of Fundamentalism and Louise Erdrich's *The Plague of Doves.*" *Literatur in Wissenschaft und Unterricht*, vol. 45, no. 1–2, 2012, pp. 5–19.

Gamber, John. "So, a Priest Walks into a Reservation Tragicomedy: Humor in *The Plague of Doves.*" *Louise Erdrich: Tracks, The Last Report on the Miracles at Little No Horse, The Plague of Doves*, edited by Deborah L. Madsen, Continuum, 2011, pp. 136–51.

Hamilton, Robert C. "'Disaster Stamps': The Significance of Philately in Louise Erdrich's *The Plague of Doves.*" *ANQ: A Quarterly Journal of Short Articles, Notes, and Reviews*, vol. 26, no. 4, 2013, pp. 266–72.

Harper, Kate. "Figuring the Grotesque in Louise Erdrich's Novels: Of Ojibwe Play, Modernist Form, and the Romantic Sensibility." *Studies in American Indian Literatures*, vol. 24, no. 2, 2012, pp. 17–38.

Ibarrola-Armendariz, Aitor. "Genre Reconsidered in Louise Erdrich's *The Round House.*" *Revista de Estudios Norteamericanos*, vol. 20, 2016, pp. 13–37.

———. "Negotiating Traumatic Memories in Louise Erdrich's *The Round House.*" *Memory Frictions in Contemporary Literature*, edited by M. J. Martínez-Alfaro and S. Pellicer-Ortín, Palgrave Macmillan, 2017, pp. 255–76.

Jacobs, Connie A. "'One Story Hinging into the Next': The Singular Achievement of Louise Erdrich's Interrelated Novels." *The Native American Renaissance: Literary Imagination and Achievement*, edited by Alan R. Velie and A. Robert Lee, U of Oklahoma P, 2013, pp. 144–60.

Kurup, Seema. "From Revenge to Restorative Justice in Louise Erdrich's *The Plague of Doves, The Round House*, and *LaRose.*" *American Revenge Narratives*, edited by Kyle Wiggins, Springer International, 2018, pp. 99–117.

Madsen, Deborah. "Discontinuous Narrative, Ojibwe Sovereignty, and the *Wiindigoo* Logic of Settler Colonialism: Louise Erdrich's Marn Wolde." *Studies in American Indian Literatures*, vol. 28, no. 3, 2016, pp. 23–51.

Martínez-Falquina, Silvia. "Re-Mapping the Trauma Paradigm: The Politics of Native American Grief in Louise Erdrich's 'Shamengwa.'" *Memory Frictions in Contemporary Literature*, edited by María Jesús Martínez-Alfaro and Silvia Pellicer-Ortín, Palgrave Macmillan, 2017, pp. 209–30.

Rainwater, Catherine. "Haunted by Birds: An Eco-critical View of Personhood in *The Plague of Doves.*" *Louise Erdrich: Tracks, The Last Report on the Miracles at Little No Horse, The Plague of Doves*, edited by Deborah L. Madsen, Continuum, 2011, pp. 152–67.

Roemer, Kenneth. "Naming Native (Living) Histories: Erdrich's Plague of Names." *Studies in American Fiction*, vol. 43, no. 1, 2016, pp. 115–35.

Schacht, Miriam. "Games of Silence: Indian Boarding Schools in Louise Erdrich's Novels."

Studies in American Indian Literatures, vol. 27, no. 2, 2015, pp. 62–79.

Strehle, Susan. "'Prey to Unknown Dreams': Louise Erdrich, *The Plague of Doves*, and the Exceptionalist Disavowal of History." *Literature Interpretation Theory*, vol. 25, no. 2, 2014, pp. 108–27.

Szeghi, Tereza M. "Literary Didacticism and Collective Human Rights in US Borderlands: Ana Castillo's *The Guardians* and Louise Erdrich's *The Round House*." *Western American Literature*, vol. 52, no. 4, 2018, pp. 403–33.

Tharp, Julie. "Erdrich's Crusade: Sexual Violence in *The Round House*." *Studies in American Indian Literatures*, vol. 26, no. 3, 2014, pp. 25–40.

Valentino, Gina. "'It All Does Come to Nothing in the End': Nationalism and Gender in Louise Erdrich's *The Plague of Doves*." *Louise Erdrich: Tracks, The Last Report on the Miracles at Little No Horse, The Plague of Doves*, edited by Deborah L. Madsen, Continuum, 2011, pp. 121–35.

Wan, Mei. "Culture Survivance and Religion Healing: On Ojibwe Spirituality in Healing Trauma in *LaRose*." *Journal of Literature and Art Studies*, vol. 8, no. 8, August 2018, pp. 1181–87.

CONTRIBUTORS

Ellen L. Arnold is an Associate Professor Emeritus in the English Department at East Carolina University, where she taught in the Multicultural and Transnational Literatures concentration and helped to design and implement an online graduate Certificate and Master's Degree in MTL. She also served as Director of Ethnic Studies for several years. She edited *Conversations with Leslie Marmon Silko* (1999) and *The Salt Companion to Carter Revard* (2007). Her essays on Silko, Revard, Linda Hogan, and Gerald Vizenor have appeared in journals such as *Modern Fiction Studies*, *Paradoxa*, and *Studies in American Indian Literatures*, and in edited collections including *Things of the Spirit: Women Writers Constructing Spirituality* (2004), *American Indian Rhetorics of Survivance: Word Medicine, Word Magic* (2006), *Cultural Sites of Critical Insight: Philosophy, Aesthetics, and Native and African American Women's Writings* (2007), and *Restoring the Mystery of the Rainbow: Literature's Refraction of Science* (2011).

Debra K. S. Barker is an enrolled member of the Rosebud Sioux Tribe (Sicangu Lakota Nation) and serves as Director of the American Indian Studies Program at the University of Wisconsin-Eau Claire. As Professor of English and American Indian Studies, she teaches and researches Lakota writing, past and contemporary;

Indigenous aesthetics; the representation of American Indians in Euromerican culture; and the rhetorics of colonial discourses. Barker has published chapters in *Critical Insights: Louise Erdrich*, edited by P. Jane Hafen; *Studies in the Literary Achievement of Louise Erdrich, Native American Writer*, edited by Brajesh Sawhney; *Approaches to Teaching the Works of Louise Erdrich*, edited by Greg Sarris, Connie A. Jacobs, and James Giles; *Introduction to Ethnic Studies*, edited by Brian Baker et al.; *American Indian Studies: An Interdisciplinary Approach to Contemporary Issues*, edited by Dane Morrison; and *After the Grapes of Wrath: Essays on John Steinbeck in Honor of Tetsumaro Hayashi*. An essay collection titled *Literary Sovereignty: Post-Indian Aesthetics*, coedited with Connie A. Jacobs, is forthcoming from the University of Arizona Press.

Gay Barton was a member of the Abilene Christian University English Department from 1990 to 2003. Receiving her PhD from Baylor University in 1999, Gay served as a beloved teacher, scholar, and colleague. Gay published her first scholarly book before her own dissertation. As the ACU English Department Culp Professor, she continued her PhD work on Native American writers, coauthoring two editions of *A Reader's Guide to the Novels of Louise Erdrich*. Louise Erdrich once said she uses *A Reader's Guide* to keep her many characters straight—a great testimony to the book. The ACU Writing Center, located in the Brown Library Learning Commons, features an art gallery honoring Gay Barton and bearing her name. Dr. Gay Barton passed away on June 2, 2020, after fighting chronic illness for seventeen years. She is survived by her brother, two children, and two grandchildren.

Peter G. Beidler is familiar to Erdrich scholars as the coauthor (with Gay Barton) of the *Reader's Guide to the Novels of Louise Erdrich* (1999, revised 2006) and as the author of *Murdering Indians: A Documentary History of the 1897 Killings that Inspired Louise Erdrich's* The Plague of Doves (2014). Although trained as a medievalist and published widely on Chaucer, he has published articles on a range of authors including Henry James, Mark Twain, and J. D. Salinger, and on subjects as diverse as self-reliance, the Civil War, pedagogy, writing, and Parkinson's disease. He was named National Professor of the Year in 1981 by the Council for Advancement and Support of Education and the Carnegie Foundation. He retired from Lehigh University in 2006.

Aitor Ibarrola-Armendariz teaches courses in ethnic relations, diversity management, academic writing, and film adaptation in the Modern Languages and Basque

Studies Department of the University of Deusto, Bilbao, Spain. He has published articles in *Atlantis, IJES, Miscelánea, Revista Chilena de Literatura,* among others, and has edited several volumes on minority and immigrant narratives, including *Fiction and Ethnicity* (1995), *Entre dos mundos* (2004), *Migrations in a Global Context* (2007), and *On the Move* (2016). He has been the Director of the Erasmus Mundus MA Programme in Migrations and Social Cohesion, and Head of the Modern Languages and Basque Studies Department at the University of Deusto.

Connie A. Jacobs is the author of *The Novels of Louise Erdrich: Stories of Her People* (2001), and a coeditor, along with Greg Sarris and James Giles, of MLA's *Approaches to Teaching the Works of Louise Erdrich* (2004). Along with her Oxford Bibliography on Erdrich, she has published chapters on Erdrich in *Louise Erdrich: Tracks, The Last Report on the Miracles at Little No Ho*rse, *Plague of Doves,* edited by Deborah H. Madsen (2011); and *The Native American Renaissance: Literary Imagination and Achievement,* edited by Alan R. Velie and A. Robert Lee (2013). Her most recent work is *The Diné Reader: An Anthology of Navajo Literature,* editors Esther G. Belin, Jeff Berglund, Connie A. Jacobs, and Anthony Webster (2021). Forthcoming in 2022 is *Literary Sovereignty: Post-Indian Aesthetics,* editors Debra K. S. Barker and Connie A. Jacobs. She is Professor Emerita at San Juan College.

Silvia Martínez-Falquina is an Associate Professor of US Literature at the University of Zaragoza, Spain. A specialist in ethnic and Native American women's fiction, she has published *Indias y fronteras: El discurso en torno a la mujer étnica* (2004). She has also coedited, with Gordon Henry and Nieves Pascual, a collection titled *Stories Through Theories/Theories Through Stories: North American Indian Writing, Storytelling, and Critique* (2009), and with Bárbara Arizti, she has coedited the collection *On the Turn: The Ethics of Fiction in Contemporary Narrative in English* (2007). Her latest articles and chapters have appeared in *Roczniki Humanistyczne, Lectora: revista de dones i textualitat, Atlantis, Iperstoria, Humanities,* and Palgrave Macmillan. Her coedited special issue on the new developments of feminism in transmodernity has been recently published in *The European Legacy.* She also serves as the editor of *Miscelánea: A Journal of English and American Studies.*

Margaret Noodin received an MFA in Creative Writing and a PhD in Linguistics from the University of Minnesota. She is a Professor at the University of Wisconsin–Milwaukee, where she also directs the Electa Quinney Institute for American Indian Education and serves as the Associate Dean of Humanities. She is author of *Bawaajimo: A Dialect of Dreams in Anishinaabe Language and Literature* (2014) and two collections of bilingual poems in Ojibwe and English, *Weweni* (2015) and *Gijigijigaaneshiinh Gikendan: What the Chickadee Knows* (2020). To see and hear current projects, visit www.ojibwe.net, where she and other students and speakers of Ojibwe have created a space for language to be shared by academics and the Native community.

Nancy J. Peterson, a Professor of English at Purdue University, focuses on contemporary American literature and culture in her research and teaching, with a particular interest in ethnic literatures, gender studies, and Indigenous studies. She is the author of *Against Amnesia: Contemporary Women Writers and the Crises of Historical Memory* (2001) and *Beloved: Character Studies* (2008), and she is the editor of *Toni Morrison: Critical and Theoretical Approaches* (1997) and *Conversations with Sherman Alexie* (2009). Her articles have appeared in such journals as *Pedagogy*, *MELUS*, *Mfs: Modern Fiction Studies*, and *PMLA*, as well as a range of edited collections.

Kenneth M. Roemer is an Emeritus Professor, University of Texas at Arlington, and an Emeritus Fellow, UT System Academy of Distinguished Teachers. Before retiring he was a Distinguished Teaching and Distinguished Scholar Professor, and a Piper Professor. He has edited two volumes on Native literature and coedited *The Cambridge Companion to Native American Literature* (2005), which won a Wordcraft Circle of Native Writers and Storytellers Writer of the Year Award. *The Obsolete Necessity* (1976), one of his four books on utopia, was nominated for a Pulitzer in American History. After twenty-five years, he is still an advisor for UTA's Native student group.

Gwen Nell Westerman, PhD, lives in the Dakota homeland where she is Professor of English and Director of the Humanities Program at Minnesota State University, Mankato. Her work in Dakota language, poetry, and history has been published in *When the Light of the World Was Subdued, Our Songs Came Through: A Norton Anthology of Native Nations Poetry*; *Words and Relations: Language Revitalization and the Promise of Indigenous Archives*; the *Albany Government Law Review*; *POETRY Magazine*; and *New Poets of Native Nations*. She is an enrolled member of the Sisseton Wahpeton Oyate.

INDEX

A

Alexander, Jeffrey C., 51, 53, 61

Allen, Chadwick, 90

American Indian Religious Freedom Act
(1978), 113

Anderson, Marcia G., 144, 145, 156 (n. 8)

Anderson, Sherwood, 25, 33

animals. *See* dogs, wolves

animal studies, 90, 102 (n. 2); and Indigenous
studies, 90–91

Anishinaabe traditions: *aadizookaanag*
(living stories), 166–67; Anishinaabe
justice, 123, 171–73; *bimaadiziwin* (the
ideal good life), 119, 123, 129; cosmology,
144, 167–68; *doodemag* (clan system), 166,
170–71; ecology and reciprocity, 83, 119,
147, 166; *manidoog* (manitous), 48, 141,
147, 150, 167–68; Nanabozho, 94, 167–68,
247; relationality and relationships, 108,
115, 129, 165; wiindigoo, 94, 168, 236–37.
See also bandolier bags, beadwork,
Ojibwe language

Antelope Wife, The, 87–88, 156 (n. 4), 160, 272,
274; and beadwork, 140–41, 142

Ateljevic, Irena, 115

Athiakis, Mark, 45, 50

Aurelius, Marcus, 1, 4

B

Baenen, Jeff, 5

Bancroft, Corinne, 137

bandolier bags (Ojibwe, *gashkibidaaganag*),
143–45, 147, 151, 155, 156 (n. 8)

Barton, Gay, 102 (n. 1), 138, 155 (n. 2), 160, 187

beadwork (Ojibwe), 140–43, 155–56 (n. 3),
156 (n. 7); in *The Antelope Wife*, 140–42;

and floral design, 140–42, 145; in the justice trilogy, 141

Beet Queen, The, 137, 261, 278

Beidler, Peter, 5–6, 102 (n. 1), 138, 155 (n. 2), 160, 187

Belcourt, Christi, 141–42

Beloved (Toni Morrison), 111–12

Bender, Jacob, 28–29, 39 (n. 8), 40 (n. 9)

Bingo Palace, The, 87

Birchbark Books, 89, 261, 277, 279–80

Birchbark House, The, 88, 166, 278–79

Blue Jay's Dance, The, 272, 276

boarding schools, 51–52, 61, 122, 264

Braithwaite, John, 173

Brave Heart, Maria Yellow Horse, 50, 61–62, 113, 152, 157 (n. 12)

Broker, Ignatia, 103 (n. 13)

Butler, Judith, 114–15

Butt, Daniel, 62

C

Carden, Mary Paniccia, 29, 39 (n. 8), 40 (n. 9), 76

Chandler, Raymond, 18, 38

Charles, Ron, 45, 54

Cicero, Marcus Tullius, 171, 180 (n. 2)

Cody, William F. (Buffalo Bill), 144

Confucius, 172–73

Crane Murdoch, Sierra, 39 (n. 5)

Crispin, Jessa, 45, 47

D

Dakota language, 183–85

Dawes Act of 1887 (allotment), xiii

Dean, Janet, 156 (n. 5)

Deane, Seamus, 10

Deloria, Vine, Jr., 63, 99

Denham, Aaron R., 44

Densmore, Frances, 155–56 (n. 3)

detective fiction. *See* Chandler, Raymond; Jameson, Fredric; Van Dine, S. S.

Dickinson, Emily, 107–08, 130

dogs: in Erdrich's fiction, 87–91; and Indigenous peoples, 102; human-dog connections, 91–93; in *LaRose*, 98–102; recent books on, 91, 102 (n. 3, 4, 5); wolves as domesticated dogs, 92

Dorris, Michael, 260, 276–78

Douglass, Frederick, 173

Drinnon, Richard, 7–8

Dubin, Lois S., 144, 156 (n. 6)

E

Erdrich, Louise: on abandonment as a theme in her works, 272; acclaimed author, xi, 45; awards, xi–xii, 260; on being a writer and a mother, 273, 276, 278; on Birchbark Books, 277, 280; on *The Birchbark House* as a critique of settler colonialism, 279; on Catholicism, 264; on changing her name from Karen to Louise, 266; on her complex character trees, 270; on the covers of her books, 271–72; on the Cree/Ojibwe story of the rolling head, 131 (n. 4); on Michael Dorris, 276–77; on Charles Eastman, 265; education experiences, 261–62, 265–66, 268–69; enrolled in Turtle Mountain Band of Chippewa, xi, 263; on evil in the world, xiv; family members, 131 (n. 6), 259–67, 273–75, 278–80; on God, 264; on the idea of justice, xii–xiii;

on justice in the trilogy, xii, xiv, 160;
on LaRose (the boy) as a character,
131 (n. 7); on local bookstores, 280–81;
as mentor, 183; on the mixture of real
and fantastic elements in her work, 131
(n. 5), 140–41, 142, 156–57 (n. 11), 274;
on the Ojibwe language, 263–64; on
Leonard Peltier, 268; on Maggie Ravich
as a character, 100; on revenge as justice,
24; on revising already published work,
272; on rewriting *The Antelope Wife*,
272; on Richard Nixon, 266; on Romeo
as a character, 22, 55; on traditional
Ojibwe adoption, xiv, 59; on traditional
(restorative) justice, 21, 23; on writing
Love Medicine, 267–69; on writing
nonfiction, 279; on writing novels for
children, 279; on writing *The Plague
of Doves*, 10, 17, 264–65, 267, 274–75;
on writing poetry, 267, 279–80; on her
writing process, x, 269–71, 275–76; on
writing *Tracks*, 268–69
Erdrich, Louise—Works: aesthetic
sovereignty, 3, 11; balancing tragedy and
healing, 44, 56, 62; counter-colonial
aesthetics, 1, 3; ethics of complexity
in, 112–13; polyvocality of her novels,
2–3; presentation of place and history,
45–46, 51; use of multiple narrators and
perspectives, 135–38, 151; weaving short
stories into novels, xi, 188. *See also justice
trilogy and entries for individual works*

F

Faulkner, William, 11, 20, 33, 45, 138, 260, 269
Fogg, Brandy R., 92–94, 103 (n. 6, 8, 10)

Forbes, Jack, 3
Four Souls, 32, 160, 272
Francioni, Francesco, 62–63
Future Home of the Living God, 160

G

Gamber, John, 69
García Márquez, Gabriel, 260
Ghost Dance, 12
glossary for Erdrich's recent novels, 174–80
Gómez-Isa, Felipe, 57
Gone, Joseph P., 61
Gonzales-Day, Ken, 6
Gordon, Mary, 22, 23, 45, 51, 54, 96
Granek, Leeat, 113
grief, theories of, 113–15
Gross, Lawrence, 94, 111, 112–14, 119, 121, 123,
129

H

Hafen, P. Jane, 51
Hallowell, A. I., 98
Haskell, David George, 82
Hertzel, Laurie, xii–xiii
Hirst, K. Kris, 91–92
Holt, Debra C., 47, 50
Howe, Nimachia, 93
Hudson, Brian K., 90

I

Ibarrola-Armendariz, Aitor, 52
Indian Citizenship Act (1924), xiii, 7
Indigenous concepts of kinship and
relationality, 83, 115–16, 130
Indigenous language preservation, 183, 185,
280

Indigenous languages. *See* Dakota language;
   Ojibwe language
Indigenous oral traditions, 44, 94, 112–13

J

Jacobs, Connie, 17, 39 (n. 2), 40 (n. 11), 49,
   56, 95
Jameson, Fredric, 18, 21–22, 35, 37
Johnston, Basil H., 79, 94
justice trilogy, xii–xvi; as an "accidental
   trilogy," xii; characters that recur in the
   novels, 238; combining murder-mystery
   elements and social justice issues, 17–18,
   38–39; comedy in, xvi–xvii; compared
   to Ojibwe beadwork, 148–49, 150–51,
   153, 155; complex storylines of, 136–37;
   diversity of characters, 162; glossary
   of non-English words and phrases
   appearing in, 174–80; kinship in 82–83;
   languages used in, 160–63; mixture of
   real and dreamlike elements, 140–41, 147;
   names in, 163–64; narrative perspective
   in, 130 (n. 1), 148–51; as one big book,
   147, 150–51, 155; settler colonialism in,
   xi, 18, 67, 114; survival as aesthetics, 14;
   theme of healing, xvii, 82–83, 151, 155;
   theme of justice/injustice, xiii–xiv, xx, 39,
   83, 136, 151–54, 159–60, 170–74; theme
   of revenge, 94–97; trauma in, xv, 46,
   67, 114, 151–52; trees as protagonists in,
   68, 82–83. *See also entries for individual
   novels of the trilogy*

K

Kohn, Eduardo, 82–83
Kurup, Seema, 52, 147, 151

L

Lakota spirituality, 14
LaRose, 237–41; Anishinaabe ceremonies in,
   20, 48, 109, 116, 127; balance between
   trauma and healing, 60–63; beadwork
   in, 141–42; boarding schools, 51–52,
   117–18, 121–22, 131 (n. 6); children raised
   by other families, 21, 48–49, 55, 57,
   110, 118, 154, 239; chronology of events,
   242–44; connections to actual events,
   51, 63, 132 (n. 10), 242, 256; dictionary of
   characters for, 244–57; dissociation in
   the novel, 119–21; ending as reparative/
   restorative, 23–24, 82–83, 126–30,
   154–55; family tree for, 244; flying in
   the novel, 80–81, 121–22, 131 (n. 5), 146,
   150, 249, 251; generations of LaRoses,
   60, 84 (n. 6), 239; Grandma Thunder's
   stories, 62–63, 94, 97, 118, 168, 247;
   kinship and relationality in, 80–81, 108,
   130; Landreaux's sense of guilt, 20, 81,
   109, 119; LaRose as a powerful name,
   46, 57, 60–61, 97, 146, 163; LaRose (boy)
   as healer, 59–60, 97, 101, 124–26; list of
   chapters, 241; location of reservation,
   238; love as medicine, 241; Maggie and
   the owl spirit, 80, 101, 120; mongrel dog,
   79, 88, 98–102, 245–46; mourning as
   transformative, 114; as a murder-mystery,
   19–24; narrative perspective, 112, 150;
   Nola's suicide attempt, 80, 99–100,
   119, 252; Ojibwemowin names in, 163;
   presence of the spirit world, 58, 80–81,
   100, 127–28, 239–40; racism in, 51, 117,
   123; rolling head, 53, 97–98, 117–18, 147,
   154, 249, 254, 257; Romeo as "dishonest

detective," 21–22; Romeo as a villain, 54–55, 96–97; sexual assault in, 52–53, 80, 117; substance abuse in, 20, 22, 119, 239; suffering and grief in, 108–10, 116–19; theme of education, 61, 122–23, 146–47, 239; theme of forgiveness, 96, 129, 240; theme of healing, 57–60, 102, 128–29; theme of justice/injustice, xiv, 24, 79, 172, 240; theme of revenge, xvi, 21–23, 46–47, 52–55, 80–81, 96–97, 126, 154; trauma in, 47–50, 79, 81, 116–17; trees in, 78–82; Wolfred's and LaRose's use of Ojibwemowin, 169; Wolfred's cabin, 45–46, 127, 238, 240, 242, 257. *See also* justice trilogy

Last Report on the Miracles at Little No Horse, The, xi, xiii, 71, 87, 139–40, 275

Lee, Harper (*To Kill a Mockingbird*), 4, 11–12

legal status of American Indians, 6–7

LeMay, Konnie, 46, 60

Leuthold, Steven, 3

Limerick, Patricia, 13

Lincoln, Kenneth, 44

Lipsitz, George, 7

literature, approaches to: ecocritical, 67–68, 82–83; ethical, 111–12

Love Medicine, ix, xi, 135, 137, 241, 260, 278; Erdrich, on writing the novel, 267–69, 272

lynchings of American Indians, 5–6

Lyons, Gene, 135

M

Madsen, Deborah L., 32, 68, 72–73, 83 (n. 1), 83–84 (n. 3)

Manifest Destiny, xiii, 2, 18, 69, 71

Marshall, III, Joseph, 93

Martínez-Falquina, Silvia, 131 (n. 2)

Masson, Jeffrey Moussaieff, 91

Master Butchers Singing Club, The, 88, 271–72, 276

Maunz-Breese, Lydia, 28–29, 39 (n. 8), 40 (n. 9)

McGrath, Charles, 21, 45, 46, 58, 59

McHugh, Susan, 90

McKee, Ian, 53

Melville, Herman, 7, 23, 32, 33

Métis (Michif), culture and language, 31, 161. *See also* Riel

Miller, Laura, 24, 28

Missing and Murdered Indigenous Women and Girls (#MMIWG), xv

"Mob Law in North Dakota" (1897), 5

Moraru, Christian, 115

Moretti, Franco, 20, 21, 24–25, 38

murder-mysteries, conventions of, 18–21, 24–25, 33, 35–36, 38

N

Nabokov, Peter, 7

"Naked Woman Playing Chopin," 274

Native history: and injustice, xiii, 5–7; termination era, 263

Neihardt, John G. (*Black Elk Speaks*), 25

Night Watchman, The, xi, xiii, 88–89, 107, 131 (n. 6)

Noodin, Margaret, 67, 79

Noori, Margaret, 2–3, 69

O

Ojibwe language (Ojibwemowin, Anishinaabemowin), 160–61; compared to English, 128, 163, 171; Erdrich on the language, 263–64; glossary of Anishinaabe words and phrases used in Erdrich's recent novels, 174–78; language and identity, 164–65; Ojibwemowin words related to justice, 170–73

Ortiz, Simon, 38–39

Owens, Jasmine, 39 (n. 5)

Owens, Louis, 116, 130

P

Painted Drum, The, 155 (n. 1), 156 (n. 5), 160, 174–78

Phelan, James, 111–12

Phillips, Ruth B., 147

"Photograph of North Dakota Triple Lynching," 6

Pierotti, Raymond, 92–94, 103 (n. 6, 8, 10)

Plague of Doves, The, 188–90; as a "braided narrative" 137; birds in, 6–70, 72–73, 190; chronology of events, 191–93; compared to *To Kill a Mockingbird*, 11–12; connections to historical events, x, 5–6, 10, 35, 188, 274–75; Cordelia as narrator, 12–13, 36–37; Cordelia's racial bigotry, 7, 37; dictionary of characters for, 196–214; Evelina as narrator, 11–12, 37, 138, 148; Evelina's interest in French, 4, 161, 170; family trees for, 193–95; hanging tree, 68–70, 72, 74, 153; kinship with the land, 71–72, 74; list of chapters, 190–91; lynch mob, 2, 35, 138, 152; Marn's killing of Billy, 32, 73; Métis culture in, 31, 161, 170; Mooshum's sense of guilt, 31, 36–37, 152–53; as a murder-mystery, 30–38; music in, 13, 30–31, 36–37, 213–15; narrative perspective, 37, 148, 190; Ojibwemowin names in, 164; Pluto, location of, 189; Pluto as a dying town, 12–13, 95, 152; racism in, 9, 14, 18, 35, 68; settler colonialism in, 2, 8–10, 32–33, 35–36, 68, 151, 189–90; as a social-justice novel, 34–38; subversiveness of, 2, 3–5; theme of guilt, 189; theme of justice/injustice, xiv–xv, 2, 8, 12, 13–14, 35–38, 71, 74, 153; trauma in, 151–52; Warren Wolde's odd behaviors, 33–34; wiindigoo, 32–33, 36, 68, 73–74. *See also* justice trilogy

Pomeldi, Michael, 101, 102

postapocalypse stress syndrome (PASS), 113–14

R

racism, in American history, xiv, 5–9

Rainwater, Catherine, 1, 82, 137

"Rape on the Reservation," xv, 39 (n. 5)

Reinventing the Enemy's Language (ed. Bird and Harjo), 38

restorative justice, theories of, 47, 57, 62–63

Riche, Maureen, 90

Ridington, Robin, 97–98

Riel, Louis, 76, 161, 173, 191

Rodríguez Magda, Rosa María, 115, 131 (n. 3)

Roemer, Kenneth M., 32, 39 (n. 1), 40 (n. 11), 83 (n. 3)

Roth, Philip, 46, 260, 269

Round House, The, 215–18; chronology of events, 218–23; clans, importance of, 77, 166, 170–71; connections to actual events, 39 (n. 6), 217, 236; dictionary of characters for, 224–37; family trees for, 223; Geraldine's rape and trauma, xv, 26–27, 95, 148, 153; Joe's sense of guilt, 29–30, 153–54; jurisdictional issues in, xv, 26, 28, 75, 95, 153; kinship and community in, 75–76; Linden Lark as a villain, 28–29; list of chapters, 218; as a murder-mystery, 24–30; narrative perspective, 25, 148–49, 216; Ojibwemowin names in, 163–64; Pearl as protector, 88, 234; round house, xiv, 29, 77–78, 217–18; *Star Trek: The Next Generation* references in, 28, 39 (n. 8), 136, 218; as a social-justice novel, 27, 30; story of Akii, Nanapush, and Old Buffalo Woman, 76–77, 149, 217–18, 233, 234; story of Liver-Eating Johnson, 29; theme of justice/injustice, xiv–xv, 29–30, 77–78, 84 (n. 4), 95; theme of revenge, 24, 75, 95; trees and seedlings in, 74–78; tribal law in, 24–25, 30, 147, 149, 221–22; wiindigoo, 28–29, 76, 147, 168, 236–37; wiindigoo justice, xiv, 77, 153, 222. *See also* justice trilogy

Russo, Maria, xiii, 25, 95

S

"Saint Marie," 269
"Scales," 268
Schacht, Miriam, 51, 131 (n. 6)
Schliephake, Christopher, 67–68
Schultz, Lydia, 137–38
Shadow Tag, x, 88, 271, 274, 275
"Shamengwa," xi, 273
Shanley, Kathryn, 20, 39 (n. 3)
Shelton, Dinah, 56, 58
Simpson, Leanne Betasamosake, 115

Sing, Pamela, 31
"Sister Godzilla" (story), xi, 262
Sotero, Michelle M., 43–44
sovereignty: Erdrich's aesthetic sovereignty, 3, 11; in Erdrich's work, xiv, xvii, xx, 18, 68, 78, 152, 221; as a legal concept, xiii, 148
Stirrup, David, 63
Strehle, Susan, 71
survivance, 19, 38–39, 44–45, 47, 89, 146–47, 156 (n. 9), 163

T

Tales of Burning Love, 88, 274
Tedrowe, Emily Gray, xii, 150
Tharp, Julie, 18, 27, 39 (n. 6, 7)
Tracks, xi, xiii, 32, 87–89, 160, 168, 271; Erdrich on writing *Tracks*, 268–69
transmodernity, 115
trauma theory (historical, intergenerational, collective), 43–44, 50, 61–62, 113–14, 152, 157 (n. 12)
trees, as sentient beings, 82–83
Treisman, Deborah, 131 (n. 4, 5, 6), 156–57 (n. 11)
tribal law, and jurisdiction, xii, xv, 18, 28, 39 (n. 5, 7)
"True Story of Mustache Maude, The," ix–xi
Turtle Mountain reservation, 183, 189, 259–60, 263
Twain, Mark, 25

U

Ursu, Anne, 13

V

Valentino, Gina, 73

Van Dine, S. S. (Willard Huntington Wright), 18, 20–21, 33, 35, 38

violence against Native women, xv, 114

Violence Against Women Act (VAWA), xv, 39 (n. 7)

Vizenor, Gerald: 19, 44–45, 156 (n. 9); critique of Erdrich's animals, 89–91. *See also* survivance

W

Wan, Mei, 47, 60–61

Washburn, Frances, 62

Washington, George, 173

West, Cornel, 159

White Hat, Sr., Albert, 14

Wilson, Shawn, 115

Wohlleben, Peter, 82

Wolfe, Art, 91

wolves: as domesticated dogs, 92; human-wolf bonds, 92–93; and Indigenous peoples, 93–94, 103 (n. 11); Indigenous stories of, 93–94, 103 (n. 9)

Woodward, Wendy, 90

"World's Greatest Fisherman, The," 260

Wyatt, Jean, 155 (n. 1)

Z

Zhang, Yan, 173

Žižek, Slavoj, 36